Visit us at

www.syngress.com

Syngress is committed to publishing high-quality books for IT Professionals and delivering those books in media and formats that fit the demands of our customers. We are also committed to extending the utility of the book you purchase via additional materials available from our Web site.

SOLUTIONS WEB SITE

To register your book, please visit **www.syngress.com**. Once registered, you can access your e-book with print, copy, and comment features enabled.

ULTIMATE CDs

Our Ultimate CD product line offers our readers budget-conscious compilations of some of our best-selling backlist titles in Adobe PDF form. These CDs are the perfect way to extend your reference library on key topics pertaining to your area of expertise, including Cisco Engineering, Microsoft Windows System Administration, CyberCrime Investigation, Open Source Security, and Firewall Configuration, to name a few.

DOWNLOADABLE E-BOOKS

For readers who can't wait for hard copy, we offer most of our titles in downloadable e-book format. These are available at **www.syngress.com**.

SITE LICENSING

Syngress has a well-established program for site licensing our e-books onto servers in corporations, educational institutions, and large organizations. Please contact our corporate sales department at corporatesales@elsevier.com for more information.

CUSTOM PUBLISHING

Many organizations welcome the ability to combine parts of multiple Syngress books, as well as their own content, into a single volume for their own internal use. Please contact our corporate sales department at corporatesales@elsevier.com for more information.

Nokia Firewall, VPN, and IPSO Configuration Guide

Andrew Hay
Peter Giannoulis
Keli Hay

Warren Verbanec Technical Editor

Foreword by
Dameon D. Welch-Abernathy
A.K.A. PHONEBOY

Unique Passcode

99385426

PUBLISHED BY
Syngress Publishing, Inc.
Elsevier, Inc.
30 Corporate Drive
Burlington, MA 01803

Nokia Firewall, VPN, and IPSO Configuration Guide

Printed and bound in the United Kingdom
Transferred to Digital Printing, 2010

ISBN 13: 978-1-59749-286-7

Publisher: Laura Colantoni
Acquisitions Editor: Andrew Williams
Developmental Editor: Matthew Cater
Technical Editor: Warren Verbanec
Project Manager: Andre Cuello
Page Layout and Art: SPI
Copy Editor: Michael McGee
Indexer: SPI
Cover Designer: Michael Kavish

For information on rights, translations, and bulk sales, contact Matt Pedersen, Senior Sales Manager, Corporate Sales, at Syngress Publishing; email m.pedersen@elsevier.com.

Library of Congress Cataloging-in-Publication Data
Hay, Andrew, 1973-
Nokia firewall, VPN, and IPSO configuration guide / Andrew Hay, Peter Giannoulis, Keli Hay.
p. cm.
ISBN 978-1-59749-286-7
1. Wireless Internet--Computer programs. 2. Nokia smartphones. 3. Extranets (Computer networks)
4. Firewalls (Computer security) 5. Software configuration management. I. Giannoulis, Peter.
II. Hay, Keli. III. Title.
TK5103.4885.H39 2009
005.1--dc22

2008044578

Authors

Andrew Hay is a recognized security expert, thought leader, presenter, and author. As the Integration Services Product and Program Manager at Q1 Labs Inc. his primary responsibility involves the research and integration of log and vulnerability technologies into QRadar, their flagship network security management solution. Prior to joining Q1 Labs, Andrew was CEO and co-founder of Koteas Corporation, a leading provider of end-to-end security and privacy solutions for government and enterprise. His resume also includes various roles and responsibilities at Nokia Enterprise Solutions, Nortel Networks, and Magma Communications, a division of Primus.

Andrew is a strong advocate of security training, certification programs, and public awareness initiatives. He also holds several industry certifications including the CCNA, CCSA, CCSE, CCSE NGX, CCSE Plus, SSP-MPA, SSP-CNSA, NSA, RHCT, RHCE, Security+, GSEC, GCIA, GCIH, and CISSP.

Andrew would first like to thank his wife Keli for her support, guidance, and unlimited understanding when it comes to his interests. He would also like to thank Dameon D. Welch-Abernathy (a.k.a. Phoneboy), Peter Giannoulis, Michael Santarcangelo, Michael Farnum, Martin McKeay, Lori MacVittie, Jennifer Jabbusch, Michael Ramm, Anton Chuvakin, Max Schubert, Andy Willingham, Jennifer Leggio, Ben Jackson, Jack Daniel, Kees Leune, Christofer Hoff, Kevin Riggins, Dave Lewis, Daniel Cid, Rory Bray, George Hanna, Chris Cahill, Ed Isaacs, Mike Tander, Kevin Charles, Stephane Drapeau, Jason Ingram, Tim Hersey, Jason Wentzell, Eric Malenfant, Al Mcgale, Sean Murray-Ford, the Trusted Catalyst Community, his past coworkers at Nokia, his current coworkers at Q1 Labs, the folks at PerkettPR, and of course his parents, Michel and Ellen Hay, and in-laws Rick and Marilyn Litle for their continued support.

Peter Giannoulis is an information security consultant in Toronto, Ontario. Over the last 10 years Peter has been involved in the design and implementation of client defenses using many different security technologies. He is also skilled in vulnerability and penetration testing, having taken part in hundreds of assessments. Peter has been involved with SANS and GIAC for quite some time as an Instructor, Authorized Grader for the GSEC certification, courseware author, exam developer, Advisory Board member, and is currently a Technical Director for the GIAC family of certifications. He currently maintains the first information security streaming video website (www.theacademy.ca), which assists organizations in implementing and troubleshooting some of the most popular security products. Peter's current certifications include: GSEC, GCIH, GCIA, GCFA, GCFW, GREM, GSNA, CISSP, CCSI, INFOSEC, CCSP, & MCSE.

Keli Hay is a certified professional instructor through Freisen, Kaye and Associates, with over 15 years experience in IT. She also has a diploma in Business Administration with a major in Information Systems. Keli is currently working as an Instructional Designer, primarily for a large, global IT client, and is based in Fredericton, New Brunswick, Canada. In other roles, Keli has provided technical support and training for company specific and third party products, provisioned client services, provided customer service, and audited IT services. Keli's employers include PulseLearning Inc., Computer Sciences Corporation (CSC), Nortel, and Magma Communications, a division of Primus. Keli also acted as a technical editor consultant on the OSSEC Host-Based Intrusion Detection Guide. She enjoys learning and writing about and helping to train people on different products.

Keli would like to thank Andrew for his support, guidance, expertise, sense of humor, and wisdom – we have shared lots of experiences and grown together. She would also like to thank her parents (Richard and Marilyn Litle) for their support, guidance, and lots of advice over the years.

Technical Editor

Warren Verbanec is a Silicon Valley native who first loaded Zaxxon from tape in 1982. He was a member of Nokia's Product Line Support group for several years, wrote Nokia's technical security courseware, and continues to consult for Nokia on various subjects. He holds a variety of industry certifications and holds a Bachelor of Science degree from the University of California.

Foreword Contributor

Dameon D. Welch-Abernathy, CISSP, a.k.a. "PhoneBoy," has provided aid and assistance to countless IT professionals since 1996. Best known as the author of two books on Check Point VPN-1/FireWall-1 as well as creator of a well-visited FAQ site on the Check Point products, Welch-Abernathy currently works in the Security Product Line Support team in Nokia's Software and Services division. In addition to assisting customers with Nokia's line of network security products, he is Editor in Chief of the Support Knowledge Base on the Nokia Support Web.

Contents

Foreword

Back when I started working with Check Point in 1996, the marketplace for firewalls was different. The market was still being educated on what firewalls were and what value they provide. Corporate firewalls typically ran on general-purpose computers with multiple network interfaces. The operating systems had to be "hardened" by administrators to ensure they did not run unnecessary services that could be used to compromise—or degrade—the firewall operation.

While Check Point still runs—and is supported—on general-purpose platforms running Solaris and Windows, a number of purpose-built platforms run Check Point software. The hard work of selecting individual components for the firewall platform and securing the underlying operating system is a thing of the past. The underlying operating system comes presecured, and the interface cards are known to work. You also get the benefit of a single source for support of the entire solution.

While a number of companies provide these platforms: Resilience, Crossbeam, and even Check Point themselves are selling their own hardware—many customers choose to run Check Point on Nokia security platforms. It's one of the most popular ways to run Check Point today.

My history with Nokia starts in 1999, when I was hired to work in their support organization. I brought the knowledge I had accumulated on the Check Point FAQ site I had on phoneboy.com and put it to use within Nokia. A lot of goodness from my own site made its way into Nokia's support knowledge base, where some of the old phoneboy.com content is still used today.

While I stopped actively supporting Check Point on Nokia in 2004, and turned over the Check Point content on phoneboy.com to cpug.org around that time, I can't entirely get away from Check Point. I still work for the same part of the company I started with, and

I have a lot of history with the product. I also read and approve the knowledgebase articles *other* people write on the Nokia solution, which show up in Nokia Support Web, our customer portal.

Having put out a couple of Check Point books myself, I know first-hand how difficult it was for Andrew, Keli, and Peter to put this book together. They've got a good book here. It should put you well on your way to getting your Nokia firewalls deployed in your network.

—Dameon D. Welch-Abernathy
A.K.A. PhoneBoy
July 2008

Chapter 1

Nokia Security Solutions Overview

Solutions in this chapter:

- Introducing Nokia IPSO
- Introducing Nokia Firewall/VPN and UTM Appliances
- Introducing Additional Nokia Security Solutions

☑ Summary

☑ Solutions Fast Track

☑ Frequently Asked Questions

Introduction

"Our aging Linux firewalls just aren't cutting it anymore, Simran," said Marty Feldman, Director of Information Security.

Simran Sing, the CISO at one of North America's premiere defense companies, knew to take Marty at his word. "All right, what are our options?"

"Well that depends." smiled Marty. "Do I have the budget for a complete overhaul? I'd like to rip these things out at the perimeter and place a trusted enterprise solution in their place."

Simran opened up her budget spreadsheet. "Well, Marty, we've got some money left for this year, but you're going to have to really convince me that the solution you select is going to give us some return on investment."

Marty smiled. "Is ROI all you care about now? I remember when you used to be all about the cool factor."

Simran laughed. "As the CISO, I really don't have that luxury anymore, Marty. We have to pick a solution that will ensure we don't lose money due to a breach."

Marty flipped through the stack of papers he always carried with him. "What about those Nokia IP Security Appliances? I was speaking to the local account manager last week and it sounds like they have a really good offering."

Simran looked down at her desk where her Nokia mobile phone sat. "I thought Nokia only dealt in mobile phones and mobile connectivity solutions?"

Marty held up a printout of a whitepaper on Nokia Security Solutions that had several images of the Nokia security platforms. "Nope." Said Marty, "They've been making firewall platforms for years. Plus, they're running on a hardened operating system that's been stripped down for performance and to run the Check Point firewall software application." Marty smiled. "You have heard of Check Point haven't you, boss?"

Simran frowned. "Don't forget, I'm still a geek at heart, Marty. Also, don't forget that I did your job for several years before I put you into my role." Simran flashed a sarcastic smile. "I brought you into this job; I can take you out of it."

Marty laughed. "Yes, boss, I remember."

Marty left Simran's office and headed back to his desk. He started scouring the Internet for any and all information about the Nokia Security Solutions offerings he could find. He watched several Webinars, read numerous technical documents, and even checked out several message boards where people were posting questions about issues they were having with their Nokia appliances and configurations. After performing his due diligence, Marty picked up the phone and called the local Nokia account manager he had spoken with the previous week.

"Josh, Marty Feldman here. I was wondering if you'd be able to drop by sometime this week to tell me more about the Nokia Security Solutions portfolio..."

When people hear the name Nokia they immediately think cellular (mobile) telephones. What most people do not know is that Nokia is also a leader in network security solutions and has been so for several years. When Nokia Corporation purchased Ipsilon Networks for $120 million, a bargain in 1997 for a technology startup that analysts valued at roughly $500 million the previous year, they found themselves forced into the IP-based network equipment business.

NOTE

Did you know that Nokia started out manufacturing pulp, paper, and rubber products? In fact, you can still find Nokia rubber boots and tires on eBay if you look hard enough. A detailed history of Nokia can be found at: http://en.wikipedia.org/wiki/Nokia.

Introducing Nokia IPSO

The IPSO operating system is the core of the Nokia IP security platform. It was designed to be a secure and lean operating system so it could operate efficiently on smaller hardware. Over time, it became the preferred operating system for applications such as the Check Point VPN-1/Firewall-1 suite of products (discussed in Chapter 8) and the ISS (now IBM) RealSecure Network Intrusion Detection Sensor software.

NOTE

The IBM RealSecure software is no longer supported on Nokia IP security platforms, but it used to be one of the most reliable platforms upon which the venerable network intrusion detection system (NIDS) software was deployed.

The original IPSO was a fork of the FreeBSD 2.2.6 operating system and has been changed so significantly over the years that you should only consider it a distant cousin of FreeBSD. A UNIX command issued at the IPSO command-line interface (CLI) will usually work, but several commands are missing newer switches. Luckily, very few administrative tasks are performed using the standard UNIX command suite. Instead, IPSO contains two powerful command-line editing utilities called *ipsctl* (pronounced *ip-skittle*) and the Command Line Interface Shell (*CLISH* pronounced klish), which can be used to configure all settings for your IPSO-based security platform. The *ipsctl* command is used mainly as a troubleshooting tool and is discussed thoroughly in Chapter 6. In recent years, the *ipsctl* command has been replaced by the powerful IPSO CLISH, which is discussed in Chapter 6.

Although IPSO can be configured directly from the CLI, it is not very user-friendly. Most Cisco administrators will love the IPSO CLI but not everyone feels comfortable configuring a network device in this manner. The Nokia Network Voyager Web-based interface lets you configure your Nokia IP security platform using your Web browser. Voyager, as it is commonly called, can be used to configure your Nokia IP security platform both at installation and throughout the life of your deployment. The Nokia Network Voyager is discussed in Chapters 4 and 5.

NOTE

The Nokia Network Voyager interface was actually developed *before* the IPSO CLISH. When was the last time that you heard about a product that had the Web interface developed before the CLI?

Introducing Nokia Firewall/VPN and UTM Appliances

Nokia offers several firewall/VPN and UTM solutions, which are covered in this section.

IP40 and IP45

The Nokia IP40 and IP45 platforms, which run on a specialized embedded operating system, were designed for remote office and branch office (ROBO) deployments. If a remote or branch office has a small number of users that need firewall protection at the perimeter, and require VPN connectivity to another ROBO or enterprise site, there may not be a need to deploy a full firewall and VPN solution.

Both platforms are sold in an 8, 16, 32, and Unlimited user node model and are shipped with the purchased license. The Tele 8 license is recommended for remote workers, such as telecommuters, who need to connect to a larger VPN infrastructure, or for remote users who need to connect back to the home office using a desktop VPN client.

NOTE

It has been rumored that Nokia executives, as well as some customers, have been known to travel with an IP40 or IP45 platform in their suitcase to simplify the remote access VPN link back to the main office.

The Satellite 16, 32, and Unlimited user node models provide firewall and VPN capabilities for ROBO, small, and medium offices. You will typically deploy a Satellite platform to interconnect small or medium enterprise locations with 16, 32, or many hosts. The Satellite user nodes models can also be deployed in a high-availability pair, connect using a dialup Internet connection, and participate in a dynamic OSPF network environment.

TIP

If you need your IP40 or IP45 to support more than the originally purchased number of hosts, you can upgrade the license.

The IP40 and IP45 platforms contain an embedded Check Point Firewall-1 stateful firewall that can be configured on each deployed device or from a centralized Check Point SmartCenter server. The embedded firewall provides network address translation (NAT), user-defined rule configuration, preset policies, Denial of Service (DoS) protection, anti-spoofing protection, attack logging, Voice over IP (H.323) support, SmartDefense service, and Application Intelligence (AI) functionality. Two additional options, which are only supported on the Satellite models, are the ability to designate a DMZ network and the support of VLANs. Figure 1.1 shows the Nokia IP40 and IP45 platforms.

Figure 1.1 Nokia IP40 and IP45 Platforms

Tools & Traps...

What Is Application Intelligence?

Application Intelligence is a set of advanced capabilities that detect and prevent application-level attacks. It integrates network and application-level defense capabilities into Check Point products, thus delivering comprehensive attack protection and network security. Application Intelligence defenses are supported by SmartDefense Services, which provide ongoing updates to keep defenses current against constantly changing threats and vulnerabilities.

Check Point provides an excellent whitepaper that describes Application Intelligence on the Product and Services section of their Web site at www.checkpoint.com/products/downloads/applicationintelligence_whitepaper.pdf.

Application-level attacks rank among the most dangerous, and most actively used, methods for exploiting security safeguards on the Internet. Application Intelligence protects your network from common:

- HTTP client attacks: worms, malicious URLs, cross-site scripting (XSS) attacks, and so on.
- HTTP server attacks: HTTP header spoofing attacks, spyware and adware attacks, LDAP injection attacks, and so on.
- FTP attacks: FTP bounce attacks, FTP port injection attacks, TCP segmentation attacks, and others.
- DNS attacks: DNS cache poisoning attacks, query-length buffer overflows, man-in-the-middle attacks, and so on.
- SNMP attacks: SNMP flooding attacks, default community attacks, brute force attacks, and others.
- Microsoft Networking attacks: worms, MS05-003 indexing service attack, MS05-010 license logging service attack, and so on.
- Microsoft SQL attacks: SQL resolver buffer overflow, MS SQL networking DoS, heap overflow attack...
- And more!

The full list of Application Layer attack prevention safeguards and blocked attacks can be found here:

www.checkpoint.com/appint/appint_application_layer.html

The VPN capabilities for the IP40 and IP45 platforms are quite robust for the size of the devices. The Tele 8 model acts as a remote access IPSec VPN client and server. It also supports X.509 certificates and RSA secure ID tokens for authentication. The Satellite models have a few additional features that make it more valuable in a small or medium site deployment. The features include site-to-site IPSec VPN capabilities, support for multiple entry point (MEP) VPN configurations, the ability to authenticate users against an external RADIUS server, and the ability to route all Internet destined traffic through a site-to-site VPN tunnel instead of the local Internet connection.

WARNING

When routing all traffic through a site-to-site IPSec VPN tunnel to a central location, keep in mind that it may impact your users' Internet experience. If your link is slow, or the site you are connecting to is slow, your users' Internet browsing might also be impacted. This method does, however, allow you to implement centralized URL and malware filtering solutions for the entire organization.

Managing the IP40 and IP45 platforms can be performed locally, using the Web-based management interface, or centrally, using Nokia Horizon Manager (NHM), SofaWare SMP, or a Check Point SmartCenter server. Additionally, the Satellite models can also be managed using the Check Point Smart LSM package. Using the management capabilities of the IP40 and IP45, numerous security services can be enabled to further protect your network. The security services include automated software updates, embedded antivirus, Web filtering, dynamic DNS configuration, centralized logging configuration, security policy customization, and management of VPN configurations.

IP60

The Nokia IP60 appliance is a Unified Threat Management (UTM) appliance based on the Check Point Embedded NGX Stateful Inspection technology. Similar to the IP40 and IP45, the IP60 is sold as an 8, 16, 32, and Unlimited host licensed platform. All IP60 appliances can be integrated into an overall enterprise security policy for maximum security. The Check Point security policy can be centrally managed and automatically deployed to an unlimited number of IP60 gateways. You can also connect IP60 appliances to security services available from select service providers, including firewall security and software updates, Web Filtering, reporting, VPN management, and Dynamic DNS.

Two IP60 platform models are available. The Nokia IP60 Internet Security Appliance is a wired device with a firewall throughput of 80 Mbps to 150 Mbps and a VPN throughput of 20 Mbps to 30 Mbps. The firewall is capable of handling up to 8,000 concurrent connections. The platform features a four-port 10/100-Mbps LAN switch, a 10/100 Ethernet WAN port, and a secondary 10/100 WAN port that is typically used as a DMZ.

The Nokia IP60 Wireless Security Appliance is the wireless brother of the wired IP60. In addition to the IP60 capabilities, it also supports the 802.11b (11 Mbps), 802.11g (54 Mbps), and Super G (108 Mbps) wireless protocols. Figure 1.2 shows the Nokia IP60 Wireless platform.

Figure 1.2 The Nokia IP60 Wireless Platform

NOTE

You can expect the IP60 wireless security appliance to work at distances up to 100 m (~328 feet) indoors and 300 m (~984 feet) outdoors. The XR model, however, works at distances up to 300 m (~984) indoors and 1 km (~0.62 miles) outdoors.

To increase the security of wireless communications, VPN over Wireless, WEP, WPA2 (802.11i), WPA-Personal, WPA-Enterprise, and 802.1x are also supported.

You Should Know...

What Do the Flashing Lights Mean?

The Nokia IP60 Security Appliance has several status LEDs on the front of the appliance. What does each mean?

The Nokia IP60 Appliance front panel has the following status indicators:

PWR/SEC

- **Off**: Power is off
- **Flashing quickly (Green)**: System bootup
- **Flashing slowly (Green)**: Establishing Internet connection
- **On (Green)**: Normal operation
- **Flashing (Red)**: Hacker attack blocked
- **On (Red)**: Error

LAN 1-4/WAN/DMZ/WAN2

- **LINK/ACT** Off, **100** Off: Link is down
- **LINK/ACT** On, **100** Off: 10-Mbps link established for the corresponding port
- **LINK/ACT** On, **100** On: 100-Mbps link established for the corresponding port
- **LINK/ACT** Flashing: Data is being transmitted/received

VPN

- **Flashing (Green)**: VPN port in use

Serial

- **Flashing (Green)**: Serial port in use

The Nokia IP60 Wireless Appliance front panel has some additional status indicators that the wired version does not:

PWR/SEC

- **Flashing (Orange)**: Software update in progress

USB

- **Flashing (Green)**: USB port in use

WLAN

- **Flashing (Green)**: WLAN port in use

IP130

The Nokia IP130 security platform is a low-cost secure network access platform for small to medium-sized organizations. They are compact, easy to install, configure, and use, and they run the Nokia IPSO secure operating system. The size of the IP130 appliance makes it ideal for installation where space is limited. You can place the appliance on a desk, table, or mount it on a wall.

You can manage the IP130 using the Nokia Network Voyager Web-based management interface, the IPSO CLI, or the Nokia Horizon Manager software image management application. Using one of these management options, you can configure any of the three onboard 10/100 Mbps Ethernet interfaces, the auxiliary (AUX) port (serial COM2), or console port (serial COM1). Figure 1.3 shows the Nokia IP130 platform.

Figure 1.3 The Nokia IP130 Platform

The Nokia IP130 security platform supports IPSO 3.7 and later, Check Point NG VPN-1/FireWall-1 FP2 and later, and IBM RealSecure v6.5 or v7.0.

WARNING

Do not expect the Nokia IP130 to perform as well as its higher-numbered brothers. The IP130 is designed for small, medium, and branch offices, not as the core firewall for a busy enterprise. Keep this in mind when detailing your requirements and planning your deployment.

Because the IP130 appliance has no user-replaceable or user-serviceable parts, other than the replaceable external power supply, only authorized service personnel should open the appliance. Opening the IP130 will likely void your warranty.

NOTE

The predecessors to the Nokia IP130, the IP110 and IP120, have been declared end of life as of 4/30/2007 and 12/31/2008, respectively. The Nokia IP130 will be declared end of service as of 12/31/2008 and end of life as of 12/31/2010. More information can be found here:

https://support.nokia.com/home/static/productsSupported_smc.htm

IP260 and IP265

The Nokia IP260 and IP265 (also known as the EM5400) security platforms provide the power of Nokia IPSO software with your choice of firewall and VPN applications, with built-in hardware-based encryption acceleration. They are ideally suited for growing companies and satellite offices that want high-performance IP routing combined with the Check Point VPN-1/FireWall-1 enterprise security suite. The small size of the appliances makes them ideal for installations that need to conserve space. As network devices, the IP260 and IP265 appliances support numerous IP-routing functions and protocols, including RIPv1/RIPv2, IGRP, OSPF, and BGP4 for unicast traffic, and DVMRP for multicast traffic. The integrated router functionality eliminates the need for separate intranet and access routers in security applications. Figure 1.4 shows the Nokia IP260 platform and Figure 1.5 shows the Nokia IP265 platform.

Figure 1.4 The Nokia IP260 Platform

Figure 1.5 The Nokia IP265 Platform

The IP260 supports 248 Mbps of firewall throughput and 5,581 firewall connections per second. The VPN is capable of 112 Mbps of throughput. The IP265 supports 256 Mbps of firewall throughput and 4,779 firewall connections per second. The VPN is capable of 113 Mbps of throughput. The main difference between the two platforms is that the IP260 has a hard disk for local storage, whereas the IP265 relies on flash cards for local storage.

The platforms provide built-in hardware-based encryption acceleration. The accelerator card has no external connections and requires no cables. The accelerator card software package is part of Nokia IPSO, so the appliance automatically detects and configures the card.

NOTE

If SecureXL is turned on, the accelerator is automatically enabled.

You can manage the IP260 and IP265 using the Nokia Network Voyager Web-based management interface, the IPSO CLI, or the Nokia Horizon Manager software image management application. Employing one of these management mechanisms, you can configure any of the four onboard 10/100 Mbps Ethernet interfaces, the AUX port (serial COM2), the console port (serial COM1), or flash-memory PC cards.

You can use the flash-memory PC card to store local system logs, Nokia IPSO images, and configuration files. The IP260 and IP265 appliances have two PC-card slots that each supports an 8-MB or greater flash-memory PC card. The two slots are located on the front panel of the appliance.

You can rack-mount the appliances as a single appliance in a one-unit space (1U) or you can rack-mount two appliances in a 1U space if you install them in a rack-mountable shell, which you can order separately.

IP290

The Nokia IP290 security platform is available as two distinct solution offerings:

The IP290 Security Platform

The IP290 is similar to the IP260 and IP265 appliances, but has some key differentiators that make this platform more desirable for larger network installations. The IP290 contains six onboard 10/100/1000-Mbps interfaces, and a PMC slot that allows for a two-port copper Gigabit Ethernet NIC or a two-port fiber-optic Gigabit Ethernet NIC. Figure 1.6 shows the Nokia IP290 platform.

Figure 1.6 The Nokia IP290 Platform

IP290 IPS

The Nokia IP290 Intrusion Prevention with Sourcefire, also referred to as Nokia IP290 IPS, is optimized for Sourcefire 3D Sensor applications. Running Nokia IPSO-LX, a specialized Linux-based operating system, the Nokia IP290 IPS comes preinstalled with Sourcefire Intrusion Prevention System (IPS) and Real-time Network Awareness (RNA). Both products can run simultaneously on the IP290 IPS platform.

Nokia IP290 IPS appliances are ideally suited for growing companies and satellite offices that want high-performance intrusion detection and protection. The small size of Nokia IP290 IPS appliances makes them attractive for installations that need to conserve space. Two Nokia IP290 IPS appliances can be rack-mounted in a 1U space if they are installed in a rack-mountable shell, which can be ordered. Figure 1.7 shows two Nokia IP290 platforms in the rack-mountable shell.

Figure 1.7 Nokia IP290 Platforms in a Rack-Mountable Shell

IP390

The Nokia IP390 security platform is available as two distinct solution offerings, described in the following sections.

IP390 Security Platform

The IP390 is a one rack–unit appliance that incorporates a serviceable slide-out tray into the chassis design and support for various network interface cards (NICs). The platform has four onboard 10/100/1000-Mbps interfaces and two PMC slots capable of supporting any combination of the following expansion cards:

- One four-port copper 10/100 Ethernet card
- One two-port copper Gigabit Ethernet (10/100/1000 Mbps) card
- One two-port fiber-optic Gigabit Ethernet card

The Nokia IPSO system is also stored in solid-state IDE compact flash memory. The IP390 appliance supports a single hard-disk drive, which provides 40GB of disk storage. You can use the hard-disk drive to store logs generated by the system, or applications installed on the system, or use one of the two PC-card slots, both of which support 1GB flash memory PC cards. Figure 1.8 shows the Nokia IP390 platform. The IP390 is an extension of the venerable *Trooper* platform that was developed to straddle the performance leap from the Pentium 3 to Pentium 4 processor architectures. The increase in processor power, along with the ratification of AES, reduced the need for onboard encryption accelerators.

Figure 1.8 The Nokia IP390 Platform

Tools & Traps...

Storing Check Point Log Messages on Flash-Based Platforms

On flash-based platforms, you can save Check Point firewall log files locally by installing and configuring an optional disk (a hard disk or external flash-memory PC card). To store firewall logs on an optional disk, your platform must be running IPSO 4.1

Continued

Build 025 or later. It also must be running a version of the Check Point firewall that supports local logging on a flash-based platform. At the time of this writing, the Check Point version that supports local logging is Check Point NGX R62 with a required hotfix installed.

To install and configure an optional disk, the following steps must be performed:

1. If necessary, install the optional disk in the platform.
2. Log in to **Nokia Network Voyager**.
3. Navigate to the **Optional Disk** configuration page (**Configuration | System Configuration | Optional Disk**).
4. Select the **Logs** option for the device.
5. Click **Apply**.
6. Wait until you see a message indicating that you should reboot the system.
7. When the status message states the operation is complete, reboot the system.
8. When the system has rebooted, log in to **Nokia Network Voyager**.
9. Navigate to the **System Logging** configuration page (System Configuration | System Logging).
10. Select the option **Logging To Optional Disk**.
11. Click **Apply** and then click **Save**.

On flash-based systems with Logging To Optional Disk enabled, the default behavior of the Check Point firewall is to normally log to a remote server and log locally to the optional disk only if the remote server fails. If the remote server becomes available again, the firewall stops logging locally and resumes logging to the remote server.

If you want to log to a remote server and an optional disk, you must first perform the following steps in your Check Point SmartDashboard application:

1. Edit the appropriate gateway.
2. Go to **Logs and Masters | Log Servers**.
3. Select the option for saving logs locally.
4. Click **OK**.
5. Push the policy to the firewall.

IP390 IPS

Similar to the IP290, the Nokia IP390 Intrusion Prevention with Sourcefire, also referred to as Nokia IP390 IPS, is optimized for Sourcefire 3D Sensor applications. Running Nokia IPSO-LX, a specialized Linux-based operating system, the Nokia IP290 IPS comes preinstalled with Sourcefire IPS and RNA. Both products can run simultaneously on the IP390 IPS platform.

This highly versatile 1RU platform is designed for growing medium businesses, remote campuses, large branch offices and securing internal network segments. The Nokia IPS PMC card slots support any combination of the following expansion cards:

- One two-port copper Gigabit Ethernet (10/100/1000 Mbps) card
- One two-port fiber-optic Gigabit Ethernet card
- One two-port fail open copper Gigabit Ethernet (10/100/1000 Mbps) card
- One four-port fail open copper Gigabit Ethernet (10/100/1000 Mbps) card
- One two-port fail open fiber-optic Gigabit Ethernet card

IP560

The Nokia IP560 security platform is a mid-range multiport security platform that is ideally suited for the enterprise data center. It is a one rack–unit disk-based or flash-based appliance that incorporates a serviceable slide-out tray into the chassis design. In its base configuration, the IP560 consists of a solid state IDE compact flash memory, a hard-disk drive in disk-based appliances, a 1GB system RAM, an encryption acceleration card to enhance VPN performance, and four PMC slots for NICs, including a single-slot PCMCIA PMC option slot in slot three and a four-port Ethernet 10/100/1000 interface in slot four.

NOTE

In disk-based appliances, the IPSO operating system and Check Point application are stored on the hard drive, and the boot manager is stored in the flash memory. In flash-based appliances, the IPSO operating system, Check Point application, and boot manager are stored in the flash memory.

For flash-based appliances, you can purchase optional 2.5-inch hard-disk drives to use for logging. The IP560 security platform is designed to meet other mid- to high-end availability requirements, including port density for connections to redundant internal, external, DMZ, and management networks. As network devices, the IP560 appliance supports numerous IP-routing functions and protocols, including RIPv1/RIPv2, IGRP, OSPF and BGP4 for unicast traffic, and DVMRP for multicast traffic. The integrated router functionality eliminates the need for separate intranet and access routers in security applications. Figure 1.9 shows the Nokia IP560 platform.

Figure 1.9 The Nokia IP560 Platform

IP690

The Nokia IP690 security platform is available as two distinct solution offerings, as described in the following sections.

The IP690 Security Platform

The IP690 is a one rack–unit appliance that incorporates a serviceable slide-out tray into the chassis design and support for various NICs. The platform consists of a solid state IDE compact flash memory, a hard-disk drive in disk-based appliances, a 2GB system RAM, redundant hot-swappable AC power supplies, an encryption acceleration card to enhance VPN performance, and four PMC slots for NICs, including a single-slot PCMCIA PMC option slot in slot three, and a four-port Ethernet 10/100/1000 interface in slot four. Figure 1.10 shows the Nokia IP690 platform.

Figure 1.10 The Nokia IP690 Platform

The IP690 security platform is designed to meet other mid- to high-end availability requirements, including port density for connections to redundant internal, external, DMZ, and management networks.

IP690 IPS

The Nokia IP690 Intrusion Prevention with Sourcefire, also referred to as Nokia IP690 IPS, is optimized for Sourcefire 3D Sensor applications. Running Nokia IPSO-LX, a specialized Linux-based operating system, the Nokia IP690 IPS comes preinstalled with Sourcefire IPS and RNA. Both products can run simultaneously on the IP690 IPS platform.

Nokia IP690 IPS is a high-end multiport security platform that offers extensive flexibility to support the threat prevention needs of high-performance segments of the enterprise networks. Nokia IP690 IPS has four PMC slots for optional NICs, including a four-port fail open copper Gigabit Ethernet NIC, and can support as many as 16 Gigabit Ethernet ports. Nokia IP690 IPS also supports dual hot-swappable power supplies to provide maximum business continuity. It is a one rack–unit appliance that incorporates a serviceable slide-out tray into the chassis design.

IP1220 and IP1260

The Nokia IP1220 Security Platform is a mid-range security platform that is ideally suited for a smaller data center. The Nokia IP1260 Security Platform is a high-end multiport security platform that is ideally suited for the enterprise data center. Both IP1200 Series Security Platforms support an encryption accelerator card to further enhance VPN performance. The IP1200 Series is a two-rack unit appliance that incorporates a serviceable slide-out tray into the chassis design. The front panel of the IP1200 Series has two I/O slots that support hot-swapping operations. A PMC carrier is provided for the I/O slots. Each PMC carrier supports two PMC NICs for a total of four NICs. Figure 1.11 shows the Nokia IP1220 platform, while Figure 1.12 shows the Nokia IP1260 platform.

Figure 1.11 The Nokia IP1220 Platform

Figure 1.12 The Nokia IP1260 Platform

The IP1220 requires IPSO 3.7 or later and ships with 512MB of system memory that is expandable to 1GB. The IP1260 requires IPSO 3.8 and later and ships with 1GB of system memory that is expandable to 2GB. Both appliances contain two storage device slots, two PCMCIA slots, a console port, a serial port, and a four-port Ethernet management interface.

The PMC expansion slots are capable of supporting the following types of cards:

- Four-port Ethernet (10 or 100 Mbps)
- Dual-port Ethernet (10 or 100 Mbps)
- Dual-port fiber-optic Gigabit Ethernet
- Dual-port copper Gigabit Ethernet (10/100/1000 Mbps)
- Single-port ISDN S/T
- Single-port V.35 or X.21
- Single-port E1
- Single-port T1

IP2255

Nokia IP2255 appliances are ideally suited to handle small packet sizes, short-lived sessions and short-lived connections, and to provide secure Internet connectivity. The appliances use accelerated data path (ADP) technology to deliver gigabit firewall and VPN forwarding performance when running Check Point VPN-1 enterprise applications. The ADP technology also allows the Nokia operating system and Check Point VPN-1 enterprise applications to accelerate other data link, network, and transport layer functions.

The IP2255 is a three-rack unit (3U) appliance that incorporates a serviceable slide-out tray into the chassis design. Nokia IP2255 appliances are designed to meet high-end availability requirements and have port density for connections to redundant internal, external, DMZ, and management networks. Figure 1.13 shows the Nokia IP2255 platform.

Figure 1.13 The Nokia IP2255 Platform

The front panel of the Nokia IP2255 appliance supports four 10/100/1000 Ethernet management ports, four NIC slots (controlled by two Nokia ADP subsystems), one console port, one serial (AUX) port for a modem connection, and two PC-card slots that support compact-flash memory.

IP2450

The Nokia IP2450 is a high-end next-generation security appliance designed for the multi-Gigabit Ethernet throughput and port-density requirements of large enterprises and carriers. The IP2450 supports dual quad-core technology and is purpose-built to run Check Point VPN-1, Check Point VPN-1 UTM, and next-generation multithreaded enterprise security applications.

The appliance is available as a disk-based or flash-based platform. In their base configurations, the IP2450 disk-based appliance ships with at least one hard-disk drive, while the flash-based appliance ships with high-capacity compact flash memory.

The IP2450 security platform is a two rack–unit appliance that incorporates a serviceable slide-out tray into the chassis design. The front panel of the IP2450 security platform has two I/O slots that support hot-swapping operations. A PMC carrier is provided for the I/O slots. Each PMC carrier supports two PMC NICs for a total of four NICs.

The front panel of the IP2450 contains two storage device slots, one console port, one serial port, and one four-port Ethernet management interface. The network interfaces in the external PMC slot are designated for management, monitoring, and high-availability traffic. Figure 1.14 shows the Nokia IP2450 platform.

Figure 1.14 The Nokia IP2450 Platform

The IP2450 security platform is designed to meet other mid- to high-end availability requirements, including port density for connections to redundant internal, external, DMZ, and management networks. In addition, the IP2450 security platform provides redundant power supplies and hot swapping from the storage and PMC NIC slots.

The Nokia disk-based IP2450 appliance supports up to two hard-disk drives. The hard-disk drives support hot swapping (when you use the Hot Swap button on the drive's front panel), and an optional RAID-1 feature.

You Should Know...

What Settings Do I Use for Console Connections?

A standard mantra is drilled into your head during the first week of training at the Nokia Technical Assistance Center (TAC). That mantra is:

"9600, 8, N, 1, None...9600, 8, N, 1, None ...9600, 8, N, 1, None ...9600, 8, N, 1, None ..."

What does this series of random numbers and letters mean? Well it is the standard console port settings required to interface with all Nokia IP Security Platforms using a console connection software package such as Microsoft HyperTerminal. If you do not use DHCP to perform the initial configuration of your Nokia appliance, you must use a serial console connection. After you perform the initial configuration, you no longer need the console connection.

You can use any standard VT100-compatible terminal, a standard null modem cable, or a standard roll-over cable depending on the platform you are using.

Continued

You must configure your terminal-emulation program to use the following settings for the console:

Bits per second: 9600

Data bits: 8

Parity: None

Stop bits: 1

Flow control: None

A null modem cable is an RS-232 serial cable where the transmit and receive lines are cross-linked. Mappings for a standard null modem cable can be found here:

http://en.wikipedia.org/wiki/Null_modem

The following IP Security Platforms use a standard null modem cable:

IP40, IP45, IP110, IP120, IP130, IP260, IP265, IP330, IP350, IP355, IP380, IP385, IP530, IP650, IP710, IP740, IP1220, IP1260, IP2250, IP2255

Rollover cable (also known as Cisco console cable) is a type of null-modem cable that is most commonly used to connect a computer terminal to a router console port. This cable is typically flat (and has a light blue color) to help distinguish it from other types of network cabling. It gets the name rollover because the pin outs on one end are literally rolled over when RJ45 plugs are used at both ends.

The following IP Security Platforms use a standard roll-over cable:

IP60, IP290, IP390, IP560, IP690, IP2450

Introducing Additional Nokia Security Solutions

Nokia has expanded its security solution offerings over the years and we thought it prudent to introduce them in this book. You may not have an immediate need for any of the following products today, but they greatly enhance your defensive posture, overall security, and ability to manage your existing Nokia infrastructure.

Nokia Integrated Firewall

Nokia integrated firewalls include a specialized Nokia IPSO release, called IPSO-VN, which has its own firewall/VPN software solution. These firewalls feature layer 2, layer 3, and mixed networking modes, integrated virtual firewall capabilities, and hardware accelerated IPSec VPN solutions. A fully integrated Nokia Network Voyager Web UI manages all aspects of these security appliances and security policies. With optional disk or flash-based storage configurations, Nokia integrated firewalls offer exceptional performance, consistent inline reliability, and simple implementation.

NOTE

Nokia integrated firewalls are only available in China and South Korea as of summer 2008.

At the time of this writing, the IP291, IP391, and IP561 platforms are capable of operating as Nokia integrated firewalls. Designed for small businesses, Nokia IP291 integrated firewall/VPN helps protect your environment with up to 1.5 Gbps of firewall throughput, 30,000 firewall connections per second, and 1 Gbps of AES256 VPN throughput. The Nokia IP391 with disk or flash-based storage configurations is a 1RU security appliance providing multigigabit performance, four integrated 10/100/1000 Ethernet interfaces, and two expansion slots for supporting up to eight additional 10/100 Ethernet interfaces, or up to four additional gigabit Ethernet interfaces. It is capable of providing up to 3 Gbps of firewall throughput, 30,000 firewall connections per second, and 500 Mbps of AES256 VPN throughput. Designed for growing mid-size to large organizations, the Nokia IP561 integrated firewall/VPN appliance helps protect your environment with up to 6 Gbps of firewall throughput, 58,000 firewall connections per second, and 1.7 Gbps of AES256 VPN throughput. The IP561 offers disk or flash-based storage options and up to 16 Gigabit Ethernet ports.

NOTE

More information about the Nokia Integrated Firewall solution can be found at:

http://asia.nokia.com/A4895072.

Nokia IP VPN

The Nokia IP VPN platform is a high-performance VPN gateway built for medium-sized enterprises that require secure connectivity between employees, customers, and partners. The platforms support site-to-site VPN tunnels and remote-access VPN connectivity. The IP VPN platform is an evolution of the VPN clustering technology inherited from the Nokia CryptoCluster product portfolio and does not require any third-party licensing like the Check Point bundled appliances.

Each gateway, with the exception of the Nokia 5i, has identical features, including support for clustered routing, which allows for multiple platforms to participate in a load-balanced architecture to enhance performance, VPN functionality, firewall protection, and a fully integrated DHCP server.

Several IP VPN platforms are available, including the 5i, 10i, 50i, 105i, and 500i. The Nokia 5i and Nokia 10i are not rack-mounted but designed rather for placement on a desk, table, or other flat surface. The 5i is meant for small offices that need secure broadband connectivity. The gateway is equipped with three configurable 10/100 Ethernet ports and a console port to connect to an external modem. The Nokia 5i is also equipped with a serial port for dial backup in the event of a network outage.

NOTE

The Nokia Mobile VPN Client is designed for mobile phones running the Symbian operating system (Symbian OS). Once the mobile VPN application is launched, a connection is established and the mobile user is prompted for proof of identity using a token such as a SecurID password or a digital certificate. If authentication to the corporate VPN occurs successfully, a VPN tunnel is established between the mobile phone and the corporate network and all data traveling to and from the device is encrypted. To see if your Symbian-based phone is capable of running the Nokia Mobile VPN Client, check the list of supported phone models from the Nokia Mobile VPN page at:

www.nokia.com/mobilevpn.

The Nokia 10i, 50i, 105i, and 500i platforms are equipped with Nokia patented IP Clustering to ensure high availability for VPN, firewall, routing, and DHCP servers. The traffic on the gateway is automatically optimized with Dynamic Load Balancing, Automatic Session Failover, and Zero-Downtime Upgrades for maximum uptime. Using the Nokia VPN Manager, IT administrators can centrally deploy, deliver, and update VPN policies and configurations for gateways and clients.

The 10i is meant for distributed large enterprises, small offices, and remote offices that require up to 80 Mbps of stateful firewall throughput and up to 50 VPN tunnels with 75 Mbps of throughput. Figure 1.15 shows the Nokia 5i and 10i IP VPN platform.

Figure 1.15 The Nokia 5i and 10i IP VPN Platform

> **You Should Know...**
>
> ### What Is Meta-Hop?
>
> Meta-Hop lets mobile users access corporate information from business-optimized devices, such as the Nokia 9500 Communicator and Nokia 9300. Users simply open an application and authenticate themselves. On the back-end, a VPN tunnel is created in accordance with corporate security policies. All of the data is secured all the way from the corporate network to the user's device.
>
> Meta-Hop also includes self-learning and self-healing properties to help ensure that secure access to business application servers is maintained. When a new application server or subnet is added to a local network, Meta-Hop automatically distributes the availability of new resources to all gateways within a VPN deployment. This saves administrators from having to manually configure all gateways in a site-to-site VPN any time there is a change to the network. If a route between two locations in a VPN fails, Meta-Hop routes the VPN around the problem automatically without IT having to manually configure any special parameters to maintain the IPSec connections. As a result, users do not know there was a problem and IT saves maintenance time.
>
> A very detailed whitepaper entitled *Nokia IP VPN Meta-Hop Basics* can be found here:
>
> www.nokia.com/.../About_Nokia/Press/White_Papers/pdf_files/whitepaper_metahopbasics_public_05apr01.pdf.

The Nokia 50i is designed to meet the needs of medium-sized businesses and enterprise branch offices requiring up to 300 Mbps of stateful firewall throughput and 500 tunnels at 156 Mbps throughput. The unique design of the gateway enables two Nokia 50i gateways to be rack-mounted side by side for easy clustering. Figure 1.16 shows the Nokia 50i IP VPN platform.

Figure 1.16 The Nokia 50i IP VPN Platform

The Nokia 105i VPN Gateway is a high-performance, fully integrated gateway. It manages wireless security issues for mid-sized enterprises, allowing mobile users to connect to business-critical resources. The 105i meets the wireless security needs of mid-sized companies that require up to 10,000 tunnels, 300 Mbps throughput, and flexible expansion options, including Gigabit-ethernet connectivity. Nokia 105i has diskless support and high MTBF components for excellent reliability. Figure 1.17 shows the Nokia 105i IP VPN platform.

Figure 1.17 The Nokia 105i IP VPN Platform

NOTE

Mean time between failures (MTBF) is the mean (average) time between failures of a system, and is often attributed to the *useful life* of the device.

The Nokia 500i VPN Gateway is a carrier-class high-performance gateway that manages wireless security issues for mobile and broadband operators and service providers. A single Nokia 500i gateway can support up to 100,000 remote access users and offers 1.5 Gbps of VPN throughput and 1.6 Gbps of firewall throughput. Figure 1.18 shows the Nokia 500i IP VPN platform.

Figure 1.18 The Nokia 500i IP VPN Platform

NOTE

More information about the Nokia IP VPN solutions can be found at: www.nokiaforbusiness.com/nfb/find_a_product/browse_security.html.

Nokia Intrusion Prevention with Sourcefire

The Nokia Intrusion Prevention solution combines Nokia IP security platforms with Sourcefire Intrusion Sensor, Sourcefire RNA Sensor, and Sourcefire Defense Center software to offer a trusted intrusion detection and prevention solution for your environment. The solution is designed to meet the demands of enterprise customers, remote campuses, or large branch offices monitoring network segments actively (inline) or passively, making it an optimal solution for internal security.

NOTE

The OEM of the Sourcefire software by Nokia started in 2006. The OEM and distributor agreement can be found at:
www.secinfo.com/dsvRq.v595.d.htm.

At the time of this writing, the IP290, IP390, IP690, and IP2450 platforms are capable of operating as Nokia Intrusion Prevention platforms. The Nokia IP290 Intrusion Prevention, operating as a 100-Mbps sensor, is designed for small to medium-sized businesses and branch offices or remote sites. The Nokia IP390 is a high-performance appliance capable of running Sourcefire Intrusion Sensor and Sourcefire RNA Sensor software. It is designed to meet the demands of enterprise customers, remote campuses, or large branch offices. With inline performance up to 1 Gbps, the Nokia IP690 Intrusion Prevention platform supports the threat prevention needs of high-performance segments of an enterprise network. With inline performance up to 4 Gbps, the Nokia IP2450 Intrusion Prevention with Sourcefire platform supports the threat prevention needs of high-performance segments of a large business or service provider network.

NOTE

More information about the Nokia Intrusion Prevention with Sourcefire solutions can be found at:
www.nokiaforbusiness.com/nfb/find_a_product/browse_security.html.

Nokia Horizon Manager

If you have one Nokia IP security platform deployed, then using the Network Voyager Web interface to manage your platform will probably be sufficient. What happens, however, if you have 10, 50, or 100 Nokia IP security platforms dropped on your desk? Will manually performing an installation on each individual platform really be an efficient allocation of your time?

Nokia Horizon Manager (NHM) was designed to act as a secure software image inventory and platform management solution to manage your Nokia IP security platforms. Using NHM, you can perform installations, upgrades, downgrades, application installations, and distribute licenses to multiple IP security platforms simultaneously.

The server component of NHM was designed to run on Microsoft Windows 2003 Server, Sun Solaris 9, or Sun Solaris 10. You can, however, use Microsoft Windows XP Professional SP1 or later as a NHM client to manage the NHM server. Network managers can access NHM, with its remote secure GUI client, from anywhere to implement configuration changes across multiple Nokia IP Security Platforms.

NOTE

A multimedia presentation on Nokia Horizon Manager can be found at: http://europe.nokia.com/A4158074.

NHM has been around for quite a while, as you can see from author Andrew Hay's early release certificate of completion in Figure 1.19. It is generally deployed in large environments where common configuration sets and backup policies are required for your Nokia deployment.

Figure 1.19 A Nokia Horizon Manager Certificate

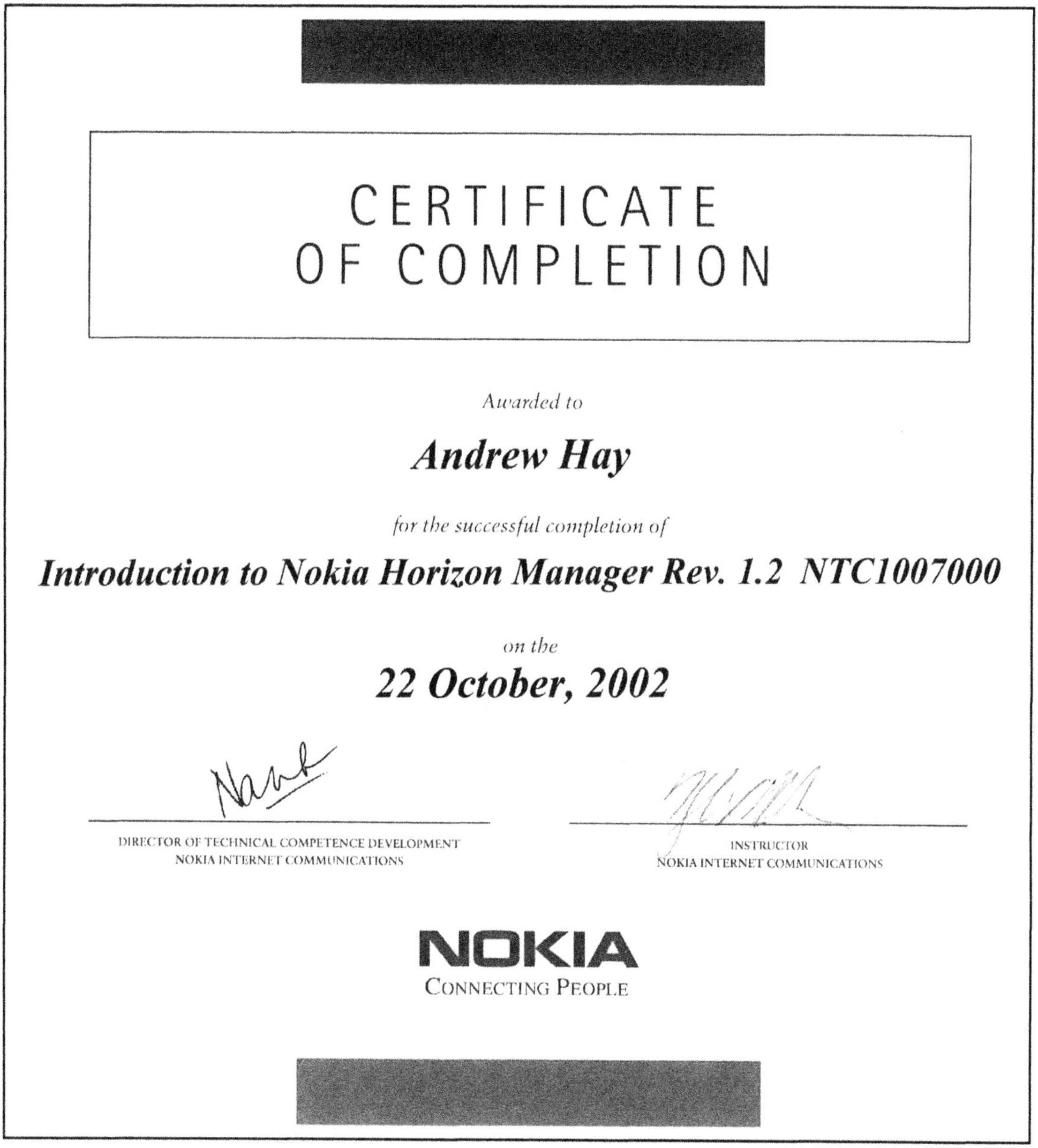

CERTIFICATE
OF COMPLETION

Awarded to

Andrew Hay

for the successful completion of

Introduction to Nokia Horizon Manager Rev. 1.2 NTC1007000

on the

22 October, 2002

DIRECTOR OF TECHNICAL COMPETENCE DEVELOPMENT
NOKIA INTERNET COMMUNICATIONS

INSTRUCTOR
NOKIA INTERNET COMMUNICATIONS

CONNECTING PEOPLE

NOTE

More information about the Nokia Horizon Manager software can be found at:

www.nokiaforbusiness.com/nfb/find_a_product/browse_security.html.

Summary

The IPSO operating system, a fork of the FreeBSD operating system, is the core of the Nokia IP security platform. It was designed to be a secure and lean operating system so it could operate efficiently on smaller hardware. IPSO contains two powerful command-line editing utilities that can be used to configure all settings for your IPSO-based security platform called ipsctl and CLISH. The Nokia Network Voyager Web-based interface lets you configure your Nokia IP security platform using your Web browser. Voyager, as it is commonly referred to, can be used to configure your Nokia IP security platform from the installation and throughout the life of your deployment.

Depending on the size of your network, a Nokia IP security appliance exists that will help protect your network. The IP40, IP45, and IP60 platforms are suited for ROBO deployments. The IP130, IP260, IP265, IP290, and IP390 platforms are suited for growing companies and satellite offices that want high-performance IP routing combined with the Check Point VPN-1/FireWall-1 enterprise security suite. The IP560, IP690, IP1220, IP1260, IP2255, and IP2450 platforms are suited for medium enterprise to large heavily trafficked network nodes, such as core datacenter connection points.

Nokia has expanded its security solution offerings over the years to include purpose-built firewall, VPN, intrusion prevention, and management solutions. Nokia integrated firewalls include a specialized Nokia IPSO release, called IPSO-VN, which has its own firewall/VPN software solution. The Nokia IP VPN platform is a high-performance VPN gateway built for medium-sized enterprises that require secure connectivity between employees, customers, and partners. The platforms support site-to-site VPN tunnels and remote-access VPN connectivity. The Nokia Intrusion Prevention solution combines Nokia IP security platforms with Sourcefire Intrusion Sensor, Sourcefire RNA Sensor, and Sourcefire Defense Center software to offer a trusted intrusion detection and prevention solution for your environment. NHM was designed to act as a secure software image inventory and platform management solution to manage your Nokia IP security platforms. Using NHM, you can perform installations, upgrades, downgrades, application installations, and distribute licenses to multiple IP security platforms simultaneously.

Solutions Fast Track

Introducing Nokia IPSO

☑ Nokia IPSO is a secure and lean operating system designed to operate as efficiently as possible.

☑ IPSO contains two powerful command-line editing utilities—ipsctl and CLISH—that can be used to configure all settings for your IPSO-based security platform.

☑ The Nokia Network Voyager Web-based interface lets you configure your Nokia IP security platform using your Web browser.

Introducing Nokia Firewall/VPN and UTM Appliances

☑ The IP40, IP45, and IP60 platforms are sold as an 8, 16, 32, and Unlimited host licensed platform, which can be upgraded using a license upgrade at any time.

☑ Some appliances, such as the IP290, can be clustered into a rack-mountable shell to save rack space and reduce clustering complexity.

☑ The standard terminal-emulation program settings for connecting to a Nokia IP series appliance is *9600, 8, N, 1, None*.

Introducing Additional Nokia Security Solutions

☑ Nokia integrated firewalls include a specialized Nokia IPSO release, called IPSO-VN, which has its own firewall/VPN software solution.

☑ The Nokia IP VPN platform is a high-performance VPN gateway built for medium-sized enterprises that require secure connectivity between employees, customers, and partners.

☑ The Nokia Intrusion Prevention solution combines Nokia IP security platforms with Sourcefire Intrusion Sensor, Sourcefire RNA Sensor, and Sourcefire Defense Center software to offer a trusted intrusion detection and prevention solution for your environment.

Frequently Asked Questions

Q: Isn't IPSO really just FreeBSD?

A: The original IPSO was a fork of the FreeBSD 2.2.6 operating system and has been changed so significantly over the years that you should only consider it a distant cousin of FreeBSD. A UNIX command, issued at the IPSO CLI, will usually work, but several commands are missing newer switches.

Q: Why would I use the CLI when I could just use the Voyager interface?

A: Because IPSO is a UNIX-like operating system, using the IPSO CLISH allows you to execute commands from remote systems or using custom scripts/applications.

Q: Can I still get IBM RealSecure for Nokia IP security platforms?

A: Unfortunately, no. IBM RealSecure has been discontinued and no further updates or revisions are being released.

Q: I bought a 16-user node IP40 platform, but I need it to support more users. What do I do?

A: Luckily, the IP40, IP45, and IP60 platforms can be upgraded to a higher user node license at any time via a simple license upgrade purchase.

Q: What is Application Intelligence?

A: Application Intelligence is a set of advanced capabilities that detects and prevents application-level attacks. It integrates network and application-level defense capabilities into Check Point products, thus delivering comprehensive attack protection and network security.

Q: My Nokia IP security platform supports flash-memory PC cards. What can I use them for?

A: You can use the flash-memory PC card to store local system logs, Nokia IPSO images, and configuration files.

Q: What is the latest supported version of IPSO?

A: At the time of this writing, the latest supported IPSO stream was IPSO 4.2.

Q: Where can I get a Nokia integrated firewall?

A: Unfortunately, at the time of this writing, the Nokia integrated firewall was only available in China and South Korea. The authors do not have any information on when this offering will be available outside of these two countries. Please contact your Nokia reseller for further information.

Q: Can I use my phone to VPN into a Nokia IP VPN appliance?

A: Yes. Using the Nokia Mobile VPN Client on your Symbian OS phone, you can establish a VPN tunnel between your mobile device and corporate network.

Q: If I can't use IBM RealSecure as an intrusion detection/prevention sensor on Nokia IP security platforms, what can I use?

A: The IP290, IP390, IP690, and IP2450 are all capable of operating as a Nokia Intrusion Prevention platform with Sourcefire Intrusion Sensor, Sourcefire RNA Sensor, and Sourcefire Defense Center software.

Q: When would I use Nokia Horizon Manager?

A: There are several scenarios where you might require a management solution like NHM, but the most likely scenario is when you have ten or more Nokia IP security appliances and the management of these individual platforms becomes laborious. NHM was designed to act as a secure software image inventory and platform management solution to manage your Nokia IP security platforms. Using NHM, you can perform installations, upgrades, downgrades, application installations, and distribute licenses to multiple IP security platforms simultaneously.

Chapter 2

Nokia IPSO Overview

Solutions in this chapter:

- Exploring the History of IPSO
- Introducing Access and Security Features
- Understanding Users and Groups
- Learning the Directory Structure
- Configuring IPSO

☑ Summary

☑ Solutions Fast Track

☑ Frequently Asked Questions

Introduction

Josh Smith arrived on Thursday to provide an overview of the Nokia Security Solutions portfolio. Accompanying him was Shin Murashima, his most seasoned sales engineer, who knew everything about the Nokia appliances. After Josh provided an overview of the Nokia portfolio, he paused to see if Marty had any questions.

"Well," said Marty, "I tried to do as much research as possible on the platforms so we weren't sitting here staring at each other when it came to the business requirements."

Josh smiled. It wasn't often that his customers were as prepared to discuss implementation as Marty.

"I figure we're going to need to implement two, or more, appliances at the perimeter to share the load going in and out of our network. We're also going to need to make sure that the operating system that they're installed on is secure out-of-the-box and easy to administer." Marty cleared his throat. "Let's just say that I don't want my security team spending days hardening the underlying platform before we implement these firewalls. Time is precious and I have a huge list of projects to complete."

Shin smiled and looked at Josh. "Shin, why don't you start your presentation on the Nokia IPSO operating system that we ship with these Nokia IP Series Appliances?"

Shin walked up to the white board, and to Marty's surprise, started drawing a flowchart of the IPSO operating system from memory.

"What no PowerPoint presentation?" Marty smirked.

"Trust me," Shin said without turning around, "you'll understand everything about IPSO features by the time I'm done explaining it."

Marty sat back and watched Shin walk through the entire feature set of the IPSO operating system, including the history of IPSO, access and security features, the user, group, and directory structure, and finally a brief overview on how to configure IPSO. Marty was impressed. He hated sitting in a conference room watching someone walk through a slide show. Whenever he had questions, he politely interrupted Shin, who expertly answered them.

After Shin's presentation was over, and Josh had completed his presentation as well, Marty and the two men went out for lunch.

While waiting for their meals, Marty turned to Josh. "I really like the solution, but, as you can imagine, we need to put it through its paces in our lab."

Josh took a drink of water. "Sure thing, Marty. I'll even throw in Shin to help you with the implementation in your lab."

Shin smiled. "Think of me as a free set of steak knives."

Marty laughed, almost spitting out his water. "Well, Shin," Marty said, "You're in for quite an adventure in our lab. When we test…we really test."

The waiter brought over their meals, placed Marty's steak in front of him, and handed him a steak knife.

"It's okay," Marty smiled, "My colleague here has already brought me a steak knife."

The waiter, confused, set the steak knife down anyway and walked away. "I guess that went over his head," Marty said laughing.

Nokia designed its Nokia IP Appliance with several goals in mind:

- To provide a stable and high-speed routing platform for integration into enterprise networks
- To provide a modern stateful network firewall
- To provide a secure platform out-of-the-box so administrators can rightfully spend their time looking after their networks and not have to worry about "hardening" their firewall platform operating system

These design goals combined to produce the Nokia IP Appliance. In the following sections, we discuss the history of the IPSO operating system and the Nokia Network Voyager interface. We will also cover what the products are based on and describe how Nokia has improved them over the years. Finally, we will discuss the basic layout of the IPSO file system, as well as some of its features.

The version of IPSO we cover in this book—and introduce in this chapter—is IPSO 4.2. This version has some new features compared with earlier releases that we discuss in detail in later chapters. This chapter concentrates on the IPSO security features and how the operating system is logically laid out.

Exploring the History of IPSO

As you learned in Chapter 1, the problem of a fast and efficient routing appliance was already solved when, in December 1997, Nokia bought Ipsilon Networks, a California-based company that developed and sold high-speed switching products. Ipsilon also developed a Web-based management tool for its products that the company named the *Network Voyager*. Nokia took the Ipsilon product line as a base and integrated its own operating system, combined with the Check Point FireWall-1 product, into an appliance designed for high-speed packet forwarding and modern stateful firewalling. The operating system Nokia engineers developed to run on the appliance was named IPSO.

The UNIX operating system had its origins at Bell Labs in 1969. Over the years, it evolved into many variants. One variant was termed 4.4BSD and was developed at the University of California at Berkeley. A portion of the core operating system source code base for 4.4BSD was made freely available and formed the basis for many modern UNIX or UNIX-like operating systems, among them FreeBSD.

NOTE

See www.freebsd.org for more information on FreeBSD, which is still an ongoing and very active operating system project.

The networking code present in the Berkeley Software Distribution (BSD)-style UNIX variants has been developed continuously in an open fashion over the last 30 years and is some of the most stable and widely used in the world.

FreeBSD version 2.2.6 was released in March 1998 and provided a solid basis for Nokia engineers to develop the IPSO operating system. IPSO has since diverged from the original FreeBSD code base, but it still remains a stable and efficient BSD-based networking platform at its core. Nokia has managed to trim down the original operating system by removing unnecessary binaries, hardening the operating system configuration, and improving the core routing and networking functionality. Modern versions of IPSO are just under 40 MB when compressed, and approximately 120 MB uncompressed.

Understanding Specialized IPSO Releases

Nokia IPSO is the all-encompassing term for the operating system that runs on Nokia IP Appliances. Several IPSO releases are available, however, that you may have heard of but were unsure of their purpose. These releases, known as IPSO LX and IPSO SX, were purpose-built IPSO releases designed to run Nokia applications that required a Linux operating system to function.

Nokia IPSO LX was the first release of a Linux-based IPSO from Nokia. It was deployed in 2002 on the now-defunct Message Protector and briefly thereafter on a short-lived appliance version of the Nokia Access Mobilizer, which was acquired from Eizel. It had a partitioning scheme somewhat reminiscent of the traditional IPSO operating system, a LILO configuration, a boot manager also somewhat inspired by IPSO, and a software package installer that made RPM packaging look more familiar to a Nokia IPSO administrator. It did not, however, include a full configuration database or a Nokia Network Voyager Web interface, the two things that normally define IPSO.

IPSO SX is the current Linux-based IPSO from Nokia, and is used on Nokia appliances sold with Sourcefire 3D. It includes a full Nokia Network Voyager and database implementation. The current Nokia Network Voyager 4.x look and feel, present in IPSO, was based on the interface implemented for IPSO SX.

NOTE

More information on these specialized releases of IPSO can be found at: http://en.wikipedia.org/wiki/Nokia_IPSO.

Introducing Access and Security Features

The primary purpose of a firewall is to protect a network segment, or segments, from unauthorized traffic as determined by your network security policy. A typical firewall deployment consists of two or more interfaces, with one interface connected to your trusted network and the other connected to the less trusted network. Figure 2.1 details a simple deployment that places your firewall between your corporate network and the Internet.

Figure 2.1 A Simple Firewall Deployment

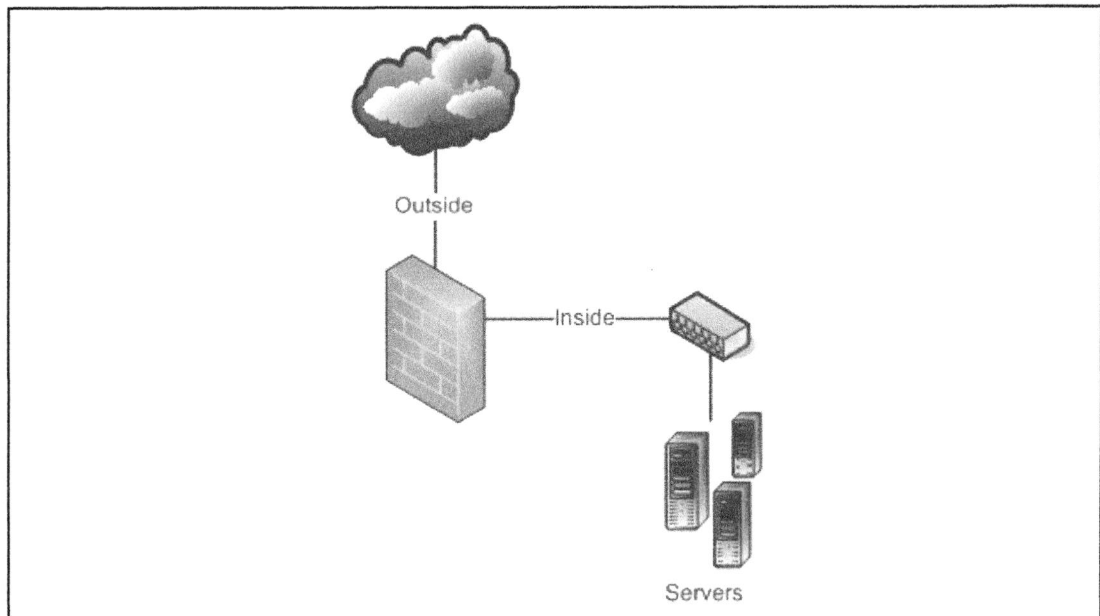

NOTE

Firewall terminology is usually very easy to relate to when compared to other security technologies. For example, a firewall with two active interfaces is typically referred to as a *two-legged firewall*. A firewall with three active interfaces is called a *three-legged firewall*.

Usually, the less trusted side of your firewall is the Internet, although this is not always the case. As with any network device that lives in such a critical network intersection, it must be installed and configured with care. The following steps detail the actions typically followed when installing a firewall:

1. Install an operating system on your hardware of choice. You might have many chances to specially configure the operating system during the installation, but most installations are automated and provide little choice along the way. You might have to add or remove hardware before the installation, and you might have to find and configure device drivers for your hardware during the installation.
2. Remove packages, networking options, and graphical user environments unless your operating system requires a graphical user interface.
3. Remove unnecessary network services, system binaries, games, and the like.
4. Configure the remaining network services so they are restricted or configured more securely.
5. Configure network interfaces and test routing and connectivity.
6. Install and configure your firewall software.
7. Install the testing and monitoring tools you use every day, which were not included with your operating system during initial installation.

NOTE

The previous list details the *how* of installing a firewall but not the *why*. Before deciding to implement a firewall, you must first put together a plan that details the business requirements and the risks you plan to mitigate by implementing the firewall. This plan is beyond the scope of this book, because we primarily focus on the *how*.

The art of removing unnecessary packages and network services from an operating system and securely configuring the remaining services is known as *hardening*. If not performed properly, your system might become more vulnerable to attack then when you started. The hardening process is not something that can easily be configured by the average user. Intimate knowledge of the operating system and services is required to properly secure the system, and care must be taken to ensure that no vulnerabilities are presented to potential attackers. Even when performed properly, the hardening process can be quite time consuming.

Nokia realized that providing a hardened operating system out of the box would appeal to most time-starved administrators. They built their hardened operating system by starting with a baseline operating system installation without any services or applications and then added binaries, libraries, and network services necessary to function as an enterprise routing platform. We discuss the details of Nokia's hardening in the following sections, and we talk about remote network access and the IPSO file system structure. By the time you are done reading this chapter, you will have a good understanding of IPSO and how it is put together.

Using Remote Access

Nokia IP Appliances have many of the standard remote and local access network protocols you would expect on a UNIX-based operating system, and each is discussed in the following sections. All available protocols leverage Transmission Control Protocol (TCP) for client/server communications. Enabling any of the listed protocols means your Nokia IP Appliance will function as a listening server, waiting for inbound connections.

Understanding the Client/Server Model and Listening Sockets

TCP forms the basis for many client/server-based communication protocols, for which reliability is paramount. A TCP connection can live in any of a dozen or so states, depending on whether the connection is being initiated, in progress, closing, or being reset.

Four pieces of data are used to uniquely identify each connection: a source IP address, a destination IP address, a source port number, and a destination port number. Ports can be in the range 1 through 65535. Which port is assigned to which application is mostly standardized, at least for certain port ranges.

TIP

You can view port assignments in the */etc/services* file on your Nokia IP Appliance.

For example, suppose an SSH server with IP address 192.168.8.1 is listening for incoming connections on TCP port 22 (the default for SSH). A client makes a connection from

192.168.8.15 and gets assigned a random high port (ports greater than 1024) by the SSH client (33090). If a new connection is established from the same client host, it will be assigned a new port number and will be considered separate from the previous connection, even though the communications are from the same host. When a system service starts, it binds to a port number, creating a *socket* that listens for incoming connections destined for that port number. You can see the status of any current network servers and connections using the *netstat -an* command. The output of this command is shown next:

```
Active Internet connections (including servers)
Proto        Recv-Q Send-Q        Local Address        Foreign Address
                (state)
tcp               0                 0                  *.22        *.*
                                 LISTEN
tcp               0                 0                  192.168.8.15.33090
                                                       192.168.8.1.22
               ESTABLISHED
tcp               0                 0                  192.168.8.15.33667
                                                       192.168.8.1.22
               ESTABLISHED
```

The first line tells you that an SSH server is listening for incoming connections on TCP port 22 on this host (or rather, something is listening for connections on TCP port 22). This is a useful debugging tool, especially when you want to know if a server is functioning properly and is listening for incoming connections. If you are using your Nokia IP Appliance as a firewall, you should see netstat results with additional services that you cannot immediately identify. Those ports are common control ports that Check Point FireWall-1 listens on by default. Examples of these ports are:

```
tcp      0      0    *.256          *.*      LISTEN
tcp      0      0    *.259          *.*      LISTEN
tcp      0      0    *.261          *.*      LISTEN
tcp      0      0    *.262          *.*      LISTEN
tcp      0      0    *.264          *.*      LISTEN
tcp      0      0    *.265          *.*      LISTEN
```

NOTE

AERAsec Network Services and Security GmbH maintain a detailed list of ports used by Check Point NGX at:

www.fw-1.de/aerasec/ngx/ports-ngx.html.

Please note this is not an official list, but is easy to quickly verify against.

Most of the services mentioned here, with the exception of SSH, have runtime configuration settings in the */var/etc/inetd.conf* file. In most UNIX systems, this file contains lists of network servers and how they should be run. In IPSO, however, this file will only have an entry for the Telnet service by default, because all other services are disabled. If you disable the Telnet service in Nokia Network Voyager, this file will contain only the following skeleton template:

```
#    This file was AUTOMATICALLY GENERATED
#    Generated by inetd_xlate on Sun Jun 1 23:22:18 2008
#
#    DO NOT EDIT
#
```

Notes from the Underground...

Port Numbers

A *port* is a special number in the header of a data packet. Ports are typically used to map data to a particular process running on a computer. The range of available ports is from 1 through 65535. This range is made up of *well-known ports, registered port numbers*, and *dynamic and/or private ports.*

The Well Known Ports are assigned by the Internet Assigned Numbers Authority (IANA) and on most systems can only be used by system (or root) processes or by programs executed by privileged users. Ports are used in TCP to name the ends of logical connections, which carry long-term conversations. For the purpose of providing services to unknown callers, a service contact port is defined. To the extent possible, these same port assignments are used for UDP communications. This list specifies the port used by the server process as its contact port. The contact port is sometimes named the "well-known port." The range for assigned ports managed by the IANA is 0-1023.

The following is an example listing from the IANA list:

```
Keyword      Decimal       Description
--------     --------      ---------------
ftp-data     20/tcp        File Transfer [Default Data]
ftp          21/tcp        File Transfer [Control]
```

The registered ports are listed by the IANA and on most systems can be used by ordinary user processes or programs executed by ordinary users. Ports are used by TCP to name the ends of logical connections, which carry long-term conversations. For the purpose of providing services to unknown callers, a service contact port is defined.

Continued

To the extent possible, these same port assignments are used for UDP communications. The list specifies the port used by the server process as its contact port and IANA registers users of these ports as a convenience to the community. The registered ports are in the range 1024-49151.

An example listing from the IANA list:

```
Keyword        Decimal         Description
-------        -------         -----------
kazaa          1214/tcp        KAZAA
kazaa          1214/udp        KAZAA
```

The dynamic and/or private ports are those from 49152 through 65535 and are not associated with common services used openly on the Internet. No ports can be registered in this range.

The IANA port list can be found at:

www.iana.org/assignments/port-numbers.

More information about the TCP protocol can be found in RFC793 located at:

www.faqs.org/rfcs/rfc793.html.

More information about the UDP protocol can be found in RFC768 at:

www.faqs.org/rfcs/rfc768.html.

Using Telnet

Telnet is a clear-text (non-encrypted) TCP-based remote login and command protocol. Nokia enables it by default in all its enterprise devices, but we recommend you disable Telnet before putting your firewall into production in favor of the Secure Shell (SSH) protocol. SSH is a secure replacement for Telnet (and FTP) that allows data to be exchanged using a secure channel. Many administrators still use Telnet on a daily basis because they are not aware that SSH clients are available for almost all UNIX and Windows platforms. If you must use Telnet, restrict it to a lab environment, but be aware of the security implications of using a clear-text remote login protocol. As an added measure of security, you can configure Telnet so the one-time password scheme *S/KEY* is mandatory.

Using File Transfer Protocol (FTP)

FTP is a way to transfer files to or from a remote server. Like Telnet, FTP is a clear-text protocol and should be used only when necessary. Unlike Telnet, the FTP server is disabled by default on new Nokia installations. FTP is commonly used as a server that allows anonymous uploads or downloads, where passwords are typically just e-mail addresses or left blank. The Nokia FTP server is not configured to accept anonymous logins and by default only allows the admin user to log in. As with Telnet, be aware of who might be listening to your network traffic as you initiate an FTP session to your Nokia firewall as user admin, because your password will be visible on the wire. S/KEY logins can also be made mandatory for incoming FTP connections.

Tools & Traps...

S/KEY

S/KEY is a one-time password system developed for authentication to UNIX-like operating systems. Each password used in the system is usable only for one authentication. Passwords cannot be reused, which means that the sniffing of passwords to determine the password being used is futile. A password is generated as follows (the *server* being the authenticating server).

1. This step begins with a secret key *w*.
   - This secret can be provided by the user or can be generated by a computer. Either way, if this secret is disclosed, then the security of S/KEY is compromised.
2. *H* is a cryptographic hash function.
3. H is applied n times to w, thereby producing a hash chain of n one-time passwords (the passwords are the results of the cryptographic hash H).
4. The initial secret w is discarded.
5. The user is provided with the n passwords, printed out in reverse order.
6. The last *n-1* passwords are discarded from the server. Only the first password, at the top of the user's list, is stored on the server.

Figure 2.2 visualizes this process.

Continued

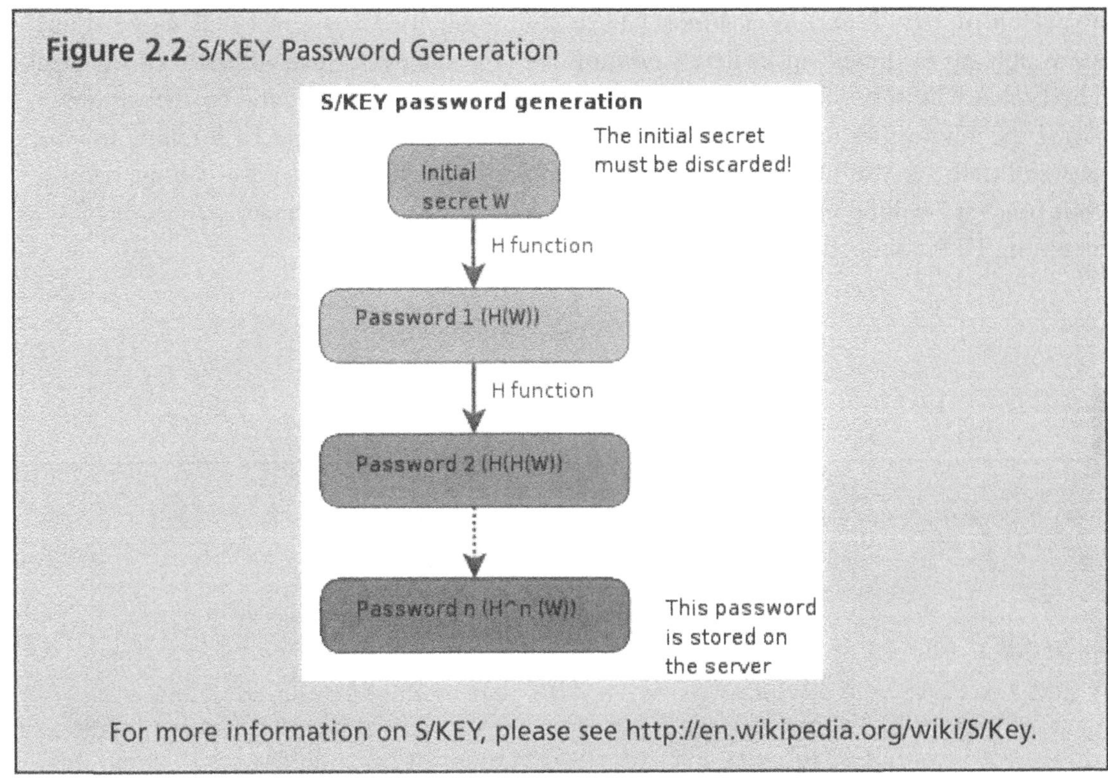

Figure 2.2 S/KEY Password Generation

For more information on S/KEY, please see http://en.wikipedia.org/wiki/S/Key.

Using Secure Shell (SSH)

As previously stated, SSH is a secure replacement for Telnet and FTP. Starting with IPSO version 3.4, Nokia began shipping OpenSSH with their operating system. OpenSSH is a free and open-source implementation of the SSH protocol available anonymously from ftp://ftp.openbsd.org. The version of OpenSSH used by Nokia, 3.1p1, is disabled by default in all IPSO versions that support it. Free SSH clients exist for many operating systems, including Windows. Most UNIX operating systems also now ship with the OpenSSH client and server by default, so there is little reason not to use SSH. OpenSSH has some useful features, including local and remote port forwarding, X11 tunneling, strong encryption by default, and scp (secure copy) that make SSH an appealing replacement for Telnet and FTP.

NOTE

One of the most popular free Windows-based SSH clients available is *Putty*. It can be downloaded from the project home page at:
www.chiark.greenend.org.uk/~sgtatham/putty/.

Using HTTP/HTTPS

The Nokia Network Voyager configuration interface is enabled by default on all IPSO releases and is configured to be accessible over standard HTTP on TCP port 80. Nokia uses the open-source Apache HTTP Server to run the Nokia Network Voyager Web user interface. It is possible (and highly recommended) to reconfigure Voyager to be only accessible using HTTPS, and you can also manually change the port number that Apache listens on. These configuration options are thoroughly covered in Chapter 4.

WARNING

Because IPSO uses third-party software for SSH and HTTP/HTTPS servers, you need to be aware that Nokia may not be as quick to adopt security fixes as the vendors of these software packages. It is a good idea to subscribe to the mailing lists provided by the OpenSSH and Apache projects to remain informed of any potential software vulnerabilities.

Gaining Console Access

Finally, if you cannot, or will not, allow remote access to your Nokia device, all models come with at least one serial port configured for local console access. Nokia provides the appropriate serial cables for your Nokia IP Appliance and are designed to work with their products. One cable is shipped with each device and if you need a replacement, standard null modem cables also work. The console port is configured to work with any standard serial client, such as Hyperterm or Minicom, at 9600/8/N/1. You can also plug a modem into your Nokia device console port, allowing for out-of-band access over phone lines in emergencies.

Notes from the Underground...

Using the AUX Port to Manage Another Device

There may be an instance where you need to connect to another system's serial port for console access for out-of-band management. Using the built-in auxiliary (AUX) port of your Nokia IP Appliance, you can connect to, and administer, the out-of-band system as needed. To do this, you must perform the following steps to change the settings of the AUX port:

Continued

- Step 1
  Connect a console cable between your Nokia IP Appliance AUX port and the serial port of the out-of-band device you want to administer.
- Step 2
  Use the following command on your Nokia IP Appliance to connect a terminal session through the AUX port:

```
nokia[admin]# tip com2
```

- Step 3
  Perform the required administrative actions on your out-of-band device. To end the connection, use one of the following command combinations:

```
nokia[admin]# ~.
```

OR

```
nokia[admin]# ~^D
```

Using Other Security Features

Nokia has made some other design decisions with IPSO that were directly related to security. The following is a list of the most visible features that emphasizes the *hardened* nature of IPSO:

- The root partition is mounted read-only.
- Sendmail is used to send mail only, through a relay server, and incoming mail is not accepted.
- A DNS server is not installed.
- Berkeley *r* commands (*rlogin*, *rsh*, *rcp*, *rexec*) are not present.
- There is no X-Windows server or libraries.
- No exportable file systems (such as NFS) or Remote Procedure Call (RPC) services are installed.
- No remote information services (finger, talk, or who) are installed.
- Chargen, echo, and daytime are disabled by default.
- There is no printing subsystem or server.
- No mail or news servers (POP or IMAP) are installed.
- Device access can be restricted to the serial console only.
- There are no extra CGI programs other than those used by Voyager under admin access.

- IPSO Dynamic routing protocols all have strong authentication capabilities using keyed MD5.
- The IPSO shadow password scheme uses MD5.
- IP access lists and rate shaping can be configured independently of Check Point FireWall-1 and can limit Denial-of-Service attacks.

Understanding Users and Groups

The IPSO operating system has only one user enabled by default at system installation time: the *admin* user. This user has a user ID (UID) of 0, like standard UNIX root accounts, and has all the privileges of the root user. The password for the admin user is chosen during the initial system configuration and must be used when the admin user logs in through Nokia Network Voyager, the console connection, or remotely using Telnet or SSH.

NOTE

The root account is present in IPSO but is not used for administrative functions. To that end, it is disabled in favor of the admin user account.

Another user is created for you during installation: the *monitor* user. This account is designed to allow read-only administrator-level access to your Nokia IP Appliance. The password for the monitor user account is disabled by default, so you must enable it, using the admin user account, prior to its first use.

You can see several other users present in the */etc/master.passwd* system password file. These are *bin*, *nobody*, and *daemon*. These users are not meant or able to be used as login accounts. They are used by system processes that need to run at a reduced privilege level as opposed to processes that run with the permissions of UID 0. For example, the Apache HTTP Server (httpd) runs as though it were started by user *nobody*. You can see which processes run with the privileges of which user account by using *ps aux* at the command prompt. The following shows what part of that output looks like:

```
pint[admin]# ps aux
USER    PID     %CPU  %MEM  VSZ   RSS   TT   STAT  STARTED  TIME     COMMAND
root    28586   0.0   0.1   440   208   p0   R+    5:15PM   0:00.06  ps -aux
root    23998   0.0   1.1   1128  2788  ??   Ss    Tue12AM  0:40.20  /bin/httpd
                                                                     -d /web
```

```
nobody  24000  0.0  1.1  2108  2784  ??  I    Tue12AM  0:02.74  /bin/httpd
                                                                 -d /web
nobody  24001  0.0  1.1  2120  2692  ??  I    Tue12AM  0:02.67  /bin/httpd
                                                                 -d /web
nobody  24465  0.0  1.1  2148  2820  ??  I    Tue09PM  0:02.67  /bin/httpd
                                                                 -d /web
nobody  24468  0.0  1.1  2132  2800  ??  I    Tue09PM  0:01.78  /bin/httpd
                                                                 -d /web
root    28520  0.0  0.2  500   380   p0  Ss   4:22PM   0:00.20  -csh (csh)
root    0      0.0  0.0  0     0     ??  DLs  1Jun08   0:03.25  (swapper)
```

Notice that all the Apache HTTP Server processes (/bin/httpd -d /web) run as user *nobody*. This is an important security feature. If someone were to gain remote access to your Nokia IP Appliance by exploiting the Apache HTTP Server running on it, after connecting they would not have admin (or root) level privileges. In fact, they would have to run a local exploit of some kind to gain root privileges after breaking into your system. The fact that Nokia has hardened IPSO by mounting the root partition as read-only and removing development tools and libraries makes finding or building a local root exploit into it very difficult.

Other nonprivileged or administrative users can be created in IPSO versions 4.2. Defining multiple user accounts on your Nokia IP Appliances aids in change auditing and may even be required for certain government or industry compliance regulations. As part of Nokia's operating system hardening process, any changes made by a user are recorded in the system log file or syslog. This includes things like logging in, mounting or unmounting file systems, password changes, and system security policy changes. Each new user you create, including new privileged users, has their own home directory, to further enable accountability.

You should not have to change the Nokia group file, */var/etc/group*, unless you add an unprivileged user account to your Nokia IP Appliance. If you want that account to be able to switch to the admin user—for example su – admin—after the user has logged in, you must add the account to the *wheel* group. Chapter 5 discusses user and group management in greater detail.

Learning the Directory Structure

The directory structure in the IPSO operating system is similar to many other UNIX operating systems. If you have any UNIX or Linux experience, you will feel right at home.

NOTE

Refer to Appendix A if you need a UNIX refresher or introduction.

Some differences exist in the way Nokia has laid out the file system. One of the major differences is that the root partition, where the kernel image and system binaries are stored, is mounted read-only by default. This means you will not be able to alter or create new files on this partition unless you change how the partition is mounted. The admin user can remount the root partition with read/write permissions using the following command:

```
pint[admin]# mount-uw /
```

When you are done making modifications, remount the root partition with read-only permissions using the following command:

```
pint[admin]# mount -o ro /
```

This was done to protect the root partition contents from accidental or malicious damage. It is harder for you, as an administrator, to make a mistake that prevents the system from booting if you must consciously make the root partition permissions read/write. This step should be unnecessary, however, because you can always place your own scripts and programs in the */opt* directory, and nothing you could change in the root partition would be persistent across a reboot, anyway. The only time you might need to remount the root partition is when you are upgrading from an old version of IPSO and you are required to upgrade the boot manager. In that case, the new boot manager image file must be placed in the */etc* directory.

NOTE

Boot manager upgrades do not happen very frequently when compared to older revisions of the IPSO operating system. You might never have to upgrade the boot manager on your Nokia IP Appliance.

The rest of the system partitions are mounted with read/write permissions, including */var*, */opt*, and */config*. Table 2.1 shows the disk partitions created in a default IPSO 4.2 installation, along with their purposes and specifications. This layout is drawn from the system file /etc/fstab.

Table 2.1 IPSO File System Details

Name	Device	Type	Read/Write?	FSCK?	Usage
/config	/dev/wd0a	ufs	YES	YES	Global system configuration
swap	/dev/wd0b	swap	N/A	NO	System swap space
/var	/dev/wd0d	ufs	YES	YES	System logs and other variable process run-time data
/opt	/dev/wd0e	ufs	YES	YES	Optional or user added software
/	/dev/wd0f	ufs	NO	YES, first	Root partition; holds kernel images and system binaries
/proc	/proc	procfs	YES	NO	Kernel configuration and runtime process data

The UFS file system is a standard on most BSD UNIX versions, including IPSO. */proc* holds runtime kernel and process data, although is generally not viewed or altered by users. Some system binaries draw data from the */proc* file system as they run.

The name in the *Device* column is the system name given to the raw device that represents the particular disk partition. On your system, these names might be different from the ones listed in the table, depending on which model appliance you have. Device names for things like Ethernet cards and disk drives will be related to the device manufacturer or device class they belong to. In this case, the *wd* portion of the disk partition name indicates a Western Digital IDE hard drive. IDE drives have four slices, which are really what most people call a DOS partition. Each slice can contain a file system, which can have any number of partitions. Nokia formats its disks with the entire drive occupying one slice, so you will not see a slice specifier in a device name as you do on Solaris or FreeBSD. The number 0 in *wd0* means this is the first disk. Disks are numbered starting at 0, so on a Nokia IP Appliance with two hard drives, they would be called wd0 and wd1, and the final letter indicates the partition you are referring to in a given slice. The partition is simply a logical piece of a disk slice that refers to a part of the file system installed on that slice. For example, the b partition on the first hard drive is written *wd0b* and refers to the system swap space.

The *FSCK* column of the table deserves some explanation. During a proper system shutdown, with the shutdown or halt commands, each partition or file system is marked to show it was cleanly unmounted and so will not be checked for errors during system startup. If for some reason the system is not shut down cleanly, for example due to a power failure, each file system will not have been properly unmounted and so will need to be checked for errors. The program that does the checking is called *fsck* (for file system check) and is run during the Nokia IP Appliance startup sequence before each partition is mounted. Most of the time, *fsck* will run and fix any errors it finds automatically, although every once in a while it needs manual attention. The root partition is always checked for errors first because it must be mounted before system startup can continue.

Understanding Special Directories and Disk Space

Several subdirectories in the IPSO file system are worth mentioning. Table 2.2 outlines these directories and their purposes. An arrow (->) in the table means that the directory to the left of the arrow is a symbolic link to the directory on the right side of the arrow. $FWDIR refers to the environment variable that holds the absolute path to the FireWall-1 base directory, if the firewall is enabled.

Table 2.2 IPSO Special Purpose Directories

Directory	Purpose
/web	Nokia Network Voyager Web pages and CGI scripts
/tmp -> /var/tmp2	Temporary file space
/var/crash	Holds crash dump files after a system crash
/var/monitor	Monitor user's home directory
/var/admin	Admin user's home directory
/etc -> /var/etc	System configuration files
/var/log	System log files
$FWDIR/log -> /var/fw/log	Firewall log files

You also might wonder how much disk space you have and how it is allocated per partition. IPSO is partitioned for you, and although the sizes of the partitions vary by model number, in general you will find that the */var* and */opt* partitions have the most space available. The other partitions are really meant to be static in size after IPSO has been configured. As a reference, the IP130 we are using as a test platform gives us the following when we run *df –k* (sizes in kilobytes):

```
pint[admin]# df -k
Filesystem   1K-blocks      Used      Avail      Capacity    Mounted on
/dev/wd0f       598029    121654     428533           22%             /
```

```
/dev/wd0a        37556     167     34385     0%    /config
/dev/wd0d     14732935   66923  13487378     0%       /var
/dev/wd0e      2561196   46809   2309492     2%       /opt
procfs               4       4         0   100%      /proc
```

Keep in mind that newer models have bigger hard drives. You can see that */var* has the most free space, which makes sense when you consider that */var* holds firewall and system logs as well as temporary file space. Nokia actually uses a set of formulas to determine disk partition sizes. Table 2.3 shows the formulas for any IPSO of version 3.4 or later.

Table 2.3 IPSO Partition Formulas

Partition	Size and/or Formula
/config	~32MB
Swap	(size of disk * 0.25)
	Note - with a max of 1 GB
leftover space	(size of disk - */config - swap)*
/	((leftover * 2) / 7)
	Note - with a max of ~600 MB
/opt	(leftover / 7)
/var	*(leftover - (/opt + /)*

NOTE

With the introduction of IPSO 3.6 and Disk Mirroring, an additional 128 KB is set aside by the installation process. Please refer to Nokia Solution ID 1132425 for more information about how IPSO partitions the disks.

Dealing with Floppy and CD-ROM Drives

Sometimes you will have to deal with floppy or CD-ROM drives based on the model of Nokia IP Appliance you are using. IPSO has support for mounting MS-DOS formatted floppy disks, but you first need to create a mount point for the floppy. Do this with the *mkdir /var/floppy* command, then run the mount command:

```
mount_msdos /dev/fd0 /var/floppy
```

After the floppy has been mounted, you can cd into */var/floppy* and access the files on it with the usual commands (*cp*, *mv*, *ls*, and so on), just like a normal file system directory. To unmount the floppy after it has been mounted, use the unmount command:

```
umount /var/floppy
```

For CD-ROMs, after a CD has been put in the drive, you can use the following command to mount it:

```
mount -t cd9660-o ro /dev/wcd0c /cdrom
```

You must unmount the CD-ROM before you can eject it. To unmount the CD-ROM, use the following command:

```
umount /cdrom
```

Make sure you move out of the floppy or CD-ROM mount point directories prior to unmounting either of those devices, or you will get an error indicating failure after running the unmount command.

Configuring IPSO

The */config* partition is where Nokia stores the */config/active* global configuration file. This file is a flat text file that contains configuration directives in a special format. It is actually a symbolic link to */config/db/initial*, which is the real configuration file. The file must be present and valid (in other words, not corrupted) at boot time for your Nokia device to get configured; otherwise, the device will go into *first-time boot mode* and attempt to configure itself using DHCP, or wait for you to configure it through the serial console port. The following is what you might see in a small part of the */config/active* file:

```
interface:eth-s2p4c0:ipaddr:192.168.0.2:mask 24
monitor:monitord:group:ifthroughput:pthroughput:binding:ipsctl:interface:
   *:stats:ipackets t
ipsrd:vrrp:interface:eth-s2p2c0:virtualrouter:40:monitor:monif:eth-s1p3c0:
   priority 10
ipsrd:vrrp:interface:eth-s1p4c0:virtualrouter:30:monitor:monif:eth-s2p2c0 t
process:sshd:path /usr/sbin
ipsrd:vrrp:interface:eth-s2p4c0:virtualrouter:60:monitor:monif:eth-s2p2c0:
   priority 10
passwd:daemon:uid 1
ipsrd:vrrp:interface:eth-s3p1c0:virtualrouter:80:advertiseinterval 1
```

Because this file is read at every system boot, and because IPSO reconfigures itself according to the contents of this file, altering this file in some way is the only way to change things like interface IP addresses or add a static route. Prior to IPSO 3.6, Nokia Network

Voyager was meant to be the only interface that would allow you to update the system configuration permanently. Nokia introduced CLISH, the command-line shell, in IPSO 3.6, and now any configuration can be done using this command shell, along with Nokia Network Voyager. You can also make backups of past configurations, as you would have made before a major configuration change. You will see the old configurations in */config/db*, along with the active file. Having global system configuration localized to one file is a security feature in that it makes it easy to restrict access to system configuration and is much simpler than using many separate files.

Apart from daily system configuration and maintenance issues, a common task for an administrator to perform is to run a custom startup script. If you ever need to run a script or executable file at system startup, you can add your commands to the */var/etc/rc.local* file. IPSO will execute the *rc.local* script after all other startup and initialization has taken place. This method could be used, for example, to start some custom monitoring scripts you have written.

Summary

All Nokia IP series enterprise appliances are based on the IPSO operating system, which was developed from a branch of the FreeBSD operating system, itself based on 4.4BSD UNIX. This basis makes for a very stable networking and routing platform. Given that most Nokia appliances are sold primarily as firewalls, Nokia made a substantial effort to harden IPSO and make it a more secure platform for firewall use. Some of the things Nokia did include shutting off unnecessary services, restricting system configuration and user accounts, logging system access, and removing development tools and libraries.

Nokia IPSO has evolved over the years to include specialized releases for new Nokia applications that could not, or rather should not, run on the standard IPSO release. These purpose-built versions of IPSO perform a specialized task and may not be needed based on your Nokia IP Appliance requirements.

Your Nokia appliance can be accessed remotely via Telnet, FTP, HTTP/HTTPS, or SSH and locally through a serial console port. Only Telnet is enabled by default, but enabling or configuring network access is easy using the Voyager interface. It is possible to change the port that the Apache Web server listens on, and you can restrict Voyager connections to HTTPS only.

The IPSO admin user is the equivalent of the UNIX root user in terms of privilege and is the only user enabled by default in a new IPSO installation. A monitor user can be enabled to allow read-only access to the Nokia IP Appliance, and it is possible to add other privileged and unprivileged users after installation. New unprivileged users must be added to the wheel group to be able to su to the admin account.

The IPSO file system is logically just like any other UNIX file system, but it features some changes that increase security. The IPSO root partition is mounted read-only, and changes to system settings and mount points are all logged using the syslog facility.

Solutions Fast Track

Exploring the History of IPSO

☑ Nokia IPSO has its roots in FreeBSD 2.2.6.

☑ Nokia has trimmed down the original operating system by removing unnecessary binaries, hardening the operating system configuration, and improving the core routing and networking functionality.

☑ IPSO SX is Nokia's current Linux-based IPSO, and is used on Nokia appliances sold with Sourcefire 3D.

Introducing Access and Security Features

- ☑ A typical firewall deployment consists of two or more interfaces, with one interface connected to your trusted network and the other connected to the less trusted network.
- ☑ The version of OpenSSH used by Nokia, 3.1p1, is disabled by default in all IPSO versions that support it.
- ☑ Because IPSO uses third-party software for their SSH and HTTP/HTTPS servers, you need to be aware that Nokia may not be as quick to adopt security fixes as the vendors of these software packages.

Understanding Users and Groups

- ☑ The IPSO operating system has only one user enabled by default at system installation time: the *admin* user.
- ☑ Defining multiple user accounts on your Nokia IP Appliances aids in change auditing and may even be required for certain government or industry compliance regulations.
- ☑ If you want to allow a user to switch to the admin user—for example, su – admin—the user must be added to the *wheel* group.

Learning the Directory Structure

- ☑ You can mount the root (/) partition with read/write permissions using the *mount -uw /* command.
- ☑ The UNIX program that is run during the Nokia IP Appliance startup to fix any errors is called *fsck*.
- ☑ Partition sizes are determined by a set formula, as described in Table 2.3 in this chapter.

Configuring IPSO

- ☑ The global configuration file, which contains all system configuration settings, is named */config/active*.
- ☑ Old configuration files are found in */config/db*.
- ☑ To execute custom scripts or commands, use the */var/etc/rc.local* file.

Frequently Asked Questions

Q: What operating system is IPSO based on?

A: IPSO is based on FreeBSD 2.2.6.

Q: Can't I just put a newer version of FreeBSD on my Nokia IP Appliance?

A: Nokia IPSO has been optimized and hardened specifically for Nokia IP Appliances. Trying to run another operating system on your appliance would not only void your warranty but may also introduce performance, security, and compatibility issues for your other software running on the system.

Q: Can I run Nokia IPSO SX with Check Point NGX?

A: Nokia IPSO SX was designed specifically to support the Sourcefire 3D product that was OEM by Nokia. It is not currently compatible with Check Point NGX and should not be installed if your plan is to install a Check Point firewall on your Nokia IP Appliance.

Q: What is the first thing I need to do before placing a firewall in my network?

A: Before even thinking about placing a piece of hardware or software into your network, you must first determine the business requirements solved and risks protected by implementing the solution.

Q: Should I use Telnet or SSH to connect to the command line of my Nokia IP Appliance?

A: Unless you have a business requirement that states Telnet must be used, it is recommended that SSH become your standard remote access administration protocol. Not only does SSH provide strong encryption but it also lets you securely copy files to and from your appliance using SCP.

Q: I have to use Telnet to administer my Nokia IP Appliance. Can I do anything to make it a stronger communications solution?

A: Although you will not be able to encrypt regular Telnet communications, you can implement S/KEY to increase the strength of your authentication process. S/KEY is a one-time password system developed for authentication to UNIX-like operating systems. Each password used in the system is usable only for one authentication.

Q: My security policy doesn't allow remote access to my Nokia IP Appliance using Telnet or SSH. How can I administer my appliance from the command line?

A: If, for any reason, you cannot connect to your Nokia IP Appliance remotely, you can always connect a console cable between your appliance and another machine. This provides a direct connection to the serial port of your appliance for any of the required administrative tasks you would perform using a remote access protocol.

Q: Why can't I log in as the root user?

A: The root account is present in IPSO but is not used for administrative functions. To that end, it is disabled in favor of the admin user account.

Q: Why does the httpd server run using the *nobody* user?

A: This is an important security feature. If someone were to gain remote access to your Nokia IP Appliance by exploiting the Apache HTTP Server running on it, once in they would not have admin (or root) level privileges.

Q: I work with three other co-workers who will need to administer my Nokia IP Appliance. Can we all use the default *admin* account?

A: Yes, but you probably should not. If each user in your group uses an individual admin-level account, you can more accurately audit changes made to your appliance.

Q: Will changes I make to the root (/) partition persist after a reboot?

A: No, they will not. Any changes you make to the root partition will be reverted back when you reboot your appliance.

Q: How can I check to see how much space is available on my Nokia IP Appliance?

A: Using the *df* command, you can see how much space is used, available, where the partition is mounted, and other things.

Q: How can I figure out how much space is going to be allocated to my partitions before I install IPSO?

A: Using the simple calculations provided in Table 2.3, you can—if you know the size of the hard drive in your appliance—determine how much space is going to be allocated to each partition.

Q: How do I mount a CD-ROM on IPSO?

A: You can use the following command to mount the CD-ROM on your system:

```
mount -t cd9660 -o ro /dev/wcd0c /cdrom
```

Q: Where are all of my IPSO configurations stored?

A: All IPSO configuration settings are stored in the */config/active* file. This is a flat-text file that, if removed, will default your IPSO installation back to the factory defaults.

Q: Where are my old configurations stored?

A: All old configurations are stored in */config/db*, along with the active file.

Q: Can I run custom scripts when my Nokia IP Appliance starts up?

A: If you have a custom script, or require that a command run at startup, you can reference it in the */var/etc/rc.local* file. This will execute your script or command when the system finishes its boot sequence.

Chapter 3

Initial IPSO Configuration

Solutions in this chapter:

- Preparing to Boot for the First Time
- Installing IPSO
- Performing the First-Time Boot Configuration
- Continuing the Configuration
- Upgrading to IPSO 4.2

☑ Summary

☑ Solutions Fast Track

☑ Frequently Asked Questions

Introduction

Shin arrived the following Monday with several Nokia appliances. With the help of Marty and two members from his team—Ming Tsai and Mark Olyphant—Shin unpacked the appliances. Mark rack-mounted them and connected the required network cables based on the prepared network diagram.

After everything was connected, Marty turned to Shin. "They're all yours, Knifey."

Mark and Ming looked at each other and then at Marty. "I'll explain later," said Marty.

Shin plugged the laptop that Marty had given him into the console port of the appliances and walked through the initial configuration. He made sure to stop and explain each step and answered any questions that came up. Mark and Ming made sure to document the entire installation process in case they needed to reference it later.

Within 30 minutes, the four appliances were racked, connected, and the initial configuration had been performed. "Wow," said Marty, "That was quick. Now what?"

Shin disconnected the laptop. "Now," Shin said, "We have to perform the more advanced configuration steps using Nokia Network Voyager."

Preparing to Boot for the First Time

When you first take your Nokia IP appliance out of the shipping box, mount it in your rack, connect the cables, and turn it on, you are not exactly finished with the installation process.

NOTE

In some older models of Nokia IP appliances, the serial number is located on the bottom of the chassis. Before mounting the appliance, you should write down the serial number because it will be needed during the installation process. There is nothing worse than racking an appliance, only to realize you need to unrack it to obtain the serial number.

As the system boots, depending on the state you received your system in, you are prompted to enter some basic configuration information before you can start configuring the system more thoroughly. In some cases, the IPSO image provided on the system is far older than the currently supported version or, depending on where it was purchased, may contain residual configuration data from the previous owner. In the latter scenario, you will probably want to perform a *fresh* or *clean* installation of the IPSO operating system.

Workstation Configuration

To prepare for the initial configuration of your Nokia appliance, you need a workstation, laptop, or VT100-capable terminal that you can directly connect to the Nokia through a console cable or perhaps indirectly (through a hub or switch), or through a standard Ethernet connection. If you choose the DHCP method of auto configuration, you need only a standard Ethernet connection. Until IPSO 3.5, a direct console connection was the only way to configure a Nokia appliance out of the box. The DHCP client on the NSP makes this process somewhat easier now.

In addition to proper cabling and network connections, you need a serial terminal emulator of some sort, such as Hyperterm (Windows) or Minicom (Linux or other UNIX platforms). Note that it is possible to do the entire Nokia base configuration through a VT100 terminal directly connected to the console port. You just will not be able to use Nokia Network Voyager through a graphical Web browser. In that case, you can continue the initial configuration through the command-line interface named CLISH.

Physical Connections

Nokia supplies a DB-9 serial cable with all its devices. This cable allows for console connections from properly configured clients. If you do not have one of the Nokia cables, you can use a standard null-modem cable for the serial connection. The local end of the serial cable plugs into one of your workstation serial ports, while the remote end plugs into your Nokia console port. The console port is always labeled Console and is usually on the front of the device for ease of use in rack-mounted installations. Your terminal emulator settings should match those shown here:

- Bits/second (BPS): 9600
- Data bits: 8
- Parity: None
- Stop bits: 1
- Flow control: None
- Terminal emulation: Auto, VT100, or VT102

If you want to continue the configuration using Nokia Network Voyager and a graphical browser, you need an Ethernet cable. You can directly connect a crossover cable from your workstation to any Ethernet port on your Nokia device, or you can indirectly connect a straight-through cable from your workstation to a hub or switch and from there to the appliance over another straight-through cable.

Installing IPSO

Performing a clean installation of IPSO is a relatively simple process. The installer configures the system based on the selections you make during the process. The standard installation procedure is as follows:

1. Power on the appliance and enter the boot manager (Bootmgr).
2. Initiate the installation process.
3. Answer the configuration questions when prompted.
4. Reboot the appliance when the initial installation is complete.
5. Continue with the initial configuration of your appliance.

Let's walk through these steps.

Booting into the Boot Manager

When the appliance is powered on, after the memory test completes, you will be presented with a menu that presents you with a boot manager (1 Bootmgr) option and an IPSO (2 IPSO) option. Entering **2** starts the standard boot process into the IPSO operating system. Because you want to perform a clean installation, you must enter the boot manager and launch the installation process. Do this by entering **1**.

```
1 Bootmgr
2 IPSO
Default: 1
Starting bootmgr
Loading boot manager..
Boot manager loaded.
Entering autoboot mode.
Type any character to enter command mode.
BOOTMGR[1]>
```

You are now presented with the BOOTMGR[1]> prompt. To begin the installation process, enter **install**.

```
BOOTMGR[1]> install
```

The IPSO installer will warn you that you will be expected to enter information during the initial configuration process, such as client IP address, netmask, system serial number, and so on. You will also be reminded that the clean installation will destroy any existing files and data on your disk. To proceed with the clean installation, enter **y**.

TIP

If you get to this point and realize there is information on this appliance you wish to keep, now would be a good time to exit the installation by entering **n**.

```
################### IPSO Full Installation ####################
You will need to supply the following information:
   Client IP address/netmask, FTP server IP address and filename,
   system serial number, and other license information.
This process will DESTROY any existing files and data on your disk.
#################################################################
Continue? (y/n) [n] y
```

TIP

To accept the default value for a menu option, shown within the [ ] braces, press **Enter**.

Part of the installation process is entering the chassis serial number. This is very important in identifying your appliance should you ever need to call into Nokia for technical support. The serial number is typically located on the back of the appliance but has been known to be on the bottom in some of the older appliances.

NOTE

Of course, you have already written down the serial number prior to racking the appliance, as per our tip earlier in the chapter, right?

Enter your serial number.

```
Motherboard serial number is NONE.
The chassis serial number can be found on a
sticker on the back of the unit with the letters
```

```
S/N in front of the serial number.
Please enter the serial number: 12345678
Please answer the following licensing questions.
```

Depending on your requirements, an enhanced license can be purchased to support IGRP and BGP routing protocols. If you do not require these routing protocols, like most Nokia installations, you can enter **n** when presented with the IGRP and BGP questions.

```
Will this node be using IGRP ? [y] n
Will this node be using BGP ? [y] n
```

Because we are performing a clean installation, it does not make sense to pull the installation image from the disk you are looking to overwrite. What the installation script does allow you to do, however, is fetch the IPSO image from a remote FTP server. Depending on your FTP server configuration, you can select from one of two options: You can install from an anonymous FTP server where no user credentials are required, by entering **1**, or you can install from an FTP server that requires a username and password, by entering **2**.

Regardless of the option you select, you are prompted to enter an IP address for your Nokia IP appliance, the IP address of the FTP server, and the default gateway your communications will use for routing. The only additional entries that require user input, if using the second menu option, are the username and password fields. To simplify the installation steps, and based on what most customers use, we will continue with the anonymous FTP server method. When prompted to choose an installation method, enter **1** and then the IP addresses you want to use. Each IP address field requires that you press **Enter** to move to the next option.

```
1. Install from anonymous FTP server.
2. Install from FTP server with user and password.
Choose an installation method (1-2): 1
Enter IP address of this client (10.3.2.5/24): 192.168.200.10/24
Enter IP address of FTP server (0.0.0.0): 192.168.200.50
Enter IP address of the default gateway (0.0.0.0): 192.168.200.1
```

After you have supplied the IP address and subnet mask information, you must select a physical interface to assign it to. Select the interface you wish to use for the FTP communications by typing the corresponding number and pressing **Enter**.

```
Choose an interface from the following list:
1) eth1
2) eth2
3) eth3
4) eth4
Enter a number [1-4]: 4
```

NOTE

The interface list may appear differently on your Nokia since it depends entirely on the types of network interface cards (NICs) installed.

Select the speed of the chosen interface by entering the corresponding number.

```
Choose interface speed from the following list:
1) 10 Mbit/sec
2) 100 Mbit/sec
Enter a number [1-2]: 2
```

Select the duplex settings for the interface using *h* for half duplex or *f* for full duplex. The duplex settings of your interface will vary depending on the device it is connected to.

```
Half or full duplex? [h/f] [h] f
```

NOTE

Switching ports almost always defaults to full-duplex operation, unless there is a requirement for interoperability with devices that are strictly half duplex.

Now that your interface is configured, you must provide the path to, and the name of, the IPSO installation package on the remote FTP server. Enter the full path to the IPSO installation package. If the installation package is located in the root directory of the FTP server you can press **Enter** or type the / character and press **Enter**.

```
Enter path to ipso image on FTP server [/]: /
```

Accept the default IPSO installation package name by pressing **Enter** or typing the full package name and pressing **Enter**.

```
Enter ipso image filename on FTP server [ipso.tgz]: ipso.tgz
```

After the installation script connects to the FTP server, you have the option of telling it what to retrieve. You can retrieve all valid packages it finds on the server, retrieve the packages it finds one at a time and prompt you to accept or reject the package, or retrieve no additional packages and only install the IPSO operating system. Select your option by entering the associated menu number.

```
1. Retrieve all valid packages, with no further prompting.
2. Retrieve packages one-by-one, prompting for each.
```

```
3. Retrieve no packages.
Enter choice [1-3] [1]: 3
```

A final confirmation screen lets you verify all of your configuration settings before proceeding. Check this carefully to ensure you have not added any incorrect information. If you are happy with your configuration settings, enter **y** to start the installation process.

```
Client IP address=192.168.200.10/24
Server IP address=192.168.200.50
Default gateway IP address=192.168.200.1
Network Interface=eth1, speed=100M, full-duplex
Server download path=[//]
Package install type=none
Mirror set creation=no
Are these values correct? [y] y
```

If the Nokia appliance is able to contact the FTP server and find the IPSO installation package, you will see the installation process status messages as the various steps are completed.

```
Downloading compressed tarfile(s) from 192.168.200.50
Hash mark printing on (1048576 bytes/hash mark).
Interactive mode off.
100% 36760KB    00:00 ETA
Checking validity of image...done.
Installing image...done.
Image version tag: IPSO-4.2-BUILD069-10.27.2007-035617-1515.
Checking if bootmgr upgrade is needed...
Need to upgrade bootmgr. Proceeding..
Upgrading bootmgr...
new bootmgr size is 2097152
old bootmgr size is 1474560
Saving old bootmgr.
Installing new bootmgr.
Verifying installation of bootmgr.
```

When the installation completes, you will see an Installation Completed message and a final instruction telling you to reset the system or press **Enter** to reboot.

```
Installation completed.
Reset system or hit <Enter> to reboot.
```

Now that the installation is complete, you must perform the first-time boot configuration steps, which are described in the next section.

NOTE

Your boot loader might be updated as part of the IPSO installation.

Performing the First-Time Boot Configuration

Now that the appliance has been clean installed, we can proceed with the first-time boot configuration settings. These settings will connect your Nokia appliance to your network and allow you to define the administrative password for further configuration. You can use two methods to perform the initial configuration:

- In an automated fashion by using the built-in dynamic host configuration protocol (DHCP) client.
- Manually by using a console (direct serial) connection.

Using DHCP to Configure the System

If you have a DHCP server in your network, you can configure it to provide your Nokia appliance with all host name, IP address, and default route information it requires for the initial configuration. If using the DHCP configuration method, please note that the default admin password will be set to *password*.

On your DHCP server, configure the minimum mappings for the following required items:

- Host name for the appliance
- Nokia appliance serial number
- IP address for the appliance

NOTE

The DHCP client accepts the lease time for the IP address that the server provides in IPSO 3.8 and later. Previously, the client accepted only IP address leases that were at least a year long.

The following provides an example of the DHCP configuration information you may need on your DHCP server:

```
ddns-update-style ad-hoc;
subnet 192.168.200.0 netmask 255.255.255.0 {
   # default gateway
   option routers 192.168.200.1;
   option subnet-mask 255.255.255.0;
   option domain-name-servers 192.168.200.155;
   range dynamic-bootp 192.168.200.10 192.168.200.100;
   host pint {
   # serial number of the box
   option dhcp-client-identifier "123456";
   fixed-address 192.168.200.10;
   option host-name "pint";
   }
}
```

The DHCP server must be on the same network as the Nokia platform, or the DHCP/BOOTP relay must be configured on the intermediate routers. Figure 3.1 shows a typical Nokia appliance placement in relation to the DHCP server.

Figure 3.1 Nokia Appliance Placement for DHCP Addressing

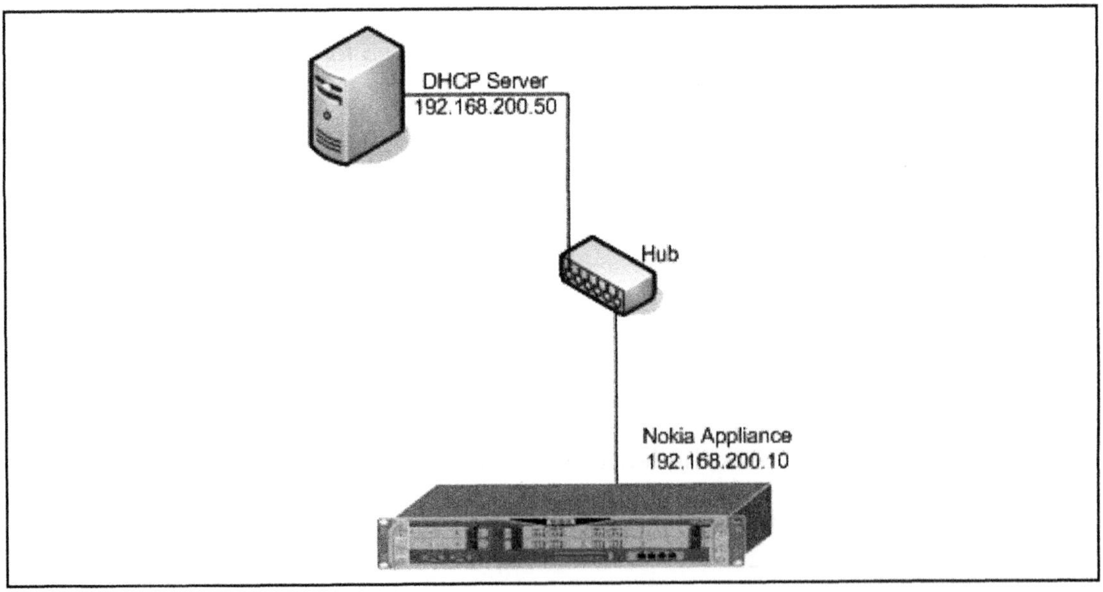

Figure 3.2 shows a typical Nokia appliance placement when using a DHCP or BOOTP relay server.

Figure 3.2 Nokia Appliance Placement for DHCP Addressing via Relay

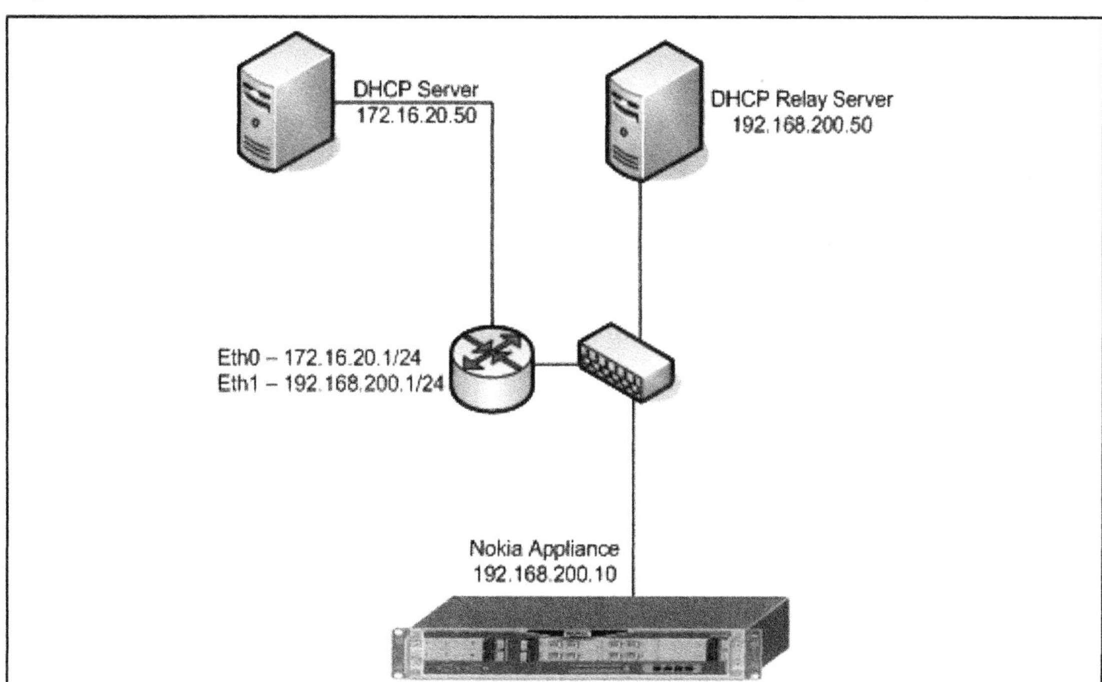

With the server-side configuration completed, you must force the Nokia appliance to obtain the information provided by the DHCP server. With the network interface of your Nokia appliance connected to the network, turn the platform on and allow the DHCP client to receive its information.

NOTE

This can take upwards of five to ten minutes to complete.

Configuring Manually with a Console Connection

The first thing you must do is provide a hostname for your Nokia appliance. Typically, this is a one-word name for the system so you can easily recognize the system when performing administrative tasks. Type your hostname and press **Enter**. You will also be prompted to confirm the setting of the hostname. Enter **y** to continue.

```
   Please choose the host name for this system. This name will be used
   in messages and usually corresponds with one of the network hostnames
   for the system. Note that only letters, numbers, dashes, and dots (.)
   are permitted in a hostname.
Hostname? pint
Hostname set to "pint", OK? [y] y
```

The admin user will require a password to authenticate you to the command line of the Nokia appliance and for Web-based administration using the Nokia Network Voyager interface. You will be asked to enter it again for validation. Enter the password you want to use.

```
Please enter password for user admin: notpassword
Please re-enter password for confirmation: notpassword
```

With the hostname and admin password set, you will be prompted to select your preferred configuration method. You can configure an interface and use Nokia Network Voyager to complete the configuration (the recommended method), or you can configure an interface by using the CLI.

The easiest, and most popular, configuration method is to configure the appliance using the Nokia Network Voyager. Enter **1** to select this method.

```
You can configure your system in two ways:
   1) configure an interface and use our Web-based Voyager via a remote browser
   2) configure an interface by using the CLI
Please enter a choice [ 1-2, q ]: 1
```

Select an interface you would like to use to configure your appliance by typing the associated menu option number and pressing **Enter**.

```
Select an interface from the following for configuration:
   1) eth1
   2) eth2
   3) eth3
   4) eth4
   5) quit this menu
Enter choice [1-11]: 4
```

Type the IP address and mask length you want to use for this interface. Press **Enter** for each option after you have input the correct information.

```
Enter the IP address to be used for eth4: 192.168.200.10

Enter the masklength: 24
```

You are asked to configure a default route for this interface to use, and to provide the IP address information for your default router. To configure the default route, enter **y**. When asked to specify your default router, type the IP address of your default gateway and press **Enter**.

```
Do you wish to set the default route [ y ] ? y

Enter the default router to use with eth4: 192.168.200.1
```

After specifying the IP address and default route information, you have the option to change the interface speed and duplex settings. Because this interface is configured for 1000 mbs and full duplex, by default, you can enter **n** to accept the current settings.

```
This interface is configured as 1000mbs by default.

Do you wish to configure this interface for other speeds [ n ] ? n
```

A final confirmation screen lets you verify all of your configuration settings before proceeding. Check this carefully to ensure you have not added any incorrect information. If you are happy with your configuration settings, enter **y**.

```
You have entered the following parameters for the eth4 interface:

         IP address: 192.168.200.10

         masklength: 24

      Default route: 192.168.200.1

              Speed: 1000M

             Duplex: full

Is this information correct [ y ] ? y
```

Optionally, you can configure the virtual local area network (VLAN) settings for this interface. Typically, you will want to answer no to this question unless the interface needs to be part of the VLAN for security or routing reasons. Enter **n** to continue.

```
Do you want to configure Vlan for this interface[ n ] ? n

You may now configure your interfaces with the Web-based Voyager by

typing in the IP address "192.168.200.10" at a remote browser.
```

At this point, you should be able to connect to your Nokia appliance using the Nokia Network Voyager Web interface with the browser of your choice.

A final optional setting is the changing of the default SNMP community string. Because this is easily performed within Nokia Network Voyager, along with more advanced SNMP configuration settings, you can type **n** and press **Enter** to complete the initial configuration.

```
Do you want to change SNMP Community string [ n ] ? n
```

Notes from the Underground...

Detecting an Installed Modem

If you have a modem installed, then during the installation process you will see a message similar to the following:

```
Modem detected on /dev/cuaa1.
Enable logins on this modem [y,n]:
```

If you want to allow remote logins through the installed modem, you can configure the modem right now or after the initial configuration through the Nokia Network Voyager or IPSO CLI interfaces.

If you choose to configure the modem for logins now, you are prompted to configure a country code for the modem. The list of valid country codes are displayed next for both Ositech Five of Clubs series modems:

Country Codes for Ositech Five of Clubs Modem

- 22 - USA
- 20 - Canada
- 1 - Australia
- 2 - Belgium
- 3 - Denmark
- 4 - Finland
- 5 - France
- 6 - Germany
- 17 - Greece
- 99 - Iceland
- 7 - Ireland
- 8 - Italy
- 9 - Luxembourg
- 10 - The Netherlands
- 11 - Norway
- 12 - Portugal

Continued

- 13 - Spain
- 14 - Sweden
- 25 - Switzerland
- 16 - United Kingdom

Country Codes for Ositech Five of Clubs II Modem

- B5 - USA
- 20 - Canada
- 09 - Australia
- 0F - Belgium
- 31 - Denmark
- 3C - Finland
- 3D - France
- 42 - Germany
- 46 - Greece
- 57 - Iceland
- 59 - Italy
- 69 - Luxembourg
- 7B - The Netherlands
- 82 - Norway
- B8 - Portugal
- A0 - Spain
- A5 - Sweden
- A6 - Switzerland
- B4 - United Kingdom

Continuing the Configuration

With the initial configuration complete, you should now launch your Web browser and connect to Nokia Network Voyager. From this interface, which is covered in detail in Chapter 4, you can configure the more advanced settings and change any of the initial installation settings you have already made.

NOTE

Remember, the default administrative user name is admin.

If you would prefer to configure the Nokia appliance using a remote access client, such as Telnet or SSH, you can. This method of configuration becomes very helpful if the Nokia appliance is deployed in a remote location and only command-line access is provided for administrative access.

When IPSO finishes the boot process, the SSH daemon is the only remote access service available. Telnet is disabled by default because it is a less secure remote access mechanism. To communicate with your Nokia system by using SSH, you must have an SSH client program installed on a workstation that has network connectivity to the Nokia appliance.

Tools & Traps...

Using a Host Key

After you perform the initial configuration, IPSO will automatically generate a host public and private key pair. You can install the public key on the workstations you will use to connect to the Nokia appliance. This allows the SSH client to verify it is really communicating with the Nokia appliance and not a system that is impersonating your appliance. The most secure way to transport the key is to use an out-of-band method, such as transporting the key on a floppy disk. This reduces the possibility that the key could be stolen in transit.

If you are unable to transfer the public key to your workstation, a message appears when you first connect to your Nokia appliance using the SSH client. At this point, you are asked to accept the public key. If you choose to accept the key, the connection is established. This procedure is potentially less secure because the SSH client cannot be sure the host key is really being supplied by the Nokia appliance. If you decide to not accept the key, you will not be able to connect to the Nokia appliance.

Continued

> More information about SSH can be found at:
> http://en.wikipedia.org/wiki/Secure_Shell
> More information about public-key cryptography can be found at:
> http://en.wikipedia.org/wiki/Public-key_cryptography

If you require that Telnet be enabled for remote access, you can enable the service using the Nokia Network Voyager or CLI interfaces.

NOTE

Detailed Nokia Network Voyager configurations are covered in Chapter 4, and the CLISH interface is covered in Chapter 11.

To use Nokia Network Voyager to enable the Telnet service:

1. Log in to the platform by using Nokia Network Voyager.
2. In the Nokia Network Voyager navigation tree, expand **Configuration** | **Security and Access** | **Network Access and Services**.
3. Click **Yes** for the Allow TELNET Access field.
4. Click **Apply**.
5. Click **Save** to make your change persistent across reboots.

To use the CLI to enable the Telnet service:

1. Establish a console connection to the platform.
2. start the CLI by entering **clish**:

   ```
   pint[admin]# clish
   ```

3. Use the ***set*** command to enable Telnet:

   ```
   NokiaIP130:9> set net-access telnet yes
   ```

4. Enter the ***save config*** command to make your changes persistent across reboots:

   ```
   NokiaIP130:10> save config
   ```

5. To exit CLISH, enter **quit**:

   ```
   NokiaIP130:11> quit
   ```

Upgrading to IPSO 4.2

You might already have a previous IPSO release installed on your Nokia platform and simply want to upgrade to IPSO 4.2.You can upgrade directly to Nokia IPSO 4.2 from the following IPSO versions:

- 3.7
- 3.7.1
- 3.8
- 3.8.1
- 3.9
- 4.0
- 4.0.1
- 4.1

Notes from the Underground...

Words of Caution When Upgrading

As with any software, there might be some caveats or warnings you should review before starting the upgrade process. Nokia IPSO is no exception and has some issues you should know about before proceeding with an upgrade.

Upgrading from IPSO 3.7.1 and Earlier

If you upgrade to IPSO 4.2 from IPSO 3.7, IPSO 3.7.1, or earlier and want to use disk mirroring, you must first install the 4.2 boot manager and then install IPSO 4.2 from the new boot manager. If you do not, you might receive messages that show the mirror set is 100 percent complete or that the *sync process* is complete when in fact the disks are still syncing. You do not need to follow this procedure if you upgrade to IPSO 4.2 from IPSO 3.8, 3.8.1, 3.9, 4.0, 4.0.1, or 4.1.

Upgrading from IPSO 4.1

Avoid using the IPSO boot manager to install IPSO 4.2 on a platform running IPSO 4.1 Build 016 or 019 if you installed the 4.1 build using the boot manager. If you attempt to upgrade in this way, the system might repeatedly panic and reboot. To upgrade these systems to IPSO 4.2, use Network Voyager, the CLI, or the *newimage* shell command.

Continued

Space Requirements

You need at least 140MB of free disk space in your root partition to install an IPSO 4.2 image. To determine the available disk space, log in to the IPSO shell through a terminal or console connection and enter **df -k**. If the first number in the Avail column (which shows the available space in the root partition) is less than 140000Kbytes, you should make more space available by deleting the temporary files specified in the following command if they are present. (These files might not be present, depending on how the upgrades were done on your system.) Execute the following commands to delete the list of unwanted files:

```
mount -uw /
rm -f /image/*/bootmgr/*.sav
rm -f /image/*/bootmgr/*.tmp
sync
mount -ur /
```

If you use the *df* command after you install IPSO 4.2 as a third image, you might see that the root partition is more than 100-percent full. If no errors were displayed while you installed IPSO 4.2, you can safely ignore this output from *df*.

Other upgrade-specific issues are covered in greater detail in the *Getting Started and Release Notes for IPSO 4.2* document available on the Nokia support site:

http://support.nokia.com/home

There are several ways to copy the IPSO installation image used to upgrade your Nokia IPSO version to your Nokia appliance. You can:

1. Use the Nokia Network Voyager to fetch the IPSO image from a remote FTP server.
2. Use the Nokia Network Voyager to upload the IPSO image from a local workstation using HTTP.
3. Use an FTP client to push the IPSO image to the Nokia appliance (if the FTP server is enabled).
4. Use secure copy (SCP) to push the IPSO image to the Nokia appliance (if the SSH server is enabled).
5. Use secure copy (SCP) to pull the IPSO image to the Nokia appliance from another server.
6. Use a floppy or CD-ROM to copy the image to the Nokia appliance (if the appliance has a floppy or CD-ROM drive).

As you can see, there is no shortage of installation image transfer mechanisms. Upgrading the image using Nokia Network Voyager (options 1 and 2) is covered in detail in Chapter 4.

If you decide to transfer the IPSO image manually (options 3, 4, 5, and 6) you can use the *newimage* command to upgrade from the CLI. The syntax of the *newimage* command is as follows:

```
newimage [[-i | -l localfile] [-b] [-R | -T]] [-r | -t imagename]
```

Table 3.1 explains the command-line switches.

Table 3.1 *newimage* Command-Line Switches

Switch	Description
-b	Force upgrade of bootmanager.
-i	Load a new image interactively.
-l *localfile*	Extract the new image from an extant file.
-r *imagename*	Specify *imagename* to run at the next boot.
-t *imagename*	Specify *imagename* to run at the next test boot.
-R	Use a newly installed image to run at the next boot.
-T	Test boot using a newly installed image.
-k	Do not deactivate existing packages.
-v	Verbose ftp.

The test boot option -t *imagename* is a method to test the newly installed image when you reboot your Nokia appliance. If it fails to boot, your Nokia appliance reverts to the previous IPSO image the next time it is started.

To add an IPSO image from the local file system, use the following *newimage* syntax:

```
pint[admin]# newimage -k -l ipso.tgz
```

You should see a response similar to the following:

```
ipso.tgz Validating image...done.
Version tag stored in image: IPSO-4.2-BUILD029-releng-1515-01.05.2007-222742
Installing new image...done [example]
```

NOTE

On some appliances, installing the image can take some time. The *newimage* command might display the message "Setting up new image..." for several minutes with no other sign of activity.

You are then prompted to choose the image to load after the next reboot. At the prompt, reboot your platform. If for some reason the package is not present, you will see a message similar to the following when trying to run the *newimage* command:

```
pint[admin]# newimage -k -l ipso.tgz
tar: can't open archive /var/emhome/admin/ipso.tgz : No such file or directory
tar: child returned status 3
tar: VERSION not found in archive
No version file in /var/emhome/admin/ipso.tgz. Possibly corrupted. Exiting
Jul 27 12:13:44 pint [LOG_ERR] Upgrade: No version file in
/var/emhome/admin/ipso.tgz. Possibly corrupted. Exiting...
```

If the IPSO image is corrupt, you will see an image similar to the following when trying to run the *newimage* command:

```
pint[admin]# newimage -k -l ipso.tgz
gzip: stdin: unexpected end of file
tar: child returned status 1
tar: VERSION not found in archive
No version file in /var/emhome/admin/ipso.tgz. Possibly corrupted. Exiting
Jul 27 12:15:52 pint [LOG_ERR] Upgrade: No version file in /var/emhome/admin/ipso.
tgz. Possibly corrupted. Exiting...
```

To verify the integrity of an IPSO image archive you can use the *openssl* command as follows:

```
pint[admin]# openssl sha1 ipso.tgz
```

You should see a response that displays the same SHA1 value that matches the SHA1 value shown at the Nokia support site. For example, you should see something like the following:

```
SHA1 (ipso.tgz)=390366ED8C53A9F1F516D2DC742331E7FE5A11C0
```

Summary

To prepare for the initial configuration of your Nokia appliance, you need a workstation, laptop, or VT100-capable terminal that you can directly connect to the Nokia using a console cable or perhaps indirectly (through a hub or switch) through a standard Ethernet connection. If you are configuring your Nokia appliance using the DHCP method, you will only need a standard Ethernet connection. Nokia supplies a DB-9 serial cable with all its devices. This cable allows for console connections from properly configured clients. If you do not have one of the Nokia cables, you can always use a standard null-modem cable for the serial connection. You can directly connect a crossover cable from your workstation to any Ethernet port on your Nokia device, or you can indirectly connect a straight-through cable from your workstation to a hub or switch and from there to the appliance over another straight-through cable.

The standard installation procedure is a five-step process. You must power on the appliance and enter the boot manager, initiate the installation process, answer the configuration questions, reboot the appliance, and then continue with the initial configuration steps.

The two methods available to perform the initial configuration carry out the procedure either in an automated fashion, by using the built-in DHCP client, or manually, by using a console (direct serial) connection. If you have a DHCP server in your network, you can configure it to provide your Nokia appliance with a host name, an IP address, and the default route information it requires for the initial configuration. If using the console connection configuration method, you must provide a hostname, password, configuration interface, interface IP address, interface netmask, and default router IP address. Optionally, can also specify interface configuration settings, such as speed and duplex, VLAN settings for the configuration interface, and a new SNMP Community string.

When the initial configuration is complete, you can continue with advanced configurations using the command line, through SSH or Telnet, or using your Web browser and the Nokia Network Voyager interface. The SSH service is enabled, and the Telnet service is disabled, by default for security reasons after a new installation. You can, however, enable the Telnet service using the CLISH interface or Nokia Network Voyager.

As with any software, there might be some caveats or warnings you should review before rushing into the upgrade process. Nokia IPSO is no exception and has some issues you should know about before proceeding with an upgrade. You can use the Nokia Network Voyager to upgrade the IPSO image or you can use the CLI. If you decide to transfer the IPSO image to your Nokia appliance manually, you can use the *newimage* command to upgrade from the CLI. On some appliances, installing the image can take some time. The *newimage* command might display the message "Setting up new image…" for several minutes with no other sign of activity.

Solutions Fast Track

Preparing to Boot for the First Time

☑ In some older models of Nokia IP appliances, the serial number is located on the bottom of the chassis. Before mounting the appliance, you should write down the serial number since it will be needed during the installation process.

☑ A standard null-modem can be used for the serial connection to the console.

☑ If you want to continue the configuration using Nokia Network Voyager and a graphical browser, you need an Ethernet cable.

Installing IPSO

☑ The clean installation will destroy any existing files and data on your disk.

☑ Depending on your requirements, an enhanced license can be purchased to support IGRP and BGP routing protocols.

☑ The interface list may appear differently on your Nokia since it depends entirely on the types of NIC installed.

Performing the First-Time Boot Configuration

☑ If you have a DHCP server in your network, you can configure it to provide your Nokia appliance with a host name, an IP address, and the default route information it requires for the initial configuration.

☑ The admin user requires a password to authenticate you to the command line of the Nokia appliance and for Web-based administration using the Nokia Network Voyager interface.

☑ The easiest, and most popular, configuration method is to configure the appliance using Nokia Network Voyager.

Continuing the Configuration

☑ The default administrative user name is admin.

☑ After you perform the initial configuration, IPSO will automatically generate a host public- and private-key pair.

☑ Enable the Telnet service from the CLI using the *set net-access telnet yes* command in CLISH.

Upgrading to IPSO 4.2

☑ Use the *newimage* command to upgrade the IPSO image from the CLI.

☑ On some appliances, installing the image can take some time. The *newimage* command might display the message "Setting up new image…" for several minutes with no other sign of activity.

☑ Verify the integrity of the IPSO image archive using the *openssl* command.

Frequently Asked Questions

Q: Where is my serial number located?

A: This depends on the model of your appliance. Most of the time it is located on the back of the chassis but in older models it is located on the bottom of the chassis.

Q: I did not receive a console cable with my appliance. What do I do now?

A: If you did not receive one of the Nokia cables, you can always use a standard null-modem (DB9) cable for the serial connection.

Q: What terminal emulation settings should I use for my console connection?

A: Use the following: BPS - 9600, Data bits - 8, Parity - None, Stop bits - 1, Flow control - None, Terminal emulation - Auto, VT100, or VT102.

Q: How to I get into the boot manager?

A: When the appliance is powered on, after the memory test completes, a menu will appear presenting you with a boot manager (1 Bootmgr) option. Use this option to gain entry to the boot manager.

Q: Will I still have my data after a clean installation?

A: No. A clean installation will destroy any existing files and data on your disk.

Q: I'm at the Choose An Interface From The Following List part of the installation, but my interfaces appear different than those listed in the chapter.

A: The interface list may appear differently on your Nokia since it depends entirely on the types of NIC installed.

Q: Can I use my DHCP server to provide the necessary information to my Nokia appliance?

A: Yes. If you have a DHCP server in your network, you can configure it to provide your Nokia appliance with the host name, IP address, and default route information it requires for the initial configuration.

Q: I'm using the DHCP configuration method but it is taking forever. How long should this take?

A: If using the DHCP configuration method, expect it to take five to ten minutes to complete.

Q: What is the preferred method for configuring my Nokia appliance after the initial configuration?

A: Due to its flexibility and ease of use, it is strongly recommended that you use Nokia Network Voyager to perform the additional configurations on your Nokia appliance.

Q: I've just finished the installation but I cannot Telnet to the Nokia appliance.

A: For security, the Telnet service is disabled after a new installation. You can, however, enable it through Nokia Network Voyager or by using the CLISH interface.

Q: Can I use SSH to connect to my Nokia appliance?

A: Yes. You can use SSH to connect to your Nokia appliance. In fact, it is enabled by default when IPSO is installed.

Q: What is the default administrative username?

A: The default administrative username is admin. The password used with this account is the same one you specified during the installation process.

Q: How much space is required to install IPSO 4.2?

A: You need at least 140MB of free disk space in your root partition to install an IPSO 4.2 image.

Q: When I try to install a new image, I receive the following error:

```
tar: can't open archive /var/emhome/admin/ipso.tgz : No such file or directory
tar: child returned status 3
tar: VERSION not found in archive
No version file in /var/emhome/admin/ipso.tgz. Possibly corrupted. Exiting
Jul 27 12:13:44 pint [LOG_ERR] Upgrade: No version file in
/var/emhome/admin/ipso.tgz. Possibly corrupted. Exiting...
```

A: This is the error you typically receive when the IPSO image specified is not present. Please check the location of your IPSO image and try the *newimage* command again.

Q: I've verified that the image is located in the correct directory but now I've received the following error:

```
gzip: stdin: unexpected end of file
tar: child returned status 1
tar: VERSION not found in archive
No version file in /var/emhome/admin/ipso.tgz. Possibly corrupted. Exiting
Jul 27 12:15:52 pint [LOG_ERR] Upgrade: No version file in /var/emhome/admin/
ipso.tgz. Possibly corrupted. Exiting...
```

A: This is likely the result of a corrupt IPSO image. Verify the SHA1 value generated by running the *openssl md5* command against the IPSO image archive to the SHA1 value posted on the Nokia support site.

Chapter 4

Nokia Network Voyager

Solutions in this chapter:

- Introducing Nokia Network Voyager
- Configuring Nokia Network Voyager Access
- Configuring a Basic System
- Applying Security Tuning
- Configuring System Options
- Managing Packages
- Configuring Static Routes
- Configuring System Backup and Restore
- Configuring System Logging
- Scheduling cron Jobs

☑ Summary

☑ Solutions Fast Track

☑ Frequently Asked Questions

Introduction

"Nokia Network Voyager?" asked Mark. "What's that?"

Shin connected his laptop's network cable to the management switch used to access the internal interface of each Nokia appliance. "The Nokia Network Voyager," explained Shin, "Is the Web user interface front-end for the configuration and day-to-day administration of the Nokia appliances." Shin brought up a Web browser and entered the IP address of the first appliance in the address field. "Using the Voyager interface, I can configure every feature of this appliance." Shin logged in using the administrator username and password he specified during installation. "I can configure basic system settings, install and manage additional software packages, back up and restore the system, and tune the security settings."

Shin moved throughout the interface, configuring the system to the test specifications. Mark ensured that the checklist he had prepared was marked as completed as Shin moved through the various sections. Ming scribbled notes throughout the entire configuration session as Marty looked over her shoulder.

"Looks fairly easy to configure," Marty said.

"It's probably one of the easiest enterprise class systems to configure and secure," responded Shin. "No more messing around at the command line in configuration files to shut down unnecessary services, add/remove users, etc."

Marty liked that idea. He knew, from personal experience, that the more you had to configure in configuration files, the higher the chance of administrative error. "I really like this user interface and I think our Ops guys are going to as well."

Introducing Nokia Network Voyager

Nokia Network Voyager is a Web-based interface that is used to manage your IPSO operating system on your Nokia appliance. The IPSO operating system software is included and is accessible using a Web browser from a client.

The commands performed using Nokia Network Voyager can also be performed at the command-line interface (CLI), letting you use the interface you are most comfortable with. For information about the CLI, see Chapter 11.

Navigating the Interface

Nokia Network Voyager access is role-based—meaning that after you have logged in, what you see and have access to depends on the role or roles assigned to you.

All information appears in a navigation tree view, similar to Windows Explorer. If you do not have access to a system item, then the item does not appear in the navigation tree. Read-only access lets you access the page, but with the buttons disabled.

NOTE

Successful and unsuccessful user access attempts are logged in the /var/log/messages file.

To open Nokia Network Voyager, perform the following steps:

1. On a computer with network access to the IPSO appliance, open a Web browser.
2. In the **Address** field, enter the IP address of the initial interface of the IPSO appliance. You are prompted for a username and password.
3. If this is the first login, enter the Admin username and password defined during the initial configuration of the IPSO appliance.

You can log in with or without an exclusive lock on configuration changes. The Acquire Exclusive Configuration Lock option is selected by default on the Login page. If the login dialog does not appear, there might not be a physical network connection between the host and your appliance, or there might be a network routing problem. Verify the appliance IP information and check all cable connections.

When you are finished with your session, or if you would like to log in as another user, click **Log Off** at the top of the Network Voyager window.

NOTE

If the Log Off link is not visible, then session management is disabled.

Using Configuration Lock

Only users with read/write access are able to log in using exclusive configuration lock. If you log in with an exclusive configuration lock, no other user can change the system configuration. If you logged in with an exclusive configuration lock and you close your Web browser without logging off, the lock remains in effect until someone overrides the lock or the session times out.

Users with one or more read/write access privileges have configuration locks when they log in, unless they deselect the Acquire Exclusive Configuration Lock option. The read/write access is limited to administrator-assigned features even though the configuration lock is in effect for all features.

To log in with the exclusive configuration lock, select **Acquire Exclusive Configuration Lock** on the **Login** page.

NOTE

By enabling the exclusive configuration lock during log in, Nokia Network Voyager prevents any user from using the CLI to configure the system while your browser session is active.

To log in without the exclusive configuration lock, deselect **Acquire Exclusive Configuration Lock** on the **Login** page.

To override a configuration lock, perform the following steps:

1. On the **Log In** page, click **Log In With Advanced Options**.
2. Verify that **Acquire Exclusive Configuration Lock** is selected. (This is the default selection.)
3. Select **Override Locks Acquired by Other Users**.
4. Type in your username and password.
5. Click **Log In**.

Navigating Nokia Network Voyager

The interface has four frames of information. The top frame information is static and includes the Nokia appliance name, the current configuration state, and the Log Off link. The Nokia appliance System directory appears on the left with possible items listed below. Clicking an item under the navigation tree returns the associated information in the upper-right frame, while the lower-right frame contains buttons for the selected item.

Under the System tab and above the navigation tree are two links:

- **Expand Tree** This expands all items and subitems under System in the tree.
- **Collapse Tree** This collapses all items and subitems under System in the tree.

In the system tree, the first item listed is always Home. Clicking Home returns the basic system information for the Nokia appliance. Figure 4.1 shows an example of the Home page, while Table 4.1 shows the basic system information that appears on the Home page.

Figure 4.1 The Nokia Network Voyager Home Page

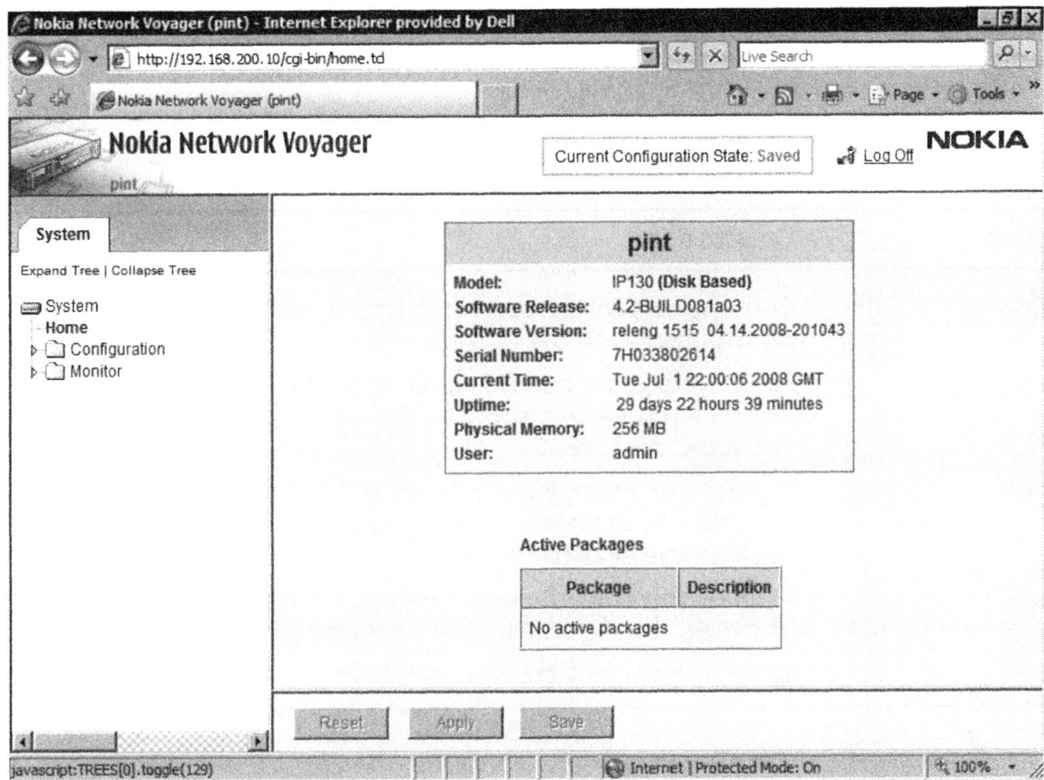

Table 4.1 Basic System Information

Item	Description
Model	Device model of the Nokia appliance
Software Release	IPSO software release
Software Version	IPSO software version
Serial Number	Serial number of the Nokia appliance
Current Time	GMT for when you clicked Home
Uptime	Duration of Nokia appliance uptime
Physical Memory	Physical memory on the Nokia appliance
User	Current user login

Understanding the Interface Buttons

The standard buttons on the interface, if you have proper access, are explained in Table 4.2.

Table 4.2 Standard Interface Buttons

Button	Description
Help	This appears in the top-right frame and provides help on the items for the current view. For example, if you clicked Change Password, the help information would apply to the settings for the Change Password feature.
Reset	If you have changed any feature settings and do not want to keep the changes, clicking Reset changes the settings back to the original state.
Apply	Applies the current page settings to the current (running) configuration file in memory.
Save	Saves the current configuration file to disk.

TIP

If you only click Apply and do not click Save, the next time you reboot the appliance the changes revert back to the previous instance.

If you enter information into any field for a feature and then click another feature in the list without applying or saving your changes, a dialog appears indicating you have not submitted your changes. You can click OK to abort the changes and leave the page or click Cancel to stay on the current page.

Understanding the Web Browser Functions

You should not use the Back and Forward buttons of your Web browser while in Nokia Network Voyager. Because the browser caches the HTML page information, the latest page information might be lost when moving from page to page. To update the page information, you can use the Web browser reload or refresh button.

Accessing Help Documentation

In addition to the interface Help button, you can find the Nokia Network Reference Guide for IPSO and the CLI Reference Guide as follows:

- At the Nokia support site: https://support.nokia.com
- On the software CD included with your Nokia appliance in the doc folder

Understanding Hardware and Software Information

The asset summary page contains three tables, which are explained in Table 4.3.

Table 4.3 Asset Summary Tables

Table	Description
Hardware	Includes the chassis serial number, the amount of memory on the appliance, and information about the CPU, disks, BIOS, and motherboard
FireWall Package Information	Includes the FireWall version, license information, and information about the host, the policy, and the date when the FireWall policy was installed
Operating System	Lists the software and version release running on the system

To view the asset summary for your system, complete the following steps:

1. Under **System**, expand **Configuration** and then expand **Asset Information**.
2. Click **Asset Summary**.

Configuring Nokia Network Voyager Access

When you set up your system for the first time, you must configure the basic Nokia Network Voyager options and change your SSL/TLS certificate from the default certificate.

Configuring Basic Nokia Network Voyager Options

Figure 4.2 shows the Network Voyager Options page. You can configure the following options for Nokia Network Voyager access:

- Allow Network Voyager access (enabled by default)
- Enable session management (enabled by default)
- Specify a Network Voyager SSL/TLS port number
- Require encryption

Figure 4.2 The Network Voyager Options Page

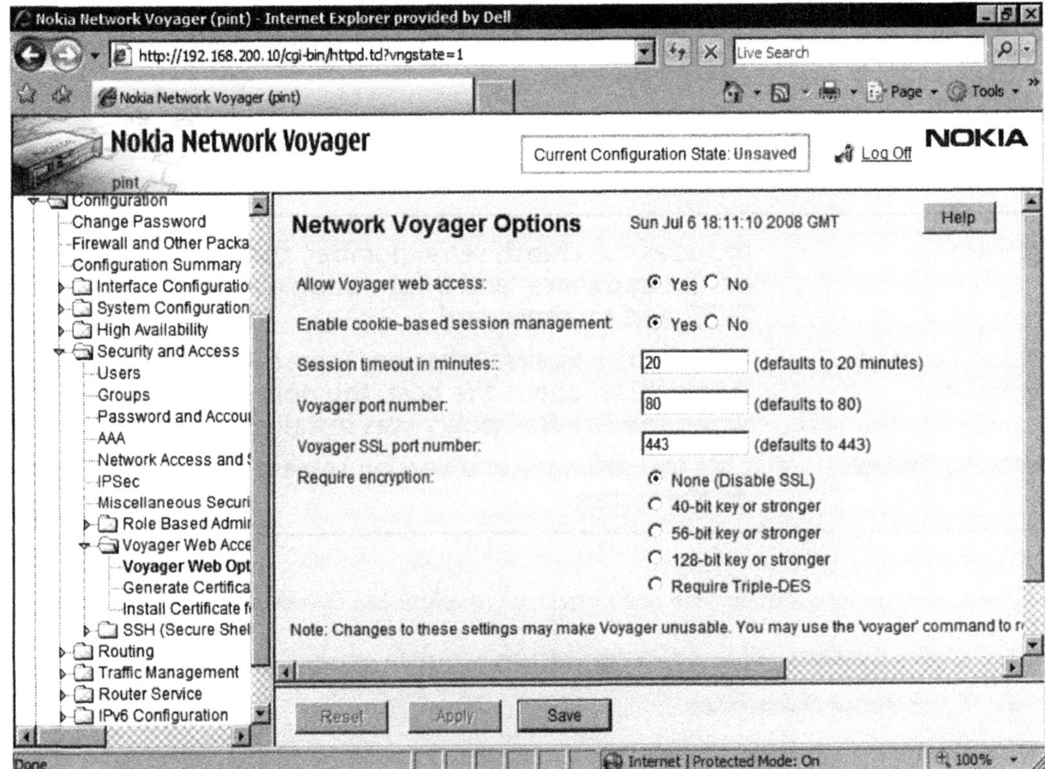

To configure web access for Nokia Network Voyager, complete the following steps:

1. In the system tree, click **Configuration | Security and Access | Voyager Web Access | Voyager Web Options**.
2. To enable access, next to Allow Voyager web access, select **Yes**. (This option is selected by default.)

WARNING

If you uncheck the check box, you must use the CLI to access your IP security platform.

3. To enable cookie-based session management, next to **Enable Cookie-Based Session Management**, select **Yes**.
4. In the **Session Timeout In Minutes** field, type the time interval for which a Nokia Network Voyager user is allowed to be logged in without activity. The default value is 20 minutes. If the user closes the browser without logging out, the exclusive configuration lock remains in effect until the session time-out interval expires.
5. In the **Voyager Port Number** field, type the port number to use for SSL/TLS-secure connections. The default is port 443. Using the default port lets users connect to Nokia Network Voyager without specifying a port number in the URL. If you change the port number, users must specify a port number in the URL—for example, https://hostname:<portnumber>/.
6. Under **Require Encryption**, select the appropriate encryption level for your security needs.

NOTE

The encryption level you enter is the minimum level of encryption you require. You might want to use stronger encryption if your Web browser supports it.

7. Click **Apply** and then click **Save**.

Generating and Installing SSL/TLS Certificates

To secure Nokia Network Voyager client connections to the IPSO system over the internet, IPSO uses the Secure Sockets Layer/Transport Layer Security (SSL/TLS) protocol. SSL/TLS, the industry standard for secure Web connections, gives you a secure way to connect to Nokia Network Voyager. Creating and keeping a unique private key a secret for your security platform is critical to preventing attacks that could compromise the platform security.

When setting up your system for the first time, change your SSL/TLS certificate from the default certificate. IPSO includes a default sample certificate and private key in the /var/etc/voyager_ssl_server.crt and /var/etc/voyager_ssl_server.key files respectively.

The certificate and private key are for testing purposes only and do not provide a secure SSL/TLS connection. To create a secure connection using SSL/TLS, you must generate a certificate, and the private key associated with the certificate, over a trusted connection. Figure 4.3 shows the Generate SSL Certificate (Request) page.

Figure 4.3 The Generate SSL Certificate (Request) Page

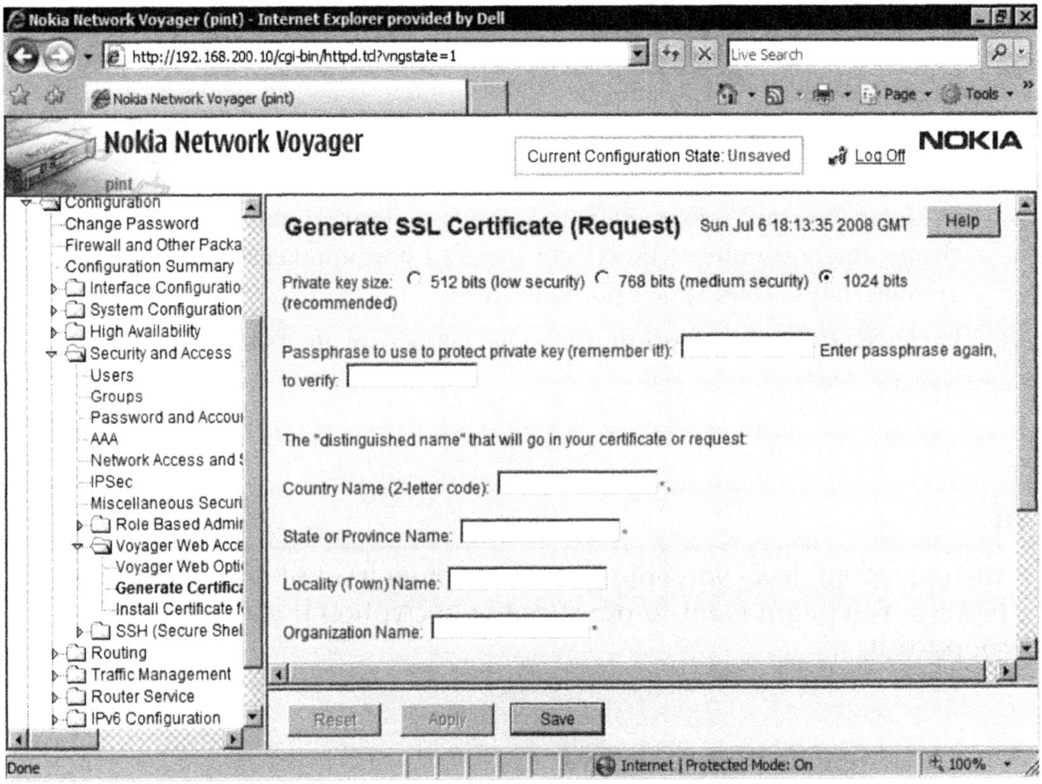

To generate an SSL/TLS certificate and keys, complete the following steps:

1. In the system tree, click **Configuration** | **Security and Access** | **Voyager Web Access** | **Generate Certificate for SSL**.
2. Next to **Private Key Size**, select the option that meets your security needs.

3. (Optional) In the **Passphrase** and **Enter Passphrase Again** fields, type a passphrase you will remember. The passphrase must be at least four characters long. If you specify a passphrase, you will have to enter the phrase later when installing your new key.
4. In the **Country Name** field, type the two-letter code of the country in which you are located.
5. In the **State Or Province Name** field, type the name of your state or province.
6. (Optional) In the **Locality (Town) Name** field, type the name of your locality or town.
7. In the **Organization Name** field, type the name of your company or organization. If you are requesting a certificate from a certificate authority, the certificate authority might require the official legal name of your organization.
8. (Optional) In the **Organizational Unit Name** field, type the name of your department or unit within your company or organization.
9. In the **Common Name (FQDN)** field, type the common name that identifies exactly where the certificate will go. The common name is most commonly the fully qualified domain name (FQDN) for your platform—for example, www.ship.wwwidgets.com. If you are generating a certificate signing request for a certificate authority (CA), that CA might impose a different standard.
10. (Optional) In the **Email Address** field, enter the e-mail address to use to contact the person responsible for this system or for its certificate.
11. Next to **What To Generate**, select one of the following:
    - A certificate signing request (CSR): Select this option if you are requesting a certificate from a certification authority. The request will be signed with a SHA-1 hash.
    - A self-signed X.509 certificate: Select this option to create a certificate you can use immediately, but that will not be validated by a certification authority. The certificate will be signed with a SHA-1 hash.
12. Click **Apply**.
13. If you generated a certificate signing request, a screen appears that contains a certificate request—New X.509 certificate signing request—and its associated private key—New private key.
    - Send the New X.509 certificate signing request to your certification authority. Include the following lines:

```
-----BEGIN CERTIFICATE REQUEST-----
```

and

```
-----END CERTIFICATE REQUEST-----
```

- Store the new private key that your certification authority securely sends. Install the private key and the certificate.

14. If you generated a self-signed certificate, a screen appears that contains a certificate (New X.509 Certificate) and its associated private key.

You must perform a cut-and-paste operation to move the certificate and the private key to the Voyager SSL Certificate page, as described in the following procedure.

To install the SSL/TLS certificate, complete the following steps:

1. In the system tree, click **Configuration** | **Security and Access** | **Voyager Web Access** | **Install Certificate for SSL**.
2. In the **New Server Certificate** box, paste the certificate information.
   Include the following lines:

   ```
   -----BEGIN CERTIFICATE -----
   ```

   and

   ```
   -----END CERTIFICATE -----
   ```

3. In the **Associated Private Key** box, paste the private key information.
   Include the following lines:

   ```
   -----BEGIN RSA PRIVATE KEY-----
   ```

   and

   ```
   -----END RSA PRIVATE KEY-----
   ```

4. If you specified a passphrase when you generated the certificate, in the **Passphrase** field, type the passphrase.
5. Click **Apply**.

Tools & Traps...

Troubleshooting SSL/TLS Configurations

You might have trouble accessing Nokia Network Voyager if SSL/TLS is not configured correctly. If you have trouble accessing Network Voyager, try the following remedies.

- Verify you are using the correct URL.
- When you enable SSL/TLS, you must use https when you connect through your Web browser, unless the Redirect HTTP Requests to HTTPS option is enabled.
- Verify you are using the correct PEM-encoded certificate and private key, and that they are installed properly with the dashed begin and end lines.
- You can view the certificate and private key in the /var/etc/voyager_ssl_server.crt and /var/etc/voyager_ssl_server.key files respectively.
- Verify the HTTP daemon error message log.
- You can find the messages in the following logs:

```
/var/log/httpd_error_log
/var/log/ssl_engine_log
```

The messages can help you troubleshoot problems and might contain important information you can use when contacting support.

Using Secure Shell (SSH)

IPSO uses the SSH program to provide secure connections for the CLI. SSH lets you securely log in to another computer over a network, execute commands on a remote platform, and move files from one platform to another. SSH provides a connection similar to Telnet or rlogin, except that the traffic is encrypted and both ends are authenticated.

The Nokia SSH implementation supports SSHv1and SSHv2. Differences between SSHv1 and SSHv2 include which part of the packet is encrypted by the protocol and how each protocol authenticates. SSHv1 authenticates with server and host keys, while SSHv2 authenticates by only using host keys. Even though SSHv1 uses server and host-key authentication, SSHv2 is a faster, securer, and more portable protocol. In some cases, however, SSHv1 might be more suitable because of your client software or your need to use the authentication modes of the protocol.

When it is properly used, SSH provides you with session protection from the following security threats:

- DNS spoofing
- Interception of passwords
- IP spoofing
- IP source routing
- Man-in-the-middle attacks (SSHv2 only)

You should use SSH, instead of utilities like Telnet or rlogin that are not secure, to connect to the system. You can also tunnel HTTP over SSH to use Nokia Network Voyager to securely manage your platform.

To use SSH, you must obtain an SSH client for the other end of the connection. SSH clients are available for several platforms.

Configuring Initial SSH

When you first activate your system, SSH is already enabled. Host keys for your platform are also generated and installed. SSH automatically authenticates users who log in with the standard password login.

No additional configuration is required unless you want users to be able to also use public-key authentication. To permit public-key authentication, you must first authorize the users' client identity keys for this system. Figure 4.4 shows the SSH Configuration page.

Figure 4.4 The SSH Configuration Page

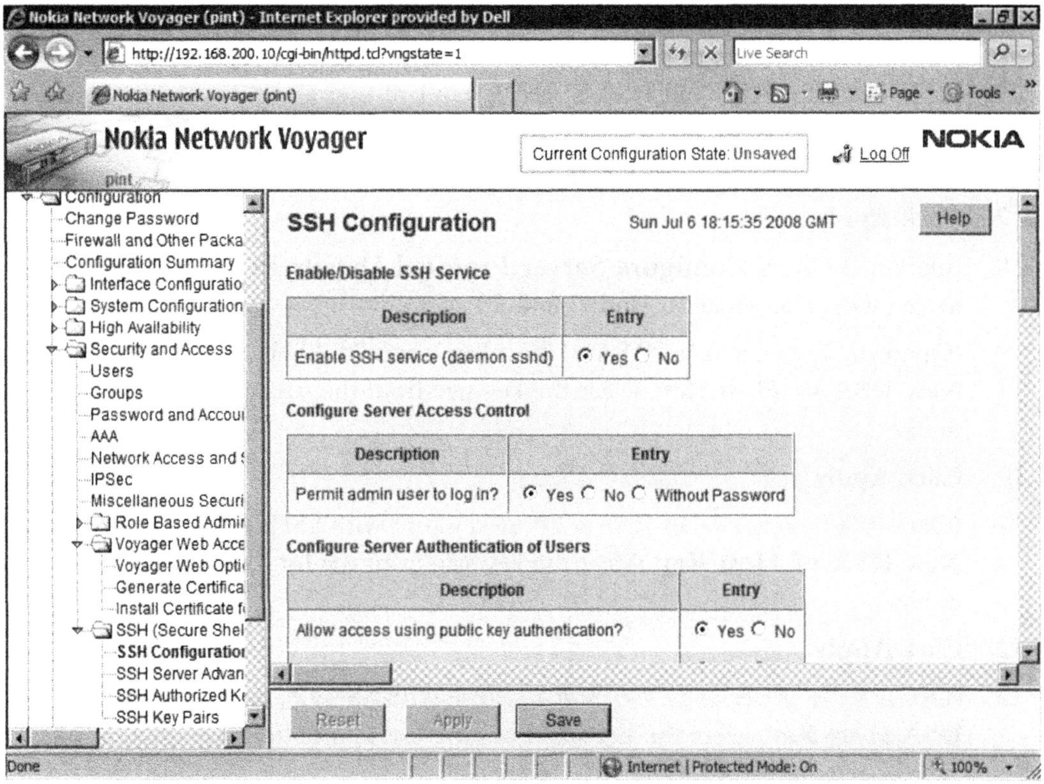

To configure SSH, complete the following steps:

1. In the system tree, click **Configuration** | **Security and Access** | **SSH (Secure Shell)** | **SSH Configuration**.
2. Under **Enable/Disable SSH Service**, click **Yes**. (The first time you enable SSH it generates RSA v1, RSA v2, and DSA host keys. This process will take a few minutes.)
3. Click **Apply**.
4. Under **Configure Server Access Control**, specify whether the admin user can log in with SSH by selecting one of the following:
   - **Yes** The admin user can log in using SSH and can use password authentication to do it. (This is the default setting.)
   - **No** The admin user cannot log in.
   - **Without Password** The admin user can log in, but must use public-key authentication to do so.

5. Click **Apply**.
6. (Optional) **Under Configure Server Authentication Of Users**, click **Yes** for each type of authentication to be used. You can authenticate SSH connections by using public keys (for RSA and DSA SSHv2), standard user and password information, rhosts files, and RSA keys (for SSHv1). You can permit any combination of these methods.
7. Click **Apply**.
8. (Optional) Under **Configure Server Protocol Details**, click the version of SSH to be used. (The default is Both 1 and 2.)
9. (Optional) To generate an RSA v1 host key (use with SSHv1), under **Generate New RSA v1 Host Key**, select the key size from the size. (The options are listed in bits.)
10. Click **Apply**.
11. (Optional) To generate an RSA v2 host key (use with SSHv2), under **Generate New RSA v2 Host Key**, select the key size from the list. (The options are listed in bits.)
12. Click **Apply**.
13. (Optional) To generate a DSA host key (use with SSHv2), under **Generate New DSA Host Key**, select the key size from the list. The options are listed in bits, and the recommended value is 1024 bits.
14. Click **Apply** and then click **Save**.

NOTE

When generating new keys, you might have to change the configurations of each client, or the clients might return errors. For more information, see your SSH client documentation.

Configuring a Basic System

When configuring interfaces, you must know the IP address and netmask of each interface you plan on using.

Notes from the Underground...

Using the IP2250 and IP2255 Management Ports

The Ethernet management ports on the IP2250 and IP2255 appliances are designed specifically for appliance management, firewall synchronization traffic, IP cluster protocol traffic, and log server connections only. The management ports are not suitable for forwarding your production data traffic for several reasons.

The major difference between these ports and the ADP (I/O) ports is that the Ethernet management ports use resources that are shared with the Nokia IPSO operating system (for example, main CPU, memory, and system PCI bus), while the ADP interfaces use separate processors for ingress (inbound) and egress (outbound) traffic, dedicated memory, and a separate PCI bus.

ADP ports are designed to accelerate network traffic through the appliance. Synchronization traffic must, by design, be processed via the main CPU. Using the ADP ports for synchronization would cause all network traffic to go through the main CPU, creating a potential bottleneck, which could result in packet loss and in certain scenarios improper failover and degradation of performance.

Using FireWall-1 synchronization and management traffic on the ADP (I/O) ports is also an inefficient way of configuring the appliance, since the synchronization and management traffic is to and from the appliance, not through the appliance.

Configuring Network Devices

Nokia Network Voyager displays network devices as physical interfaces. Physical interfaces exist for each physical port on a network interface card (NIC) installed on the appliance. The interface names have the following form:

```
<type>-s<slot>p<port>
```

- **<type>** The prefix for the device type.
- **<slot>** The slot number for the device on the appliance.

- `<port>` The NIC port number. The first port on a NIC is port one. A two-port Ethernet NIC in slot two is represented by two physical interfaces: eth-s2p1 and eth-s2p2.

Several interface names exist, which are explained in Table 4.4

Table 4.4 Prefix Interface Names

Type	Prefix
Ethernet	Eth
FDDI	Fddi
ATM	Atm
Serial	Ser
T1/E1	Ser
HSSI	Ser
Token Ring	Tok
ISDN	Isdn
Loopback	Loop0

You can use Nokia Network Voyager to set interface attributes, and each communications port has exactly one physical interface.

Configuring Ethernet Interfaces

You can configure several parameters for each Ethernet interface, including:

- Enable or disable the interface
- Change the IP address of the interface
- Change the speed and duplex mode

Figure 4.5 The Interface Configuration Page

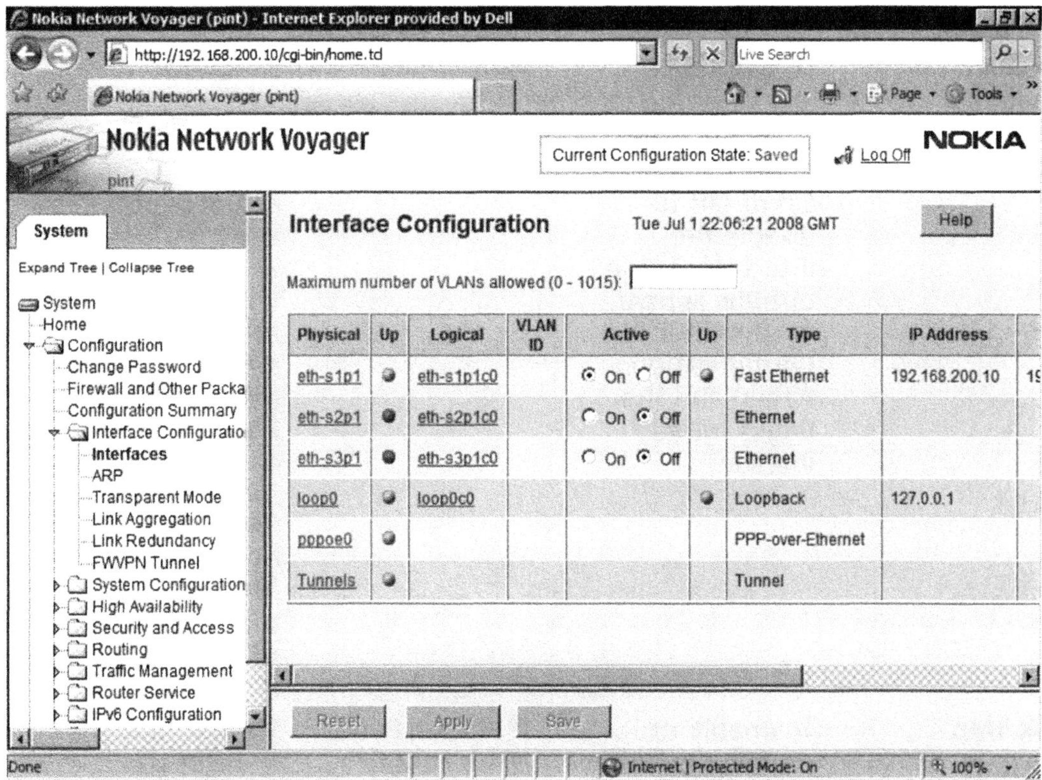

Figure 4.5 shows the Interface Configuration page.

The physical and logical interfaces have different configuration parameters, which are explained in Table 4.5.

Table 4.5 Physical and Logical Interface Configuration Parameters

Physical Interface Parameters	Description	Logical Interface Parameters	Description
Active	To enable the interface, select On or Off to disable the interface. These options appear on the Interface Configuration screen and the pages for each interface.	ARP Mirroring for HA	If you enable Virtual Router Redundancy Protocol (VRRP) on this interface, specify whether it should learn the same ARP information as the master if it is on a backup router. Enabling this option can speed VRRP failovers because the new VRRP master does not need to learn the MAC addresses that correspond to its next hop IP address before it can forward traffic.
Link Trap	To enable or disable the linkup/ linkdown traps for the interface, select On or Off. For all physical interfaces, the default is On.	IP Address and Mask Length	You can add multiple IP addresses. **Note**: Do not change the IP address you use in your browser to access Nokia Network Voyager because you will no longer be able to access the IP security platform with Nokia Network Voyager.
Link Speed	Select 100 Mbit/sec or 10 Mbit/sec. This setting must be the same for all hosts on the network to which the device connects.	Logical Name	Specify a different name for the logical interface. **Note**: It is generally a good idea to not change the default logical name.

Continued

Table 4.5 Continued. Physical and Logical Interface Configuration Parameters

Physical Interface Parameters	Description	Logical Interface Parameters	Description
Duplex	Select Full or Half. This setting must be the same for all hosts on the network to which the device connects.	Comments	Specify an optional comment to associate with the interface name.
Flow Control	To enable or disable flow control, select On or Off. Enabling flow control can reduce receiving-buffer overflows and therefore reduce the number of dropped packets. If you enable flow control, interfaces can send flow-control packets and respond to received packets. This option is not available for all Ethernet interfaces.		
Autoadvertise	To enable or disable autoadvertising, select On or Off. If set to On, the device advertises its configured speed and duplicity by using Ethernet negotiation.		

Continued

Table 4.5 Continued. Physical and Logical Interface Configuration Parameters

Physical Interface Parameters	Description	Logical Interface Parameters	Description
Link Recognition Delay	Specify how many seconds a link must be stable before the interface is declared up. The default is 6 and the range is 1–255.		

To configure an Ethernet interface, complete the following steps:

1. In a Web browser, open and log in to the Nokia Network Voyager interface.
2. In the system tree, click **Configuration** | **Interface Configuration** | **Interfaces**.
3. Click the physical interface to configure.
4. Specify the configuration parameters for speed and duplex mode.
5. Click **Apply**.
6. In the **Logical Interfaces** table, click the logical interface.
7. Specify the IP address and mask length.
8. Click **Apply**. (Each IP address and mask length are added to the table when you click Apply. The page refreshes with blank fields.)
9. (Optional) Change the logical interface name to something more meaningful by typing information into the **Logical Name** field and then clicking **Apply**.
10. (Optional) To further define the logical interfaces, add a comment in the **Comment** field and then click **Apply**.
11. For the logical interface you configured, click **On**.
12. Click **Apply**. The Ethernet interface will now be available for IP traffic and routing.
13. To permanently save your changes, click **Save**.

Configuring IP Addresses

You assign IP addresses to logical interfaces, which are created for the physical interface of a device, and then route to the IP address.

Ethernet, FDDI, and Token Ring devices have one logical interface. You create a new logical interface every time you configure an RFC1483 PVC for ATM devices.

Serial, T1/E1, and HSSI devices have one logical interface when running PPP or Cisco HDLC. However, they have one logical interface for each PVC configured on the port when running point-to-point Frame Relay. For point-to-point interfaces, you have the option of configuring an unnumbered amount, while tunnels cannot be configured as unnumbered interfaces.

By default, logical interfaces are named after the physical interface they are created for. You can override the name if you want something more descriptive or familiar to you. Comments can also be associated with logical interfaces to further define the network relationship. Default logical interface names have the form:

```
<type>-s<slot>p<port>c<chan>
```

The <type>, <slot>, and <port> values are the same as the corresponding physical interface, while <chan> is the logical interface channel number.

The channel number is always zero for automatically created logical interfaces. The channel number for manually created logical interfaces is the identifier of the virtual circuit (VC) for which the interface is created, such as the Frame Relay DLCI. Table 4.6 outlines the supported logical interface channels on a physical interface.

Table 4.6 Logical Interface Channels

Physical Interface	Logical Interface			
	Default	**Cisco HDLC**	**PPP**	**Frame Relay**
Ethernet	One (c0)			
FDDI	One (c0)			
ATM	One per VCI (c#)			
Serial (X.21 or V.35)		One (c0)	One (c0)	One per DLCI (c#)
T1/E1		One (c0)	One (c0)	One per DLCI (c#)
HSSI		One (c0)	One (c0)	One per DLCI (c#)
Token Ring	One (c0)			
ISDN			One (c#)	

Examples:

- Physical interface eth-s1p1 = logical interface eth-s1p1c0
- PVCs 15 and 20 on an ATM NIC in slot 1 = logical interfaces atm-s1p1c15 and atm-s1p1c20

If a logical interface exists for a device, you can assign it an IP address. For Ethernet, FDDI, and token ring, you must indicate the IP address of the local interface and the length, in bits, of the subnet mask of the subnet to which the device connects.

For multiple subnets on the same physical network, you can configure more addresses and subnet masks on the single logical interface connected to that network. You do not have to create additional logical interfaces to run multiple subnets on a single physical network.

For point-to-point media, you can assign IP addresses or configure an unnumbered interface. If assigning IP addresses, you must specify the IP address of the local interface and the point-to-point interface of the remote system.

Only one local or destination IP address pair can be added to a point-to-point logical interface. To assign IP address to multiple VCs, you must create a logical interface for each VC because IP subnets are not supported on point-to-point interfaces.

Whenever an unnumbered interface generates a packet, it uses the interface address specified by the user as the source address of the IP packet. Therefore, for a router to have an unnumbered interface, it must have at least one IP address assigned. The Nokia implementation of unnumbered interfaces does not support virtual links.

TIP

IP address changes or interface deletion is not always reflected when you receive the firewall topology. If the changes do not appear, stop and restart the firewall.

To add an IP address to an interface, complete the following steps:

1. In a Web browser, open and log in to the Nokia Network Voyager interface.
2. In the system tree, click **Configuration** | **Interface Configuration** | **Interfaces**.
3. Click the logical interface to which you want to assign an IP address.
4. To make the interface active, next to **Active**, click **On**.
5. Specify the new IP address and mask length for your browser. (All netmasks configured through Nokia Network Voyager are in aggregate or bit mask format.)

6. (Optional) To make the interface easier to identify, change the logical name of the interface.
7. Click **Apply**. The changes will take effect immediately.
8. Click **Save**. (You must save your configuration for the setting to be retained after a system reboot.)
9. To return to the previous interface configuration page, click **Up**.

You should now see your new interface in the table.

Applying Security Tuning

The outlined configurations are for specific purposes. In most circumstances, you should not change any default settings.

Tuning the TCP/IP Stack

Established TCP connections have a maximum segment size (MSS) at each end. The MSS setting is the value presented by your system. You can change this value to tune TCP performance by allowing your system to receive the largest possible segments without fragmentation.

The MSS configuration:

- Is only applicable to TCP.
- Sets the TCP MSS for packets generated and received by the system. If a remote terminating node has a higher MSS than the MSS configured on your system, your system sends packets with the segment size configured with this feature. For example, if you set the MSS to 512, but the remote system has 1024, then your system sends packets with a TCP segment size of 512.
- Is only relevant to Check Point security servers or similar products requiring the Nokia appliance to terminate the connection.

Only the remote terminating node responds to the MSS value you set. In other words, intermediate nodes do not respond. Typically, however, intermediate nodes can handle 1500-byte MTUs.

Your system presents the MSS value that you set, and the remote terminated notes respond by sending segments in packets that do not exceed your set value. The MSS presented by your system should be 40 bytes less than the smallest MTU between your system and the outgoing interface. The 40-byte difference allows for a 20-byte TCP header and a 20-byte IP header, which are included in the MTU.

Figure 4.6 shows the Advanced System Tuning page.

Figure 4.6 The Advanced System Tuning Page

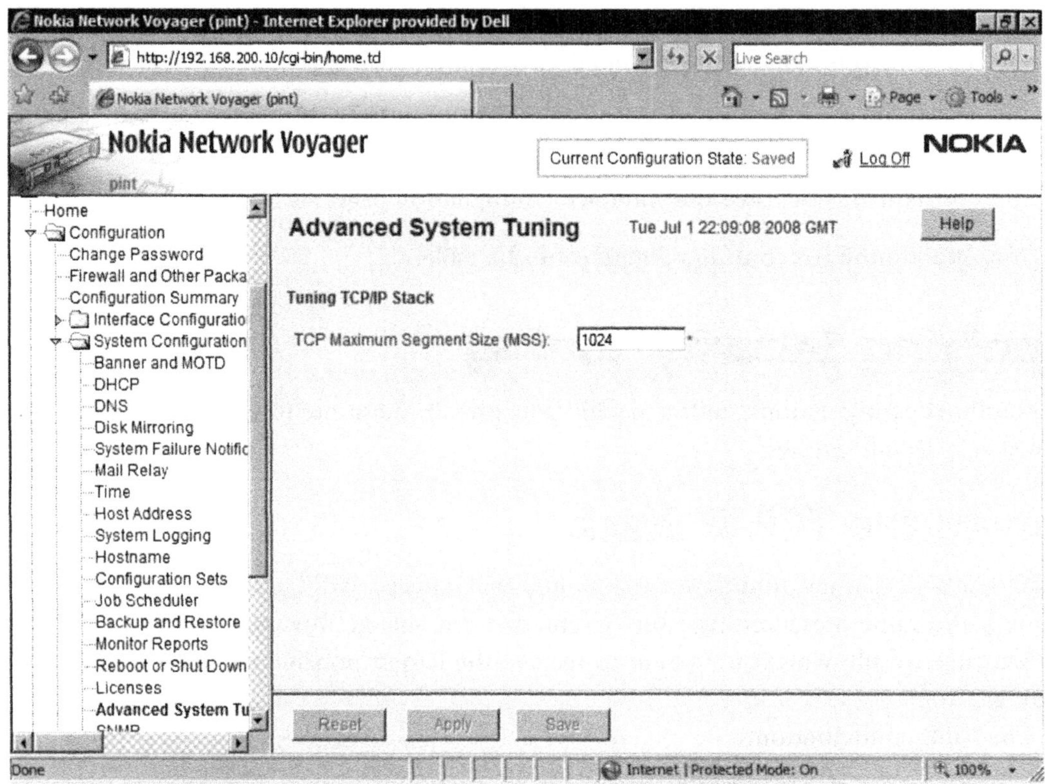

To set the TCP MSS, complete the following steps:

1. In the system tree, click **Configuration | System Configuration | Advanced System Tuning**.
2. In the **TCP Maximum Segment Size (MSS)** field, type your MSS value.

The range is 512 to 1500 and the default value is 1024. If you enter a value out of the range, you will receive an out-of-range error.

3. Click **Apply** and then, to permanently save the value, click **Save**.

Controlling SecureXL

You can enable or disable some SecureXL features in IPSO if Check Point NGX is installed on your system. These features are listed in the SecureXL TCP box, which appears on the Advanced System Tuning page of Nokia Network Voyager.

Enabling Sequence Validation

For enhanced security, IPSO supports the SecureXL sequence validation (TCP state detection version 2) functionality. This feature allows the firewall to stop exploits that make use of out-of-sequence TCP packets.

To use sequence validation, enable it on SmartDashboard and in IPSO—for stand-alone systems and high-availability configurations. This feature is disabled by default.

1. On the **Advanced System Tuning** page, click the button to enable sequence validation.
2. Enable sequence validation in SmartDashboard.
3. Push the new policy to the IPSO platform.

Setting Delayed Notification and Auto-Expiry

You can improve performance using delayed notification and auto-expiry to reduce the amount of required communication between IPSO and the firewall. You can also reduce the amount of synchronization between the IP cluster members or VRRP groups, reducing overhead processing.

By default, delayed notification is enabled on stand-alone systems and it does not require configuration in SmartDashboard. Delayed notification is also enabled by default in high-availability configurations (IP clusters or VRRP groups), but you also need to enable delayed synchronization (for each service) in SmartDashboard using the Advanced TCP Service Properties dialog box for the service, such as HTTP.

Delayed synchronization is automatically disabled for any connections matching a rule that uses any of the logging, accounting, and worm catcher Check Point features.

You can configure delayed synchronization in high-availability configurations so connections do not expire before a set time. For example, if you configure HTTP traffic to be synchronized after 15 seconds, then HTTP connections expiring before this time are not synchronized to the other systems. If failover happens, the unsynchronized connections do not survive. Delayed notification and synchronization are useful for systems that process many short-lived connections.

Auto-expiry is enabled by default. This option improves performance by allowing IPSO to terminate certain connections.

Using the Router Alert IP Option

The router alert IP option can be used to indicate if IPSO should strip the router alert IP option before passing packets to the firewall. The router alert IP option is typically enabled in IGMP packets.

Using Optimize for Two-Port IP1260

The Optimize For Two-Port Ip1260 option can be used to optimize the performance of IP1260 Gigabit Ethernet interfaces when they forward unidirectional IDP traffic. Enabling this option does not optimize throughput for other traffic types or interfaces and is not available on the IP1220. This option only optimizes throughput if there are two Gigabit Ethernet interfaces installed on the platform.

WARNING

Do not enable the Optimize For Two-Port IP1260 option if more than two Gigabit Ethernet interfaces are installed on the platform, because this can impair system performance.

Configuring System Options

Under the system tree Configuration section, several items for configuration are located under the System Configuration subsection. This section provides information about some items and the steps required to properly configure each.

Configuring Banner and Login Messages

On the login page, when a user connects to an IPSO system or logs out, the system displays the message "This system is for authorized use only" by default. On the Banner And MOTD Configuration page, you can change or disable this message. You can also configure a MOTD Message (Message of the Day) and an FTP welcome message. Figure 4.7 shows the layout of the Banner And MOTD Configuration page.

Figure 4.7 The Banner and MOTD Configuration Page

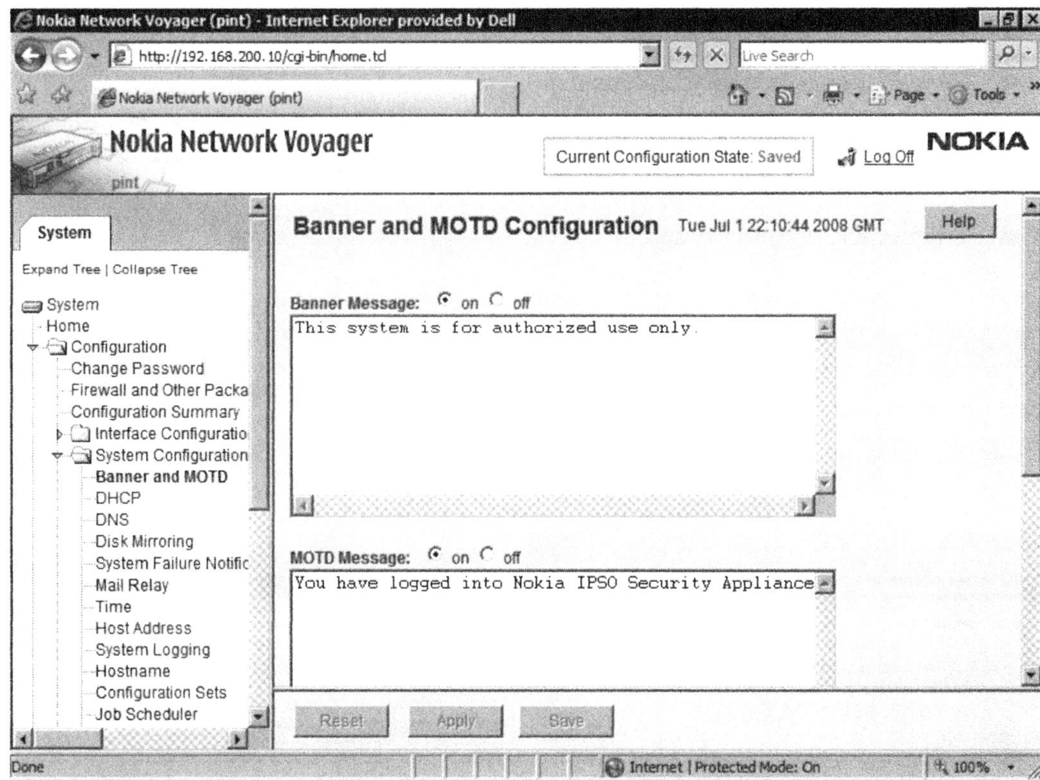

To configure messages, complete the following steps:

1. In the system tree, click **Configuration** | **System Configuration** | **Banner And MOTD**.
2. Create or modify the messages.
3. Click **Apply** and then click **Save**.

Configuring Dynamic Host Configuration Protocol (DHCP)

Nokia IPSO provides complete DHCP client and server capabilities for your Nokia appliance. DHCP enables you to configure network parameters through a server to clients requiring the parameters to operate on the network. DHCP eliminates the need to manually configure each client and reduces configuration errors.

The Nokia IPSO implementation of DHCP includes the following:

- DHCP client enabling
- DHCP client interface configuration
- Dynamic and fixed IP address allocation from the DHCP server
- Automatic DNS server updates from the DHCP server
- Support for VLAN clients

It also enables you to specify various client parameters, including the servers for different services, such as DNS, NTP, and SMTP. You can also configure NetBIOS over TCP/IP, which includes identifying WINS and Datagram Distribution (DD) servers available to clients. Figure 4.8 shows the DHCP Configuration page.

Figure 4.8 The DHCP Configuration Page

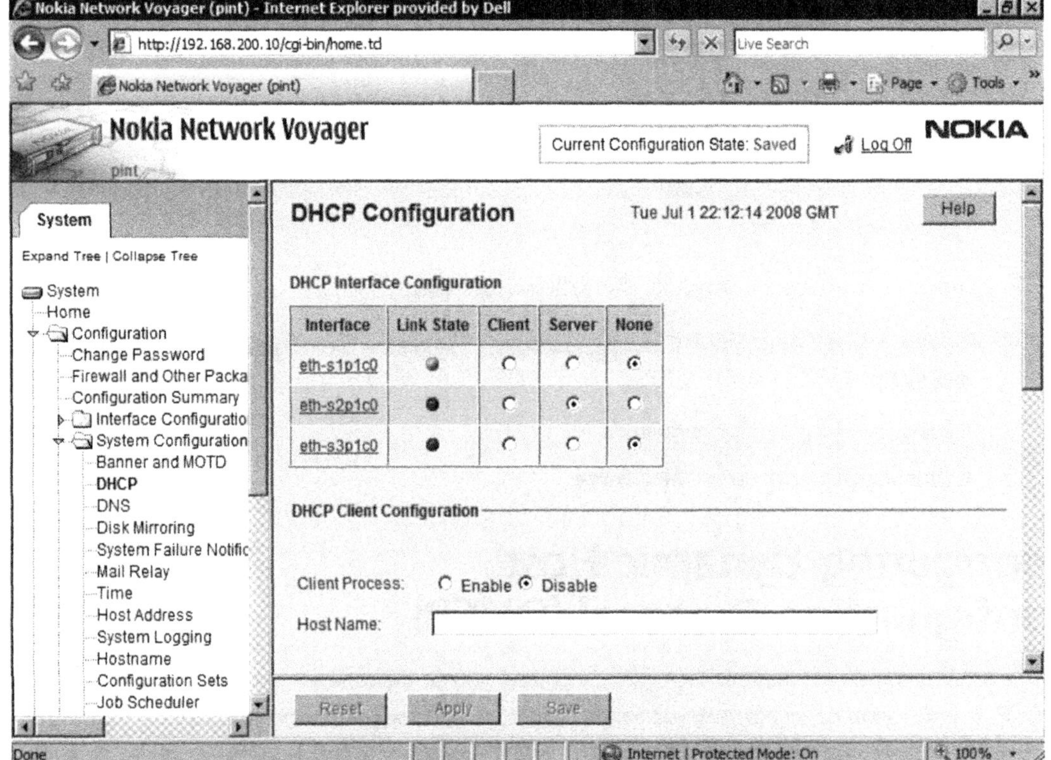

WARNING

If you enable the IPSO DHCP server, the Nokia appliance still receives and accepts DHCP requests even if there is a firewall rule blocking DHCP requests. If you enable the DHCP server, but do not want external DHCP requests to be accepted, enable DHCP on internal interfaces only.

To configure DHCP client interfaces, complete the following steps:

1. In the system tree, click **Configuration** | **System Configuration** | **DHCP**.
2. Under **DHCP Interface Configuration**, click the link of the logical interface for configuration. (The Ethernet interface must be enabled before you enable the client.)
3. (Optional) In the **Client ID** field, enter a unique name. (The name is used in request packets instead of the interface MAC address.)
4. In the **Timeout** field, enter a value in seconds. The default value is 60 seconds.
5. In the **Retry** field, enter a value in seconds. The default value is 300 seconds.
6. In the **Lease** field, enter a value in seconds for the length of time the IP address will be leased to the interface.
7. In the **Reboot** field, enter a value in seconds for the client to reacquire an expired lease address before it attempts to discover a new address.
8. Click **Apply** and then click **Save** to make your changes permanent.

To enable the DHCP client process, complete the following steps:

1. In the system tree, click **Configuration** | **System Configuration** | **DHCP**.
2. Under **DHCP Interface Configuration**, click **Client** for the logical interface for configuration.
3. Under **DHCP Client Configuration**, click **Enable**. (The Ethernet interface must be enabled before you enable the client.)
4. In the **Host Name** field, enter a host name.
5. Click **Apply** and then click **Save**.

To configure the DHCP server process, complete the following steps:

1. In the system tree, click **Configuration** | **System Configuration** | **DHCP**.
2. Under **DHCP Interface Configuration**, click **Server** for the logical interface for configuration.

3. Click **Apply**.
4. Under DHCP Server Configuration, DHCP Server Subnet Configuration, click **Add a New Subnet Entry**.
5. In the **Subnet** field, enter the subnet address of the Ethernet interface configured for the DHCP server process.
6. In the **Mask Length** field, type in the mask length.
7. Under **IP-Pool Configuration**, type the IP address range in the **Start** and **End** fields.
8. Under **System Setup Configuration**, in the **Router** field, type the IP address of the default router for clients.
9. In the **DNS Servers** field, type in the DNS server used by clients to resolve domain names.
10. In the **NTP Servers** field, type in the NTP servers in order of preference and separated by commas.
11. In the **SMTP Servers** field, type in the SMTP servers, each separated by a comma.
12. If you configured NetBIOS, under **NET BIOS Configuration for Windows Client**, complete the following steps:
    - In the **Wins Server** field, type in the WINS available to clients.
    - In the **DD Servers** field, type in the DD servers available to clients.
    - From the **Node Type** list, select the node type the client will configure as.
    - In the **Scope** field, type in the client scope.
13. Click **Apply** and then click **Save**.

Optional fields for configuration are explained in Table 4.7.

Table 4.7 Optional Fields

Field	Description
Default Lease	This field contains the lease length, in seconds, for client IP addresses. This is only applied if clients do not require a specific lease time. The default value is 43,200 seconds.
Maximum Lease	This field contains the maximum lease length, in seconds, for client IP addresses. This value is the longest lease the server will allow. The default value is 86,400 seconds.

Continued

Table 4.7 Continued. Optional Fields

Field	Description
TFTP Server	This field contains the Trivial File Transfer Protocol (TFTP) for server clients.
File Name	This field contains the file name of the boot file for diskless clients.
Extensions Path	This field contains additional configuration options. You must configure TFTP to use the Extensions Path option because clients will use TFTP to transfer the configuration options from the server.
Root Filename	This field contains the root path where diskless clients mount a network file system (NFS).
Domain	This field contains the domain name you want clients to use.
Time Offset	This field contains the time offset for clients.
Swap Server	This field contains the IP address or name of the swap server for diskless clients to use.

To enable the DHCP server process, complete the following steps:

1. In the system tree, click **Configuration | System Configuration | DHCP**.
2. Under **DHCP Interface Configuration**, click **Server** for the logical interface for configuration.
3. Click **Apply**. (You must configure an Ethernet interface and specify the subnet address and mask length on which the interface is listening before enabling the DHCP Server Process.)
4. Under **DHCP Server Configuration**, next to **DHCP Server Process**, click **Enable**.
5. Click **Apply** and then click **Save**.

To change the DHCP service, complete the following steps:

1. In the system tree, click **Configuration | System Configuration | DHCP**.
2. Under **DHCP Interface Configuration**, click the link of the logical interface for the configuration.
3. Under **DHCP Interface**, click the service for which you want to configure your appliance.
4. Click **Apply** and then click **Save**.

To add DHCP address pools, perform the following steps:

1. In the system tree, click **Configuration** | **System Configuration** | **DHCP**.
2. Under **DHCP Server Subnet Configuration**, click the IP address link to which you want to add address ranges.
3. Under **IP-Pool Configuration**, in the **Start** and **End** fields, type the range of IP addresses that the server will assign to clients. (If you are configuring a large number of VLANs, there might be a delay when assigning IP addresses to VLAN interfaces.)
4. Click **Apply** and then click **Save**.

TIP

To enable or disable a DHCP address pool, on the DHCP page, next to the subnet IP address link, click **Enable** or **Disable**. Click **Apply** and then click **Save** to make the changes permanent.

To assign a fixed IP address to a client, complete the following steps:

1. In the system tree, click **Configuration** | **System Configuration** | **DHCP**.
2. Under **Fixed-IP-Address Client Configuration**, click **Add A New Fixed-IP Entry**.
3. Under **New Fixed-IP Entry**, in the **Client ID** field, enter the client identification, or in the **Client MAC Address** field, enter the MAC address of the client.
4. In the **IP Address** field, enter the IP address you want to assign to the client.
5. Under **System Setup Configuration**, in the **Router** field enter the IP address of the default router for clients.
6. In the **DNS Servers** field, enter the DNS server used by clients to resolve domain names.
7. In the **NTP Servers** field, enter the NTP servers in order of preference and separated by commas.
8. In the **SMTP Servers** field, enter the SMTP servers separated by commas.
9. If you configured NetBIOS, under **NET BIOS Configuration For Windows Client**, complete the following steps:

- In the **Wins Server** field, enter the WINS available to clients.
- In the **DD Servers** field, enter the DD servers available to clients.
- From the **Node Type** list, select the node type that the client will configure as.
- In the **Scope** field, enter the client scope.

10. Click **Apply** and then click **Save**.

Optional fields for configuration are explained in Table 4.7.

Configuring DNS

IPSO uses DNS to translate host names into IP addresses. To enable DNS lookups, you must specify the primary DNS server for your system. You can also specify secondary and tertiary DNS servers. The system consults the primary DNS server first, then the secondary and finally the tertiary DNS servers if a failure or timeout occurs when resolving host names.

1. In the system tree, click **Configuration** | **System Configuration** | **DNS**.
2. In the **Domain Name** field, enter the new domain name.
3. In the **Primary Name Server** field, enter the IP address of the primary DNS server.
4. (Optional) In the **Secondary Name Server** and **Tertiary Name Server** fields, enter the IP addresses for the secondary and tertiary DNS servers.
5. Click **Apply** and then click **Save**.

Configuring Disk Mirroring

The Nokia disk mirroring feature (RAID Level 1) protects against downtime in the event of a hard-disk failure on your Nokia appliance (for platforms that support the feature), but you must have a second hard disk drive installed on your appliance.

Disk mirroring allows you to configure a mirror set composed of a source hard disk drive and a mirror hard disk drive that uses Nokia Network Voyager. The source drive is where IPSO is installed. When configuring a mirror set, the hard disk drives are synchronized (the source hard disk drive is fully copied to the mirror hard disk drive) and all new data written to the source drive is also written to the mirror hard disk drive. If the source hard disk drive fails, the mirror hard disk drive automatically replaces your source hard disk drive without an interruption of service on the Nokia appliance.

The source and mirror hard disk drives can be warm-swapped on appliances other than the IP500 series, meaning you can replace a failed hard disk drive without shutting down your Nokia appliance. You can also monitor the status of a mirror set, the synchronization time, and the system log entries. Figure 4.9 shows the Disk Mirroring Configuration page.

Figure 4.9 The Disk Mirroring Configuration Page

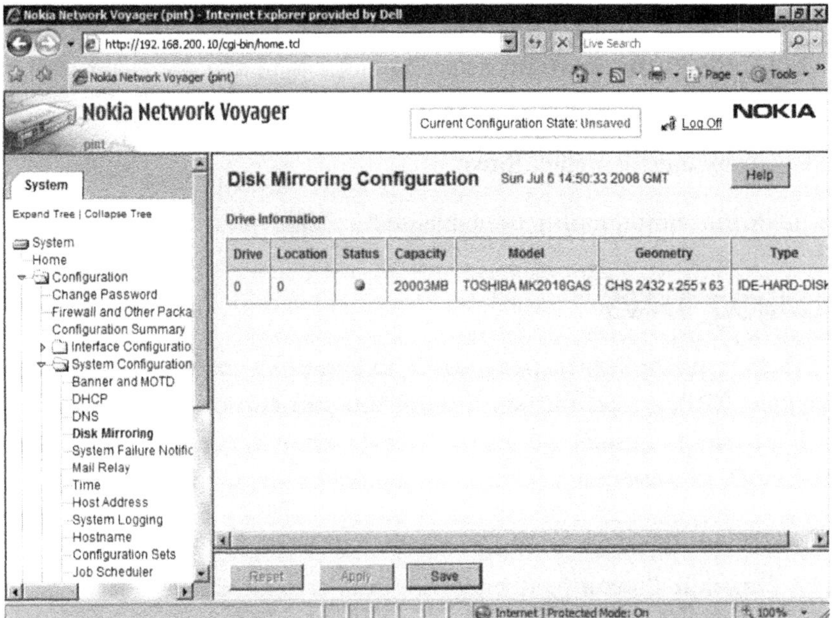

To create a mirror set or enable disk mirroring, perform the following steps:

1. In the system tree, click **Configuration** | **System Configuration** | **Disk Mirroring**.
2. Under **Mirror Set**, select **Create**. (The source and mirror hard disk drives should have identical geometries.)
3. Click **Apply**.

A message indicating that a mirror set was created appears. Numbers indicate which hard disk drive is the source and which is the mirror, and that mirror synchronization is in progress.

NOTE

The synchronization percent value in the Mirror Set table indicates the percentage of synchronization zones that are copied from the source to the mirror disk. A zone is equivalent to contiguous disk sectors. When all zones are copied to the mirror disk, the synchronization percent value is 100. For a 20GB disk, the synchronization time is approximately 20 to 30 minutes.

To delete or disable disk mirroring, on the Disk Mirroring page, next to the item for removal or deactivation, select **Delete**. Click **Apply** and then click **Save** to make the changes permanent.

NOTE

You can only delete a mirror set that is 100-percent synchronized.

Configuring System Time

Synchronized clock times are critical for several reasons, including distributed applications requiring time synchronization, analyzing event logs from different devices, ensuring cron jobs execute at the correct time, and making sure applications using system time to validate certificates find the correct time. For example, for audit logs, the timestamps on different network devices should be accurate to within a second of each other to correlate events across multiple devices.

The current system time appears across the top of all Nokia Network Voyager pages. You can set the system time using any of these methods:

- Set the date and time (manually)
- Access a time server (once)
- Configure NTP to access time servers for continuing clock synchronization

You can also configure rules for daylight savings time changes.

Setting System Time

You can set the system time manually or by using a time server when you initially configure the system. You might need to set the time again if you bring the system back up after it has been down for a while. You can also use the following procedure to specify the local time zone.

WARNING

When you reset the system time, the routing table is reset and existing connections might be terminated.

1. In the system tree, click **Configuration | System Configuration | Time**.
2. Under Set Time Zone, select the appropriate city. (By default, the time zone is set to GMT.)
3. (Optional) Under **Manually Set Time And Date**, enter the appropriate time and date values.
4. (Optional) Under **Set Time And Date From Time Server Once Only**, in the **Time Server** field, enter the time server name.
5. Click **Apply** and then click **Save**.

Configuring Daylight Savings Time

IPSO allows you to create and configure rules for daylight savings time (DST) changes. You can configure multiple DST rules for each time zone. When creating a DST rule, you must specify if it is recurring or nonrecurring, according to the following definitions:

- Recurring (always occurs, with no defined stopping point). For example, the United States started using recurring daylight savings rules in 2007.
- Nonrecurring (defined for a specific period of time). For example, the United States used daylight savings rules that expired after 2006.

You can access DST settings by clicking the Timezone DST Rule Configuration link on the Time Configuration page.

Configuring Host Addresses

Click **Host Address** under **Configuration | System Configuration** to perform any of the following tasks:

- View the entries in the hosts table.
- Add an entry to the list of hosts.
- Modify the IP address of a host.
- Delete a host entry.

You should add host addresses for systems that will communicate frequently with the system you are configuring. Figure 4.10 shows the Host Address page.

Figure 4.10 The Host Address Page

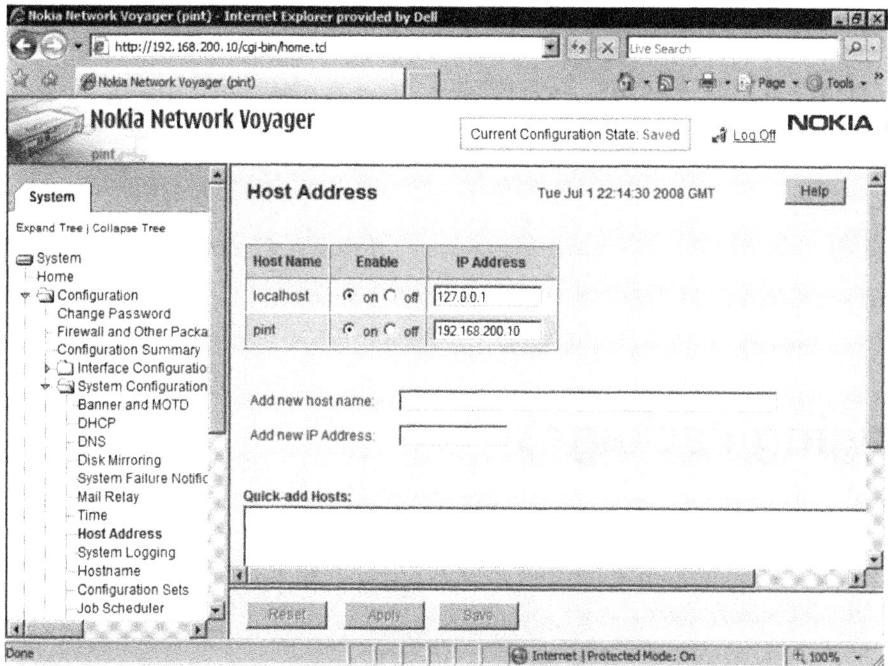

To add a static host entry using Nokia Network Voyager fields, complete the following steps:

1. In the system tree, click **Configuration** | **System Configuration** | **Host Address**.
2. In the **Add New Host Name** field, enter the host name.
3. In the **Add New IP Address** field, type the host IP address.
4. Click **Apply** and then click **Save**.

To add a static host entry using the quick add method, perform the following steps:

1. In the system tree, click **Configuration** | **System Configuration** | **Host Address**.
2. Under **Quick-add Hosts**, enter host names and IP addresses using the following format (you can enter as many pairs as you want):

   hostname IP-address

   hostname IP-address
3. Click **Apply**. The new host name appears in the list of Current Host Address Assignments.
4. Click **Save** to make your changes permanent.

To delete a static host, on the **Host Address** page, under the **Enable** column for the host name, select **Off**. Click **Apply** and then click **Save** to make the changes permanent.

Changing the Host Name

You set the host name during the initial configuration. The host name is also displayed in each page header.

1. In the system tree, click **Configuration** | **System Configuration** | **Hostname**.
2. In the **Change It To** field, type the new host name.
3. Click **Apply** and then click **Save**.

Managing Packages

Packages are ready-to-install software bundles for IPSO systems. Each package is installed as a subdirectory of the /opt directory.

You can use Nokia Network Voyager to install, upgrade, and remove packages. Figure 4.11 shows the Install Package page.

Figure 4.11 The Install Package Page

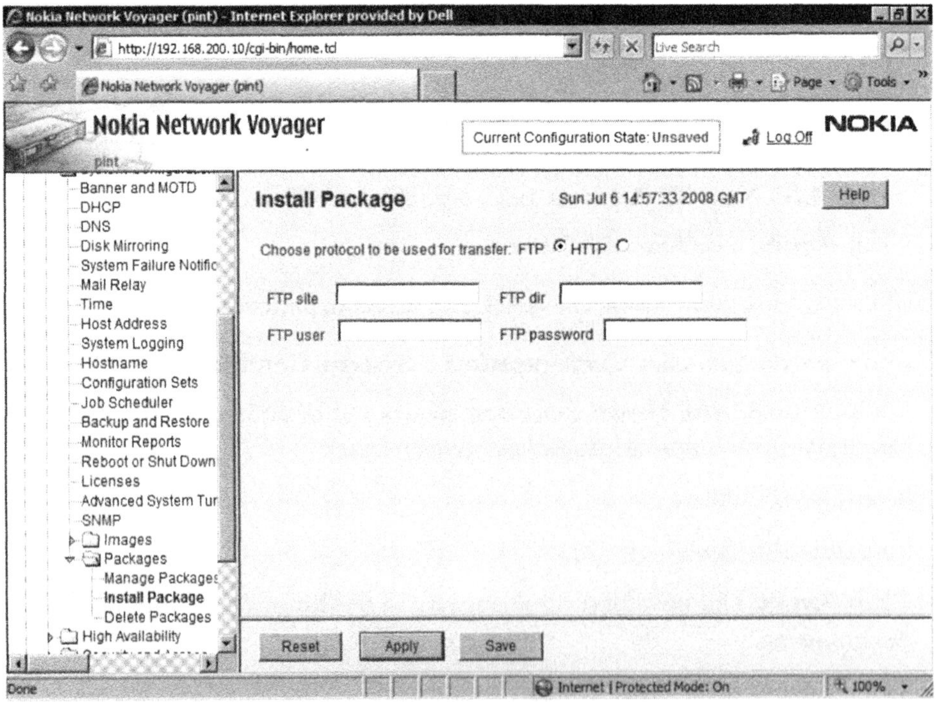

Installing and Enabling Packages

You can use Nokia Network Voyager to enable, disable, and delete packages. You can also use Nokia Network Voyager to delete files you no longer need to maintain on your local system.

Notes from the Underground...

Restrictions for Flash-Based Platforms

At a maximum, you can install two versions of Check Point VPN-1 Pro/Express on flash-based systems. If your platform runs Check Point NGX, the only supported Check Point packages are Check Point VPN-1 Pro/Express NGX R60 and Check Point CPinfo.

If your platform runs NG with Application Intelligence (R55) for IPSO 3.8, the only packages you can install are:

- Check Point VPN-1 NG with Application Intelligence (R55) for IPSO 3.8 (or later)
- Check Point SVN Foundation NG with Application Intelligence (R55) for IPSO 3.8
- Check Point Policy Server NG with Application Intelligence (R55) for IPSO 3.8
- Check Point CPinfo NG with Application Intelligence (R55) for IPSO 3.8

To install packages, complete the following steps:

1. In the system tree, click **Configuration** | **System Configuration** | **Packages** | **Install Package**.
2. For an FTP transfer, complete the following steps:
    1. Select **FTP**.
    2. Enter the FTP information in the appropriate fields. (The FTP site can be the host name or IP address and the FTP dir is the directory containing the package on the FTP site.)
3. For an HTTP transfer, complete the following steps:
    1. Select **HTTP**.
    2. Click **Browse**.

    3. Navigate to and select the location of the package file.
    4. Click **Open**.
4. Click **Apply**. A list of files ending with extensions TGZ, Z, and GZ from the specified directory appear in the Site Listing field.
5. Select a package to download.
6. Click **Apply**. The package is downloaded to the local Nokia IPSO system. After the download completes, the package appears in the **Unpack New Packages** field.
7. Select the package and then click **Apply**. The package is unpacked into the local file system.
8. Click **Click Here to Install/Upgrade [File Name]**.
9. (Optional) Click **Yes** to display all packages and then click **Apply** to display all installed packages.
10. (Optional) Click **Yes** next to **Install** and then click **Apply** to perform a first-time installation.
11. (Optional) Under **Choose One Of The Following Packages To Upgrade From**, click the button for the package to upgrade.
12. Click **Apply** and then click **Save**.

To enable or disable a package, complete the following steps:

1. In the system tree, click **Configuration** | **System Configuration** | **Packages** | **Manage Packages**.
2. Next to the package you want to enable or disable, click **On** or **Off**.
3. Click **Apply** and then click **Save**.

Deleting a Package

To delete a package, on the **Delete Packages** page, next to the package you want to delete, click **Delete**. Click **Apply** and then click **Save** to make the changes permanent.

Configuring Static Routes

Static routes are routes that you manually configure in the routing table. They do not change and are not dynamic. Static routes cause packets addressed to the destination to take a specified next hop. They enable you to add routes to destinations unknown by dynamic routing protocols and consist of the destination, type, and next-hop gateway parameters.

Figure 4.12 shows the Static Routes page. Static routes can be one of the following types:

- **Normal** A normal static route is one used to forward packets for a given destination in the direction indicated by the configured router.
- **Black hole** A black hole static route is a route that uses the loopback address as the next hop. This route discards packets that match the route for a given destination.
- **Reject** A reject static route is a route that uses the loopback address as the next hop. This route discards packets that match the route for a given destination and sends an ICMP unreachable message back to the sender of the packet.

Figure 4.12 The Static Routes Page

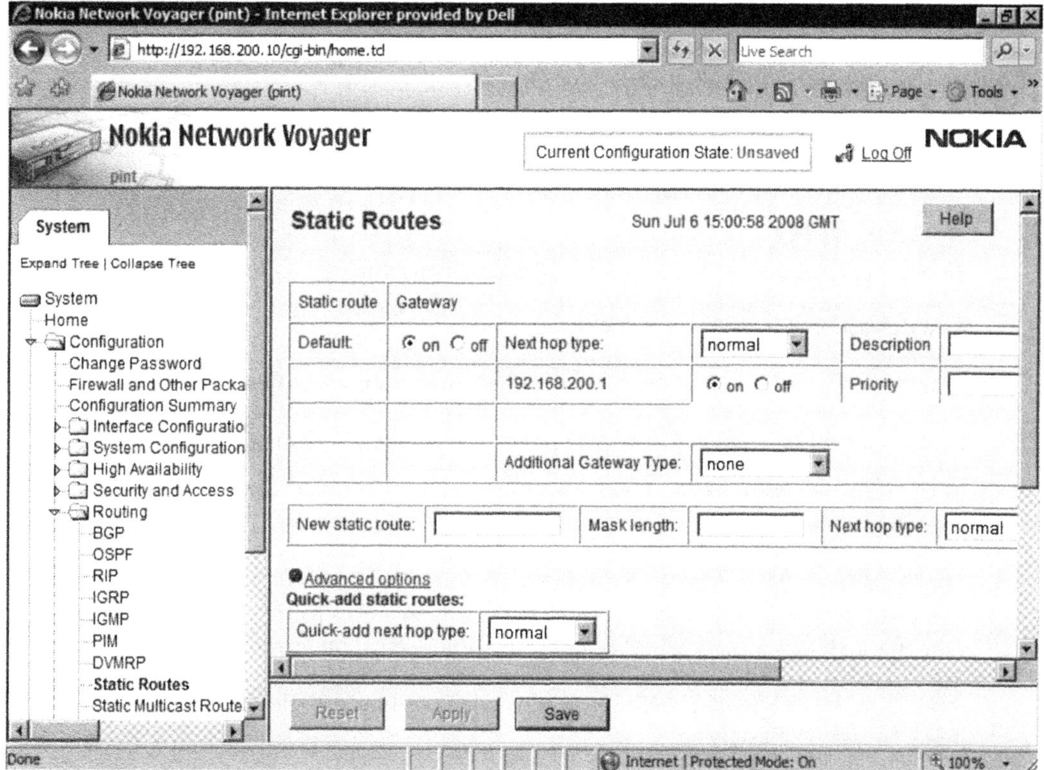

To configure a default or static route, complete the following steps:

1. In the system tree, click **Configuration** | **Routing** | **Static Routes**.
2. To enable a default route, click **On** in the **Default** field, and then click **Apply**.

3. To configure a new static route, complete the following steps:
    1. In the **New Static Route** field, type the network prefix.
    2. In the **Mask Length** field, type the mask length (number of bits).
    3. In the **Next Hop Type** list, select the type of next hop the static route will take.
    4. In the **Gateway Type** list, select the gateway type of the next hop router. (The Gateway Address specifies the IP address of the gateway to which forwarding packets for each static route are sent. This must be the address of a router that is directly connected to the system you are configuring.)

NOTE

Gateway Logical Name is valid only if the next-hop gateway is an unnumbered interface and you do not know the IP address of the gateway.

    5. Click **Apply**.
4. In the **Gateway** field, type the IP address of the default router.
5. Click **Apply** and then click **Save**.

To add and configure many static routes at the same time, complete the following steps:

1. In the system tree, click **Configuration** | **Routing** | **Static Routes**.
2. In the **Quick-Add Next Hop Type** list, select **Normal**, **Reject**, or **Black hole**. The default is Normal.
3. In the **Quick-Add Static Routes** field, type an IP address, its mask length, and add one or more next-hop IP addresses for each static route you want to add. Use the following format: IP address/mask length next hop IP address.

   The IP addresses must be specified in a dotted-quad format and the range for the mask length is 1 to 32.

   For example, to add a static route to 205.226. 10.0 with a mask length of 24 and next hops of

   10.1.1.1 and 10.1.1.2, enter:

   205.226.10.0/24 10.1.1.1 10.1.1.2
4. Press **Enter** after each entry you make for a static route.

NOTE

You cannot configure a logical interface through the Quick-Add Static Routes option.

5. Click **Apply**. The newly configured additional static routes appear in the Static Route field at the top of the Static Routes page.

NOTE

The text box displays any entries that contain errors. Error messages appear at the top of the page.

6. Click **Save**.

Creating Backup Static Routes

Static routes can become unavailable if the interface related to the currently configured gateway is down. If this happens, you can use a backup static route instead.

To implement backup static routes, you must prioritize them. The priority values range from 1 to 8, with 1 being the highest priority. If multiple gateways belong to the same priority, a multipath static route is installed. If a directly attached interface is down, all the gateways that belong to the interface are deleted from the list of next-hop selections.

Creating Aggregate Routes

Route aggregation lets you take several specific routes and combine them into one inclusive route. Route aggregation can reduce the number of routes a given protocol advertises. The aggregates are activated by contributing routes. For example, if a router has many interface routes subnetted from class C and is running Routing Information Protocol (RIP) 2 on another interface, the interface routes can be used to create an aggregate route (of the class C) that can then be redistributed into RIP. Creating an aggregate route reduces the number of routes advertised using RIP.

An aggregate route is created by first specifying the network address and mask length. Next, you must provide a set of contributing routes. A contributing route is defined when a source, such as a routing protocol, a static route, or an interface route, and a route filter, or a prefix, are specified. An aggregate route can have many contributing routes, but at least one of the routes must be present to generate an aggregate.

Aggregate routes are not used for packet forwarding by the originator of the aggregate route, only by the receiver. A router receiving a packet that does not match one of the component routes that led to the generation of an aggregate route responds with an ICMP network unreachable message. This message prevents packets for unknown component routes from following a default route into another network where they would be continually forwarded back to the border router until their TTL expires. Figure 4.13 shows the Route Aggregation page.

Figure 4.13 The Route Aggregation Page

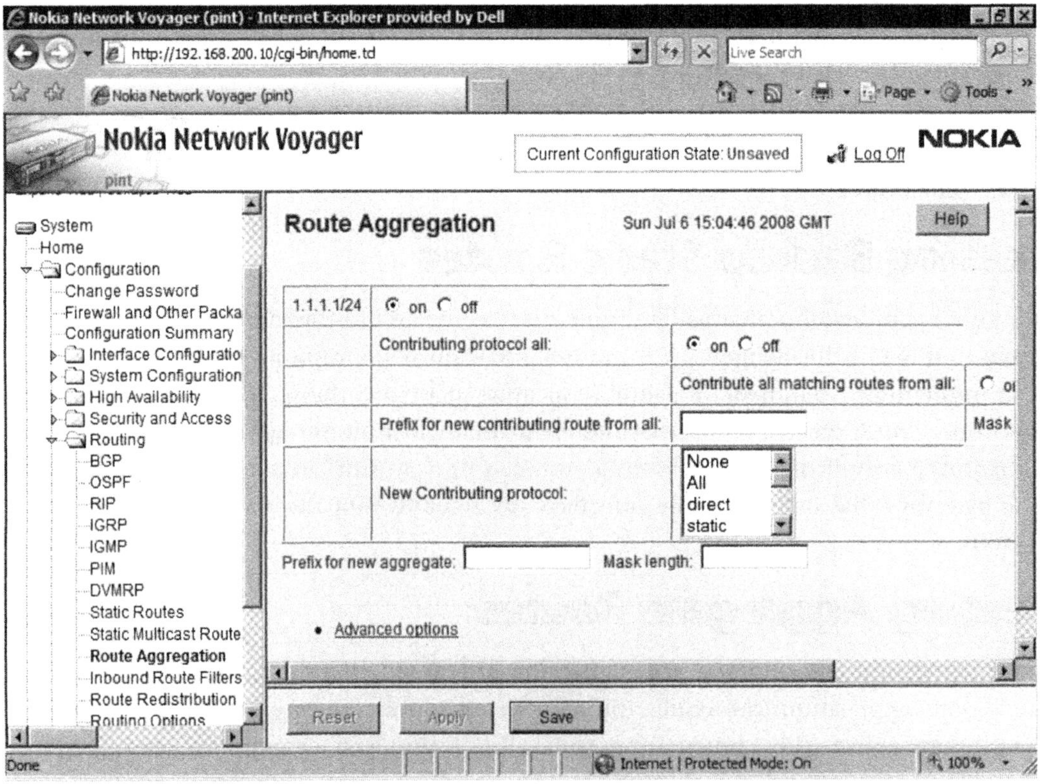

1. In the system tree, click **Configuration** | **Routing** | **Route Aggregation**.
2. In the **Prefix For New Aggregate** field, type the prefix for the new contributing route.

3. In the **Mask Length** field, type the mask length (number of bits) and then click **Apply**. (The mask length is the prefix length that matches the IP address to form an aggregate to a single routing table entry. By default, the aggregate route is on.)
4. Scroll through the New Contributing protocol list, click the protocol to use for the new aggregate route, and then click **Apply**.
5. (Optional) If you want to specify a prefix, in the **New Contributing Route From *Protocol*** field type the IP address and then click **Apply**.
6. To make your changes permanent, click **Save**.

TIP

You can also remove aggregate routes on the Route Aggregation page. In the table for the aggregate route, click **Off** and then click **Apply**.

Defining Route Rank

The *route rank* is an arbitrarily assigned value that the routing subsystem uses to order routes from different protocols to the same destination in a single routing database. Each route has only one rank associated with it, even though rank can be set in several locations in the configuration. The route derives its rank from the most specific route match among all configurations.

You cannot use the rank to control the selection of routes within a dynamic interior gateway protocol (IGP). This is accomplished automatically by the protocol and is based on the protocol metric. You can use the rank to select routes from the same external gateway protocol (EGP) learned from different peers or autonomous systems.

The active route is the route installed into the kernel forwarding table by the routing subsystem. If the same route is contributed to by more than one protocol, the one with the lowest rank becomes the active route.

Some protocols, such as Border Gateway Protocol (BGP) and aggregates, allow for routes with the same rank. To choose the active route in these cases, a separate tie breaker is used. This tie breaker is called LocalPref for BGP and weight for aggregates.

Assigning Ranks

A default rank is assigned to each protocol. Rank values range from 0 to 255, with the lowest number indicating the most preferred route.

Table 4.8 summarizes the default rank values.

Table 4.8 Default Rank Values

Preference	Default
Interface routes	0
OSPF routes	10
Static routes	60
IGRP routes	80
RIP routes	100
Aggregate routes	130
OSPF AS external routes	150
BGP routes	170

NOTE

You can set the route rank by clicking **Configuration | Routing | Routing Options.** Figure 4.14 shows the Routing Options page.

Figure 4.14 The Routing Options Page

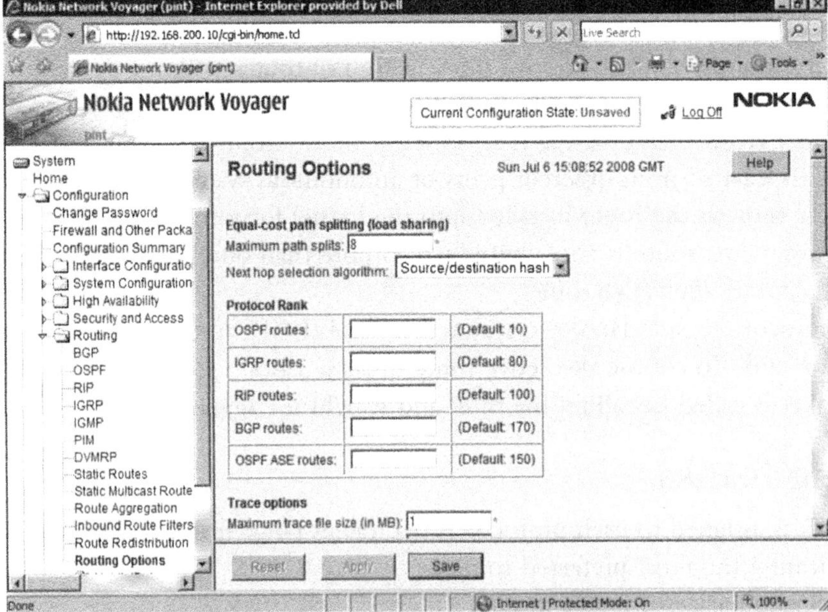

Configuring System Backup and Restore

You can manually back up files or you can configure the system for scheduled backups. Nokia Network Voyager can also be used to manage your backup files, including restoring from local files, transferring and restoring backup files on a remote server, and deleting backup files stored on a local system.

You can also view the Configuration Summary under IPSO Configuration for a list of backup files. Figure 4.15 shows the Backup And Restore Configuration page.

Figure 4.15 The Backup and Restore Configuration Page

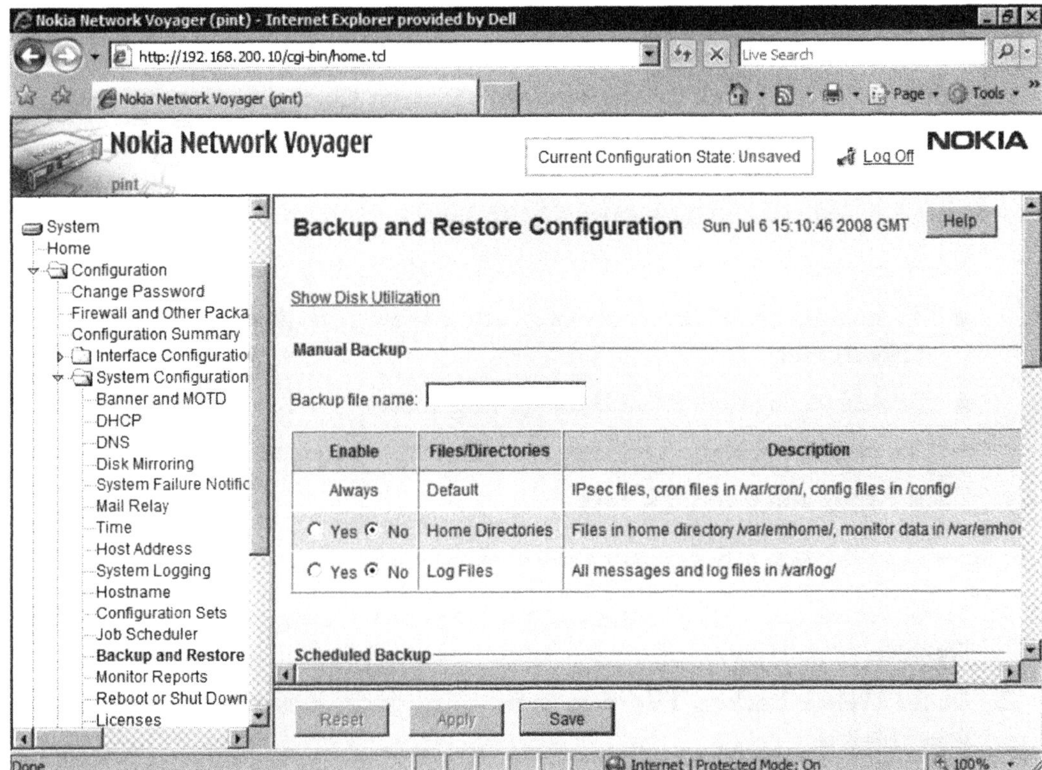

Creating Backup Files

By default, the backup file contains information in the following directories:

- configuration (/config)
- cron (/var/cron)

- etc (/var/etc)
- IPSec files (/var/etc/IPSec)

NOTE

Export versions of Nokia IPSO do not include IPSec files.

You also have the option to include the user home directories (/var/emhome) and log files (/var/logs) in your backup file.

To manually create a backup file, complete the following steps:

1. In the system tree, click **Configuration** | **System Configuration** | **Backup And Restore**.
2. In the **Backup File Name** field, type a name for your backup file. (If you do not provide a name, the backup file is not created.)
3. Select any additional directories to include in the backup file.
   - To back up home directories of all active users, select **Backup Home Directories**.
   - To include log files, select **Backup Log Files**.
   - To include application package files, select the corresponding package.
4. Click **Apply** and then click **Save**.

To delete local backup files, perform the following steps:

1. In the system tree, click **Configuration** | **System Configuration** | **Backup and Restore**.
2. Under **Delete Backup File**, next to the name of the backup files for deletion, select **Delete**.
3. Click **Apply** and then click **Save**. The backup file entry disappears.

To configure scheduled backups, perform the following steps:

1. In the system tree, click **Configuration** | **System Configuration** | **Backup And Restore**.
2. Under **Scheduled Backup**, in the **Frequency** list, select how often you want to perform a regular backup. The options are Daily, Weekly, or Monthly.

3. Click **Apply**. Depending on the frequency you selected, more fields and options appear for completion.
4. In the **Backup File Name** field, type a name for your backup file. (If you do not provide a name, the backup file is not created.)
5. Select any additional directories to include in the backup file.
   - To back up home directories of all active users, select **Backup Home Directories**.
   - To include log files, select **Backup Log Files**.
   - To include application package files, select the corresponding package.
6. Click **Apply** and then click **Save**.

To cancel scheduled backups, navigate to the Backup And Restore page. Under **Scheduled Backup**, in the **Frequency** list, select **None**. Click **Apply** and then click **Save** to make the changes permanent.

Transferring Backup Files

You can transfer backup files to remote servers or download the files to the workstation running Nokia Network Voyager. Backup files are removed from the system when you transfer the files to a remote server.

To configure automatic transfers of archive files to a remote server, complete the following steps:

1. In the system tree, click **Configuration | System Configuration | Backup And Restore**.
2. Under **Automatic Transfer Of Archive Files**, select the transfer protocol. (If you select FTP, verify that your server accepts anonymous FTP logins.)

WARNING

The TFTP option does not work with TFTP servers running on many UNIX-based operating systems if the target directory on the remote system does not contain a file with the same name as the backup file being transferred.

3. In the **Enter IP Address For Remote Machine** field, type the IP address of your remote server.

4. (For the FTP protocol only) In the **Enter FTP Directory** field, type the path and directory of the FTP server.
5. Click **Apply** and then click **Save**.

To transfer backup files manually, complete the following steps:

1. In the system tree, click **Configuration | System Configuration | Backup And Restore**.
2. Under **Manual Transfer Of Archive Files**, enter the following:
   - The IP address of the FTP server
   - The directory location for the saved backup file
   - The user account for connecting to the FTP server
   - The password for connecting to the FTP server (You must change the password if you change the FTP server, directory, or user.)

NOTE

The password is not stored in the database. Specify the password every time you want to transfer files to a remote server; even if using the same FTP server.

3. From the **Manual Backup File** or **Scheduled Backup File** lists, select the file you want to transfer.
4. Click **Save**.

Restoring Files from Locally Stored Backup Files

You can restore files stored locally or on a remote server. When restoring files from backup, the existing files are overwritten.

Before you can restore files, you must make sure the following prerequisites are met:

- Enough disk space is available (If you attempt a restore and not enough space is available, you can damage the operating system.)

- Your system is running the same operating system version and same packages as the backup files being restored. Running incompatible versions can cause problems with configuration and data files, which might not be immediately detected.

To restore files, complete the following steps:

1. In the system tree, click **Configuration | System Configuration | Backup And Restore**.
2. If restoring locally, under **Restore From Local**, in the **Manual Backup File** or **Scheduled Backup File** lists, select the file you want to restore. (Manually backed-up files are located in the /var/backup directory, and scheduled backed-up files are located in the /var/backup/sched directory.)
3. If restoring from a remote server using FTP, complete the following steps:
    1. Click **FTP** and then enter the following:
        - The IP address of the FTP server
        - The directory location to save the backup file
        - The user account for connecting to the FTP server
        - Password for connecting to the FTP server
    2. Select the files to restore.
4. If restoring from a remote server using HTTP, complete the following steps:
    1. Click **HTTP**.
    2. Click **Browse**.
    3. Navigate to the server's location and select the backup file.
5. Click **Apply** and then click **Reboot**.

NOTE

You must reboot your system after restoring from backed-up files.

Tools & Traps...

How Often Should I Test Backup/Restore?

The correct answer is that this depends entirely upon the information security policy within your organization. A better answer is that you should be performing backup and restore tests as often as possible to ensure that your archived data can be restored in the event of a disaster. All too often an administrator will trust their backup mechanism only to find out, after an incident, breach, or system failure that they cannot restore their last full backup because it is corrupt or, even worse, missing.

Always keep in mind the following considerations when planning for your backup and restore exercises:

- **Scope of Backups** Do you need to back up everything or just key files?
- **Responsibility for Backups** Who is responsible for managing the backups? Who ensures that the backups have completed successfully?
- **Backup Storage and Retrieval** How much space is required to store the backup? Do you have enough space on your device to restore the backup?
- **Testing the Integrity of Backups** How often are you validating the integrity of the backup? Will it work in a time of need?

A detailed backup and restore policy, which includes "dry runs" to test the integrity and accuracy of backups, should be included in any organization's operations planning and disaster recovery exercises.

More information about the back up and restoration of data can be found here:

http://en.wikipedia.org/wiki/Backup.

Configuring System Logging

System logging is configured differently on flash-based (or diskless) systems and disk-based systems. Figure 4.16 shows the System Logging Configuration page.

Figure 4.16 The System Configuration Logging Page

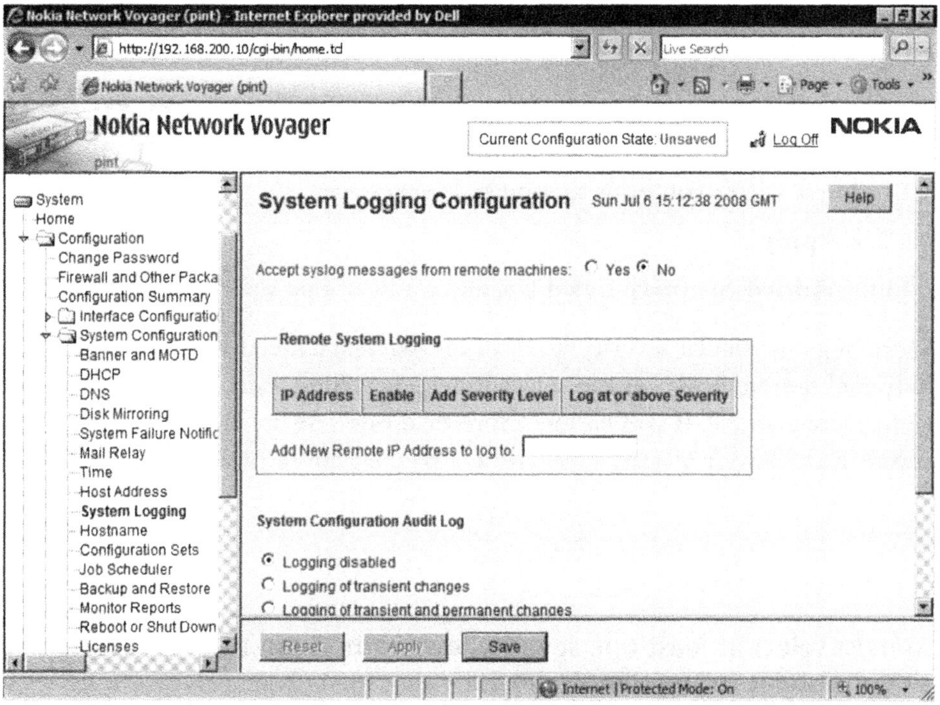

Configuring Logging on Disk-Based Systems

Disk-based systems automatically store IPSO log files on the local hard disk. You can configure system logging to send logging messages to a remote device or accept unfiltered system log messages from remote devices.

WARNING

Do not configure two devices to send system logging messages to each other directly or indirectly because it creates a forwarding loop, causing any system log message to be repeated indefinitely on both devices.

Logging to a Remote System

Any log messages sent to remote devices are also stored in the local log directories. You can use remote system logging to send log messages to a device that is configured for more secure storage, or to reduce the risk of losing log information if you max out the disk space on your IPSO appliance. You can also send all logs from multiple computers to one central log server, which could be configured for high availability, and select the severity levels of messages to send to remote devices.

To send syslog messages to a remote system, complete the following steps:

1. In the system tree, click **Configuration | System Configuration | System Logging**.
2. In the **Add New Remote IP Address To Log To** field, type the host machine IP address where you want to send syslog messages.
3. Click **Apply**.
4. In the **Added Security Level** list, select at least one severity level.

By specifying a particular severity level, all messages that are at least that severe are sent to the associated remote host. You can select Emergency, Alert, Critical, Error, Warning, Notice, Info, Debug, or All. If you choose more than one severity level, all messages that are least as severe as the lowest severity level are sent to the remote host.

NOTE

You must select at least one severity level, otherwise the system will not send syslog messages to the remote host.

5. Click **Apply**. The name of each severity level appears in the **Log At Or Above Severity** field.
6. To disable any of the severity levels, next to the severity level to delete, click **No**.
7. Click **Apply** and then click **Save**.

Accepting Log Messages

You can enable your system to accept unfiltered system log messages from remote devices. If you enable logging from remote systems, then system log packets are tagged with the host name of the sending device. The log packets are also logged as if the messages were generated locally. Network system log packets are ignored if logging from remote systems is disabled.

To set the system to accept syslog messages from a remote system, complete the following steps:

1. In the system tree, click **Configuration | System Configuration | System Logging**.
2. Next to **Accept Syslog Messages From Remote Machines**, click **Yes**.
3. Click **Apply** and then click **Save**.

WARNING

It is not a good idea to make your Nokia appliance a syslog server because processing of remote syslog might impact the performance of more critical system processes.

Configuring Logging on Flash-Based Systems

On flash-based (or diskless) systems, log files do not persist across system reboots unless they are stored on an appropriate device.

You can store log files on either or both the remote log servers (primary and secondary) and an optional disk.

If you want to use remote systems, you must configure the systems to store the log files.

An optional disk can be an internal hard disk (on some systems) or an external flash memory card. The disk must be installed and configured before you can use it.

Log messages are stored temporarily in system memory and stored to remote log servers or an optional disk according to a schedule, which you can configure.

Log messages are stored in the following files:

- **/tmp/tmessages (in memory)** Stores most log messages temporarily.
- **/var/log/messages** Stores most log messages when an optional disk is installed. When an optional disk is not installed, this directory links to the /tmp/tmessages directory.

NOTE

Messages stored in http_error_log or httpd_access_log are stored in the messages files on flash-based systems of other platforms.

- **/var/log/wtmp** Stores messages about shell logins and logouts. When an optional disk is installed, /var/log/wtmp is automatically stored on the drive.

Configuring Logging to Remote Log Servers

You must configure remote systems before you can use them to store log files.

1. In the system tree, click **Configuration | System Configuration | System Logging**.

2. Next to **Network Logging**, click **On**.
3. Enter the IP address of the primary remote log server. Make sure the flash-based system has connectivity to the remote server.
4. If you want to use a secondary remote log server, enter the IP address. If the primary log server is unreachable, there is a several-minute delay before log messages are sent to the secondary server. The messages are stored in a buffer during this time and are sent when connectivity is established with the secondary server.
5. Set the threshold percentage for saving log messages to the remote server. Flash-based systems can hold 512 log messages in a specific memory buffer. Use this configuration option to control when the messages are saved to the remote server and the buffer is cleared. For example, assume that 50 is the threshold percentage. When there are 256 messages in the buffer, the messages are transferred to the remote server and the buffer is cleared.
6. Use the Flush Frequency option as an additional control for saving messages. When the Flush Frequency interval expires, log messages are transferred to the remote server, and the log buffer is cleared regardless of how many messages are in the buffer.
7. Click **Apply** and then click **Save**.

Configuring Logging to an Optional Disk

If an optional disk is installed and enabled, you can configure the system to save log files by selecting the option **Logging To Optional Disk**. If you enable local logging, log messages are saved in the /var/log/message and /var/log/wtmp directories on the memory card. The messages are saved to the optional disk according to the settings of the Threshold % and Flush Frequency options, and you can save log files to a remote log server and an optional disk simultaneously.

The system displays a console message if an optional disk is full and stops saving log messages to the device, but messages previously saved on the optional disk are not affected. If you have configured the system to send messages to a remote log server, the system continues to send the messages.

NOTE

If you use SNMP, the system sends SNMP traps when the flash memory file system is 90 and 95 percent full to alert you of the impending issue.

You can delete log files stored in PC card flash memory using the *rm* command to delete files in the /var/log/ directory.

Configuring Audit Logs

You enable and configure the audit logs for both disk-based and flash-based systems in the same manner. To make specific log messages more useful, you can configure the system so messages about system configuration changes are displayed in a textual format instead of the configuration database bindings format. Examples that show log messages in the configuration database style and in the textual format are outlined in Table 4.9.

Table 4.9 Log Message Formats

Configuration Database Format	Textual Format
process:pm:coreaction t	PROCESS_CONFIG: Enabled system failure notification
ipsrd:instance:default:vrp: nomonitorfw t	VRRP_CONFIG: Disabled VRRP Monitor Firewall State
mcvr:vrid:123	Deleted Monitored-Circuit Virtual Router with vrid 123

If you enable the Voyager Audit Log option, every time Apply or Save is clicked, the name of the user, the Network Voyager page, and the name of the clicked button are recorded in the log. The log records the actions regardless of whether the operation succeeds. For Nokia Network Voyager configuration pages that do not include Apply and Save buttons, the log records the relevant action, such as clicking Reboot. To see the log, view the System Message Log page.

To set the system configuration audit log, complete the following steps:

1. In the system tree, click **Configuration | System Configuration | System Logging**.
2. In the **System Configuration Audit Log** area, select from the following:
   - **Logging disabled** The system writes minimal messages to the system log that a configuration change was made, including the name of the host from which the change was made, and the name of the user who made the change.
   - **Logging of transient changes** The system writes messages to the system log every time a user applies a configuration change to the running system.

Transient changes only apply to the currently running system. Transient changes are equivalent to clicking Apply Only in Nokia Network Voyager.

- **Logging of transient and permanent changes** The system writes messages to the system log every time a user applies a configuration change to the running system or changes the configuration files. Permanent changes are changes that remain active after the system is rebooted. These changes are equivalent to clicking Save in Nokia Network Voyager after you apply a configuration change.

3. Click **Apply**. If you are using a disk-based system, a Destination Log Filename text box appears after you enable the system configuration auditlog. The box contains the name of the file to which syslog messages for this feature are sent. The default is /var/log/messages.
4. To change the file, in the **Destination Log Filename** field, type the new file name. (On flash-based systems, you cannot save the messages to another file.)

NOTE

The system configuration audit log setting is not saved in the configuration file. You must reset it after rebooting to enable logging again.

You must provide a destination file name to view log messages in the Management Activity Log. The default destination file logs messages in the standard system log file. To access the Management Activity Log page, click **Monitor** on the **Home** page in Nokia Network Voyager and under **System Logs**, click the **Management Activity Log** link.

To enable logging in textual format, complete the following steps:

1. In the system tree, click **Configuration | System Configuration | System Logging**.
2. Select the textual format option in the **System Configuration Audit Log** area.

To set logging of all Nokia Network Voyager apply and save actions, complete the following steps:

1. In the system tree, click **Configuration | System Configuration | System Logging**.
2. In the **Voyager Audit Log** field, select **Enabled** or **Disabled**.
3. Click **Apply** and then click **Save**.

The Voyager Audit Log feature does not record any operations performed using the CLI. To log configuration changes made using Nokia Network Voyager or the CLI, enable the system configuration audit log.

Configure the system configuration audit log to record transient and permanent configuration changes. You can view the syslog messages to determine if only authorized users are making configuration changes to the system.

Scheduling cron Jobs

You can use Nokia Network Voyager to access the crontab file and schedule regular jobs. The cron daemon executes jobs upon the dates and times you specify. Figure 4.17 shows the Job Scheduler page.

Figure 4.17 The Job Scheduler Page

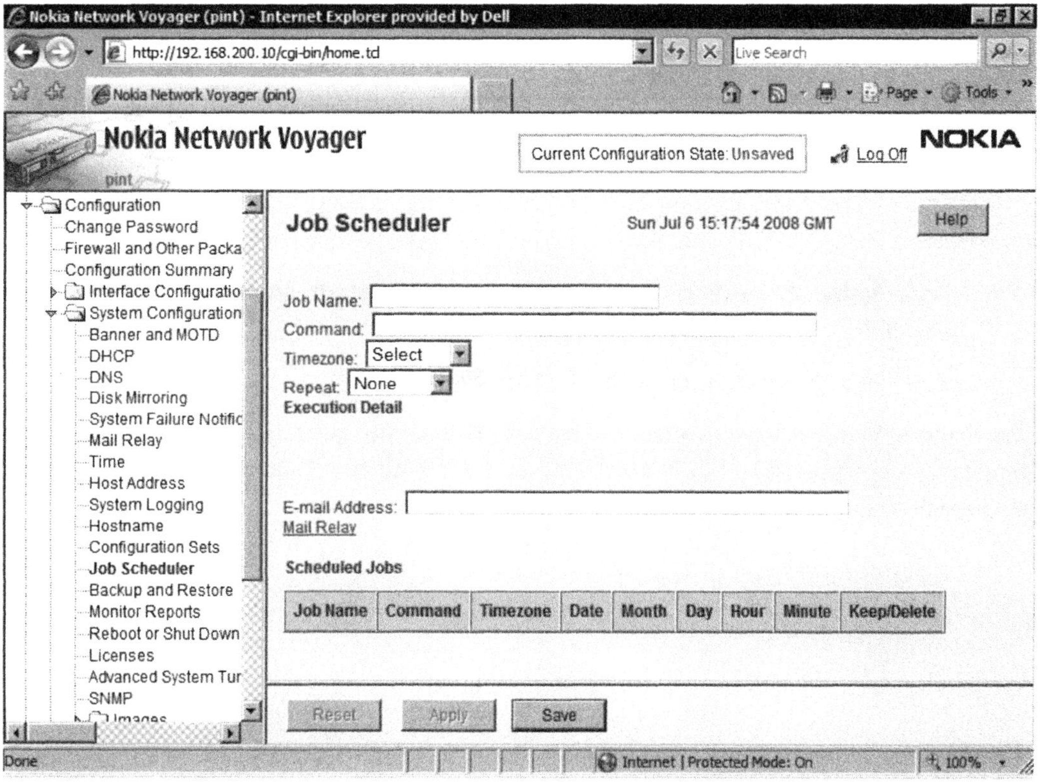

To schedule jobs, complete the following steps:

1. In the system tree, click **Configuration | System Configuration | Job Scheduler**.

2. In the **Job Name** field, type a name for the job you want the cron daemon to execute. Use alphanumeric characters only, and do not include spaces.
3. In the **Command** field, type the name of the command you want the cron daemon to execute. The command can be any UNIX command.
4. In the **Timezone** list, select **Local** or **Universal**.
5. In the **Repeat** list, select the frequency (**Daily**, **Weekly**, **Monthly**, or **WildCard**) that you want the job to execute.
6. Click **Apply**.
7. Under **Execution Detail**, specify when the job will execute.
8. To receive e-mails regarding your scheduled jobs, in the **E-mail Address** field, type your e-mail address.

TIP

Click **Mail Relay** to verify that a mail server is configured.

9. Click **Apply**. If your configuration is successful, the job appears in the Scheduled Jobs table.
10. To make your changes permanent, click **Save**.

To delete scheduled jobs, navigate to the **Job Scheduler** page. In the **Scheduled Jobs** table, next to the name of each job for deletion, select **Delete**. Click **Apply** and then click **Save** to make the changes permanent.

Summary

Nokia Network Voyager is a role-based application provided in a Web-based interface. You can use Nokia Network Voyager to manage your IPSO operating system on your Nokia appliance. The IPSO operating system software is included and is accessible using a Web browser from a client.

All information appears in a navigation tree view, similar to Windows Explorer and is split across four frames. If you do not have access to a system item, then the item does not appear in the navigation tree. Read-only access gives you access to the page, but with the buttons disabled. Remember to not use the Back and Forward buttons of your Web browser while in Nokia Network Voyager because the browser caches the HTML page information and the latest page information might be lost when moving from page to page.

When you set up your IPSO system for the first time, configure the basic Nokia Network Voyager options and change your SSL/TLS certificate from the default certificate. To secure Nokia Network Voyager client connections to the IPSO system over the Internet, IPSO uses the SSL/TLS protocol. When setting up your system for the first time, change your SSL/TLS certificate from the default certificate. IPSO includes a default sample certificate and private key in the /var/etc/voyager_ssl_server.crt and /var/etc/voyager_ssl_server.key files, respectively. IPSO uses the SSH program to provide secure connections for the CLI. SSH allows you to securely log in to another computer over a network, execute commands on a remote platform, and move files from one platform to another.

When configuring interfaces in Nokia Network Voyager, you must know the IP address and netmask of each interface. Nokia Network Voyager displays network devices as physical interfaces, and physical interfaces exist for each physical port on a NIC installed on the appliance. The interface names have the following form:

```
<type>-s<slot>p<port>
```

- **<type>** The prefix for the device type.
- **<slot>** The slot number for the device on the appliance.
- **<port>** The NIC port number. The first port on a NIC is port one.

When applying security tuning in Nokia Network Voyager, you can set the MSS value to tune TCP performance by allowing your system to receive the largest possible segments without fragmentation. For enhanced security, IPSO supports the SecureXL sequence validation (TCP state detection version 2) functionality. This feature allows the firewall to stop exploits that make use of out-of-sequence TCP packets.

To use sequence validation, enable it on SmartDashboard and in IPSO—for stand-alone systems and high-availability configurations. Remember, this feature is disabled by default.

You can improve performance using delayed notification and auto-expiry to reduce the amount of required communication between IPSO and the firewall. You can also reduce the amount of synchronization between the IP cluster members or VRRP groups, reducing overhead processing.

Nokia Network Voyager provides GUI access to configure several items for your Nokia appliance. You can create banner and login messages to provide informative responses to users, configure DHCP to configure network parameters to operate on the network, configure DNS to translate host names into IP addresses, and configure disk mirroring to protect against downtime in the event of a hard-disk failure. Other configurable items include system time, host address, and host names.

Using Nokia Network Voyager, you can install, upgrade, and remove IPSO packages. You can also use Nokia Network Voyager to enable, disable, and delete packages and to delete files you no longer need to maintain on your local system.

Static routes are also configurable through Nokia Network Voyager. Static routes cause packets addressed to the destination to take a specified next hop. They enable you to add routes to destinations unknown by dynamic routing protocols and consist of destination, type, and next-hop gateway. You can configure one or more static routes and implement backup static routes. You also create aggregate routes to combine multiple static routes into one inclusive route, reducing the number of routes advertised by a given protocol. You can use a route rank, which is an arbitrarily assigned value that the routing subsystem uses to order routes from different protocols to the same destination in a single routing database, to select routes from the same EGP on autonomous systems.

Nokia Network Voyager can also be used to manage your backup files, including restoring from local files, transferring and restoring backup files on a remote server, and deleting backup files stored on a local system. By default, the backup file contains information in the following directories:

- configuration (/config)
- cron (/var/cron)
- etc (/var/etc)
- IPSec files (/var/etc/IPSec)

You can restore files stored locally or on a remote server. When restoring files from backup, the existing files are overwritten. Before you can restore files, you must make sure there is enough disk space available on your system and that your system is running the same operating system version and packages as the backup files being restored.

In Nokia Network Voyager, you can configure system logging to send logging messages to a remote device or accept unfiltered system log messages from remote devices. You can use remote system logging to send log messages to a device that is configured for more secure storage, or to reduce the risk of losing log information if you max out the disk space on your IPSO appliance. You can also send all logs from multiple computers to one central log server, which could be configured for high availability, and select the severity levels of messages to send to remote devices.

Finally, you can also use Nokia Network Voyager to access the crontab file and schedule regular jobs, which lets you execute jobs at specific dates and times.

Solutions Fast Track

Introducing Nokia Network Voyager

☑ Nokia Network Voyager access is role-based, meaning that after you have logged in, what you see and have access to depends on the role or roles assigned to you.

☑ All information appears in a navigation tree view, similar to Windows Explorer.

☑ If you do not have access to a system item, then the item does not appear in the navigation tree. Read-only access gives you access to the page, but with the buttons disabled.

Configuring Nokia Network Voyager Access

☑ When you set up your IPSO system for the first time, configure the basic Nokia Network Voyager options and change your SSL/TLS certificate from the default certificate.

☑ To secure Nokia Network Voyager client connections to the IPSO system over the internet, IPSO uses the SSL/TLS protocol.

☑ IPSO uses the SSH program to provide secure connections for the CLI, which allows you to securely log in to another computer over a network, execute commands on a remote platform, and move files from one platform to another.

Configuring a Basic System

☑ When configuring interfaces, you must know the IP address and netmask of each interface.

☑ Nokia Network Voyager displays network devices as physical interfaces, and physical interfaces exist for each physical port on a network interface card (NIC) installed on the appliance.

☑ You assign IP addresses to logical interfaces, which are created for the physical interface of a device, and then route to the IP address.

Applying Security Tuning

- ☑ Established TCP connections have a maximum segment size (MSS) at each end, which you can change to tune TCP performance by allowing your system to receive the largest possible segments without fragmentation.
- ☑ You can enable or disable some SecureXL features in IPSO if Check Point NGX is installed on your system.
- ☑ You can configure delayed synchronization in high-availability configurations so connections do not expire before a set time.

Configuring System Options

- ☑ Nokia IPSO provides complete DHCP client and server capabilities for your Nokia appliance, which enables you to configure network parameters through a server to clients requiring the parameters to operate on the network and eliminates the need to manually configure each client and reduces configuration errors.
- ☑ IPSO uses DNS to translate host names into IP addresses.
- ☑ Disk mirroring lets you configure a mirror set composed of a source hard disk drive and a mirror hard disk drive that uses Nokia Network Voyager.

Managing Packages

- ☑ Packages are ready-to-install software bundles for IPSO systems.
- ☑ Each package is installed as a subdirectory of the /opt directory.
- ☑ You can use Nokia Network Voyager to install, upgrade, and remove packages.

Configuring Static Routes

- ☑ Static routes are routes that you manually configure in the routing table.
- ☑ To implement backup static routes, you must prioritize them.
- ☑ Route aggregation allows you to take several specific routes and combine them into one inclusive route.

Configuring System Backup and Restore

- ☑ You can manually back up files or you can configure the system for scheduled backups.

- ☑ Nokia Network Voyager can also be used to manage your backup files, including restoring from local files, transferring and restoring backup files on a remote server, and deleting backup files stored on a local system.
- ☑ Backup files are removed from the system when you transfer the files to a remote server.

Configuring System Logging

- ☑ Disk-based systems automatically store IPSO log files on the local hard disk.
- ☑ You can configure system logging to send logging messages to a remote device or accept unfiltered system log messages from remote devices.
- ☑ You can enable your system to accept unfiltered system log messages from remote devices.

Scheduling cron Jobs

- ☑ You can use Nokia Network Voyager to access the crontab file and schedule regular jobs.
- ☑ The cron daemon executes jobs upon the dates and times you specify.
- ☑ The cron daemon can execute any UNIX command.

Frequently Asked Questions

Q: When I log in to Nokia Network Voyager, will I be able to manage everything on the appliance?

A: Nokia Network Voyager is role-based. Depending on the account you log in with, you might be able to manage all or only specific items for the appliance.

Q: How can I determine what I have access to?

A: If you do not have access to a system item, then the item does not appear in the navigation tree. Read-only access gives you access to the page, but with the buttons disabled.

Q: How can I prevent another user from making system changes while I am logged in to Nokia Network Voyager?

A: If you log in with an exclusive configuration lock, no other user can change the system configuration.

Q: I went back one Web page and my changes are gone. What happened?

A: You should not use the Back and Forward buttons of your Web browser while in Nokia Network Voyager. Because the browser caches the HTML page information, the latest page information might be lost when moving from page to page. To update the page information, you can use the Web browser reload or refresh button.

Q: I am about to use my IPSO system for the first time. Is there anything I should know?

A: When you set up your IPSO system for the first time, configure the basic Nokia Network Voyager options and change your SSL/TLS certificate from the default certificate.

Q: What does IPSO use to secure client connections?

A: To secure Nokia Network Voyager client connections to the IPSO system over the internet, IPSO uses the Secure Sockets Layer/Transport Layer Security (SSL/TLS) protocol.

Q: I cannot access the Nokia Network Voyager interface. What could the problem be?

A: Verify you are using the correct URL, that you are using the correct PEM-encoded certificate and private key, and that the certificate and private key are installed properly with the dashed begin and end lines. Finally, verify the HTTP daemon error message log.

Q: What do I need to know about an interface to be able to configure it?

A: When configuring interfaces, you must know the IP address and netmask of each interface.

Q: What if I have multiple subnets on the same physical network?

A: For multiple subnets on the same physical network, you can configure more addresses and subnet masks on the single logical interface connected to that network. You do not have to create additional logical interfaces to run multiple subnets on a single physical network.

Q: How do I configure point-to-point media?

A: For point-to-point media, you can assign IP addresses or configure an unnumbered interface. If assigning IP addresses, you must specify the IP address of the local interface and the point-to-point interface of the remote system.

Q: Do all nodes respond to the MSS value I set?

A: Only the remote terminating node responds to the MSS value you set. In other words, intermediate nodes do not respond. Typically, however, intermediate nodes can handle 1500-byte MTUs.

Q: I have Check Point NGX installed. Can I manage the SecureXL features through Nokia Network Voyager?

A: Yes. You can enable or disable some SecureXL features in IPSO if Check Point NGX is installed on your system. These features are listed in the SecureXL TCP box, which appears on the Advanced System Tuning page of Nokia Network Voyager.

Q: Why would I use delayed notification or auto-expiry?

A: You can improve performance using delayed notification and auto-expiry to reduce the amount of required communication between IPSO and the firewall. You can also reduce the amount of synchronization between the IP cluster members or VRRP groups, reducing overhead processing.

Q: I do not like the message "This system is for authorized use only." Can I change it?

A: Yes. This is considered the Banner message. It can be changed by clicking **Configuration | System Configuration | Banner And MOTD**.

Q: Will the Nokia appliance still receive and accept DHCP requests if I have enabled the IPSO DCHP server?

A: If you enable the IPSO DHCP server, the Nokia appliance still receives and accepts DHCP requests even if there is a firewall rule blocking DHCP requests. If you enable the DHCP server, but do not want external DHCP requests to be accepted, enable DHCP on internal interfaces only.

Q: How can I enable DNS lookups?

A: To enable DNS lookups, you must specify the primary DNS server for your system. You can also specify secondary and tertiary DNS servers. The system consults the primary DNS server first, then the secondary, and finally the tertiary DNS servers if a failure or timeout occurs when resolving host names.

Q: I am concerned about downtime if the Nokia appliance encounters a hard-disk failure. Is there anything I can configure to help minimize downtime?

A: The Nokia disk mirroring feature (RAID Level 1) protects against downtime in the event of a hard-disk failure on your Nokia appliance (for platforms that support the feature), but you must have a second hard disk drive installed on your appliance.

Q: I just installed the latest IPSO package. Where is it?

A: Each package is installed as a subdirectory of the /opt directory.

Q: I have been using my Nokia appliance for a while now and I know there are extra files I should probably delete. What can I use to clean the system?

A: You can use Nokia Network Voyager to enable, disable, and delete packages. You can also use Nokia Network Voyager to delete files you no longer need to maintain on your local system.

Q: What transfer method can I use to install the latest IPSO package?

A: You can use FTP or HTTP.

Q: Why would I indicate a static route as "reject"?

A: A reject static route is a route that uses the loopback address as the next hop. This route discards packets that match the route for a given destination and sends an ICMP unreachable message back to the sender of the packet.

Q: Can I use a backup static route?

A: Yes. To implement backup static routes, you must prioritize them. The priority values range from 1 to 8, with 1 being the highest priority. If multiple gateways belong to the same priority, a multipath static route is installed. If a directly attached interface is down, all the gateways that belong to the interface are deleted from the list of next-hop selections.

Q: Is there anything I can do to reduce the number of multiple static routes defined?

A: Route aggregation lets you take several specific routes and combine them into one inclusive route. Route aggregation can reduce the number of routes that a given protocol advertises. The aggregates are activated by contributing routes.

Q: Can I configure backing up and restoring through Nokia Network Voyager?

A: Yes. Nokia Network Voyager can be used to manage your backup files, including restoring from local files, transferring and restoring backup files on a remote server, and deleting backup files stored on a local system.

Q: Can I delete local backup files using Nokia Network Voyager?

A: Yes. You can delete files, by clicking **Configuration | System Configuration | Backup And Restore**. On the **Backup And Restore Configuration** page, under **Delete Backup File**, next to the name of the backup files for deletion, select **Delete**

Q: Where can I transfer backup files?

A: You can transfer backup files to remote servers or download the files to the workstation running Nokia Network Voyager. Backup files are removed from the system when you transfer the files to a remote server.

Q: Is system logging handled the same for all system types?

A: System logging is configured differently on flash-based (or diskless) systems and disk-based systems.

Q: What can I do to back up and securely store remote system logs?

A: You can use remote system logging to send log messages to a device that is configured for more secure storage or to reduce the risk of losing log information if you max out the disk space on your IPSO appliance. You can also send all logs from multiple computers to one central log server, which could be configured for high availability, and select the severity levels of messages to send to remote devices.

Q: Is there anything I must do or know about before I can log files to a remote system?

A: You must configure remote systems before you can use them to store log files.

Q: How can I configure a job to run every Monday at 8 a.m.?

A: You can use Nokia Network Voyager to access the crontab file and schedule regular jobs. The cron daemon executes jobs upon the dates and times you specify.

Q: Which type of commands will the cron daemon run?

A: The cron daemon will execute any UNIX command.

Q: Can I specify a different time zone for the cron job?

A: Yes. You can specify Local or Universal.

Chapter 5

Security and Access Configuration

Solutions in this chapter:

- Managing Accounts and Passwords
- Managing Groups and Access
- Configuring Authentication, Authorization, and Accounting (AAA)
- Configuring IPSO VPN

☑ Summary

☑ Solutions Fast Track

☑ Frequently Asked Questions

Introduction

Shin had configured the first system but, at Marty's request, let Mark and Ming configure the other appliances.

"Wow," said Mark after he finished his configuration, "that was easy." Ming nodded in agreement. "Now that we have the base system configured, how do we manage the security and access settings?" Mark turned to Shin. "And how would we go about creating a site-to-site VPN tunnel between HQ and the remote offices?"

Marty looked at Mark with a surprised look on his face. "You're not the only one who researches products before we install them Marty," Mark said as he winked at Marty.

"No problem," said Shin. "I was just going to get into that. Let's start with the user and group access configurations and then move into the configuration of VPN tunnels." Shin paused. "That being said, you might want to use the Check Point VPN functionality, so I'll show you how to configure it in case you want to use the IPSO method instead."

Managing Accounts and Passwords

When you log in to Nokia Network Voyager, the features available in the navigation tree depend on the role or roles assigned to your user account. If the roles do not provide access to a feature, you will not see a link to the feature in the tree. If you have read-only access to a feature, you will see a link and be able to access the page, but the controls will be disabled.

Password and Account Management

An important aspect when securing your Nokia network security platform is establishing user passwords and creating an effective password policy. Remember that having users create strong and unique passwords using a variety of character types and creating a password policy requiring users to change their passwords are often key factors to overall network security.

When configuring your platform with Nokia Network Voyager, you want to:

- Enforce the creation of strong passwords
- Force users to change passwords regularly
- Track and prevent password reuse
- Lock out users after failed login attempts
- Lock out accounts that have been inactive for a period of time

The password policies you establish with password and account management are sharable across a cluster. The password and account management features do not apply to non-local users, whose login information and passwords are managed by authentication servers such as RADIUS servers. The features also do not apply to non-password authentication, such as the public-key authentication supported by SSH. Figure 5.1 shows the Password And Account Management Controls page where you can modify the password length, complexity, and history requirements.

Figure 5.1 Password and Account Management Controls Page

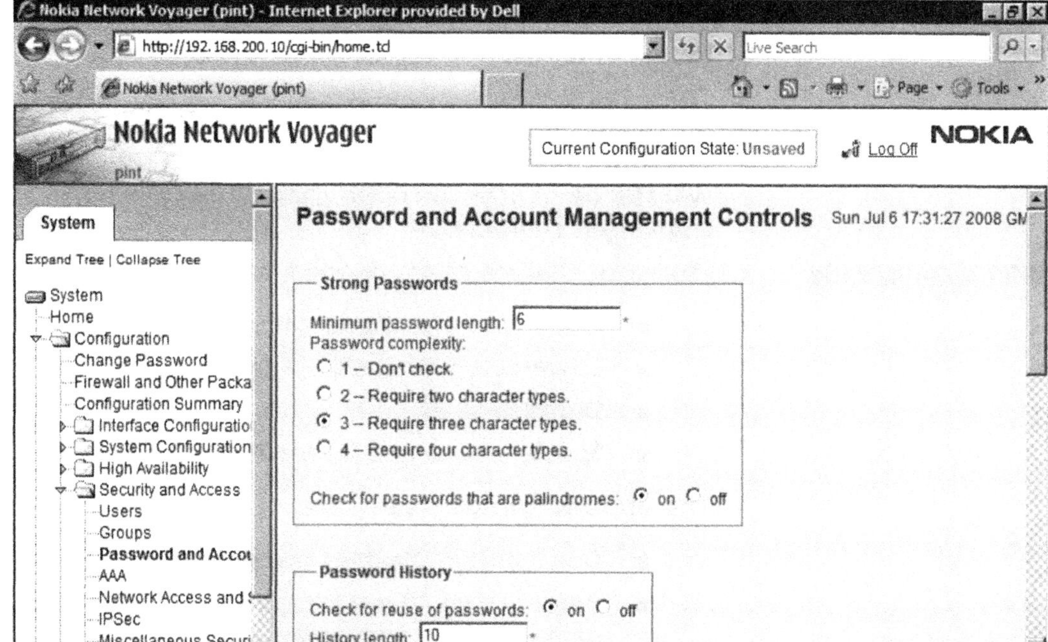

Configuring Password Strength

To create an effective security policy, you must make sure users create strong and unique passwords. You can configure a policy that requires strong passwords by making certain the passwords:

- Are a certain length (the default minimum is six characters)
- Use more than one character type (the default is three character types)
- Are not palindromes (palindromes are words that can be read the same forward or backwards, such as refer or racecar)

Table 5.1 describes the available password strength options.

Table 5.1 Password Strength Options

Option	Description
Minimum password length	Specifies the minimum number of characters for a password. Default: 6 Range: 6 to 128 The minimum passphrase length for SNMPv3 USM users is always eight characters. If you set this option to fewer than eight characters, SNMP users will still be unable to create passphrases of fewer than eight characters.
Password complexity	Password characters are divided into four types: ■ Uppercase alphabetic (A to Z) ■ Lowercase alphabetic (a to z) ■ Digits (0 to 9) ■ Special characters (everything else) The options for complexity are: ■ *Don't check*: Disables complexity checking ■ *Require two character types*: Requires that passwords are composed of two character types at minimum. For example, abcABC ■ *Require three character types*: Requires that passwords are composed of three character types at minimum. For example, ab1ABC ■ *Require four character types*: Requires that passwords are composed of four character types at a minimum. For example, ab1AB# Default: Require three character types.
Check for palindromes	Checks for passwords with characters that can be read the same when written left to right or right to left. This check is not case-sensitive, so racecar is still considered a palindrome. Default: On

In the system tree, click **Configuration | Security And Access | Password And Account Management Controls** to access the Password And Account Management screen. To set the minimum password length, complete the following steps:

1. Under **Strong Passwords**, in the **Minimum Password Length** field, specify the length.
2. Click **Apply** and then click **Save**.

To set the number of character types required in a password, complete the following steps:

1. Under **Strong Passwords**, select the number of character types you want to enforce in passwords.
2. Click **Apply** and then click **Save**.

To configure the palindrome check, complete the following steps:

1. Under **Strong Passwords**, next to **Check For Passwords That Are Palindromes**, click **On**.
2. Click **Apply** and then click **Save**.

Configuring Password History Check

Use the password history feature to check for password reuse in order to force users to create unique passwords every time they change their password. The number you specify in the history length is the number of previous passwords the feature checks against.

The forced password change and password history features work together to make sure unique passwords are created at particular intervals. By default, the password history check feature is enabled.

The password history check feature checks against all passwords, including the administrator and cluster administrators, but it does not apply to SNMPv3 user passphrases.

WARNING

Be careful when using this feature on systems with IP clustering enabled because sometimes cluster administrators need to re-create cluster configurations and might want to reuse the original cluster administrator password when they do. By enabling this feature, they will not be able to reuse the password.

The following are considerations you might want to be aware of when using this feature:

- The password history file for a user is only updated when the user successfully changes their password. For example, if you changed the history length from ten to five, the number of passwords stored in the password history file does not immediately change. The next time the user attempts to change their password, the new password is checked against all the passwords in the file, regardless of how many are stored. After the password change succeeds, the password file is updated to store only the five most recent passwords.
- A password is only stored in a user password history file if the password history feature is enabled when the user creates the password.
- The password history feature always checks the new password against the most recent password, regardless of whether the previous password is in the password history file or not. For example, when a user changes a password for the first time after the password history check is enabled, the previous password is still checked.

Table 5.2 explains the available password history options.

Table 5.2 Password History Options

Option	Description
Check for reuse of passwords	Enables password history checking Default: On
History length	Specifies how many passwords are kept and checked against Default: 10

You can change the Password and Account Management Controls by clicking **Configuration | Security And Access | Password And Account Management Controls**. Under **Password History**, verify that **Check For Reuse Of Passwords** is set to **On**. By default, it is on. In the **History Length** field, type the number of history checks you want to perform on the password history. The default is 10 and the range is 1 to 1,000. Click **Apply** and then click **Save**.

Configuring Mandatory Password Change

Another important aspect when implementing a strong security policy is forcing users to change their passwords at regular intervals and to change to the administrator-assigned password to a unique password. Using Nokia Network Voyager, you can:

- Set user passwords to expire after a specified number of days.
  - When a password expires, the user is forced to change the password the next time they log in. This feature works in conjunction with the password history check to force users to use new passwords at regular intervals.
- Force a user to change their password immediately after an administrator has given the user a new password.
- Force new users to change their password from their initial password when logging in the first time.
- Lock out users if they do not change expired passwords within a certain number of days after password expiration.
  - After a user is locked out, you can unlock the account using the User Management screen located under **Configuration | Security And Access | Users**. Figure 5.2 shows the User Management page.

Figure 5.2 The User Management Page

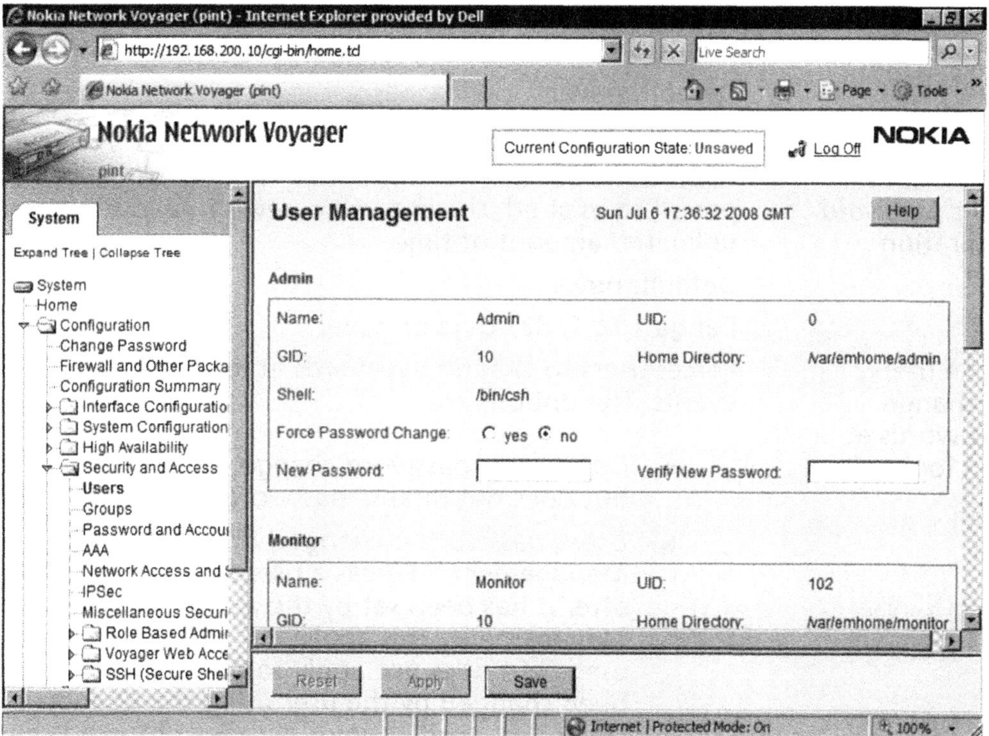

For mandatory password change to work, the password history checking and session management must be enabled. You can also force a user to change the password the next time they log in, independent of any policy you have set up using the Force Password

Change option on the User Management page. Users with access to the User Management page can override a forced password change.

Although the mandatory password change settings can be shared across a cluster, changes to local user passwords do not propagate over a cluster. Also, the cadmin user cannot be forced to change their password, which eliminates the risk of having different cadmin passwords on different cluster nodes complicating cluster management.

This feature does not apply to SNMPv3 USM user passphrases. Table 5.3 describes the mandatory password change options.

Table 5.3 Mandatory Password Change Options

Option	Description
Password expiration lifetime	Specifies the length of time, in days, between forced password changes. The value *never* disables the feature. Default: never Range: 1 to 1,827 days or never
Warn users before password expiration	Specifies the number of days before a password expires that users start receiving a password expiration warning. Default: never Range: 1 to 366 days or never
Lock out users after password expiration	Locks users out after the specified number of days since the password expired. Use the value *never* to allow users an unlimited amount of time. Default: never Range 1 to 1, 827 days or never
Force users to change passwords at first login after	Forces users to change passwords at login after specific events. The options are: ■ *Don't force password change*: Disables this feature, but does not disable password expiration lifetime. ■ *User's password is changed from "User Management"*: Forces a user to change passwords after it has been set by the administrator in User Management. This applies to existing users and new users, but does not apply to passwords that have been changed by the user using the Change Current User's Password page or because of forced change at login. ■ *First password change*: Forces a new user to change passwords the first time they log in after the account has been created and the password set.

To configure password expiration, complete the following steps:

1. In the system tree, click **Configuration | Security And Access | Password And Account Management Controls**.
2. Under **Mandatory Password Change**, in the **Password Expiration Lifetime** field, type the number of days before a password expires.
3. In the **Warn Users Before Password Expiration** field, type the number of days before expiry that the user will start receiving warnings.
4. In the **Lock Out Users After Password Expiration** field, type the number of days after expiry that the account will lock.
5. Click **Apply** and then click **Save**.

To configure mandatory user password change, complete the following steps:

1. In the system tree, click **Configuration | Security And Access | Password And Account Management Controls**.
2. Under **Mandatory Password Change**, under **Force Users To Change Passwords At First Login After**, select an option that satisfies your security needs.
3. Click **Apply** and then click **Save**.

Notes from the Underground...

Denying Access After Failed Login Attempts

You can lock out users for a specified number of failed login attempts. You can configure the length of time the user is locked out and the number of failed login attempts that trigger a lockout.

A locked account can be unlocked in two ways:

- The user issues no login attempts during the lockout period and then logs in successfully on the first attempt after the lockout period expires. If the user issues a login attempt during the lockout period, the lockout period is restarted, regardless of whether the attempt would have been successful. After the lockout period expires, if the user's first attempt to log in is unsuccessful, the user is locked out again for the full period.

Continued

- The administrator manually unlocks the account. When a user is locked out, a control appears in the user account information on the User Management page that allows you to manually unlock the account with a reason for the lockout.

This function leaves the system vulnerable to Denial-of-Service (DOS) attacks. An attacker can lock out an account by issuing the specified number of failed login attempts and then repeatedly issuing login attempts during the lockout period to extend the lockout indefinitely.

Table 5.4 describes the failed login attempt options.

Table 5.4 Failed Login Attempt Options

Option	Description
Deny access after failed login attempts	Locks out users after a specified number of failed logins Default: off
Maximum number of failed attempts allowed	Sets the number of failed logins before a user is locked out Default: 10 Range: 2 to 1,000
Allow access again after time	Sets the duration a user is locked out after failed login attempts Default 1,200 seconds (20 minutes) Range: 60 to 604,800 seconds (7 days)

To deny access after failed login attempts, complete the following steps:

1. In the system tree, click **Configuration | Security And Access | Password And Account Management Controls**.
2. Under **Deny Access After Failed Login Attempts**, next to **Deny Access After Failed Login Attempts**, select **On**.
3. In the **Maximum Number Of Failed Login Attempts Allowed** field, type the allowable number of failed attempts.
4. In the **Allow Access Again After Time** field, type the number of seconds for an account to be locked.
5. Click **Apply** and then click **Save**.

Denying Access to Unused Accounts

You can deny access to accounts that have been inactive for a specified length of time. An account is considered inactive when there has been no logins with the account. Account lockout for inactivity does not apply to the admin user or to users logging on to the serial console. Table 5.5 describes the available unused account options.

Table 5.5 Unused Account Options

Option	Description
Deny access to unused accounts	Locks out user accounts after a specified period of inactivity
Days of non-use before lockout	Specifies the number of days an account can be inactive before it is locked out Default: 365 days Range: 30 to 1,827 days

Changing Passwords

Any user can change their password. Users with privileges to the Users feature can change passwords for any users, including the admin user.

WARNING

Because users with read/write permissions to the Users feature can change all passwords, be careful when granting this type of access.

To change your password, complete the following steps:

1. In the system tree, click **Configuration | Change Password**.
2. In the **Old Password** field, type your current password.
3. In the **New Password** and **Confirm New Password** fields, type your new password.
4. Click **Apply** and then click **Save**.

To change another user's password, complete the following steps:

1. Log in as a user with read/write permission to the Users feature.

NOTE

Admin users or any user with read/write access to the Users feature can change a user password without providing the existing password.

2. In the system tree, click **Configuration | Security And Access | Users**.
3. Locate the username you want to change the password for.
4. In the username table, in the **New Password** and **Verify New Password** fields, type the new password.
5. Click **Apply** and then click **Save**.

Managing User Accounts

You can use Nokia Network Voyager to add users to your IPSO system and to edit the user ID, group ID, home directory, and default shell for a user. You can also change user passwords and force users to change passwords on next log in.

The following users are created by default and cannot be deleted.

- **admin** This account has full read/write capabilities to all features accessible through Nokia Network Voyager and the CLI. This user has a User ID of 0, and therefore has all privileges of a root user.
- **monitor** This account has read-only capabilities for all features in Nokia Network Voyager and the CLI. You must establish a password for monitor before the account can be used.
- **cadmin** This account has full read/write capabilities to all features on every node of the cluster. This user only appears if clustering is configured on your system.

When you create a new user, the user is given read-only privileges to the Nokia Network Voyager home page and CLI prompt. The user cannot access other Nokia Network Voyager pages or execute commands from the CLI prompt.

NOTE

You can assign administrative privileges or any read/write roles without assigning a user ID of 0. If you assign a user ID of 0 to a user account, the user is equivalent to the Admin user and the roles assigned to that account cannot be modified.

Table 5.6 describes the attributes associated with each user account.

Table 5.6 User Account Attributes

Attribute	Description
Name	This attribute is the name used to identify the user. The valid characters are alphanumeric characters, dash (_), and underscore (_). Range: 1 to 32 characters
User ID	This is the unique ID number for the user account. The system does not allow the creation of a user with a duplicate user ID. Range: 0 to 65,535 Values 0 to 102 and 65,534 are reserved for system use. The admin user is UID 0, the monitor user is UID is 102, and the cadmin user is UID 101.
Group ID	This is the primary group for the user. The user can be assigned to other groups and the files and directories owned by the user are assigned the permissions of the user's primary group. Range: 0 to 65,535 Values 0 to 10 are reserved for the predefined Wheel and Other groups respectively. GIDs 65,533 and 65,534 are also reserved.
Home directory	This is the full UNIX path name for the users log in directory. The home directory for all users must be in /var/emhome/.
Shell	By default, all users except the admin user are assigned to the CLI shell (/etc/cli.sh).

Continued

Table 5.6 Continued. User Account Attributes

Attribute	Description
Force Password Change	This attribute forces the user to set a new password on the next log in. The initial setting of this attribute reflects the global password management policy regarding forced password changes. If there is no global password policy or if the conditions of the password policy that forces a password change have not been met, then this attribute is set to No. If a policy is in place and the conditions that force a password change are met, this attribute is set to Yes. You can manually override this setting. The attribute is automatically reset to no when the user changes the password on the next log in. **Note:** If a mandatory password change is in effect for users when their passwords are set or changed by the administrator, the system automatically sets this option to yes after you successfully change a user password.
Locked Out; Unlock	This attribute unlocks the user account. This option only appears if the user is locked out. If the user is locked out because of an expired password and you unlock the account, the user is given the currently configured amount of time to change the expired password. If the user again fails to change the password before it expires, they will be locked out again.
New Password and Verify New Password	These attributes are used to change the password.

Adding and Deleting Users

You can create regular users, with access to Nokia Network Voyager features and the CLI, and you can create SNMP users. SNMP users are only visible on the Manage SNMP Users page of Nokia Network Voyager.

When adding a user with cluster permissions, the user is not automatically created on the other nodes of the cluster. You must log in to each node as a system admin user (cluster admin users do not have RBA access) to add this user to other nodes of the cluster.

To add a user, complete the following steps:

1. In the system tree, click **Configuration | Security And Access | Users**.
2. Under **Add New User**, in the **Username** field, type an alphanumeric username.

3. In the **UID** field, type the user ID for the account.
4. In the **Home Directory** field, type the home directory for the user. The format is /var/emhome/*username*.
5. Click **Apply**.
6. (Optional) Next to **Force Password Change**, select **Yes**.

TIP

If you have a password management policy that forces all new users to change passwords on first login, then the Force Password Change attribute is automatically set to Yes after you click Apply.

7. In the **New Password** and **Verify New Password** fields, type the password for the account.
8. (Optional) Change the GID and Shell values.
9. Click **Apply** and then click **Save**.

To remove a user, in the system tree, click **Configuration | Security And Access | Users**. Next to the username, select **Off**. Click **Apply** and then click **Save**.

NOTE

When you remove a user, the user can no longer log in, but the user's home directory is still on the system. You must use the UNIX shell to remove the user's home directory. Also, because the user accounts for SNMP are maintained separately, you might also have to delete the SNMP account for the user—if it exists.

Managing S/Key

S/Key is a one-time password system that you can enable to protect the password of the admin or monitor accounts when users connect through Telnet or FTP. You must first enable S/Key and then enter an S/Key password. After you configure the S/Key for a user, a sequence number and a seed appear before each Telnet or FTP password prompt. Enter these two items as arguments to the S/Key program running on a secure machine. After you enter these arguments and your S/Key secret key, the key program produces a password that you use only once to log in.

1. In the system tree, click **Configuration | Security And Access | Users**.
2. Under **S/Key Configuration**, do the following:
   - To enable the Admin S/Key, under **Admin S/Key**, select **Allowed**.
   - To enable the Monitor S/Key, under **Monitor S/Key**, select **Allowed**.
3. Click **Apply**. (The current password and secret password fields appear for each account with S/Key enabled.)
4. Under **Generate New S/Key**, in the **Current Standard Password** field, type the current password.
5. In the **S/Key Secret Password** and **Verify S/Key Secret Password** fields, type a new password. This must be four to eight alphanumeric characters long. Repeat step 4 for the other key if necessary.
6. Click **Apply** and then click **Save**.

Using S/Key

To generate the S/Key one-time password (OTP), you must have an S/Key calculator on your platform. Many UNIX-derived and UNIX-like systems include the S/Key calculator command key and several GUI calculators include support for MD4 (S/Key) algorithms and MD5 (OPIE) algorithms. You should configure MD5 calculators to use MD4 algorithms.

The OTP is typically a string, or strings, containing a series of words. You must enter all the words in the valid string at the password prompt.

1. Open a Telnet or FTP client.
2. Log in to the firewall.
3. At the prompt, enter **admin** or **monitor** as a username. (The server returns an S/Key challenge, which contains the S/Key sequence number and seed—for example, 95 ma74213. The server also returns a prompt for a password.)
4. Copy the S/Key sequence number and seed into the S/Key calculator on your platform.
5. Copy the S/Key challenge into the S/Key calculator on your local platform.
6. Enter the S/Key Secret Password. The calculator returns the OTP for this session.
7. Copy the OTP into the Telnet or FTP session.

To disable S/Key, in the system tree, click **Configuration | Security And Access | Users**. Under S/Key Configuration, for the appropriate account, select **Disabled**. Click **Apply** and the sequence number and seed disappear. To make the changes permanent, click **Save**.

Managing Groups and Access

You can define and configure groups with IPSO similarly to UNIX-based systems. This capability is retained under IPSO for advanced applications and for retaining compatibility with UNIX.

You can view a list of existing groups, under **Configuration | Security And Access | Groups In The Tree View**. Figure 5.3 shows the Group Management page.

Figure 5.3 The Group Management Page

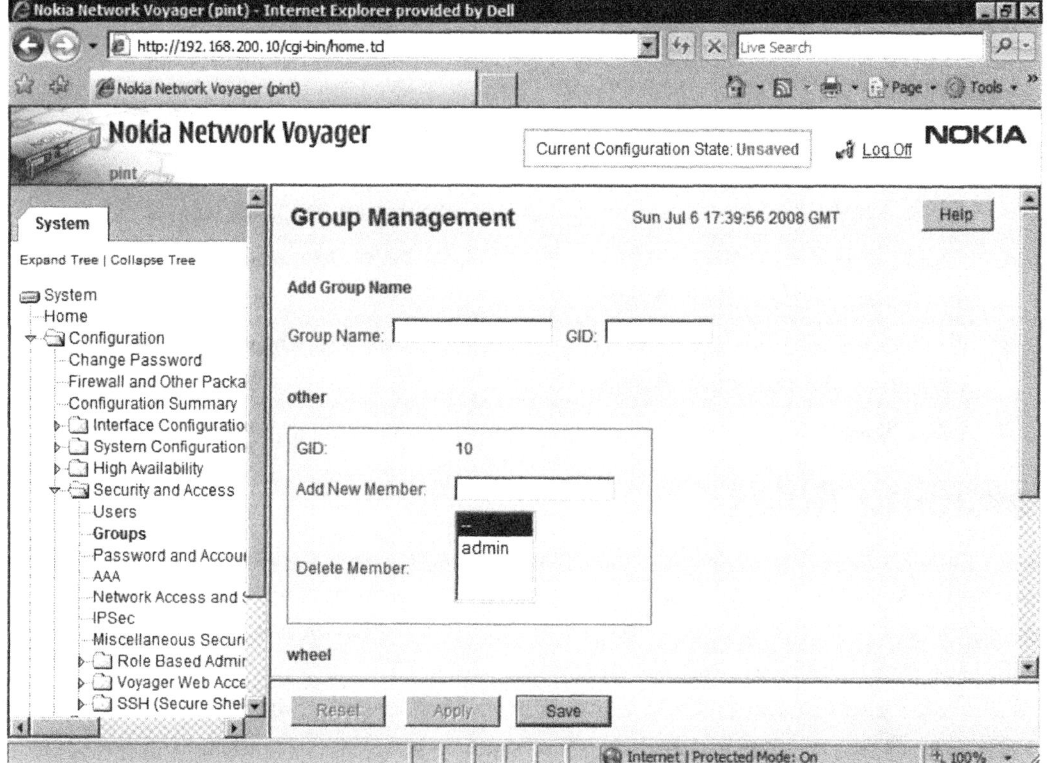

By default, two groups are created and cannot be deleted:

- **Other group** By default, all users are assigned to the Other group. If you edit the primary group ID for a user to something other than the default, you can use the Edit Group page to add the user to the Other group. All users in the Users group might not appear in the list of current members because the list only shows users who are explicitly added, not users added by default.
- **Wheel group** Controls which users have root access to the system. Users must be members of the wheel group to use the *su* command to log in as root.

You can use groups for the following reasons:

- To specify UNIX file permissions. By default, all users are assigned to the Other group.
- Use the Wheel group to control which users have root access to the system.
- Control who can log in through SSH.

To add or edit a group, complete the following steps:

1. In the system tree, click **Configuration | Security And Access | Groups**.
2. In the **Group Name** field, type a name for the group. (This must be less than eight characters long.)
3. In the GID field, type a group ID number. (The group ID must be unique. Suggested values are between 101 and 65000.)
4. Click **Apply**. The new group information appears on the page.
5. To add a new member to a group, in the **Add New Member** field, type the username and then click **Apply**.
6. To delete a member from the group, in the **Delete Member** list, select the username and then click **Apply**.
7. Click **Save**.

Managing Roles

When you add a new user to Nokia Network Voyager, the user is given read-only privileges to the Nokia Network Voyager home page and the CLI prompt. The user, however, cannot access other Nokia Network Voyager pages or execute commands from the CLI prompt. For the user to gain more access, you must assign roles.

Role-based administration (RBA) allows IPSO administrators to create and use separate roles. By using RBA, an administrator can allow users to access specific features by including the features in a role and assigning the role to users. Each role can include a combination of administrative (read/write) access to some features, monitoring (read-only) access to other features, and no access to other features. This feature also provides improved auditing capabilities.

To assign a set of access permissions to a user, create a role that specifies access levels to features you want to include, and then assign this role to the relevant user. You can also specify the access mechanisms (Nokia Network Voyager or CLI) available to the user when you assign a role.

If your system is part of a cluster, you can create and assign roles that provide access to the entire cluster for the associated features.

You can view a list of existing roles, under **Configuration | Security And Access | Role Based Administration** in the tree view. Figure 5.4 shows the Manage Roles page.

Figure 5.4 The Manage Roles Page

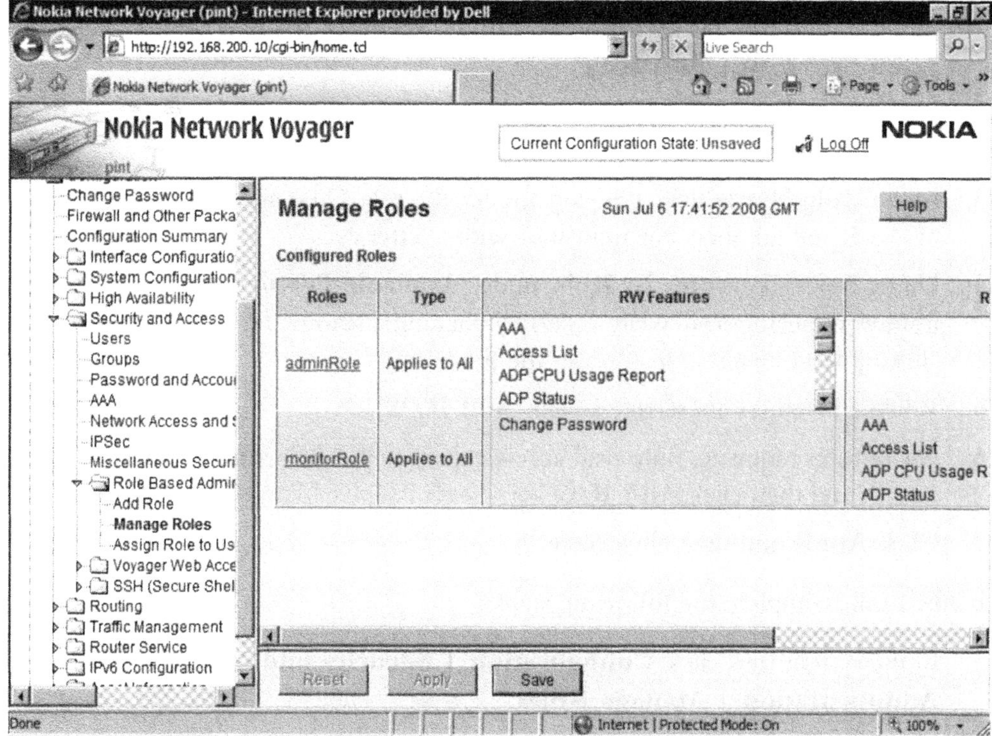

The following roles are predefined:

- **adminRole** Gives the user read/write access to every feature on the system.
- **monitorRole** Gives the user read-only access to every feature on the system.
- **clusterAdminRole** Gives the user read/write access to every feature on every node in the cluster except for role-based administration. To configure role-based administration, you must log in to each node of the cluster as an admin instead of the cluster admin.

When you create a new role, you can select only system access or cluster access features, but not a combination of both. Also a single user can only be assigned system or cluster roles, you cannot assign a system and a cluster role to the same user.

NOTE

When you assign a user a role that has access to a feature, the user gains access to the configuration pages for that feature, but not the monitor pages. To provide access to the monitor pages, you must include the monitor privilege for the feature in the role definition.

To add a role, complete the following steps:

1. In the system tree, click **Configuration | Security And Access | Role Based Administration | Add Role**.
2. In the **Role Type** list, select the appropriate type. Cluster only appears in the list if clustering is enabled.
3. In the **Role Name** field, type a name for the role. (The name can be a combination of letters and numbers but must start with a letter.)
4. Under **Select Features In Role**, under **Available Features**, select the appropriate features requiring read/write access by clicking a feature, pressing **Ctrl**, and then clicking the remaining features in the list.
5. When all features are selected, click **Add R/W ->**.
6. For features requiring only read access, repeat step 4 (selecting features for read-only access), and then click **Add R-O ->**.
7. Click **Apply** and then click **Save**.

To edit a role, complete the following steps:

1. In the system tree, click **Configuration | Security and Access | Role Based Administration | Manage Roles**.
2. Under **Configured Roles**, in the **Roles** column, click the role for editing.

To add features:

1. In the section **Select Features In Role**, under **Available Features**, select the appropriate features requiring read/write access by clicking a feature, pressing **Ctrl**, and then clicking the remaining features in the list.
2. When all features are selected, click **Add R/W ->**.
3. For features requiring only read access, repeat step 4 (selecting features for read only access), and then click **Add R-O ->**.

To remove features:

1. Under **Read/Write Features**, select the roles to remove and then click **<- Remove**.
2. Under **Read-Only Features**, select the roles to remove and then click **<- Remove**.
3. Click **Apply** and then click **Save**.

To delete a role, complete the following steps:

1. In the system tree, click **Configuration | Security And Access | Role Based Administration | Manage Roles**.
2. Under **Configured Roles**, locate for the role for deletion.
3. Under the **Delete** column, click the box.
4. Click **Apply** and then click **Save**.

NOTE

You cannot delete the adminRole, clusterAdminRole, or monitorRole default roles.

Assigning Roles and Access Mechanisms to Users

To give users permissions to various features, assign the role or roles containing the feature permissions to the user. You can also specify whether a user can use Nokia Network Voyager and the CLI by assigning access mechanisms to the user from the Assign Roles To User page.

When you create a role, you associate a role type. The role types are:

- **System** A system role assigned to a user provides the user with access to the associated features on this machine only.
- **Cluster** A cluster role assigned to a user provides the user with access to the associated features on every node in the cluster.

1. In the system tree, click **Configuration | Security And Access | Role Based Administration | Assign Role to Users**.
2. Under **Users Permissions**, click the role to which you want to assign roles.
3. To add access mechanisms, under **Assign Access Mechanisms To User**, under **Available Access Mechanisms**, click the access mechanism and then click **Assign ->**.
4. To remove any access mechanisms, under **User's Access Mechanisms**, click the access mechanism and then click **<- Remove**.

5. To assign roles, in the section **Assign Roles To User**, under **Available System Roles**, click the role and then click **Assign ->**. (You cannot change the roles assigned to the admin, cadmin, or monitor users.)
6. To remove any roles, under **User's Roles**, click the role and then click **<- Remove**.
7. Click **Apply** and then click **Save**.

Creating Cluster Administrator Users

You can create and make a user a cluster administrator by assigning the user a cluster role. To create cluster administrators, note the following constraints:

- You must log in as a system user to use role-based administration.
  - This feature is not accessible if you log in as a user with a cluster role. (This is also true if you log in as cadmin.)
- If you do not assign the default cluster administrator role (clusterAdminRole) to the users you create, assign them a role of type Cluster.
  The implications of this choice are explained next.
  - Users with the role clusterAdminRole automatically log in to Cluster Voyager or the CCLI and have full access to all clustering features.
  - Users with the role type Cluster automatically log in to Cluster Voyager or the CCLI and have access to the features you assign to the role.
- To allow a user to administer a cluster, you must assign them the domain value that matches the appropriate cluster ID.
- If you want to log in to a node as a cluster administrator, you must create the user on that node. For example, if you create a cluster administrator user on node A, but not on node B, you cannot log in to node B as the user. However, any changes you make to node A using Cluster Voyager or the CCLI are also implemented on node B.
- You can log in to all nodes as cadmin because this user is created automatically on each node.

NOTE

If you assign the clustering feature to users with System role types, the users can configure clustering on individual nodes but cannot use Cluster Voyager or the CCLI.

Configuring Authentication, Authorization, and Accounting (AAA)

You can use the AAA component of the system to manage user access to the appliance. Typically, AAA includes authentication, which identifies a user; authorization, which determines what a user is permitted to do; and accounting, which tracks aspects of user activity.

Nokia IPSO implements Pluggable Authentication Modules (PAM), an industry-standard framework for authenticating and authorizing users. Using PAM, authentication, account management, and session management algorithms are contained in shared modules that you configure on your appliance.

Configuring AAA Service Modules

To configure a new AAA service on your appliance, you configure a service module. The service module is then shared by applications that need to invoke authentication, account management, or session management algorithms. When you create or modify a service module profile, you specify the service profile to use. Each service profile is composed of the authentication, account management, and session profiles it uses. For each profile type, you can specify multiple service profiles using stacking. Service module names and profiles can be composed of alphanumeric and underscore (_) characters.

WARNING

Nokia strongly recommends you adopt a naming convention.

The following service modules are included by default and cannot be deleted:

- httpd
- login
- other
- snmpd
- sshd

You can, however, modify any of these service modules by modifying the service profiles it uses, or by modifying the authentication, account management, or session profiles that are likewise used by a service profile.

You cannot delete services or profiles referenced by other definitions. You can delete a service and any or all of its profiles at the same time. Figure 5.5 shows the AAA Configuration page.

Figure 5.5 The AAA Configuration Page

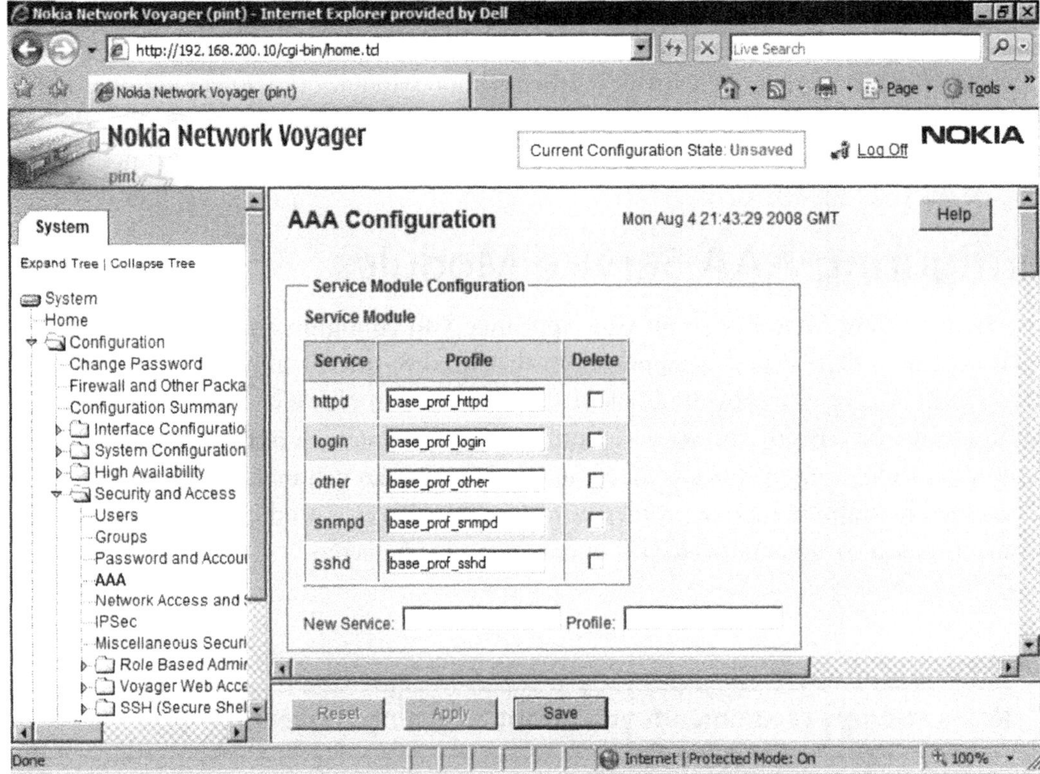

To configure a service module, complete the following steps:

1. In the system tree, click **Configuration | Security And Access | AAA.** (You can use an existing session profile, modify an existing session profile, or create a new one. The session profile contains information about how to assign IP addresses to sessions.)
2. If you are creating a new session profile, scroll down to **Session Profile Configuration** and in the **New Sess. Profile** field, type a name profile. The name must not match the name of any existing session profiles.
3. In the **Type** list, select the profile type.
4. In the **Control** list, select a value.
5. Click **Apply**.

You can use or modify existing account management or authentication profiles or create new ones.

1. Scroll to Account Management Profile Configuration or Authentication Profile Configuration.
2. Modify the existing profile by using the associated lists, or, if you are creating a new profile, in the **New Auth. Profile** field, type a name that does not match any existing profile names.
3. In the **Type** list, select the profile type.
4. In the **Control** list, select a value.
5. Click **Apply**.

You can use or modify an existing service profile or define a new one. Service profiles describe the characteristics of the PAM service module, by referencing specific authentication, accounting, and session profiles.

1. Scroll to **Service Profile Configuration**.
2. If you are creating a new service profile, in the **Service Profile** field, type a name that does not match any existing service profile names.
3. If you are modifying an existing service profile, type the name of the profile you want to modify.
4. Enter names of the existing authorization, account, and session profiles you want this service profile to use.
5. Leave any fields blank if the service requirements do not include them. (You can include multiple services of any type: authentication, account management, or session.)

NOTE

Profiles are invoked in the order in which they appear in the relevant list—from top to bottom. New profiles are added to the end of the list. To change the order, delete the profiles that are out of order and add them back in the proper order.

6. Click **Apply**.
7. To modify an existing service module, in the **Profile** field, type the name of the service profile you want the service module to reference.
8. Click **Apply**.
9. Click **Save** to make your changes permanent.

NOTE

If multiple authentication servers are configured for the same user, the roles for the user should be identical on all servers. If the roles are different, then the role assigned in the last server (the one lowest in the list) is used.

Tools & Traps...

Deleting and Removing a Service Module or Service Profile

You cannot delete a profile that is used by a service module or another profile. You also cannot delete any of the default service modules or profiles.

To delete a service module or service profile, select the **Delete** check box for the module or profile you want to delete. Click **Apply** and then click **Save** to make your changes permanent.

To remove a profile (authentication, accounting, or session) from a service profile, select the authentication, accounting, or session profile in the appropriate service profile. Then, select the **Delete** check boxes for the service profile. Click **Apply** and then click **Save** to make your changes permanent.

NOTE

The authentication and accounting profiles that begin with *tally* and *nonuse* are used by certain Password and Account Management features and are required for the features to work.

Table 5.7 describes the profile control types used to determine how the results of multiple authentication, accounting, or session algorithms are handled. It also indicates when multiple items are defined in the authentication, account, or session profile lists for a given service profile. This is a feature known as stacking. Values other than those required are effective only when the service requires more than one profile.

Table 5.7 Profile Control Types

Type	Description
Required	The result is retained and the next algorithm is invoked. If the algorithm is at the end of the list, the result is combined with the results of previous algorithms such that any failure result causes failure to be reported.
Requisite	A result of failure is reported immediately and no further algorithms are invoked. If the algorithm is at the end of the list, the result is reported immediately.
Sufficient	If no previous algorithm reported failure, a result of success is reported immediately and no further algorithms are invoked. A result of failure for this algorithm is discarded. If a previous algorithm has reported failure or the result of this algorithm is failure, the next algorithm is invoked. If the algorithm is at the end of the list, the result is reported immediately.
Optional	A result of failure is ignored and a result of success is retained. The next algorithm is always invoked. If the algorithm is at the end of the list, a result of success is reported.
nokia-server-auth-sufficient	Used in Auth. Profiles only. It is the same as sufficient, except that a result of "authentication error" for this algorithm is reported immediately and no further algorithms are invoked. This type is intended for use with algorithms that access remote servers and where the modules have different result codes for "authentication error" and "server not reachable."

Table 5.8 describes the authentication algorithms that are available when you create a new authentication profile.

Table 5.8 Authentication Profile Types

Type	Description
HTTP	Logs a message to indicate that a session has started or stopped. It also authenticates the user and verifies the username and password. Module: pam_httpd_auth.so.1.0
PERMIT	Does not do any authentication. Is considered to succeed when invoked. Module: pam_permit.so.1.0
RADIUS	A client/server authentication system which offloads authentication processing and some other management functions from the IPSO system to a RADIUS server. Defined in RFC2865. Module: pam_radius_auth.so.1
ROOTOK	Performs one task: if the user ID is 0, it returns success. It can be used to allow password-free access to some services for root. Caution: This module can bypass password checking, which in some cases might be undesirable. Module: pam_rootok_auth.so.1.0
SECURETTY	Allows root logins only if the user is logging in on a secure TTY. Module: pam_securetty_auth.so.1
SKEY	Implements the S/Key algorithm. The user provides the one-time passphrase, which is used to authenticate the user by using the password database. Module: pam_skey_auth.so.1.0
SNMPD	Authenticates the SNMP packets from a user (Management Station). When an SNMP user is added in the system through Network Voyager, a corresponding authentication and privacy key is created and kept in the usmUser database, /var/ucd-snmp/snmpd.conf. When an SNMP packet is received, the username in the packet is used to retrieve the user information from the database and imported to the SNMP agent local store by this module. This information is then used to authenticate the packets. Module: pam_snmpd_auth.so.1.0

Continued

Table 5.8 Continued. Authentication Profile Types

Type	Description
TACPLUS	A client/server authentication system, which offloads authentication processing and some other management functions from the IPSO system to a RADIUS server. Module: pam_tacplus_auth.so.1.0
TALLY	Maintains a count of attempted accesses and resets count on success. Module: pam_tally_auth.so.1.0
UNIX	Uses the local password database to authenticate the user. When the user enters username and password, this module is called to authenticate the user. Module: pam_unix_auth.so.1.0

NOTE

Modules are located in the /usr/lib directory.

Configuring RADIUS

Remote Authentication Dial-In User Service (RADIUS) is a client/server authentication software system that supports remote-access applications. This service allows you to maintain user profiles in a centralized database that resides on an authentication server. A host contacts a RADIUS server that determines who has access to that service. IPSO will accept users configured on a RADIUS server even if there is no corresponding local account on the Nokia system (assuming you configure the RADIUS server and IPSO appropriately).

You can configure RADIUS as an AAA module so your appliance functions as a RADIUS client. Nokia systems do not include RADIUS server functionality.

You can configure your appliance to contact more than one RADIUS server. If the first server in the list is unreachable, the next RADIUS server in the priority ranking is contacted to provide the functionality. You can remove servers at any time by clicking the Delete check box next to the row for the server you want to remove.

Tools & Traps...

Configuring RADIUS on Your Appliance

On the **AAA Configuration** page, under **Authentication Profile Configuration**, you must create a new RADIUS type authentication profile. Then, under **Service Profile Configuration**, select the **Servers** link for the new profile.

On the **AAA RADIUS Authorization Server Configuration** page, complete the following fields:

- **Priority** Enter a unique integer to indicate the priority of the server in the Priority field. There is no default, but you must enter a value. You can configure multiple servers for a profile, and the priority value determines which server to try first. A smaller number indicates a higher priority.
- **Host address** Enter the IP address of your RADIUS server. RADIUS supports only IPv4 addresses.
- **Port number** Enter the port number of the UDP port to contact on the server host. The default is 1812, which is specified by the RADIUS standard. The range is 1 to 65535. Firewall software often blocks traffic on port 1812. To ensure that RADIUS packets are not dropped, make sure any firewalls between the RADIUS server and IPSO devices are configured to allow traffic on UDP port 1812.
- **Secret** Enter the shared secret used to authenticate the authorization profile between the RADIUS server and the local client. Enter a text string without a backslash. You must also configure this same value on your RADIUS server. For more information, see RFC 2865. The RFC recommends that the shared secret be at least 16 characters long. Some RADIUS servers limit the shared secret to 15 or 16 characters. Consult the documentation for your RADIUS server.
- (Optional) **Timeout** Enter the number of seconds the system waits for a response after contacting the server. The default value is 3. Depending on your client configuration, if the client does not receive a response, it retries the same server or attempts to contact another server.
- (Optional) **Max Tries** Enter the maximum number attempts to contact the server. The default is 3. If all the attempts do not make a reliable connection within the timeout period, the client stops trying to contact the RADIUS server.

Continued

You must configure a RADIUS authentication server for each profile, even if you associate the new profile with a server you previously configured for an existing RADIUS authentication profile.

Under **Service Profile Configuration**, you also need to complete the following fields:

- **Service Profile**
- **Acct. Profile**
- **Session Profile**

Then, you must associate the service module with the profile. Finally, to test the setup, on the RADIUS server configure a locally configured account, and then log in to Nokia Network Voyager with that account.

Configuring Non-Local RADIUS Users

To allow access by non-local users, which are users defined on a RADIUS server, but not defined on the Nokia system, you must configure the RADIUS server and Nokia system appropriately.

1. Copy the file nokiaipso.dct (for Steel-Belted RADIUS servers) or dictionary.nokia (for freeRADIUS servers) to your RADIUS server. (These files are in /etc on the Nokia system.)
2. Define the user roles by adding the following Nokia vendor-specific attribute (VSA) for the appropriate users in your RADIUS user configuration file:

```
Nokia-IPSO-User-Role = "role1[:domain1;domain2;.....],role2[:domain1:...
```

For example:
Nokia-IPSO-User-Role = "foorole, barrole"
Nokia-IPSO-User-Role = "foorole:foodomain, barrole"
Nokia-IPSO-User-Role = "foorole:foodomain;bardomain, barrole: foodomain;bardomain"

NOTE

Make sure the role names match existing roles in the IPSO system.

3. Specify whether the Nokia users should have superuser access to the IPSO shell by adding the following VSA:

```
Nokia-IPSO-SuperUser-Access = <0|1>
```

Where:
0 provides nonsuperuser access
1 provides superuser access

To configure a Nokia system for non-local users, complete the following steps:

1. On your Nokia system, create the roles that are to be assigned to the non-local users.
2. Create a RADIUS type authentication profile and set the control level to sufficient.
3. Add the new authentication profile to each appropriate service profile.
4. Make the RADIUS authentication profile the first authentication mechanism for each appropriate service by deleting the other authentication profiles for each service and then adding them back again. (The other profiles are then added after the RADIUS authentication profile.)
5. For critical users, you should configure the Nokia system to allow access even if the RADIUS server is unavailable, by creating local accounts for these users and then, if necessary, adding a local authentication profile after the RADIUS profile for all the service profiles.

To log in as a superuser, complete the following steps:

If the Nokia Superuser VSA is set to 1 for a non-local user, they can log in to the IPSO shell with superuser privileges if they perform the following procedure:

1. Log in to the system using the command line. The default shell is the IPSO CLI.
2. To access the IPSO shell, type **shell** and press **Enter**.
3. Type in **sudo /usr/bin/su –** and press **Enter**.

The user should now have superuser privileges.

Configuring TACACS+

The Terminal Access Controller Access Control System (TACACS+) authentication protocol allows a remote server that is not part of IPSO to authenticate users on behalf of the IPSO system. IPSO will accept users configured on a TACACS+ server, even if there is no corresponding local account on the Nokia system, if you configure the TACACS+ server and IPSO appropriately.

All data sent to the TACACS+ server are encrypted. IPSO supports TACACS+ for authentication only, and not for accounting. Challenge-response authentication, such as S/Key, over TACACS+ is not supported.

You can configure TACACS+ support separately for various services. The Nokia Network Voyager service is one of those for which TACACS+ is supported and is configured as the httpd service. When TACACS+ is configured for use with a service, IPSO contacts the TACACS+ server each time it needs to check a user password. If the server fails or is unreachable, the password is not recognized and the user is not allowed access. Before you change the Nokia Network Voyager configuration, confirm any new configuration.

To configure TACACS+ servers for a single authentication profile, complete the following steps:

1. In the system tree, click **Configuration | Security And Access | AAA**.
2. Scroll to the **Authentication Profile** section.
3. In the **New Profile** field, enter a name that does not match any existing profile names.
4. In the **Type** list, select **TACPLUS**.
5. In the **Control** list, select a control.
6. Click **Apply** and then click **Save** to make your changes permanent. The name of the TACACS+ authentication profile appears in the Auth. Profile table. A link labeled Servers also appears in the new row.
7. In the **Auth. Profile** table, click the **Servers** link in the row for the TACACS+ authorization profile you configured. The AAA TACACS+ Authorization Servers Configuration page appears.
8. Complete the following fields:
   - **Priority** Enter a unique integer to indicate the priority of the server in the Priority field. There is no default, but you must enter a value. You can configure multiple servers for a profile, and the priority value determines which server to try first. A smaller number indicates a higher priority.
   - **Host address** Enter the IP address of the TACACS+ Server. TACACS+ supports only IPv4 addresses.
   - **Port number** Enter the port number of the TCP port to contact on the server host. The default is 49, which is specified by the TACACS+ standard. The range is 1 to 65535.

- **Secret** Enter the shared secret used to authenticate the authorization profile between the TACACS+ server and the local client. You must also configure this same value on your TACACS+ server. Enter a text string without a backslash.
- (Optional) **Timeout** Enter the number of seconds to wait for a response after contacting the server. Depending on your client configuration, if the client does not receive a response, it retries the same server or attempts to contact another server. The default value is 3.

9. Click **Apply** and then click **Save**.
10. Repeat steps 2 to 6 to configure additional TACACS+ authentication profiles. You must configure a TACACS+ authentication server for each profile even if you associate the new profile with a server that you previously configured for an existing TACACS+ authentication profile.
11. Repeat steps 7 to 9 to configure additional AAA TACACS+ authentication servers for existing TACACS authentication profiles.
12. Associate the service module httpd with the name of the TACACS+ authorization profile you created.

Configuring Non-Local TACACS+ Users

To allow access by non-local users (users defined on a TACACS+ server but not defined on the Nokia system), you must configure the TACACS+ server and Nokia system appropriately.

To configure a TACACS+ server for non-local IPSO users, complete the following steps:

1. Define the following IPSO-specific service in your TACACS+ server:

```
service = nokia-ipso {
Nokia-IPSO-User-Role = "role_name_on_IPSO"
Nokia-IPSO-SuperUser-Access = <0|1>
}
```

NOTE

Make sure the role name matches an existing role in the IPSO system. 0 provides nonsuperuser access, and 1 provides superuser access.

2. Configure the appropriate user accounts in the TACACS+ server.

The following is an example:

```
#key = password
group = ipso-admin {
    service = nokia-ipso {
        Nokia-IPSO-User-Role = "adminRole"
        Nokia-IPSO-SuperUser-Access = 1
      }
    }
#IPSO admin users
user = admin {
        member = ipso-admin
        login = cleartext changeme
      }
user = Landon {
        member = ipso-admin
        login = cleartext changeme
      }
#Cluster administrator role for cluster ID 100
group = cluster-admin {
    service = nokia-ipso {
        Nokia-IPSO-User-Role = "ClusterRole:100"
        Nokia-IPSO-SuperUser-Access = 1
      }
    }
#Cluster administrator users
user = cadmin {
    member = cluster-admin
    login = cleartext changeme
}
user = Mia{
    member = cluster-admin
    login = cleartext changeme
}
```

To configure a Nokia system for non-local users, complete the following steps:

1. On your Nokia system, create the roles that are to be assigned to the non-local users.
2. Create an authentication profile of type TACACS+ and set the control level to sufficient.

3. Add the new authentication profile to each appropriate service profile.
4. Make the TACACS+ authentication profile the first authentication mechanism for each appropriate service by deleting the other authentication profiles for each service and then adding them back again. The other profiles are then added after the TACACS+ authentication profile.

For critical users, you should configure the Nokia system to allow access even if the TACACS+ server is unavailable, by creating local accounts for these users and then if necessary, adding a local authentication profile after the TACACS+ profile for all the service profiles.

Logging in as a Superuser

If TACACS+ allows a non-local user superuser access, the user must also perform the following procedure to obtain superuser privileges in the IPSO shell:

1. Log in to the system using the command line. (The default shell is the IPSO CLI.)
2. To access the IPSO shell, type in **shell** and press **Enter**.
3. Type in **sudo /usr/bin/su –** and press **Enter**.

The user should now have superuser privileges.

Configuring IPSO VPN

IPSec (IP Security) is a suite of protocols that includes protocols for cryptographic key establishment, and for securing IP communications by authenticating and/or encrypting each IP packet in a data stream. IPSec is the industry standard that ensures the construction of secure virtual private networks (VPNs), which are private and secure networks implemented on public and insecure networks.

NOTE

IPSec VPN functionality is included in the Check Point VPN-1/Firewall-1 product suite. It is generally a good idea to decide which product will be used for IPSec VPN configurations.

The IPSec protocol suite provides three protocols for IP:

- An authentication header (AH) that provides connectionless integrity and data origin authentication. The IP header is included in the authenticated data. It does not offer encryption services. Table 5.9 shows an AH packet diagram.

Table 5.9 AH Packet Diagram

0–7 bit	8–15 bit	16–23 bit	24–31 bit
Next header	Payload length	RESERVED	
Security parameters index (SPI)			
Sequence number			
Authentication data (variable)			

- An encapsulation security payload (ESP) that provides authentication and confidentiality through symmetric encryption, and an optional anti-replay service. ESP does not include the IP header in the authentication/confidentiality. Table 5.10 shows an ESP packet diagram.

Table 5.10 ESP Packet Diagram

0–7 bit	8–15 bit	16–23 bit	24–31 bit
Security parameters index (SPI)			
Sequence number			
Payload data (variable)			
Padding (0–255 bytes)			
		Pad Length	Next Header
Authentication Data (variable)			

- A protocol negotiation and key exchange protocol (IKE) for easier administration and automatic secure connections. IKE introduces two negotiations. Phase 1 negotiation authenticates both peers and sets up the security for the Phase 2 negotiation. IPSec traffic parameters are negotiated in Phase 2.

Understanding Transport and Tunnel Modes

The basic building blocks of IPSec, AH, and ESP use symmetric cryptographic techniques for ensuring data confidentiality, and data signatures for authenticating the source of the data. IPSec operates in two modes: Transport mode and Tunnel mode.

You use transport mode for host-to-host communications. In transport mode, the data portion of the IP packet is encrypted, but the IP header is not. The security header is placed between the IP header and the IP payload. This mode offers some light bandwidth savings, at the expense of exposing the original IP header to third-party elements in the packet path. It is generally used by hosts—communication endpoints. This mode can also be used by routers if they are acting as communication endpoints.

With IPSec transport mode:

- If AH is used, selected portions of the original IP header and the data payload are authenticated. Figure 5.6 shows a diagram of AH in transport mode.

Figure 5.6 AH in Transport Mode

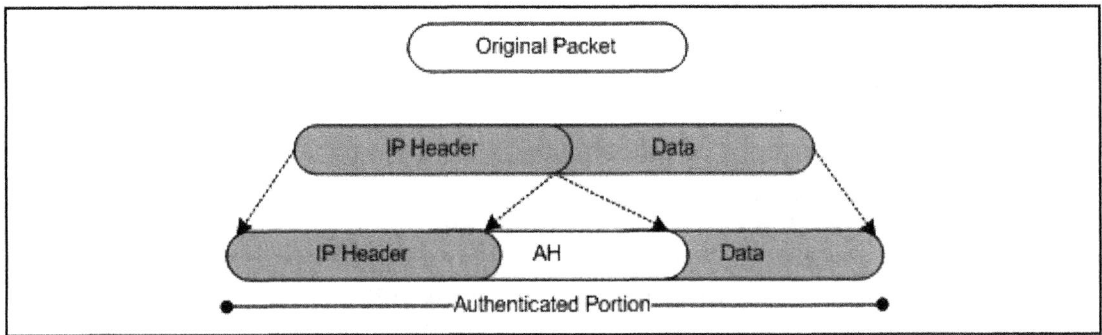

- If ESP is used, no protection is offered to the IP header, but data payload is authenticated and can be encrypted. Figure 5.7 shows a diagram of ESP in transport mode.

Figure 5.7 ESP in Transport Mode

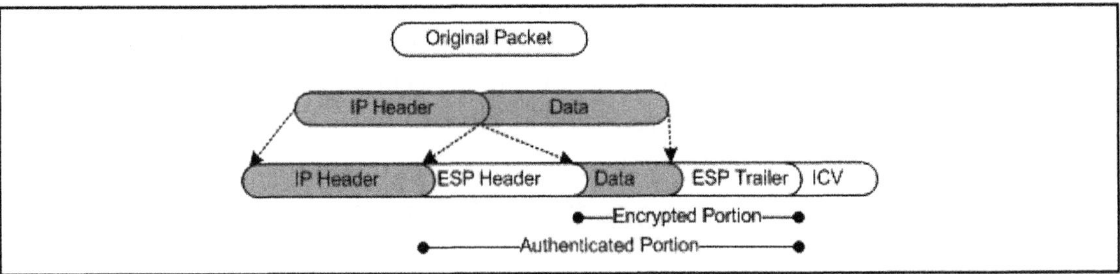

Use tunnel mode for network-to-network communications or host-to-network and host-to-host communications over the Internet. In tunnel mode, the entire IP packet (data, plus the message headers) is encrypted and/or authenticated. It must then be encapsulated into a new IP packet for routing to work. In tunnel mode, the original IP datagram is placed inside a new datagram, and AH or ESP are inserted between the IP header of the new packet and the original IP datagram. The new header points to the tunnel endpoint, and the original header points to the final destination of the datagram. Tunnel mode offers the advantage of complete protection of the encapsulated datagram and the possibility to use private or public address space. Tunnel mode is meant to be used by routers—gateways. Hosts can operate in tunnel mode, too.

With IPSec tunnel mode:

- If AH is used, the outer header is authenticated as well as the tunneled packet. Figure 5.8 shows a diagram of AH in Tunnel mode.

Figure 5.8 AH in Tunnel Mode

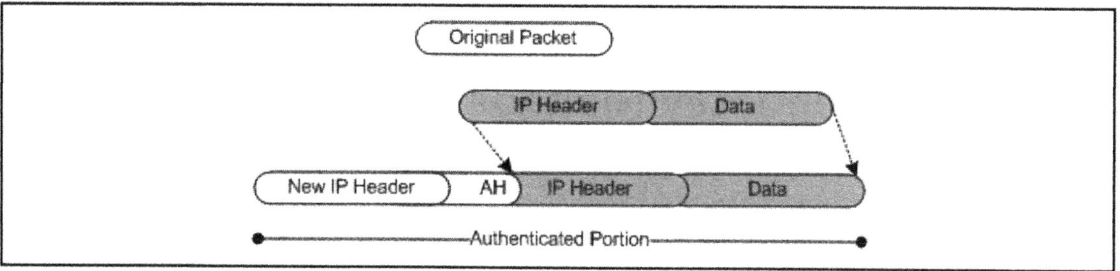

- If ESP is used, the protection is offered only to the tunneled packet, not to the new outer IP header. By default, ESP, providing the highest level of confidentiality, is used in this release. Figure 5.9 shows a diagram of ESP in Tunnel mode.

Figure 5.9 ESP in Tunnel Mode

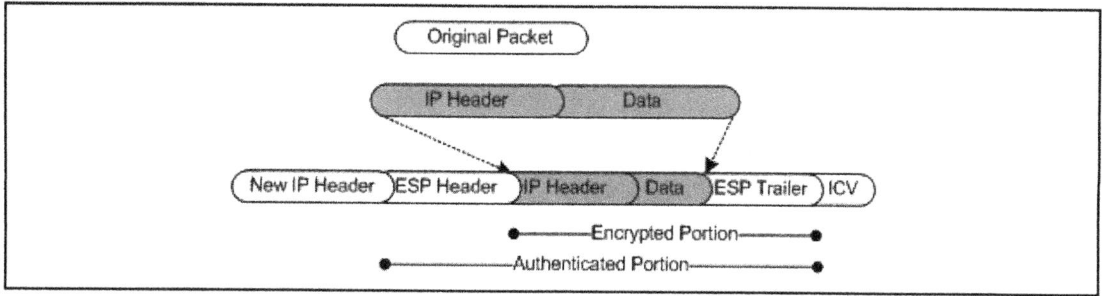

Notes from the Underground...

Building a VPN on ESP

Tunneling takes the original IP header and includes it in ESP. Then it adds a new IP header, containing the address of a gateway, to the packet. Tunneling allows you to pass non-routable and private (RFC 1918) IP addresses through a public network that otherwise would not be accepted. Tunneling with ESP using encryption also has the advantage of hiding the original source and destination addresses from the users on the public network, which reduces the chances of traffic analysis attacks. Tunneling with ESP can conceal the addresses of sensitive internal nodes, protecting them from attacks and hiding their existence to outside computers.

Understanding Protocol Negotiation and Key Management

For you to successfully use the IPSec protocol, two gateway systems must negotiate the algorithms used for authentication and encryption. The gateways must self-authenticate and choose session keys that will secure the traffic. The exchange of this information creates a security association (SA), which is a policy and set of keys used to protect a one-way communication. To secure bidirectional communication between two hosts or two security gateways, you require two SAs—one in each direction.

Security Architecture for IP (RFC 2401) defines a model with the following two databases:

- The security policy database that contains the security rules and security services to offer to every IP packet going through a secure gateway.
- The SA database that contains parameters associated with each active SA. Examples are the authentication algorithms, encryption algorithms, keys, lifetimes for each SA (by seconds and bytes), and modes to use.

The Internet Key Exchange (IKE) is implemented on top of UDP, port 500. IKE provides authenticated secure key exchange with perfect forward secrecy (based on the Diffie-Hellman protocol) and mutual peer authentication using public keys or shared secrets.

The IKE protocol defines two phases:

- Phase 1: To safely set an IPSec SA, the two peers first establish a secure channel, which is an encrypted and authenticated connection. The two peers agree on authentication and encryption methods, exchange keys, and verify the other's identity. The secure channel is called ISAKMP Security Association. Unlike IPSec SAs, ISAKMP SAs are bidirectional and the same keys and algorithms protect inbound and outbound communications. IKE parameters are negotiated as a unit and are termed a protection suite. Mandatory IKE parameters are:
  - Symmetric Encryption algorithm.
  - Hash function.
  - Authentication method: Pre-Shared Key and X.509 Certificates.
  - Group for Diffie-Hellman.
  - Other optional parameters such as SA lifetime can also be part of the protection suite.
- Phase 2: IPSec SAs are negotiated after the secure ISAKMP channel is established. Every packet exchanged in phase 2 is authenticated and encrypted according to keys and algorithms selected in the previous phase.

The one method to complete phase 1 is Main Mode.

  - The Main Mode negotiation uses six messages, in a triple two-way exchange. The messages containing the identity information are not authenticated or encrypted. One mode is defined for phase 2. This mode is called Quick Mode. Quick Mode uses three messages, two for proposal parameters and a third to acquit the choice. With "perfect forward secrecy" enabled, the default value in Nokia's configuration, a new Diffie-Hellman exchange must take place during Quick Mode. Consequently, the two peers generate a new Diffie-Hellman key pair.

Using PKI

For Phase 1 negotiation of IKE, your IPSec systems can use X.509 Certificates for authentication. IPSO IPSec implementation supports Entrust VPN connector and Verisign IPSec on site services.

To use the X.509 Certificates, the IPSec system should follow these steps:

1. Install the trusted CA certificates for all peer IPSec systems.
2. Make a certificate request with the information required to identify the system, such as your IP address, a fully qualified domain name, organization, organization unit, city, state, country, and contact e-mail address.

3. Forward the certificate request to the CA or corresponding RA (Registration Authority) using the Web interface or another file transfer mechanism. CA or RA verifies the identity of the IPSec system and generates the approved certificate. A certificate is valid only for a certain period of time.
4. Download and install the approved device certificate and the CA certificate on the IPSec system.
5. Link the certificate to an IPSec policy.

NOTE

This information is also explained in Chapter 4.

Using IPSec

The IPSO operating system provides a native IPSec implementation supporting ESP in tunnel mode. This implementation is compliant with the RFCs explained in Table 5.11.

Table 5.11 IPSec RFCs

RFC	Description
2401	Security Architecture for the Internet Protocol
2402	IP authentication header
2406	IP Encapsulating Security Payload (ESP)
	Supports algorithms: 3DES, DES, and Blowfish for encryption, and SHA-1 and MD5 for authentication.
2407	The Internet IP Security Domain of Interpretation for ISAKMP
2408	Internet Security Association and Key Management Protocol (ISAKMP)
2409	The Internet Key Exchange (IKE)
2411	IP Security Document Roadmap
2412	The OAKLEY Key Determination Protocol
2451	ESP CBC-Mode Cipher Algorithms

The IPSec configuration in Nokia Network Voyager is based on three IPSec objects:

- **Proposals** Define the combination of encryption and authentication algorithms that secure phase 1 negotiation (Main Mode), phase 2 negotiations (Quick Mode), and IPSec packets.
- **Filters** Determine which packets relate to certain proposals. The filters are matched against the source or destination fields in the packet header depending on if the filters are source or destination filters. If applicable, Protocol and Port fields are also used.
- **Policies** Link the type of IPSec security proposals with the defined traffic. The traffic is defined by a list of filters specified for the source address and a second list specified for the destination address. If the source address of a packet matches a filter from the source filter list and the destination address matches a filter from the destination filter list, IPSec is applied to the traffic.

Tools & Traps...

Defined Traffic Security

The kind of security applied to a defined traffic is specified by a list of proposals ordered by priority. This list is offered to the other peer beginning with the lowest priority value proposal.

Proposals and filters can be reused in different policies. Other elements defined in a policy are authentication methods (Pre-Shared Keys or X.509 Certificates) and lifetime attributes.

Defining Tunnel Requirements

IPSec tunnels are defined by local and remote tunnel addresses. The tunnel requires a policy to define which traffic is encapsulated by the tunnel and which security to use in the encapsulation. The traffic that matches filters associated to the policy is encapsulated by using tunnel addresses. Policies can also be reused in different tunnels. An IPSec tunnel cannot function without an associated policy.

NOTE

Native IPSO IPSec tunnels cannot coexist in the same device with Check Point IPSec software. Before you use IPSO IPSec software, make sure no Check Point software is running. Likewise, before you use Check Point IPSec software, ensure no IPSO IPSec software is running.

You can create IPSec tunnel rules with or without a logical interface for all IPSO platforms except the IP3000 Series. For the IP3000 Series platform, you must create a logical interface with each tunnel rule. You can create tunnel rules without logical interfaces if you require a large number of tunnels. However, creating IPSec tunnels without interfaces can slow down non-IPSec traffic.

For IPSO, the Phase 1 encryption and authentication algorithms are the same as those used in Phase 2. However, if Phase 2 encryption is NULL, such as with an AH proposal or NULLencryption-ESP proposal, IPSO uses 3DES as Phase 1 for the encryption algorithm.

NOTE

Onboard hardware accelerators assist phase 2 negotiations if you're using the 3DES encryption algorithm. Check your Nokia platform documentation to see if it supports onboard VPN acceleration.

The values set in the Lifetime table are used as the hard lifetime of the Phase 2 SA. Phase 1 lifetimes are calculated as Hard Phase 1 lifetime (seconds) = 5* Hard Phase 2 lifetime (seconds). Depending on whether the device is working as a session initiator or responder, the soft limit value is approximately 80–90 percent of the hard-limit value.

If you create tunnels between IPSO and non-IPSO systems, configure the non-IPSO system so the Phase 1 lifetime is five times the Phase 2 lifetime. You should also set the encryption to 3DES, and set the authentication so it is the same as the Phase 2 algorithm.

Tools & Traps...

IPSec Parameters

The two IPSec peers should agree on authentication and encryption methods, exchange keys, and verify each other's identities. While configuring the peer IPSec devices, consider the following:

- At least one proposal (encryption algorithm and hash function) should match on the peer devices.
- Authentication method:
- If you are using Shared Secret, then both devices should have the same shared secret.
- If you are using X.509 Certificates, then both devices should install all the trusted CA certificates in the trust hierarchy.
- Some IPSec systems require that the SA lifetimes (seconds and megabytes) match on both devices.
- IKE and PFS groups should match on both devices.
- The Diffie-Hellman key exchange uses the IKE group during the establishment of Phase 1 ISAKMP SA. Value options are 1, 2, or 5; 2 is the default value.
- The Diffie-Hellman key exchange uses the PFS group in Phase 2 to construct key material for IPSec SAs. The value options are 1, 2, 5, or none; 2 is the default. Setting the value to none disables PFS.

When IPSO is acting as the responder of the Phase 2 negotiation, it always accepts the PFS group proposed by the initiator.

Creating an IPSec Policy

An IPSec policy is a set of rules that govern when and how IPSO uses the IPSec protocol. The IPSec policy interacts directly with the IPSec driver. The policy tells IPSO things, such as which data to secure and which security method to use. Figure 5.10 shows the IPSec Configuration page.

Figure 5.10 The IPSec Configuration Page

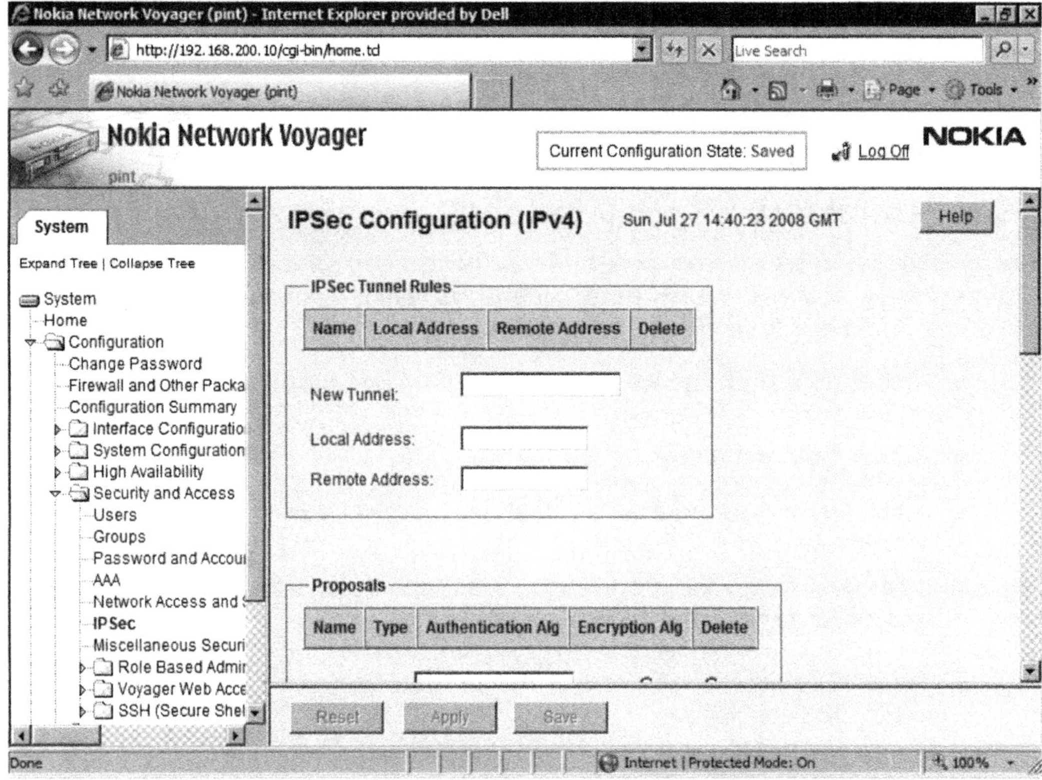

1. In the system tree, click **Configuration | Security And Access | IPSec**.
2. Access the appropriate IPSec Configuration page:
   - To display the IPv4 IPSec Configuration page, click the **IPSec** link.
   - To display the IPv6 IPSec Configuration page, first click the **IPv6 Configuration** link. This takes you to the main IPv6 page. Next, click the **IPSec** link. This takes you to the IPv6 IPSec Configuration page.

NOTE

Application procedures are the same for both configuration page types. The primary difference is the format of the IP addresses. IPv4 uses dotted quad format, while IPv6 uses the canonical address format. Selected range values might be different. Consult the inline Help option for specifics.

Create Proposals and Filters:

3. Under **Proposals**, in the **New Proposal** field, type a name for a new proposal.
4. Click **ESP** or **AH**.

TIP

If you click AH, the Encryption Alg (algorithm) must always be set to NONE. If this is not done, an error message appears when you click Apply.

5. From the **Authentication Alg** and **Encryption Alg** lists, select the necessary algorithms.
6. Click **Apply**.
7. Under **Filters**, in the **New Filter** field, type a new filter name for the subnetwork you want to control.
8. In the **Address** and **Mask Length** fields, type the subnet address and the mask length.

NOTE

Destination filters across multiple rules (tunnel or transport) should not overlap, but source filters *can* overlap.

9. Click **Apply**. The new filter information is added to the Filters list. If needed, you can then define a protocol or a port. Defaults are assumed. Repeat this operation for as many networks you need.

Create a Trusted CA Certificate:

10. Under **Trusted CA Certificates**, in the **New CA** field, type a name.
11. Click **Apply**. An "Apply Successful" message appears and the name of the CA you just entered appears under Trusted CA Certificates.
12. Click the link with the name you entered in Step 10. This action takes you to the IPSec Certificate Addition page for that specific certificate.

13. On the **Certificate Addition** page, you have two choices:
    - If you have the PEM (base64) encoded certificate, select the **Paste The PEM Certificate** option.
    - If you know the URL to the certificate (including the local file), select the **Enter URL To The Certificate** option.
14. Click **Apply**.
15. If you are asked to enter the PEM coded certificate, use the copy and paste function of your browser to copy the PEM text of the certificate into the **Paste The PEM Encoded Certificate** field and then click **Apply**. This action should print a Success message. To return to the main IPSec configuration page, click the **IPSec Configuration** link.
16. If you are prompted for the certificate URL information, enter the URL of the certificate.

    Examples are:

    http://test.acme.com/dev1.cert

    ftp://test.acme.com/dev1.cert

    file://tmp/dev1.cert

    1dap://test.acme.com/cn=dev1.acme.com?pem_x509?sub
17. Enter the HTTP realm information (only for the HTTP protocol). Enter the username and password if needed to connect to the FTP/HTTP server.
18. Click **Apply**. This action should print a Success message. Click the link titled **IPSec Configuration Page** to return to the main IPSec Configuration page. Repeat the steps in this procedure for every trusted CA certificate that needs to be installed.

NOTE

On successful completion, a green button appears under the Certificate File column. The green button indicates that the certificate file is present on the machine and it is also a link to view the installed certificate.

Create Device Certificates:

19. Under **Device Certificates**, in the **New Certificate** field, type a name and then click **Apply**. An Apply Successful message appears, and the name of the CA you just entered appears under Device Certificates.

20. Click the link with the name you entered in the previous step. This takes you to the IPSec Certificate Enrollment page for that named item.
21. Enter all the fields on the page that identifies the IPSec system and then click **Apply**. You should be taken to the page where a PEM-encoded certificate request is shown.
22. Click **Save**.
23. If you have access to the CA/RA enrollment page, open the page in a separate browser window.
24. Use the copy and paste function or your browser to paste the PEM certificate request into the CA/RA certificate enrollment page or copy the text in a file and send the file to the CA/RA by FTP or some other file transfer mechanism that is supported. Contact the CA for details.

NOTE

Some CAs do not expect the header (----BEGIN CERTIFICATE REQUEST----) and the footer (----END CERTIFICATE REQUEST----) lines in the text.

25. If you successfully make the certificate request, select **Completed The Certificate Request At The CA Site** or select **Will Do It Later**.
26. Click **Apply**.
27. If you selected the Completed The Request At The CA Site, a new link **Click Here To Install The Certificate** appears near the bottom of the page. (To install the certificate, refer to the steps under *Create a Trusted CA Certificate*.)

TIP

Before you install the certificate, make sure that CA approved the certificate and that you know how to access the approved certificate. If you must wait for the approval, you can click the link with the certificate name in the IPSec Configuration page to install the certificate.

28. If you selected Will Do It Later, the link on the main IPSec Configuration still points to the certificate request page. You can repeat steps 22 through 26 to install the certificate. If you finished all the steps, two green buttons appear. You can click the button under the **Certificate** column to view the certificate.

Notes from the Underground...

Advanced IPSec

The following options are available through the IPSec Advanced Configuration page. The link is at the bottom of the IPSec Configuration page:

- **Log Level** IPSO IPSec provides three levels of message logging through the syslog subsystem:
- **Error** (default value) Only error messages or audit messages are logged.
- **Info** Provides minimum information about the successful connections to the system. Also includes error messages.
- **Debug** Besides the informational messages, gives full details of the negotiations that the subsystem performs.

In any of the log level options, confidential information (such as secrets or session keys) are not shown.

- **Allowing tunnels without logical interfaces** This option allows for the creation of IPSec tunnels that are not associated with a logical tunnel interface. You can create tunnels without logical interfaces if you want to achieve scalability and want a greater number of tunnels. The Create A Logical Interface field appears only if the Allow Tunnels Without Logical Interface field is set to On on the Advanced Configuration page. Enabling this option might slow down forwarding of non-IPSec packets.
- **LDAP servers** IPSO IPSec implementation supports automatic CRL retrieval following the LDAPv2/3 protocol specification (RFC 2251). To retrieve CRL automatically from the centralized directory, enter the URL of the directory server. Because of different implementations, the internal configuration of the directory server might not be compatible with IPSO that has implemented LDAP query formats.

Complete IPSec Policy Creation:

29. Under **Policies**, in the **New Policy** field, type a name for the new policy and then click **Apply**. An Apply Successful message appears and the policy name appears in the Policies table.
30. Under **Policies**, click the policy name. The IPSec Policy Configuration page for the name appears.

31. Under **Linked Proposals**:
    1. In the **Add A Proposal** list, select the name of the proposal to use in this policy.
    2. Assign a priority in the **Priority** text box and then click **Apply**.
    3. Repeat this step for every proposal that must be offered to the other peer. The proposals are offered starting with the lowest priority value (one).
32. Select the authentication method (Pre-Shared Secrets or X.509 Certificates) needed in this policy, and then click **Apply**.

NOTE

Only one method can be active at a time.

33. If you selected Pre-Shared Secret, in the **Enter Shared Secret** and **Shared Secret (Verify)** fields, type the shared secret.
34. Click **Apply**. If the secret has been entered correctly, the red light of the Secret Status field turns green after you click Apply.
35. If you selected X.509 Certificates, select the certificate name from the list of device certificates that identifies this machine.
36. In the **Lifetime** table, if the default lifetime values are not appropriate, modify the values in the **Seconds** and **Megabytes** fields.

NOTE

Lifetimes must be set to the same value between peers when negotiation is initiated. If they are not set the same, IPSO IPSec might deny the negotiation.

37. In the **Diffie-Hellman Groups** table, if the default values in the **IKE Group** and **PFS Group** fields are not appropriate, modify the values and then click **Apply**.

To create an IPSec tunnel rule, complete the following steps:

1. In the system tree, click **Configuration | Security And Access | IPSec**.
2. Under **IPSec Tunnel Rules**, in the **New Tunnel** field, type a name for the tunnel.

3. In the **Local Address** field, type the IP address of the local end of the IPSec tunnel. The local address must be one of the system interface addresses and must be the remote endpoint configured for the IPSec tunnel at the remote gateway.
4. In the **Remote Address** field, type the IP address of the remote interface to which the IPSec tunnel is bound. The remote endpoint cannot be one of the system interface addresses and must be the local endpoint configured for the IPSec tunnel at the remote gateway.
5. Click **Apply**. An Apply Successful message appears and an entry for the new tunnel appears in the IPSec Tunnel Rules table.

NOTE

IPSO can support up to 1,500 rules. However, each Nokia Network Voyager page displays a maximum of ten. If you create more than ten rules, they are continued on new pages. Access these pages by clicking the link directly below the rule section.

6. In the **IPSec Tunnel Rules** table, click the link with the name you created in step 2. The IPSec Tunnel page appears.
7. (Optional) Activate Hello Protocol inside the tunnel and then click **Apply**. The hello protocol determines the connectivity of an end-to-end logical tunnel. As a result, the hello protocol modifies the link status of the logical interface. If the connectivity of an unavailable tunnel is restored, the hello protocol brings up the link.

NOTE

This and the following two steps are not applicable for tunnels without logical interface parameters.

8. (Optional) If the hello protocol is active, type values for the **Hello Interval** and **Dead Interval** fields and then click **Apply**. The Hello Interval field specifies the interval (number of seconds) between the Hello packets being sent through the tunnel. The Dead Interval field determines the interval (number of seconds) in which you do not receive a Hello packet before the link status changes to unavailable.

9. (Optional) Change the logical name of the interface to a more meaningful one by typing the preferred name in the **Logical Name** field and then clicking **Apply**.
10. From the **Select Policy** list, select the policy name that is needed and then click **Apply**. This action displays a new table, Linked Policy.
11. In the **Source Filters** list, select a filter name that corresponds to the source of the traffic that this policy will protect, and then click **Apply**.
12. Repeat this operation to add as many filters as necessary, clicking **Apply** after each selection.

NOTE

If there are 40 or more source or destination filters, they do not appear as a list on the Nokia Network Voyager page. To view a filter that is not displayed, type the name of the filter in the appropriate field.

14. In the **Destination Filters** list, select a filter name that corresponds to the destination of the traffic that will be protected by this policy and then click **Apply**.
15. Repeat this operation to add as many filters as necessary, clicking **Apply** after each selection.
    (Optional) In the **Options** table, select the option **Include End-Points In The Filters** and then click **Apply**.
16. Click **Save**.

To create a transport tunnel rule, complete the following steps:

1. In the system tree, click **Configuration | Security And Access | IPSec**.
2. Click the **IPSec Transport Rules Configuration** link at the bottom of the page. The IPSec Transport Rules page appears. The structure of this page is common to both IPv4 and IPv6.
3. In the **New Transport Rule** field, type the name of the new rule.
4. In the **Select A Policy** list, select the desired option and then click **Apply**. The new entry appears in the IPSec Transport Rules table.
5. (Optional) To change the policy entry without changing the name of the associated transport rule, perform the following steps:
    1. Select the current policy entry and then click **Apply**. The policy name is removed.

2. In the **Policy** list, select a policy option and then click **Apply**. The new policy is entered without changing the associated transport rule.

6. In the **Source Filters** list, select the filter name that corresponds to the source of the traffic that will be protected by this policy and then click **Apply**.
7. Repeat this operation to add as many filters as necessary, clicking **Apply** after each selection.

NOTE

Select as source filters only filters that present a single host but no subnet. If you have 40 or more source or destination filters, they are not displayed as a list on the Nokia Network Voyager page. To view a filter that is not displayed, type the name of the filter in the appropriate field.

8. In the **Destination Filters** list, select the filter name that corresponds to the destination of the traffic to be protected by this policy.
9. Click **Apply** and then click **Save** to make your changes permanent.
10. To delete any entries, select the **Delete** check box and click **Apply**.
11. Click **Save** to make the delete permanent.

NOTE

Each Network Voyager page displays a maximum of ten transport rules. If you create more than ten rules, they are continued on new pages. Access the new pages by clicking the link directly below the rule section. The link to more pages appears only after you create more than ten transport rules.

To change the local/remote address or local/remote, complete the following steps:

1. In the system tree, click **Configuration | Security And Access | IPSec**.
2. Under the Name column, click the name link for which you want to change the IP address. Example: tun0c1

You are taken to the IPSec Tunnel page.

3. (Optional) In the **Local Address** field, type the IP address of the local end of the IPSec tunnel. The local address must be one of the system interfaces and must be the same as the remote address configured for the IPSec tunnel at the remote router.
4. (Optional) In the **Remote Address** field, type the IP address of the remote end of the IPSec tunnel. The remote address cannot be one of the system interfaces and must be the same as the local address configured for the IPSec tunnel at the remote router.
5. Click **Apply** and then click **Save**.

To remove an IPSec tunnel, complete the following steps:

1. In the system tree, click **Configuration | Security And Access | IPSec**. The IPv4 IPSec Configuration page appears by default. If the IPv6 General Configuration page is desired, scroll to the bottom of the page and click the IPv6 IPSec Configuration link.
2. Under **IPSec Tunnel Rules**, under the **Delete** column, mark the boxes of the tunnel names you wish to delete.
3. Click **Apply**. An Apply Successful message appears and the tunnels selected for deletion are removed from the IPSec Tunnel Rules table.
4. To make your changes permanent, click **Save**.

Using Miscellaneous Security Settings

The Miscellaneous Security Settings page under Configuration | Security And Access lets you change the handling of TCP packets. The default behavior for IPSO is to drop TCP packets that have SYN and FIN bits set.

You must change the default configuration if you want your Nokia platform to accept packets that have both the SYN and FIN bits set. Complete the following procedure to configure your platform to accept packets that have both SYN and FIN bits set. Figure 5.11 shows the Miscellaneous Security Settings page.

Figure 5.11 The Miscellaneous Security Settings Page

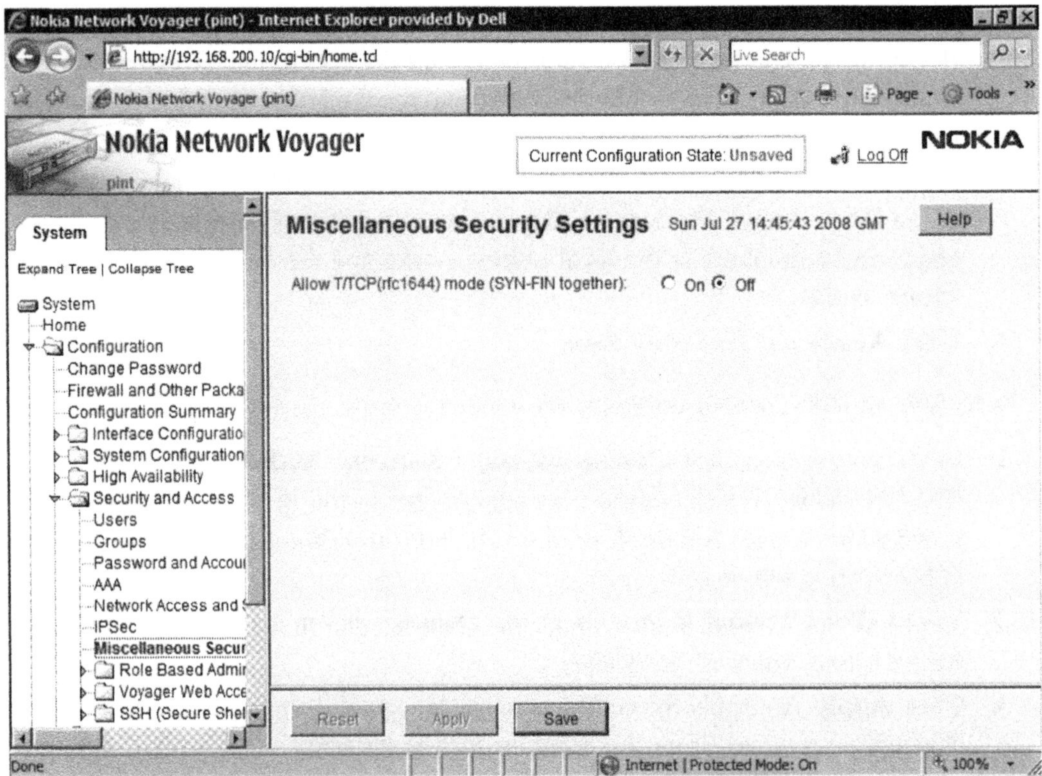

To set TCP flag combinations, complete the following procedure:

1. In the system tree, click **Configuration | Security And Access | Miscellaneous Security Settings**.
2. Next to **Allow T/TCP(rfc1644) Mode (SYN-FIN together)**, click **On**. To return to the default configuration if you have enabled your platform to accept packets that have both SYN and FIN bits set, click **Off**.
3. Click **Apply** and then, to make your change permanent, click **Save**.

Summary

When users log in to Nokia Network Voyager, the features available in the navigation tree depend on the role or roles assigned to their user account. If the roles do not provide access to a feature, the user will not see a link to the feature in the tree. If the user has read-only access to a feature, they will see a link and be able to access the page, but the controls will be disabled.

An important aspect when securing your Nokia network security platform is establishing user passwords and creating an effective password policy. Remember that having users create strong and unique passwords using a variety of character types and creating a password policy requiring users to change their passwords often are key factors to your overall network security. To create an effective security policy, you must make sure users create strong and unique passwords. You can configure a policy that requires passwords to be a certain length, use more than one character type, and not be palindromes.

You can lock out users for a specified number of failed login attempts and configure the length of time the user is locked out, as well as the number of failed login attempts that trigger a lockout. You can also deny access to accounts that have been inactive for a specified length of time. Using Nokia Network Voyager, you can add users to your IPSO system and edit the user ID, group ID, home directory, and default shell for a user. You can also change user passwords and force users to change passwords on their next login.

For group access, you can define and configure groups with IPSO similarly to UNIX-based systems. This capability is retained under IPSO for advanced applications and for retaining compatibility with UNIX.

When you add a new user to Nokia Network Voyager, the user is given read-only privileges to the Nokia Network Voyager home page and the CLI prompt. The user, however, cannot access other Nokia Network Voyager pages or execute commands from the CLI prompt. For the user to gain more access, you must assign roles.

RBA allows IPSO administrators to create and use separate roles. By using RBA, an administrator can allow users to access specific features by including the features in a role and assigning the role to users. Each role can include a combination of administrative (read/write) access to some features, monitoring (read-only) access to other features, and no access to other features. This feature also provides improved auditing capabilities.

To assign a set of access permissions to a user, create a role that specifies access levels to features you want to include, and then assign this role to the relevant user. You can also specify the access mechanisms (Nokia Network Voyager or CLI) available to the user when you assign a role.

You can use the AAA component of the system to manage user access to the appliance. Typically, AAA includes authentication, which identifies a user; authorization, which determines what a user is permitted to do; and accounting, which tracks aspects of user activity.

Nokia IPSO implements Pluggable Authentication Modules (PAM), an industry-standard framework for authenticating and authorizing users. Using PAM, authentication, account management, and session management algorithms are contained in shared modules that you configure on your appliance.

To configure a new AAA service on your appliance, you configure a service module. The service module is then shared by applications that need to invoke authentication, account management, or session management algorithms.

IPSec is a suite of protocols that includes protocols for cryptographic key establishment, and for securing IP communications by authenticating and/or encrypting each IP packet in a data stream. IPSec is the industry standard that ensures the construction of secure VPNs, which are private and secure networks implemented on public and insecure networks. The basic building blocks of IPSec, AH, and ESP use symmetric cryptographic techniques for ensuring data confidentiality and data signatures for authenticating the source of the data. IPSec operates in two modes: Transport mode for host-to-host communications, and Tunnel mode for network-to-network communications or host-to-network and host-to-host communications over the Internet

The IPSec configuration in Nokia Network Voyager is based on three IPSec objects:

- **Proposals** Defines the combination of encryption and authentication algorithms that secure phase 1 negotiation (Main Mode), phase 2 negotiations (Quick Mode), and IPSec packets.
- **Filters** Determines which packets relate to certain proposals. The filters are matched against the source or destination fields in the packet header depending on whether the filters are source or destination filters. If applicable, Protocol and Port fields are also used.
- **Policies** Links the type of IPSec security with the defined traffic. The traffic is defined by a list of filters specified for the source address, and a second list specified for the destination address. If the source address of a packet matches a filter from the source filter list and the destination address matches a filter from the destination filter list, IPSec is applied to the traffic.

An IPSec policy is a set of rules that govern when and how IPSO uses the IPSec protocol. The IPSec policy interacts directly with the IPSec driver. The policy tells IPSO things, such as which data to secure and which security method to use.

Solutions Fast Track

Managing Accounts and Passwords

- ☑ When users log in to Nokia Network Voyager, the features available in the navigation tree depend on the role or roles assigned to their user account.
- ☑ An important aspect when securing your Nokia network security platform is establishing user passwords and creating an effective password policy.
- ☑ You can lock out users for a specified number of failed login attempts and configure the length of time the user is locked out and the number of failed login attempts that trigger a lockout.

Managing Groups and Access

- ☑ You can define and configure groups with IPSO similarly to UNIX-based systems.
- ☑ RBA allows IPSO administrators to create and use separate roles.
- ☑ To assign a set of access permissions to a user, create a role that specifies access levels to features you want to include, and then assign this role to the relevant user.

Configuring Authentication, Authorization, and Accounting (AAA)

- ☑ You can use the AAA component of the system to manage user access to the appliance.
- ☑ Typically, AAA includes authentication, which identifies a user; authorization, which determines what a user is permitted to do; and accounting, which tracks aspects of user activity.
- ☑ Nokia IPSO implements Pluggable Authentication Modules (PAM), an industry-standard framework for authenticating and authorizing users.

Configuring IPSO VPN

- ☑ IPSec is a suite of protocols that includes protocols for cryptographic key establishment, and for securing IP communications by authenticating and/or encrypting each IP packet in a data stream.
- ☑ The basic building blocks of IPSec, AH, and ESP use symmetric cryptographic techniques for ensuring data confidentiality, and data signatures for authenticating the source of the data.
- ☑ An IPSec policy is a set of rules that govern when and how IPSO uses the IPSec protocol.

Frequently Asked Questions

Q: Do users automatically gain access to every component of Nokia Network Voyager?

A: No. Access is role-based, meaning the features available in the navigation tree depend on the role or roles assigned to their user account.

Q: Can users reuse their passwords?

A: Yes, but how often is up to you. You use the password history feature to check for password reuse and force users to create unique passwords every time they change their password. The number you specify in the history length is the number of previous passwords that the feature checks against.

Q: Can I force users to change their password?

A: Yes. You can force users to change their passwords at regular intervals and immediately after the password has been reset by an administrator.

Q: How can I define user groups?

A: You can define and configure groups with IPSO similarly to UNIX-based systems.

Q: Why would I want to use a group?

A: You would create a group to specify UNIX file permissions, use the Wheel group to control which users have root access to the system, and control who can log in through SSH

Q: I have added a new user, but the user can't do anything in the system. Why?

A: When you add a new user to Nokia Network Voyager, the user is given read-only privileges to the Nokia Network Voyager home page and the CLI prompt. The user however cannot access other Nokia Network Voyager pages or execute commands from the CLI prompt. For the user to gain more access, you must assign roles.

Q: Can I delete and modify the default service modules?

A: No. You cannot delete them, but you can modify any of these service modules by modifying the service profiles it uses, or by modifying the authentication, account management, or session profiles that are also used by a service profile.

Q: Can I delete any service or profile at any time?

A: You cannot delete services or profiles referenced by other definitions, but you can delete a service and any or all of its profiles at the same time.

Q: Can I change the order of the profiles I just created?

A: Profiles are invoked in the order they appear in the relevant list—from top to bottom. New profiles are added to the end of the list. To change the order, delete the profiles that are out of order and add them back in the proper order.

Q: Can I create an IPSec policy in Voyager?

A: Yes. In the system tree, click **Configuration | Security And Access | IPSec**.

Q: The IPSec Configuration page indicates I am using IPv4. Can I switch to IPv6?

A: Yes. Scroll to the bottom of the page and click **IPv6 IPSec General Configuration**.

Q: Can I change how the appliance handles TCP packets?

A: Yes. The Miscellaneous Security Settings page under **Configuration | Security And Access** lets you change the handling of TCP packets.

Chapter 6

Advanced System Administration and Troubleshooting

Solutions in this chapter:

- Understanding the Boot Manager
- Introducing CLISH
- Troubleshooting

☑ Summary

☑ Solutions Fast Track

☑ Frequently Asked Questions

Introduction

"Let's take a minute so I can explain how the IPSO boot manager works, as well as some of the things we can do at the command line," said Shin.

"Can you explain how Mark can reset his password when he locks himself out?" asked Marty.

"Very funny," responded Mark. "It only happened the one time."

Marty laughed. "How long did that take again?"

Mark frowned.

"Only 4 days," responded Ming, rolling her eyes.

"I figured it out, Ming," Mark quickly replied. "It just took...some time."

"I'll also introduce you to the Command Line Interface Shell, more commonly referred to as CLISH," said Shin. "I hear from Marty that you both are fairly handy at the Cisco PIX command interface." Shin wanted to make sure Mark's pride wasn't hurt and thought it might do well to stroke his ego a bit.

"Why, yes," Mark replied. "Ming and I have been working with Cisco hardware for years."

Shin smiled. "Well, I think you will really enjoy this method of configuring the system then."

Understanding the Boot Manager

The *boot manager* is a small program that runs just after system startup, but before the IPSO kernel is loaded into memory. The Nokia boot manager is present on the system hard drive or in flash memory depending on the model. Without any interruption, the boot manager will bootstrap the system with the default kernel image, but it can be interrupted and given options from a rudimentary command shell. This functionality is typically useful to boot into single-user mode for system maintenance, or for reinstalling the operating system to factory defaults.

Understanding Boot Manager Variables

The boot manager operates by referencing some user-definable variables that are given sensible defaults when your Nokia device is shipped. Table 6.1 lists each variable and its purpose. This section discusses how to change the values of these variables.

Table 6.1 User-Definable Boot Manager Variables

Variable Name	Meaning	Factory Default Value
autoboot	Do we wait for *bootwait* seconds at the boot manager prompt during startup before continuing unattended?	Yes
boot-device	Device to load the boot-file from.	wd0
boot-file	Kernel image path.	/image/current/kernel
boot-flags	Flags to pass to the kernel.	-x
-x	Do not identify the flash disk as wd0.	N/A
-d	Enter the kernel debugger as soon as possible during startup.	N/A
-s	Single-user mode; admin password may be needed if console is marked "insecure" in /etc/ttys.	N/A
-v	Verbose mode.	N/A
bootwait	The amount of time to wait at the boot manager prompt for user input before continuing.	5 seconds

NOTE

If you set autoboot to *No*, your Nokia device stops at the boot manager prompt during startup and waits indefinitely for your keyboard input. In this case, you need to manually enter the *boot* command from a console connection to get the system up and running.

Understanding Boot Manager Commands

When you are at the boot manager prompt, you can enter various commands. The following is a list of those commands with sample uses:

- ***printenv*** Prints all variables and their values to the screen.
- ***showalias*** Shows alias list in volatile memory. Eight aliases are available.

- ***sysinfo*** Shows CPU, memory, and device information.
- ***ls*** The syntax of this command is *ls device path*. This will display the contents of a directory given by *path* on the device *device*. For example, *ls wd0 /image/current* lists the contents of the currently active IPSO directory tree.
- ***setenv*** This command is used to set environment variables. The syntax you should use is *setenv name value*. For example, to change the default five-second boot timeout to ten seconds, enter ***setenv bootwait 10***.
- ***unsetenv*** This command unsets or clears the environment variable given to it by name. So, for example, *unsetenv boot-file* clears the *boot-file* variable. Note that unsetting autoboot will not clear it but will set it to *No*. Similarly, unsetting *boot-wait* will set that variable to 0.
- ***set-defaults*** Resets the given environment variable back to its default value, so *set-defaults bootwait* would set bootwait back to five seconds. If you use set-defaults with no arguments, the system resets all boot manager environment variables to their default values.
- ***setalias*** Used to set an alias. An alias allows you to substitute one name for another. The syntax for this command is *setalias <name device>*, where *name* is the alias you want to create, and *device* is the name of the device you want to alias. Note that *disk* is a predefined alias for *wd0*.
- ***showalias*** Displays a list of all the currently defined aliases.
- ***unsetalias*** Used to delete or undefine an alias. The syntax for this command is *unsetalias <name>*, so the command *unsetalias disk* deletes the alias named *disk* that you defined earlier.
- ***halt*** Used to halt the system, which is typically followed by the system being powered off. Note that *halt* can also be used from a multiuser or single-user shell and is the safest way to power off your Nokia device since it makes sure that all mounted file systems are unmounted.
- ***help*** Shows help for the various boot manager commands.
- ***boot*** The *boot* command is used to boot the system manually. It allows you to specify that you would like to boot from a specific device, with a specific kernel image, using explicit kernel flags. It is sometimes useful to restore a system that has been rendered unbootable by a failed upgrade or corrupt kernel image. The syntax of the boot command is *boot <boot-device> <boot-file> <boot-flags>*. For example, entering ***boot wd0 /image/current/kernel.old*** would boot the kernel named *kernel.old* in the /image/current directory on device *wd0*. Entering just the word ***boot*** here has the same effect as if you had entered *boot wd0 /image/current/kernel* (/image/current/ ·

kernel always points to the kernel image of your most recently installed IPSO). Typing ***boot –s*** boots your Nokia into single-user mode.

- ***install*** Performs a factory default installation. This command is discussed later in the section.
- ***passwd*** Normally, access to the *install* command in the boot manager is open to anyone with physical access to your Nokia appliance; no password is necessary. If you are not confident in the physical security measures at your workplace, it is probably a good idea to set a password for access to this command. The first time you use *passwd*, it will prompt you for a new password twice. After the *install* password has been set, you will be prompted for the current password before being allowed to change it again.

WARNING

If you lose or forget the *install* password, to get access to it again you have to remove your hard drive(s), reboot your Nokia appliance, change the install password, reinstall your hard drive(s), and reboot. Some older appliances without the boot manager in flash memory must be returned to Nokia to have the password reset.

Performing a Factory-Default Installation

You might find it necessary to reinstall IPSO as though the Nokia just came from the factory—perhaps if you are configuring a previously used Nokia device or have to repair a damaged installation. This procedure will reformat and repartition your hard drive, so make sure you have performed appropriate backups before starting. The procedure is as follows:

1. Set up an FTP server and make sure the Nokia appliance you are reinstalling has physical network connectivity to it. Test your FTP server from another host to make sure it works.
2. Download the necessary IPSO package (ipso.tgz) from the Nokia Web site, and if desired, additional packages can be obtained from the vendor site (FireWall-1 from the Check Point Web site for example).
3. Connect and verify serial console connection to the Nokia.
4. Boot the Nokia and interrupt the boot sequence to get the boot manager prompt.
5. Enter **install** from the boot manager prompt.
6. Enter the install password if you set it up previously.

7. Follow the prompts, which will have you enter your device serial number, specify both your IP address and the IP address of your FTP server, and specify the username and login for your FTP server
8. After IPSO has been transferred and installed on your Nokia, reboot with the **reboot** command.
9. After a reboot, you are back at the *Hostname?* prompt, as if this were a freshly unpacked box.

Tools & Traps...

Rapid Install

When building multiple Nokia appliances that share the same packages, you might find it easier to put all of the packages in the same directory as the IPSO image. When doing the factory default installation, you will be prompted to download all the packages as they are discovered by the installer. If you answer yes to the installation of a particular package, it will be fetched and installed immediately after the IPSO image.

This saves you time, effort, and allows you to baseline your appliances using the same IPSO image version and software package versions.

Using Single-User Mode

To get into single user mode, during the startup sequence, interrupt the boot sequence at the prompt *Type any character to enter command mode* while booting with the console cable attached. Press any key before the five-second timeout to get to the boot manager prompt BOOTMGR[0]>. Enter **boot –s**. After the system boots, it will ask you to *Enter pathname of shell or RETURN for sh:*. Press **Enter** to get a command shell. When you have finished with the single-user commands you can exit single-user mode by typing **exit** or pressing **Ctrl + D**. Both methods exit and restart the system.

TIP

It is also possible to enter single-user mode from a running system. Type **kill –TERM 1** (you must be logged in as admin on a console for this to work) to send the init process a TERM signal and force entry into single-user mode. The same thing can be accomplished by typing **shutdown now** from a console login.

Resetting the Admin Password

At some point, you will encounter a Nokia that needs to have work done on it, but the admin password has been forgotten. The password cannot be recovered, but a new one may be set as long as console access to the Nokia is available.

1. Boot into single-user mode from a directly attached console connection by entering **boot –s** at the BOOTMGR prompt.
2. Select **sh** for the shell by pressing **Enter** when prompted
3. Type **/etc/overpw** at the # prompt, and confirm that you want to reset the admin password.
4. Enter the new admin password when prompted, or leave it blank.
5. Press **Ctrl** + **D** and allow the system to come up into full multiuser mode.
6. Login as admin. If a dmin password was set to blank, set it now.
7. Use the *dbpasswd* command to change the password for Voyager:

   dbpasswd admin *newpassword* ''

8. Save the new voyager password:

   dbset :save

The following is what the receding procedure looks like when run through on IPSO 3.6:

```
Enter pathname of shell or RETURN for sh:
# /etc/overpw
   This program is used to set a temporary admin password when you have
   lost the configured password. You must have booted the machine into
   single user mode to run it. The configured password will be changed.
   Please change the temporary password as soon as you log on to your system
   through voyager.
```

```
Please enter password for user admin:
Please re-enter password for confirmation:
Continue? [n] y
Running fsck…
/dev/rwd0f: clean, 65453 free (2461 frags, 7874 blocks, 0.6% fragmentation)
/dev/rwd0a: clean, 36154 free (42 frags, 4514 blocks, 0.1% fragmentation)
/dev/rwd0d: clean, 5802929 free (625 frags, 725288 blocks, 0.0% fragmentation)
/dev/rwd0e: clean, 902680 free (992 frags, 112711 blocks, 0.1% fragmentation)
   Admin password changed. You may enter ^D to continue booting.
   THIS IS A TEMPORARY PASSWORD CHANGE.
   PLEASE USE VOYAGER TO CREATE A PERMANENT PASSWORD FOR THE USER ADMIN.
```

Introducing CLISH

Command-line configuration before IPSO 3.6 was difficult on Nokia firewalls given the way IPSO handled system configuration. However, user demand for a scriptable interface that could enable remote configuration changes caused Nokia to release the *Command Line Interface Shell*, or *CLISH*. CLISH provides a command-line interface to all Voyager configuration options that can be accessed interactively, from the command line or from a file containing CLISH command sequences.

Understanding CLISH Basics

To enter CLISH, at a command prompt enter **clish**. You will see a Nokia> prompt, which is ready to accept commands. The help operator (?) can be used in the middle of a command string, to give context-sensitive help on the argument you just typed and what needs to follow. Some of the other nice features CLISH offers are tab completion of commands, command history perusal with the **Up**- and **Down-arrow keys**, basic command-line editing with the **Right**- and **Left-arrow keys**, and C-shell style history searches with the ! operator. Pressing **Ctrl** + **u** erases the current line, while pressing **Ctrl** + **c** aborts the current command. Quit or exit causes you to leave CLISH.

To see the commands available from one of the main sections shown on the basic help screen, type the command and press **Tab**. You will see a list of valid command arguments that can follow whatever you just typed. For example, if you want to see what the *show* command has to offer, type **show** and press **Tab**. (Notice the *More* reminder at the bottom of the screen. It indicates there are more completion choices, which you can access by pressing the **Spacebar**.)

NOTE

CLISH has multiple outputs: pretty, structured, and XML. If you are taking the output of CLISH commands as inputs into other programs, the structured and XML options may provide for cleaner parsing.

Using *show* Command Completions in CLISH

If you press **q**, you are put back at the *show* command you just typed, with a trailing space added for whatever you want to type next. You only need to type just enough of the command or argument for it to be unique before pressing the **Tab** key again. Type **fowar**, press **Tab**, and then press **Enter**. When you press **Tab**, the phrase *forwarding-table* is completed for you. To get this command with the least amount of typing, you could have typed **sho**, pressed **Tab**, typed **fo**, pressed **Tab**, and then pressed **Enter**.

CLISH also has the capability to execute just one or multiple commands from a file in *batch mode*. To execute just one command, type **clish –c "command"** at a shell prompt. To execute more than one command, place the commands (one per line) in a text file and execute them by typing **clish –f *filename.txt***. The same file can be loaded and executed from within CLISH by typing **load commands *filename.txt***.

Commands entered using CLISH are immediately applied to the running system, but they are not persistent across reboots. Any configuration changes you make must be *saved* to be permanent—much like the Voyager apply and save semantics. To permanently save all your configuration changes from within the interactive shell, type **save config**. To save your configuration changes to a separate file named *configfile.txt*, type **save cfgfile configfile.txt**. This will be a valid system configuration file and is saved in /config/db with all the other system configuration files. This new configuration file is linked to /config/active after it is saved, altering the active configuration of your system. If you are using the one-off command form or the batch file form of CLISH, add the switch *–s* to the command to force a configuration save after the command or batch file executes, as in **clish –s –f commandfile.txt** or **clish –s –c "set vrrp accept-connections on"**.

In general, CLISH commands are formatted as *operator feature argument(s)*, where *operator* is usually one of *show*, *set*, *add*, or *delete*. Yes or no arguments are generally specified *yes* or *no* on the command line, similarly for *on* or *off*. If you know a feature name, using the word *default* for the argument always sets the system default value.

Tools & Traps...

CLISH for Compliance

Often firewalls are added to the environment one at a time, and installed manually. Using CLISH to script the common installation options required allows your Nokia appliances to be consistently baselined. Common options would be settings for Syslog destinations, SNMP trap destinations, backup schedules, alerting, and so on. Having a baseline for your firewalls also helps in troubleshooting should something like a breach or failure occur.

Combining a common script with a firewall-specific CLISH script allows for rapid recovery if a Nokia needs to be replaced due to hardware failure. Running two CLISH scripts, instead of building the entire platform configuration by hand, can restore the previous configuration. This saves both time and unnecessary effort in the long run.

Troubleshooting

When solving problems that eventually come up, it is nice to know that IPSO provides common tools you have access to on other platforms that can help you get enough information to solve problems yourself or at least assist your support provider in fixing the problem. Many of these commands are UNIX commands that we use together in the way they were intended, and some are creations of Nokia that allow you to gather information for them should the need arise.

Managing Logs

The IPSO operating system provides several command-line utilities and many log files that can be used to troubleshoot problems or monitor user or process behavior. Most of the log files created and maintained by IPSO are in the /var/log directory, although some are in other subdirectories of /var. Check Point FireWall-1 logs are kept in the directory $FWDIR/log.

Searching and Displaying Log Files

One of the contents of the /var/log directory contains the *messages* file, this is the global system log to which programs send messages by default. The system program that controls these log messages is called *syslog*, and is configured through the settings in /etc/syslog.conf. In addition to the messages file are several compressed files named messages.*x*.gz. These are the compressed system log files that have been archived as part of the *log rotation* process. messages.0.gz is the latest archive, followed by messages.1.gz, and so on. IPSO also rotates some other logs in /var/log, so look for this pattern in the /var/log directory and its subdirectories.

The *more* command can be used to page through a text file one screen at a time with the **Spacebar**, and you can combine *gzip* and *more* to display the compressed logs, without permanently decompressing the gzipped archive. *Tail* is useful to watch logs in real time, and *grep* is a powerful search tool. The following are some basic examples of using these commands:.

- **more /var/log/messages** Pages through /var/log/messages one screen at a time
- **gzip –cd /var/log/messages.6.gz | more** Decompresses /var/log/messages.6.gz and sends the output through a pipe to *more*.
- **tail –f /var/log/httpd_access_log** Watches the HTTP access log in real time.
- **grep –E '\<10\.100\.6\.1\>' /var/log/messages** Displays all the lines in / var/log/messages that contain the IP address 10.100.6.1. (The \< and \> character sequences are necessary so you do not match IP addresses such as 110.100.6.11).
- **grep –E –v 'LOG_INFO|LOG_NOTICE' /var/log/messages | more** Prints all the lines in /var/log/messages that do *not* contain the strings LOG_INFO or LOG_NOTICE and pages through the output.
- **grep 'LOG_CRIT' /var/log/messages | grep –E –v 'FW-1|ex_expire' | more** Displays all the lines in /var/log/messages that contain the string LOG_CRIT but do *not* contain the strings FW-1 or ex_expire and pages through the output.
- **fw log –nft** Displays the firewall logs in real time.
- **fw log –nft | grep –i 'icmp' | grep –i 'drop'** Displays in real time firewall log entries for the service icmp that are dropped by the firewall. (The *-i* tells the system to do a case-insensitive string match.)
- **fw log –nft | grep –E '\<10\.100\.6.\1\>' | grep –v 'domain'** Shows all real-time firewall log entries containing the IP address 10.100.6.1 that are not DNS traffic.

Using *tcpdump*

Log files are great resources for troubleshooting your firewall, but frequently they do not contain the information needed to troubleshoot user problems. A common troubleshooting technique is to *follow the packet* through the firewall to make sure everything is behaving as expected. This requires tools that can see the packets, on IPSO this is *tcpdump*. It is a network sniffer that can be used to display packet information on any interface on the Nokia.

A simple example of *tcpdump* is to examine all the traffic the firewall sees on a network interface. The level of detail can be enhanced later if the default settings do not show enough information. The syntax for this command is *tcpdump –i <interface name>*. For example, if the internal (physical) interface of the Nokia was named eth-s1p3, you would use *tcpdump –i eth-s1p3* to see all the traffic coming across that interface.

The easiest way to learn is to see some examples of *tcpdump* in use. Table 6.2 shows the most common *tcpdump* command-line arguments, whereas Table 6.3 shows some useful command sequences you can try yourself.

Table 6.2 *tcpdump* Command-Line Arguments

Option	Meaning
-a	Converts numeric addresses to names.
-c <number>	Stops after processing <number> packets.
-e	Displays the Layer 2 header information.
-i <interface name>	Listens on interface <interface name>.
-n	Instructs to not convert numeric addresses to names.
-q	Prints less information.
-r <filename>	Reads packets from file <filename>, which was created with the –w option.
-S	Prints absolute, as opposed to relative, TCP sequence numbers.
-v, -vv, -vvv	Various levels of output verbosity, in increasing order.
-w <filename>	Writes output to the binary file <filename>.

Table 6.3 *tcpdump* Examples

This Command...	Will Capture...
tcpdump –i eth-s1p3 host 10.100.6.153 and not port 80	All the traffic to or from the host 10.100.6.153 that is not on port 80 over the interface eth-s1p3.
tcpdump –i eth-s1p3 src host 10.100.6.153 and tcp dst port 22	All the TCP traffic to port 22 from the host 10.100.6.153 over the interface eth-s1p3.

Continued

Table 6.3 Continued. *tcpdump* Examples

This Command...	Will Capture...
tcpdump –i eth- s1p3 –w vrrp.out proto vrrp	All the VRRP traffic across the interface eth-s1p3. This will be written to the binary file vrrp.out.
tcpdump –i eth-s1p3 –r vrrp.out	All the data from the file vrrp.out, collected from the preceding.
tcpdump –i eth- s1p3 udp port 500	IKE key negotiation across the interface eth-s1p3.

Warning

Running *tcpdump* places your firewall at risk because it exposes IPSO to packets that would otherwise be blocked by Check Point. It is recommended that *tcpdump* is only run for short periods of time when the problem is occurring. If a longer packet capture is required, running commands such as *fw monitor* are better options.

Note

In the commands described in Table 6.3, the output file generated by the *–w* switch is not a text file and can only be read by *tcpdump* or some other software written to parse the binary file format such as Wireshark for Windows.

Troubleshooting Flows

Firewall *flows* are a feature Nokia added to the IPSO operating system to specifically work in conjunction with and increase the throughput for certain types of FireWall-1 traffic. To understand how flows work, we need to understand how IPSO and FireWall-1 normally work together to inspect and route packets at the kernel level.

The traditional name for the path that packets take through the IPSO kernel is *slowpath*. First, a packet comes in through a network interface and gets a kernel route lookup at the device driver level. It is then passed up to the FireWall-1 kernel module, where it is checked against the connection table. If the packet is not in the table, it gets checked against the firewall rule base. Assuming that the packet is part of an existing connection or is accepted by the rule base, it gets passed back down to the network interface device driver (now as an outbound packet), where it gets another route lookup. Then, the connection table/route lookup process is repeated again, before the packet is sent on to its destination. This means two connection table lookups and three routing table lookups for every packet. Nokia found that the bottleneck in this *slowpath* process was the connection table lookups, which are very slow compared with packet routing.

In an attempt to increase FireWall-1 throughput, Nokia implemented what is essentially a copy of the connection table at the device driver level. In what Nokia terms *flowpath*, incoming packets now get a connection table lookup at the same time they get a routing table lookup from the network interface device driver. The connection table lookup is done with the cached copy, not the FireWall-1 copy. If the packet matches an established connection, it is immediately forwarded on to its destination. If the packet does not match a connection table entry, it is passed up to the FireWall-1 kernel module, where it continues with the *slowpath* process as normal. Changes to the FireWall-1 connection table (for example, for new connections) are immediately propagated to the cached copy so it is always up to date. This process results in a throughput increase for firewall traffic, with the best performance increase seen with small (64-byte) packets that are part of long-term existing connections (such as large FTP or SCP transfers). Nokia claims a four-fold increase in throughput in the best case, with performance gains decreasing as the packet size increases. A small amount of overhead is incurred when a new connection is established, because of the need to update the cached copy of the connection table, but this overhead is offset by the performance gains described, so throughput actually increases, even if only slightly, in almost all cases.

Firewall flows have some limitations. Flows are not used at all for encrypted, ICMP, multicast, or authentication (security server) traffic. If you want to increase throughput of your VPN traffic, install a hardware accelerator. The combination of flows and a hardware VPN accelerator is the reason that Nokia's IP series devices attain such high firewall throughput numbers (refer back to Chapter 1). Note that NAT and antispoofing configuration data *is* cached by flows.

You can always check whether flows are enabled with the *ipsofwd list* command:

```
hostname[admin]# ipsofwd list
net:ip:forward:noforwarding = 0
net:ip:forward:noforwarding_author =
net:ip:forward:switch_mode = flowpath
net:ip:forwarding = 1
hostname[admin]#
```

In this case, you can see that flows are enabled by looking at the net:ip:forward:switch_mode line, shown in bold type. If flows were disabled, the word *flowpath* would be replaced by *slowpath*.

Using the Configuration Summary Tool (CST)

The term *cst* refers to the command provided for you to assist Nokia or your support provider in troubleshooting, should the need arise. It is somewhat similar to Check Point *cpinfo*, but *cst* includes much more information. In fact, if the *cpinfo* command is found when the *cst* command is run, it includes the *cpinfo* output in the file it generates. All you need to do to run the command is to enter **cst** when logged in as the admin user. After a while, the command completes and leaves a tarred gzipped file named *cst-hostname-mm.dd.yyyy-time.tar.gz* in the admin home directory. The *cst* contains the following files and directories along with many other commands:

- A system summary file
- A *dmesg* output
- A cpinfo output, if that command is present
- The ipsctl.log file, which tracks changes made through *ipsctl*
- The contents of the /var/etc, /var/log, /var/crash, and /var/tmp directories
- The contents of the /opt and /config/db directories

This file gives you or your support provider lots of information about your system configuration and is generated when the firewall is having issues so the support provider can have a snapshot of the "broken" configuration.

Understanding Memory and Processes

It is useful when you are troubleshooting any system to have a good grasp of what the system processes are actually doing behind the scenes. This section covers some of what the IPSO system daemons do. Where appropriate, we discuss CLISH and how to display this information from a CLISH shell.

The *ps* command gives you a useful snapshot of what is happening on your Nokia system, if it is used with the right arguments. The output of the *ps -auxwm* command displays statistics about all processes running on your Nokia device, in order of memory consumption.

What do these processes do? Some, like *csh*, have obvious functions, but others, like */bin/pm*, are more mysterious. The following is a list of the most important processes you are likely to see running on your Nokia appliance. They are presented in alphabetical order by process name:

- ***cron*** Executes scheduled commands as configured per user in a crontab file. The system crontab is in /etc/crontab.
- ***csh*** The default command shell run when you log in to IPSO remotely or through a serial console.

- ***fmd*** The Fault Management daemon.
- ***getty*** Monitors serial ports for user logins.
- ***httpd*** The Apache HTTP daemon as used by Voyager.
- ***ifm*** Monitors all interfaces for changes and maintains consistency with /config/active.
- ***ifwd*** Monitors network interfaces for changes and reloads the firewall security policy so it enforces the policy on the new interfaces. Nokia recommends disabling this daemon on firewalls in its final interface configuration. This can be done through Voyager in the Check Point configuration section. *ifwd* can be useful on systems with hot-swappable NICs, such as the Nokia 600 or 700 series devices.
- ***inetd*** A daemon that listens for network connections for the servers it has enabled in its configuration file, /etc/inetd.conf. In a default Nokia installation, the only network server enabled is Telnet.
- ***init*** The first process started by the kernel after system boot. It starts all the *getty* processes that listen for console logins and also starts the *inetd* process that listens for network logins.
- ***ipsrd*** The IPSO routing daemon. It modifies routing tables after dynamic routing protocol updates or static route changes.
- ***monitord*** Collects real-time statistics on interfaces and routing.
- ***pagedaemon*** Manages the movement of memory pages into and out of main memory.
- ***pccard*** The PC Card Daemon. Handles the insertion and removal of PCMCIA cards.
- ***pm*** A daemon that monitors certain critical processes and restarts them if they die.
- ***rcm*** Controls the run level of a system (single- or multiuser).
- ***snmpd*** A daemon that responds to queries through SNMP.
- ***sshd-x*** Secure Shell daemon. Listens for incoming secure shell connections.
- ***swapper*** Manages the system swap space.
- ***syslogd*** Daemon that logs system messages.
- ***update*** This daemon flushes file system caches to disk periodically.
- ***mdaemon*** Memory daemon. It manages virtual memory.
- ***xpand*** Implements operating system changes to the global configuration file /config/active.

Sometimes during testing or network troubleshooting, it is useful to have a historical view of process and memory data. If you need a synopsis of memory and swap space usage at any given moment, you can use the command *vmstat –ism | more* to get very detailed memory and swap statistics, including how much memory each process in your system is using. This form of *vmstat* is actually run as part of the *cst* command.

Look at the *vmstat* output. If the MemUse or HighUse column is greater than the Limit column for any of the categories, you might need to upgrade your physical memory.

Tools & Traps...

System Monitoring Over Time

Tools like *vmstat* are best used to monitor the Nokia over time. Nokia has provided some scripts (see Vantive Resolutions ID: 1130911) that can be used to build a picture of the behavior of the firewall by appending the output of the command to a file. Running the command every 90 seconds will allow a picture to develop over time as to what is occurring on your appliance before the system becomes non-responsive.

Download the *memmon.csh.gz* archive listed in the resolution ID, upload it to your Nokia Security Appliance, and then extract the archive using the following command:

```
Nokia[admin]# gunzip memmon.csh.gz
```

Make the script executable using the following command:

```
Nokia[admin]# chmod a+x memmon.csh
```

Execute script using the following syntax:

```
Nokia[admin]# ./memmon.csh
```

To stop the *memmon* script, use the **Ctrl + C** keyboard combination when you have collected enough statistics:

```
Nokia[admin]# ^C
```

Submit the output file to Nokia Support to help diagnose any problems you are experiencing.

Summary

The IPSO boot manager is a valuable tool, knowledge of which is a large part of troubleshooting problems from boot failures to lost administrative passwords. The main function of boot manager is to load the IPSO kernel into main memory, and it does this if left to function unattended. If the boot sequence is interrupted, however, the boot manager gives you access to a rudimentary command shell, from which you can set and clear environment variables that control its function. The boot manager can be upgraded or reinstalled if the need arises.

CLISH gives you the functionality of Voyager from a command shell. It can be used in shell mode to enter interactive commands, or it can be used in batch- or single-command mode. Changes to the global configuration file /config/active can be made by saving your changes from the CLISH shell, much like the Save button in Voyager. It is possible for administrators to get exclusive access to the CLISH shell if they maintain a Nokia appliance with other administrators.

Nokia appliances can provide high levels of firewall throughput when *flows* are enabled. The biggest performance gain is seen in long-lasting connections with small packet sizes, such as large FTP transfers. *Flows* are enabled by default in IPSO 3.3 and later and can be disabled if needed with the command *ipsofwd slowpath*.

Troubleshooting problems can be made easier with the right command-line tools. Anything that can be seen or done from a GUI interface, such as Voyager or the Check Point log viewer, is also possible from the shell. Managing and searching log files, in particular, benefits from the flexibility of tools like *grep*. If your disk runs out of space or you need to more closely examine a log file, SSH (SCP) can be used to initiate secure unattended log file transfers to remote hosts.

Other tools IPSO offers to make your life as an administrator easier include *cst*, *dmesg*, *ps*, *vmstat*, and *tcpdump*. The *cst* command is used to collect detailed system data for troubleshooting by your support provider or Nokia, whereas *dmesg* will show you boot-time messages or frequent console errors. The commands *ps* and *vmstat* can be used to diagnose memory or swap space problems, and *tcpdump* provides for detailed network packet header analysis.

Solutions Fast Track

Understanding the Boot Manager

☑ The boot manager is responsible for loading the operating system kernel into memory.

☑ The Nokia boot manager can be kept in flash memory or on the hard drive

☑ Single-user mode can be accessed through the boot manager with the *boot –s* command.

- ☑ You can change the operation of the boot manager by changing the value of various environment variables with the *setenv* command.
- ☑ The *set-defaults* command sets all the environment variables back to their default values.
- ☑ You might have to upgrade your boot manager prior to upgrading your IPSO version.
- ☑ You can perform a factory-default installation using the *install* command.

Introducing CLISH

- ☑ CLISH has all the functionality of Nokia Network Voyager, from a command-line interface.
- ☑ CLISH can be run in shell mode or batch mode or used to execute single commands.
- ☑ CLISH provides context-sensitive help with the **?** key and command completion with the **Tab** key.
- ☑ Remember to save your configuration changes with the *–s* flag or the *save config* command.
- ☑ It is possible to block other administrators from making changes with CLISH with the *set config-lock on* command.

Troubleshooting

- ☑ Most of the IPSO system log files are kept in /var/log, except for firewall logs, which are in /var/fw/log.
- ☑ IPSO rotates system logs monthly so they do not grow uncontrollably in size.
- ☑ *grep*, *more*, *tail*, and *gzip* can be used together to provide powerful log searching capabilities.
- ☑ SCP can be used to automate the transfer of log files in a secure way.
- ☑ It is possible to recover a lost admin password with the */etc/overpw* command.
- ☑ *tcpdump* can be used to show detailed packet-level data moving across a network interface.
- ☑ *cst* is used to generate a detailed system summary, which can be useful to your support provider.
- ☑ The *ps* and *vmstat* commands can be used to troubleshoot memory or swap space problems.

Frequently Asked Questions

Q: When installing a new image from an anonymous FTP server, the image does not download. What should I do?

A: When using Boot Manager to install from an anonymous FTP server, Boot Manager uses the account name *ftp* instead of the usual *anonymous*. Make sure that the ftp account has the correct permissions.

Q: How can I find out which version of Boot Manager is running?

A: The boot manager version can be displayed in one of two ways. If the Nokia is currently booted, log in and run the command ***ipsctl -ax kern:bootmgr:revision***. You can also boot the Nokia into boot manager and run the command ***printenv*** and look for the BOOTMGR version.

Q: How do I get into single-user mode?

A: To get into single user mode, during the startup sequence, interrupt the boot sequence at the prompt *Type any character to enter command mode* while booting with the console cable attached. Press any key before the five-second timeout to get to the boot manager prompt BOOTMGR[0]>. Enter **boot –s**. After the system boots, it will ask you to *Enter pathname of shell or RETURN for sh:*. Press **Enter** to get a command shell. When you have finished with the single-user commands, you can exit single-user mode by typing **exit**, or press **Ctrl + D**. Both methods exit and restart the system.

Q: What happened to the command *lynx*?

A: When Nokia released IPSO 4.0 the text-based browser *lynx* was not included in the IPSO operating system because the new voyager interface was unable to be correctly displayed in the browser. CLISH is now the preferred method for making any changes to the IPSO configuration using the command line.

Q: How do I set static routes in clish?

A: The syntax for setting static routes in clish is:

```
set static-route ip_prefix nexthop gateway <address | logical> gateway_address
priority <1-8> on
```

So if the next hop to network 192.168.2.0/24 is 192.168.1.254, the command would appear as:

```
set static-route 192.168.2.0/24 nexthop gateway address 192.168.1.254
priority 1 on
```

If the default gateway is 192.168.1.1, use the keyword ***default*** instead of *ip_prefix*:

```
set static-route default nexthop gateway address 192.168.1.1 priority 1 on
```

Q: What's the best way to make sure a set of commands is implemented at the same time?

A: CLISH has an option to enter Transaction mode where the changes will only be applied if ALL the changes can be successfully applied. To enter Transaction mode, enter the command ***start transaction*** and at the prompt have the characters [XACT] added to it to indicate these commands are part of one transaction. Enter all commands that are part of the change and then exit Transaction mode by issuing the ***commit*** command. If there are problems with the commands entered in Transaction mode, you can *roll back* the changes.

Q: When rebooting the Nokia with a console cable monitoring boot, a fast-blinking cursor appears and nothing else. What should I do?

A: This commonly happens on IP130s when a carriage return is received before Boot Manager takes control of the boot sequence. When booting the IP130, make sure no keys are pressed until the boot manager prompt is displayed on screen.

Q: When booting, the error message "Bootmgr version is older than running kernel" appears. How can I resolve this error?

A: This is a bug that occurs on 100 and 300 series hardware and can be resolved by starting oot manager and issuing the command ***set-defaults***.

Q: The Nokia hangs without creating any kernel panic information. What can I do about this?

A: Nokia has an option to force the kernel into debugging mode. Connect a console cable to the Nokia and issue a *break* key sequence (check your terminal emulator for the correct key combination), followed by the command ***ddb***. This puts you in the serial debugging shell. Enable console logging and run the command ***ps*** and ***trace***, then exit ddb by typing ***continue***. Wait a few seconds and repeat the process. After at least three dumps of ps and trace information, enter the ***panic*** command. This forces a core file to be written to disk. Upload the output of all of the *trace* and *ps* commands, along with the core file, to your support provider for further debugging.

Chapter 7

Advanced Routing Configuration

Solutions in this chapter:

- Introducing Dynamic Routing
- Configuring RIP
- Configuring OSPF
- Configuring BGP

☑ Summary

☑ Solutions Fast Track

☑ Frequently Asked Questions

Introduction

"What about dynamic routing protocols?" asked Ming. "Our entire network uses OSPF to distribute routes dynamically. Can our Nokia appliances participate in this?"

Shin brought up the Routing menu within the Nokia Network Voyager interface.

"Yes, from within this configuration," explained Shin, "you can configure the dynamic routing configurations for your appliances." Shin clicked through the items. "If you're using any external routing protocols, such as BGP, you can also configure them within this section. We should probably set up all of our routing before we start working with the Check Point software. That way we know what types of traffic the firewall should be expected to pass."

Introducing Dynamic Routing

Firewalls deal with redundancy using a number of different methods. All of the methods center on the process of using a virtual IP address that is shared by all firewall members to receive all network traffic, and then from that virtual IP address the traffic is allocated to one of the members of the cluster. Redundancy in different parts of the network can also be obtained in this fashion, if two routers are doing HSRP, for example. But sometimes redundancy requires us to manipulate the routing tables of the firewall. For instance, two VPN devices can be added into the DMZ, and tunnels can move between these devices depending on the DNS. For the firewall to know which VPN device to send the correct traffic, we can use a dynamic routing protocol to keep the routing table on the firewall accurate.

Some firewalls do not support dynamic routing protocols because certain people consider dynamic routing protocols to be insecure. This scenario can be resolved by re-architecting your firewall implementation to add a routing device between the firewall and the dynamic devices. Nokia appliances support a wide range of dynamic routing protocols, and Check Point firewalls are flexible enough to handle them once you have your spoofing groups properly defined.

Dynamic routing is typically a rare requirement for firewall implementations unless the customer has revenue-generating partners that require always-up connections via VPN or Frame Relay connections with backup links. This level of redundancy requires dynamic routing labs to be set up since the equipment that is in production cannot have routing errors in it.

Understanding RIP

RIP, which stands for *routing information protocol*, is a commonly used interior gateway protocol (IGP). IGPs, as opposed to exterior gateway protocols (EGPs), distribute routing information within one autonomous system, such as your LAN.

RIP is a distance-vector protocol, meaning it determines distance to other network devices by hop count. Hop count, which is stored in each TCP packet header, is simply the number of routers (or other devices, in some cases) a packet must traverse before reaching its final destination.

The distribution of routing information from one RIP router to another is accomplished when each RIP router sends its routing table to all neighboring routers. This transmission occurs on a regular interval, usually every 30 seconds, and whenever a router receives an update to its routing table.

When a router receives an update from another router, it increments the hop count by one. It then adds the route to its routing table and sets the gateway to the router from which it received the update. The update is then broadcast to all neighboring routers. This process of route transmission continues from router to router until the network reaches a state of convergence, when all routers have been updated with the latest routes.

Tools & Traps...

Redistributing RIP and OSPF

When introducing routing protocols into your network, make sure all equipment is capable of using the same protocols. Some equipment only supports RIP or OSPF.

It's possible to redistribute one protocol with another but if all interior routing protocols are the same, the only time you will be required to redistribute routing protocols is when you need to transfer from an Interior Routing Protocol to an Exterior routing protocol—OSPF to BGP, for example.

To avoid routing loops, where a group of routers update each other continuously regarding the same route, RIP considers any hop count above 15 to be invalid, and a route with such a hop count will not be retransmitted.

There are two versions of RIP: 1 and 2. RIP v2 provides several enhancements over v1, including authentication and additional amounts of information to be transferred per packet, such as subnet mask, which is not included in a RIP v1 packet.

WARNING

RIP routers have a tendency to synchronize their broadcasts over time. This could cause issues if many routers are in the same broadcast domain. It is essential that time be spent planning how to implement any dynamic routing protocol.

Understanding OSPF

OSPF, which stands for *open shortest path first*, is a more advanced interior gateway protocol than RIP, and that allows you to design a more sophisticated local network. OSPF works on the basis of dividing your network into areas. An *area* consists of network nodes and routers that can logically be grouped together.

Tools & Traps...

OSPF Terminology

When reading about OSPF, you'll see many new acronyms and terms introduced. The following are some common ones:

Area An OSPF administrative zone is one area. For example, the group of routers in a lab could be one area, and all of the production routers in the building another.

Area border router (ABR) A router that connects one or more areas to the OSPF backbone.

Autonomous system border router (ASBR) A router that is connected to one or more logical entities (AS), usually through an exterior routing protocol such as BGP.

Autonomous system number (ASN) A number that defines all the devices as belonging to the same logical entity (usually the same company)

Backbone (a.k.a., Area Zero) The area that all routing information travels through. The routing "spine"—all routers must connect to this backbone physically or via a virtual circuit.

Backbone router A router that is part of the OSPF backbone.

Internal router A router that only has information about one OSPF area.

Stub area An area that does not receive any external routes except for the default gateway. Intra area routers are updated regularly.

Not so stubby area (NSSA) A type of stub area that can import AS routes and forward them to the backbone, but that cannot receive external AS routes from the backbone.

Types of routes:

- **Intra-area** Has destinations within the same area.
- **Interarea** Has destinations in other OSPF areas.
- **Autonomous system external (ASE)** Has destinations external to the autonomous system (AS). These are the routes calculated from Type 5 LSAs.
- **NSSA ASE router** Has destinations external to AS. These are the routes calculated from Type 7 LSAs.

Unlike RIP, which is a distance-vector protocol, OSPF is a link-state protocol, which means it transmits information about the state of its *links*, or connections. These transmissions, called *link-state advertisements* (*LSAs*), are used to determine the short path from one router to another. This determination is accomplished via an algorithm called the *shortest path first* (*SPF*) algorithm, for which OSPF is named.

NOTE

The *Open* in OSPF means that the source code used to write the protocol is freely accessible in the public domain.

OSPF routers routinely send LSAs to routers in the same area to provide information about state changes. Then, each router uses the LSAs it has received to generate a routing table based on the SPF algorithm. Due to the nature of OSPF, it is able to detect failed routers very quickly, which results in minimal network disruption in case of failure.

A key advantage of OSPF over RIP is a significantly reduced amount of network traffic required to keep routing tables up-to-date. This is the case because routing information within each area is restricted to that area; routers in other areas do not receive these updates. In addition, if there are more than two routers in an area, one router is elected the designated router (DR), while another is elected the backup designated router (BDR), and only the active designated router transmits LSAs. This is possible because all routers within an area contain the same routing table, so it is not necessary for all of them to be transmitting updates.

Understanding BGP

Border gateway protocol (*BGP*) is the most popular exterior gateway protocol (EGP) in use on the Internet today. As an EGP, BGP is used to transmit routing information between autonomous systems (ASs). This contrasts with RIP and OSPF, which are both generally used as IGPs and therefore only transmit routing information within an AS.

An AS is simply a collection of network devices that are controlled by one network administrator or group. There is a common network and routing policy in place in an AS, and it is has controlled ingress and egress points where traffic flows to and from other ASs in a controllable fashion. Unlike RIP or OSPF, BGP does not transmit routing updates at any scheduled interval. Instead, BGP routers only transmit routing information to other routers when their routing table has changed. Initially, when a BGP router starts up, an entire routing table is transmitted to it, and this routing table contains information on how to connect to literally every reachable network on the Internet. Then, the router receives incremental updates to this routing table as other BGP routers' tables are updated.

The metric used for BGP is not based on distance vector or link state. Instead, the metric is a number based on a variety of factors, such as speed, number of ASs traversed, stability, and other items. As a network administrator, you also have the ability to affect this metric through manual configuration of your router so you can fine-tune route preference.

Every BGP router has neighbors, which are simply other BGP routers that communicate with it. Communication sessions between neighbors can be *internal*, meaning the two routers are within the same AS, or *external*, meaning the two routers are in two different ASs.

WARNING

BGP routing on the Internet is not something that should be taken lightly. BGP routing affects many systems, and if possible the configuration should be verified with your peer before changes are applied to production systems.

Understanding Other Supported Protocols

Nokia supports many routing protocols, picking the right one for the right job is important. This is an overview of the other routing protocols.

IGRP

Interior Gateway Routing Protocol (IGRP) was developed by Cisco to overcome problems with RIP in large networks. IGRP is a distance vector protocol, but uses multiple routing metrics (not just hop count) to determine the distance to the destination. IGRP provides features designed to enhance stability such as hold-downs, split horizons and poison-reverse updates. IGRP should only be used if your current environment is all IGRP and you do not want to introduce another routing protocol into it.

IGMP

Internet Group Management Protocol (IGMP) is used to join Multicast sessions. When a multicast session is ongoing, members can join by sending IGMP messages to the router to participate in the multicast streams. IGMP v3 is defined in RFC 3376. If multicast traffic is being passed through your Nokia, enabling IGMP on the Nokia and downstream switches would allow efficient use of network bandwidth by allowing clients to subscribe and unsubscribe to multicasts.

PIM

Protocol Independent Multicast (PIM) is a family of routing protocols that assist many-to-many and many-to-one multicasting sessions. PIM is defined in RFC 4601 and RFC 3973. When combined with protocols like IGMP, PIM allows routers to communicate with one another to control multicast traffic.

DVMRP

Distance Vector Multicasting Routing Protocol (DVMRP) is used to synchronize routes to transport multicast packets. DVMRP is defined in RFC 1075. The protocol is based on RIP but is used to transmit multicast session information. DVMRP looks ahead to the next hop to see if it really is the shortest path and will prune out excess multicast branches if possible.

Understanding Routing Options

Use the Routing Options page to configure a variety of miscellaneous options that affect how routing behaves on the Nokia. The Routing options page allows the setting of the following global properties:

- **Maximum Path Splits** The default is the maximum value of 8. If you want the Nokia to allow less redundant paths for a destination, that can be set here.
- **Next Hop Selection Algorithm** This option determines when the Nokia should perform a routing lookup for a packet. The default selection is *source/destination hash* which allows the Nokia to keep the same route for each TCP *conversation* based on the source IP, source port, destination IP, and destination port. The entire conversation will use the same network path for the duration of the conversation. Other options are Source Hash where only the source IP and source port are used, destination hash, which only uses the destination IP, and destination port and round robin. Round robin is not recommended because it may cause packets to arrive at their destination out of order.
- **Protocol Rank** This allows the default priority of the routing protocols. By default, OSPF routes have a rank of 10, and RIP has a rank of 100 (from 1–255). The protocol with the lowest cost (rank + routing information) will determine the next hop for the specific destination.
- **Trace Options** By default, the Nokia will keep ten log files (/var/log/ipsrd.log) each 1MB in size to assist in troubleshooting. If more data is required, the maximum number of files or the size of each file can be increased to provide the correct amount of logging for your situation.

- **Protocol Specific Logging** When troubleshooting issues with a specific protocol, you can select from the drop-down menu to log specific parts of the protocol (such as OSPF's "Hello" packets), or you can enable logging for "All" parts of the routing protocol.

NOTE

Enabling logging on routing protocols options is suggested when performing dynamic routing troubleshooting and initial setup, and is disabled once normal operations have been tested.

These logs can be referred to for understanding what the Nokia logs as normal operations. This is key when troubleshooting errors that occur after initial testing is completed.

Configuring RIP

You can configure RIP versions 1 and 2 from the **Configuration** | **Routing** | **RIP** section of the Nokia Network Voyager. After initially configuring RIP, you may want to tune the RIP timers and route auto-summarization as it applies to your network. These configuration steps are discussed next.

Stepping through the Initial RIP Configuration

1. In the system tree, click **Configuration | Routing | RIP**.
2. Click **On** for each interface you wish RIP to be enabled for and then click **Apply**.
3. Click **1** or **2** in the **Version** field to select RIP 1 or RIP 2, respectively, for each interface. Then, click **Apply**.
4. (Optional) Enter a new cost in the **Metric** field for each interface, and then click **Apply**.
5. (Optional) To configure the interface to not accept updates, click the **On** radio button in the **Accept updates** field, and then click **Apply**.
6. (Optional) If you want to configure the interface to not send updates, click **On** in the **Send updates** field, and then click **Apply**.

NOTE

If you selected RIP 2 for an interface, make sure that *Multicast* is turned on for that interface.

7. (Optional) If you selected RIP 2 for an interface, select the type of authentication scheme to use from the **AuthType** drop-down list, and then click **Apply**. For simple authentication, select **Simple** from the **AuthType** drop-down window. Enter the password in the **Password** edit box, and then click **Apply**. For MD5 authentication, select **MD5** from the **AuthType** drop-down list. Enter the password in the **MD5 key** field, and then click **Apply**.

TIP

The password for the *Simple* AuthType must be from 1 to 16 characters long.

8. (Optional) If you selected MD5 as your authentication type and want to ensure interoperability with Cisco routers running RIP MD5 authentication, click **YES** in the **Cisco Interoperability** field. The default is no, which means that RIP MD5 is set to conform to Nokia platforms. Click **Apply**.
9. To enable RIP on the virtual IP address associated with this interface, click **On**, and then click **Apply**. This option functions only if this router is a VRRP master. You must also configure VRRP to accept connections to VRRP IPs.

NOTE

You must use Monitored Circuit mode when configuring virtual IP support. Do not use VRRPv2 when configuring virtual IP support.

10. To make your changes permanent, click **Save**.

Figure 7.1 shows the RIP configuration section within Nokia Network Voyager.

Figure 7.1 The RIP Configuration Page

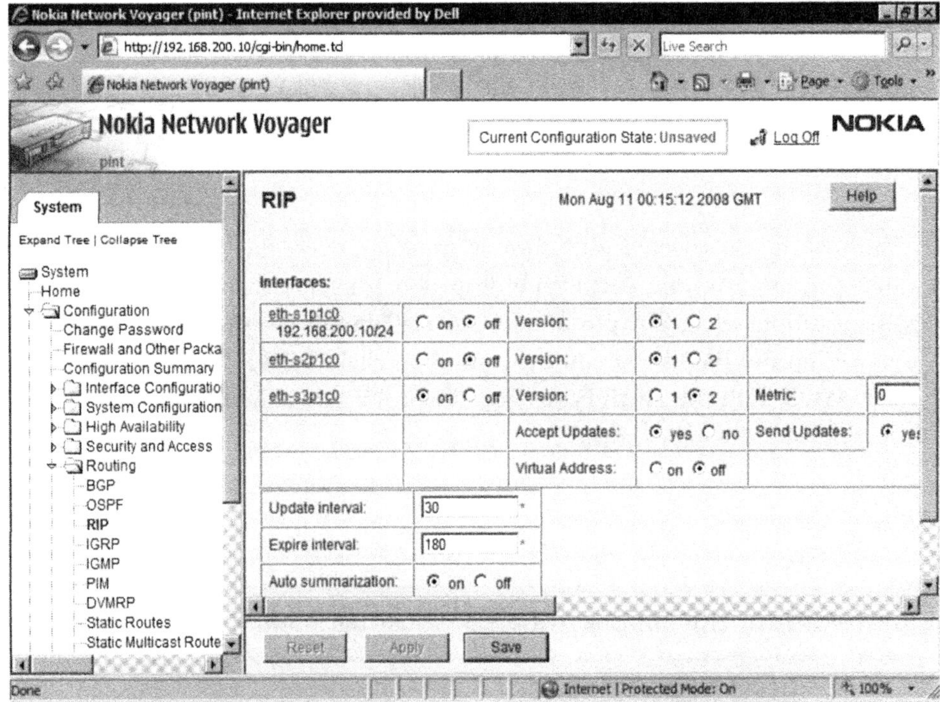

Configuring RIP Timers

Configuring RIP timers lets you vary the frequency with which updates are sent and when routes are expired. To configure RIP timers:

1. In the system tree, click **Configuration | Routing | RIP**.
2. To modify the update interval, enter the new update interval in the **Update Interval** field, and then click **Apply**.
3. To modify the expire interval, enter the new expire interval in the **Expire Interval** field, and then click **Apply**.
4. To make your changes permanent, click **Save**.

NOTE

By default, the update interval is set to 30 seconds, and the expire interval is set to 180 seconds.

Configuring Auto-Summarization

If using RIP version 1, auto-summarization lets you aggregate and redistribute non-classful routes. You can enable or disable auto-summarization from the **Configuration | Routing | RIP** menu using the **On** or **Off** radio buttons in the **Auto-Summarization** field.

Configuring OSPF

At first glance, one might think that configuring a dynamic routing protocol like OSPF need be a complicated process. Using the Nokia Network Voyager, however, makes this a relatively easy task to accomplish. You need follow only three steps to configure OSPF on your Nokia appliance:

1. Specify a router ID.
2. Define the OSPF areas and global settings.
3. Configure each interface that participates in OSPF.

Additionally, depending on your OSPF environment, virtual links may need to be configured. All of these configurations are detailed in the following sections.

Stepping through the Initial OSPF Configuration

1. In the system tree, click **Configuration | Routing | OSPF**.
2. Enter the router ID in the **Router ID** field.

NOTE

Although you do not need to use an IP address as the router ID, you must enter a dotted quad value ([0–255].[0–255].[0–255].[0–255]. Do not use 0.0.0.0 as a router ID.

3. If you want to define additional OSPF areas besides the backbone area:
    1. Enter each name in the **Add New OSPF Area** field and click **Apply**.
    2. Select an **Area Type**: **Normal**, **Stub**, or **NSSA**.

3. If you select a stub area type, configure the additional parameters that appear, as described in Table 7.1.
4. If you select a NSSA area type, configure the additional parameters that appear, as described in Table 7.2.

Table 7.1 Stub Area Parameters

Parameter	Description
Cost for Default Route	Enter a cost for the default route to the stub area. Range: *1–16777215*.
Import Summary Routes	Specifies if summary routes (summary link advertisements) are imported into the stub area or NSSA. Default: *On*.

Table 7.2 NSSA (Not So Stubby Area) Parameters

Parameter	Description
Translator Role	Specifies whether this NSSA border router will unconditionally translate Type-7 LSAs into Type-5 LSAs. When role is **Always**, Type-7 LSAs are translated into Type-5 LSAs regardless of the translator state of other NSSA border routers. When role is **Candidate**, this router participates in the translator election to determine if it will perform the translations duties. If this NSSA router is not a border router, then this option has no effect. Default: *Candidate*.
Translator Stability Interval	Specifies how long in seconds this elected Type-7 translator will continue to perform its translator duties once it has determined that its translator status has been assumed by another NSSA border router. This field appears only if an area is defined as an NSSA with translator role as Candidate. Default: *40* seconds.

Continued

Table 7.2 Continued. NSSA (Not So Stubby Area) Parameters

Parameter	Description
Import Summary Routes	Specifies if summary routes (summary link advertisements) are imported into the stub area or NSSA. Default: *On*.
Cost for Default Route	Enter a cost associated with the default route to the NSSA.
Default Route Type	Specifies the route type associated with the Type-7 default route for an NSSA when routes from other protocols are redistributed into OSPF as ASEs. If a redistributed route already has a route type, this type is maintained. If summary routes are imported into an NSSA, only then is a Type-7 default route generated (otherwise, a Type-3 default route is created). This field appears only if an area is defined as an NSSA into which summary routes are imported. The route type can be either 1 or 2. A type 1 route is internal and its metric can be used directly by OSPF for comparison. A type 2 route is external and its metric cannot be used for comparison directly. Default: *1*.
Redistribution	Specifies if both Type-5 and Type-7 LSAs or only Type-7 LSAs will be originated by this router. This option will have an effect only if this router is an NSSA border router and this router is an AS border router. Default: *On*.
Type 7 Address Ranges	An NSSA border router that performs translation duties translates Type-7 LSAs to Type-5 LSAs. An NSSA border router can be configured with Type- 7 address ranges. Use these ranges to reduce the number of Type-5 LSAs. Many separate Type-7 networks may fall into a single Type-7 address range. These Type-7 networks are aggregated, and a single Type-5 LSA is advertised. By definition, a Type-7 address range consists of a prefix and a mask length.

4. (Optional) For each area, you can add one or more address ranges if you want to reduce the number of routing entries that the area advertises into the backbone.
5. Configure virtual links for any area that does not connect directly to the backbone area, as described in the "Configuring Virtual Links" section.
6. Configure the OSPF interfaces, as described in the "Configuring OSPF Interfaces" section.

Figure 7.2 shows the OSPF configuration section within Nokia Network Voyager.

Figure 7.2 The OSPF Configuration Page

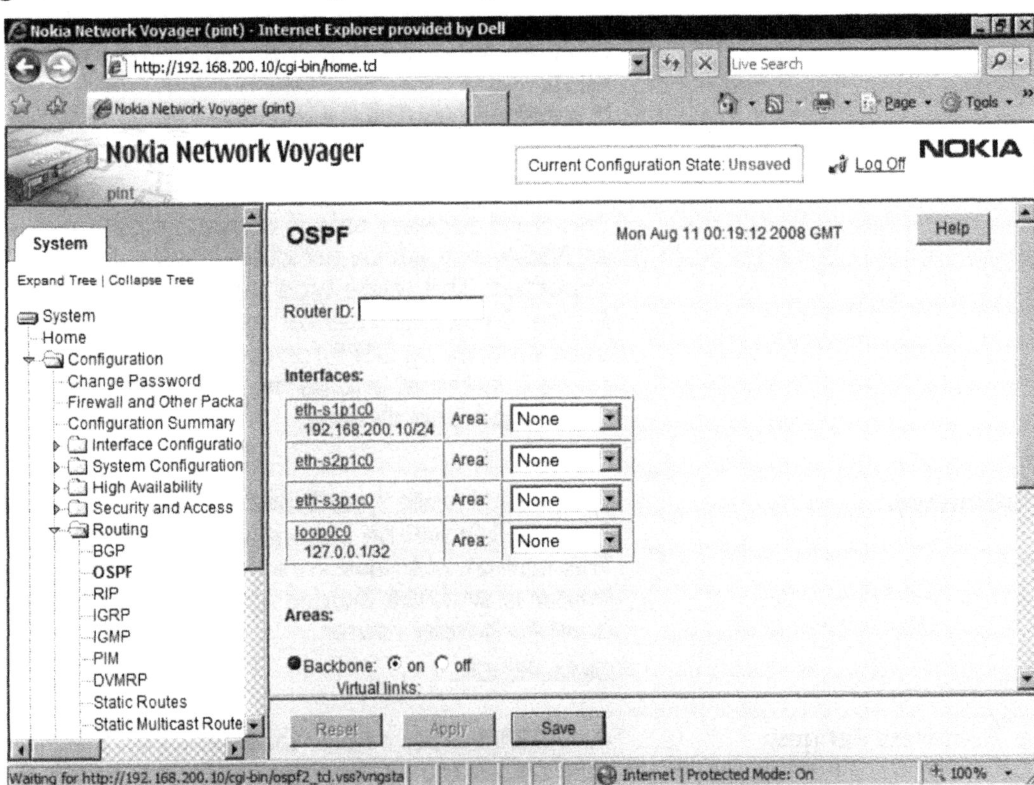

Configuring Virtual Links

As mentioned in step 5 of the "Stepping through the Initial OSPF Configuration" section, you must configure a virtual link for any area that does not connect directly to the backbone area. You configure the virtual link on both the ABR for the discontiguous area and another ABR that connects to the backbone. The virtual link acts like a point-to-point link.

NOTE

The routing protocol traffic that flows along the virtual link uses intra-area routing only.

1. Create an area that does not connect directly to the backbone area, and configure an interface to be in that area.
2. In the **Add A New Virtual Link** field, enter the router ID of the remote endpoint of the virtual link.
3. Select the transit area from the drop-down box. This is the area that connects both to the backbone and to the discontiguous area. Additional fields will appear.
4. Configure the following parameters for the virtual link:
    1. **Hello interval** Length of time, in seconds, between hello packets that the router sends on the interface. For a given link, this field must be the same on all routers, otherwise adjacencies do not form. The default *hello interval* value is 30 seconds.
    2. **Dead interval** Number of seconds after the router stops receiving hello packets that it declares the neighbor is down. For a given link, this value must be the same on all routers, or adjacencies do not form. The value must not be zero and must fall within the range of 1–65535. The default *dead interval* value is 120 seconds.

TIP

Typically, the value of this field should be four times that of the hello interval.

3. **Retransmit interval** Specifies the number of seconds between LSA retransmissions for adjacencies belonging to this interface. This value is also used when retransmitting database description and link state request packets. Set this value well above the expected round-trip delay between any two routers on the attached network. Be conservative when setting this value to prevent unnecessary retransmissions. Range: 1–65535 in number of seconds. The default *retransmit interval* value is five seconds.

4. **Auth Type** Type of authentication scheme to use for a given link. In general, routers on a given link must agree on the authentication configuration to form neighbor adjacencies. This feature guarantees that routing information is accepted only from trusted routers. The available options are *None*, *Simple*, and *MD5*. The default *auth type* value is *None*.

5. If you selected MD5 for the auth type, you must also configure the following parameters:

    1. **Add MD5 Key** If the Auth type selected is *MD5*, the *Key ID* and *MD5 Secret* fields appear. Specify the Key ID and its corresponding MD5 secret to configure a new MD5 key.

NOTE

If you configure multiple Key IDs, the Key ID with the highest value is used to authenticate outgoing packets. All keys can be used to authenticate incoming packets.

    2. **Key ID** The *Key ID* is included in the outgoing OSPF packets to enable the receivers to use the appropriate MD5 secret to authenticate the packet. The available *Key ID* range is 0–255.
    3. **MD5 Secret** The MD5 secret is included in encrypted form in outgoing packets to authenticate the packet.

6. Click **Apply**.
7. To make your changes permanent, click **Save**.

NOTE

Repeat this procedure on both the ABR for the discontiguous area and an ABR that connects to the backbone area.

Configuring OSPF Interfaces

Now that the virtual links are correctly defined, you must configure your OSPF interfaces. To configure an OSPF interface:

1. Assign the appropriate area to each interface by selecting the OSPF area that this interface participates in from the Area list for the interface, and then click **Apply**.

NOTE

The OSPF interface configuration parameters are displayed showing the default settings. If you want to accept the default settings for the interface, no further action is necessary.

2. (Optional) Change any configuration parameters for the interface, described in Table 7.3, and then click **Apply**.
3. To make your changes permanent, click **Save**.

Table 7.3 Configuration Parameters for OSPF Interfaces

Parameter	Description
Area	The drop-down list displays all of the areas configured and enabled on your platform. An entry for the backbone area is displayed even if it is disabled. An OSPF area defines a group of routers running OSPF that have the complete topology information of the given area. OSPF areas use an area border router (ABR) to exchange information about routes. Routes for a given area are summarized into the backbone area for distribution into other non-backbone areas. An ABR must have at least two interfaces in at least two different areas.
Hello interval	Specifies the length of time in seconds between hello packets that the router sends on this interface. For a given link, this value must be the same on all routers, or adjacencies do not form. Range: *1–65535* in seconds. Default: For broadcast interfaces, the default hello interval is *10* seconds. For point-to-point interfaces, the default hello interval is *30* seconds.

Continued

Table 7.3 Continued. Configuration Parameters for OSPF Interfaces

Parameter	Description
Dead interval	Specifies the number of seconds after the router stops receiving hello packets that it declares the neighbor is down. Typically, this value should be four times the hello interval. For a given link, this value must be the same on all routers, or adjacencies do not form. The value must not be 0. Range: *1–65535* in seconds. Default: For broadcast interfaces, the default dead interval is *40* seconds. For point-to-point interfaces, the default dead interval is *120* seconds.
Retransmit interval	Specifies the number of seconds between LSA retransmissions for this interface. This value is also used when retransmitting database description and link state request packets. Set this value well above the expected round-trip delay between any two routers on the attached network. Be conservative when setting this value to prevent necessary retransmissions. Range: *1–65535* in seconds. Default: *5* seconds.
OSPF cost	Specifies the weight of a given path in a route. The higher the cost you configure, the less preferred the link as an OSPF route. For example, you can assign different relative costs to two interfaces to make one more preferred as a routing path. You can explicitly override this value in route redistribution. Range: *1–65535*. Default: *1* second.
Election priority	Specifies the priority for becoming the designated router (DR) on this link. When two routers attached to a network both attempt to become a designated router, the one with the highest priority wins. If there is a current DR on the link, it remains the DR regardless of the configured priority. This feature prevents the DR from changing too often and applies only to a shared-media interface, such as Ethernet or FDDI. A DR is not elected on point-to-point type interfaces. A router with priority 0 is not eligible to become the DR. Range: *0–255*. Default: *1* second.

Continued

Table 7.3 Continued. Configuration Parameters for OSPF Interface

Parameter	Description
Passive mode	Specifies that the interface does not send hello packets, which means that the link does not form any adjacencies. This mode enables the network associated with the interface to be included in the intra-area route calculation rather than redistributing the network into OSPF and having it as an ASE. In passive mode, all interface configuration information, with the exception of the associated area and the cost, is ignored. Options are *On* or *Off*. Default: *Off*.
Virtual address	Makes OSPF run only on the VRRP Virtual IP address associated with this interface. If this router is not a VRRP master, then OSPF will not run if this option is *On*. It will only run on the VRRP master. You must also configure VRRP to accept connections to VRRP IPs.
Authorization type	Specifies which type of authentication scheme to use for a given link. Options are *Null*, *Simple*, and *MD5*.

Figure 7.3 shows the OSPF interface configuration section within Nokia Network Voyager.

Figure 7.3 The OSPF Interface Configuration Page

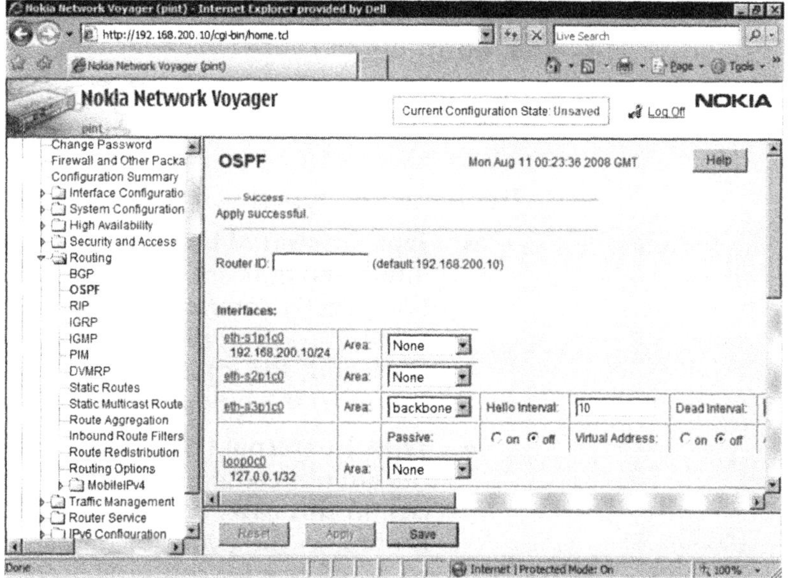

Configuring Global Settings

Your Nokia appliance also contains some global settings specific to the way OSPF operates. In the system tree, click **Configuration | Routing | OSPF** and then scroll down to see the global settings. These settings are detailed in Table 7.4.

Table 7.4 Global Settings for OSPF

Parameter	Description
RFC1583 Compatibility	The Nokia implementation of OSPF is based on RFC2178. If your implementation is running in an environment with OSPF implementations based on RFC1583 or earlier, enable RFC 1583 compatibility to ensure backwards compatibility.
SPF Delay	Specifies the time in seconds the system will wait to recalculate the OSPF routing table after a change in topology. Range: *1–60* seconds. Default: 2 seconds.
SPF Hold	Specifies the minimum time in seconds between recalculations of the OSPF routing table. Range: *1–60* seconds. Default: *5* seconds.
Default ASE Route Cost	Specifies a cost for routes redistributed into OSPF as ASEs. Any cost previously assigned to a redistributed route overrides this value.
Default ASE Route Type	Specifies a route type for routes redistributed into OSPF as ASEs, unless these routes already have a type assigned. There are two types: ▪ **Type 1 external** Used for routes imported into OSPF that are from IGPs whose metrics are directly comparable to OSPF metrics. When a routing decision is being made, OSPF adds the internal cost to the AS border router to the external metric. ▪ **Type 2 external** Used for routes whose metrics are not comparable to OSPF internal metrics. In this case, only the external OSPF cost is used. In the event of ties, the least cost to an AS border router is used.

Figure 7.4 shows the OSPF global settings section within Nokia Network Voyager.

Figure 7.4 OSPF Global Settings

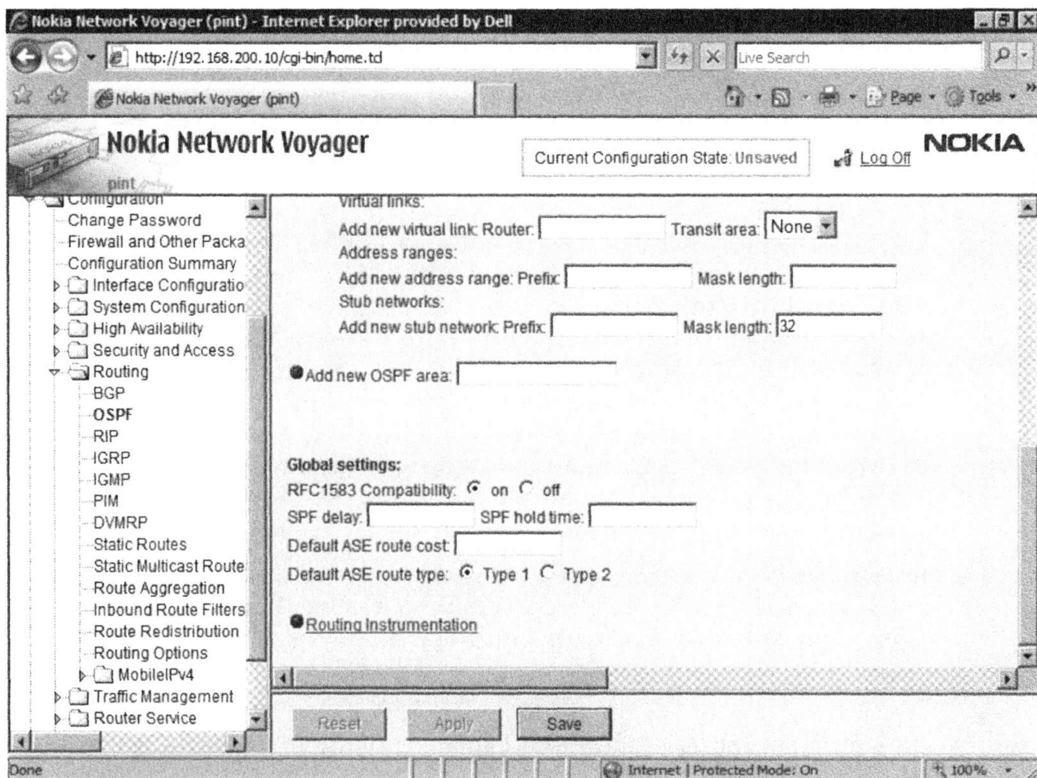

Notes from the Underground...

How Do I Exchange Routes between RIP and OSPF?

When a Nokia appliance needs to communicate with different routers via different routing protocols, a network administrator may need to "Redistribute" routes learned via one routing protocol into the routes advertised by the other routing protocol. The procedure is documented in the online documentation, but we will outline the steps and some of the issues that customers have experienced.

Continued

The following example describes redistributing routes between the OSPF and RIP protocols. It assumes that RIP and OSPF are configured properly and that the Nokia device is exchanging routing information with neighboring routers.

1. In the system tree, click **Configuration | Routing | Route Redistribution**.
2. Under the heading **Redistribute To OSPF External**, select **RIP**.
3. Set **All RIP Routes Into OSPF External** to **Accept**, and then click **Apply**.

Let's take a break here since there are two concerns related to this configuration:

- The Metric field will set the base OSPF Cost for the routes redistributed into OSPF domain. An in-depth discussion of OSPF Cost is outside the scope of this sidebar, but the value set in the Metric field will need to be coordinated with the configuration of other routers in the OSPF domain in order to assure that traffic flows through the network according to the network design. The network administrator should also remember that these redistributed routes will be handled as *OSPF External* routes, not as *native* OSPF routes. When designing the network topology and routing, it is therefore important to consider for each router in the design the effects of intra-protocol metric calculations as well as inter-protocol interactions guided by each router's *Protocol Rank*, or similar, configuration.
- An administrator can configure a complex policy for the redistribution of routes learned via RIP into the OSPF routing domain. Individual prefixes can be handled differently with a different metric value for each.

Now, back to the configuration steps:

4. On a different router in the OSPF domain, verify that the Nokia device is advertising the routes learned via RIP.
5. In the system tree, click **Configuration | Routing | Route Redistribution**.
6. Under the heading **Redistribute To RIP** select **OSPF**.
7. Set **All OSPF Routes Into RIP** to **Accept** and then click **Apply**.
8. On a different router in the RIP domain, verify that the Nokia device is advertising the routes learned via OSPF.

Some of the routes learned through OSPF may be marked by the protocol as *OSPF External* routes. Such routes would not be redistributed into RIP with the preceding procedure. To redistribute OSPF External routes into the RIP domain, select **OSPF External** under the **Redistribute To RIP** heading. OSPF External redistribution is configured the same way as OSPF redistribution.

Continued

Also, consider the scenario where two high-availability Nokia appliances are learning *OSPF External* routes from an external OSPF domain and are both redistributing the information into an internal RIP domain. One of the Nokia devices will begin advertising routes first. By default, the *Protocol Rank* of RIP is lower to the *Protocol Rank* of OSPF External. This means that the second router will prefer the route learned via RIP from the first router rather than the actually closer route learned via OSPF. To correct this problem, set the *Protocol Rank* of OSPF External routes to a value lower than the rank of RIP routes.

Configuring BGP

Before you can configure BGP on a Nokia device, you must purchase a BGP license that lets you use this functionality. To install the license, open and log in to your Nokia Network Voyager interface. Click **Configuration | System Configuration | Licenses** and you will see a list of features that require licensing, including BGP.

Enter the license key you obtained from Nokia under **BGP**, click **Apply**, and then **Save**. Then return to the main Configuration screen, and you will notice that under Routing Configuration, BGP now appears.

Click **BGP**, and you will see the main BGP configuration screen, as shown in Figure 7.5.

Figure 7.5 The BGP Configuration Page

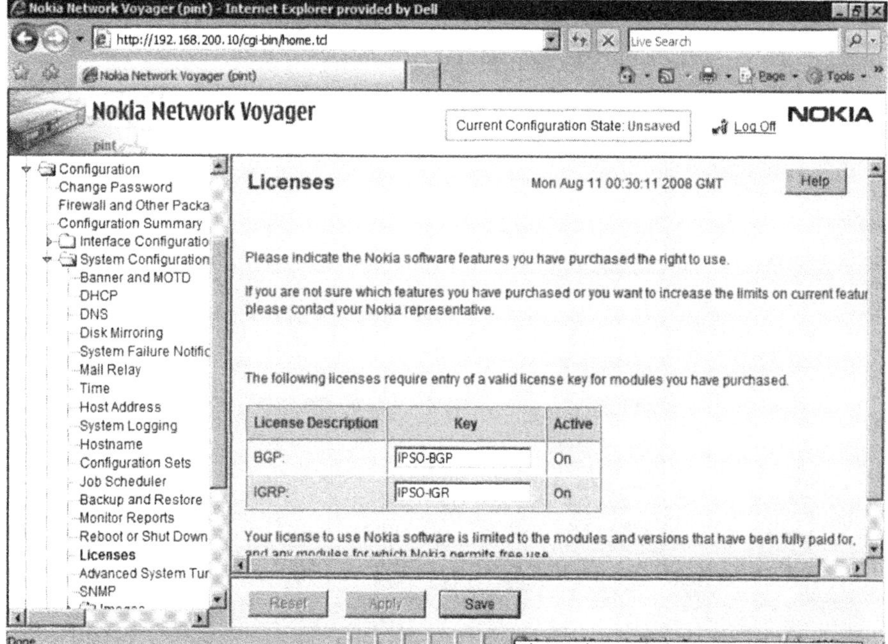

Here, set the Router ID to a valid IP address you have configured on your Nokia. This can be an address from any interface. Even better, you can configure a loopback interface via the Interface Configuration section (do not use 127.0.0.1—you will need to add another IP to the loopback interface that is routed to the Nokia), and use this loopback address as the router ID. The advantage to this approach is that even if one interface goes down, as long as the Nokia is still reachable via another interface, the loopback address should still respond.

Next, set the Local Autonomous System to a valid AS number. To obtain an AS number, you can apply to an AS authority such as ARIN, or you have the option of using a private AS number. Private AS numbers, like private IP blocks, are reserved for internal use, so there is no risk of AS number conflict. Using a private AS assumes your service provider, with which you will establish a BGP session, has a public AS, which is what will actually be used to distribute your routes to the rest of the Internet.

We will look at the advanced BGP options later, but first let's skip to the peer settings. Set the peer autonomous system number to the AS number of the BGP router with which you are peering or establishing a session. For peer group type, select **Internal** if the peer is within the same AS as your Nokia, or select **External** otherwise. The Description field is a convenient place for you to enter a brief description of this peer.

Now let's go back and click **Advanced BGP Options**, which will bring you to the screen shown in Figure 7.6.

Figure 7.6 The Advanced BGP Options Page

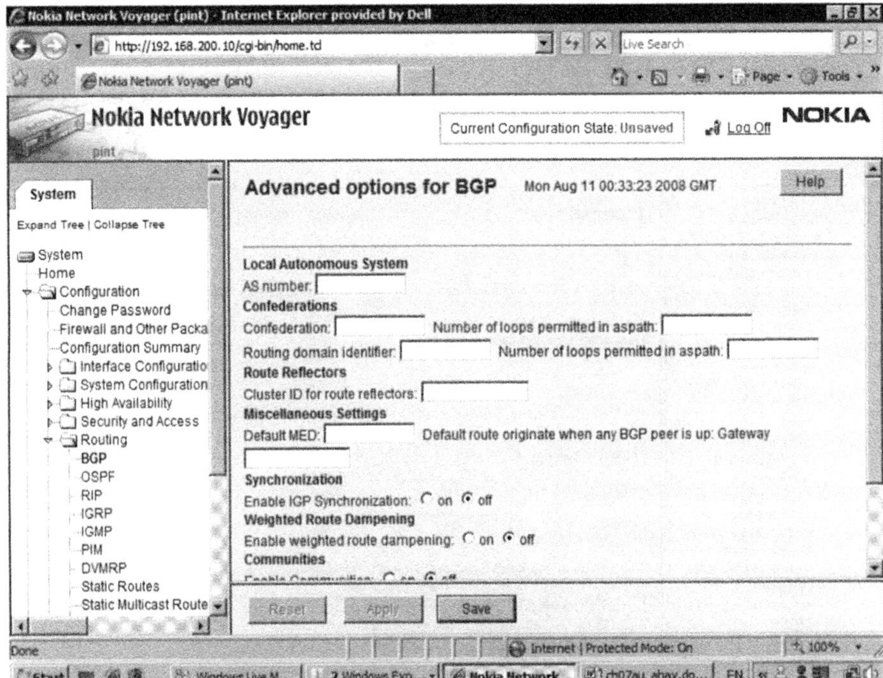

Here, you have the option to set up a number of interesting BGP features. Notice that you again have the option of setting your local autonomous system number. This field will already be populated if you entered and applied this information on the previous screen. Note that if you are using confederations, you should not set the AS number here.

Next is the Confederations section. A *BGP confederation* is a method of reducing the need to have all routers within an AS connected to each other. That is, normally in order for BGP to function, all routers within an AS must connect to all other routers—this is referred to as a *fully meshed configuration*. With a confederation, routers within an AS are subdivided into additional ASs, and then all these sub-ASs are assigned to one confederation. All routers within a sub-AS are fully meshed, and each sub-AS has a connection to each sub-AS. Confederations are not visible to outside ASs—they are an internal function.

To configure a confederation, first enter the confederation ID, which should be your AS number as it appears to your BGP peers. *Number Of Loops Permitted In Aspath* is simply a method of avoiding routing loops—if the local AS number appears more than the specified number of times, the route in question is discarded. *Routing Domain Identifier* is the internal AS number that will be used within the confederation. Be sure this is different from the confederation ID set earlier. Finally, the *Number Of Loops Permitted In Aspath* option is, again, a method of avoiding routing loops, but this time it relates to the confederation ID.

Next is the Route Reflectors section. A BGP route reflector is simply a BGP router that sends routes it learns from one internal BGP router to another internal BGP router—it reflects routes from one to the other. This further reduces the need for fully meshed routers within an AS. The *Cluster ID For Route Reflectors* option is normally set to the router ID, unless you have a specific reason to set it otherwise.

Under Miscellaneous settings, the default MED is the default metric to be used for routes that will be transmitted to other BGP routers. The *Gateway* option adds the specified default route to the routing table when the Nokia is connected to at least one other BGP router.

Weighted Route Dampening instructs the Nokia to ignore route updates and not transmit route updates for routes that constantly move from being reachable to unreachable. Such a route is said to be *flapping*.

The *Communities* option, when turned on, allows you to configure options in groups rather than per individual peer.

Next, we will look at the options available when you add an internal and external peer. Enter a peer autonomous system number, select **External** for peer group type, and click **Apply**. The peer group options appear, as shown in Figure 7.7.

Figure 7.7 The External BGP Group

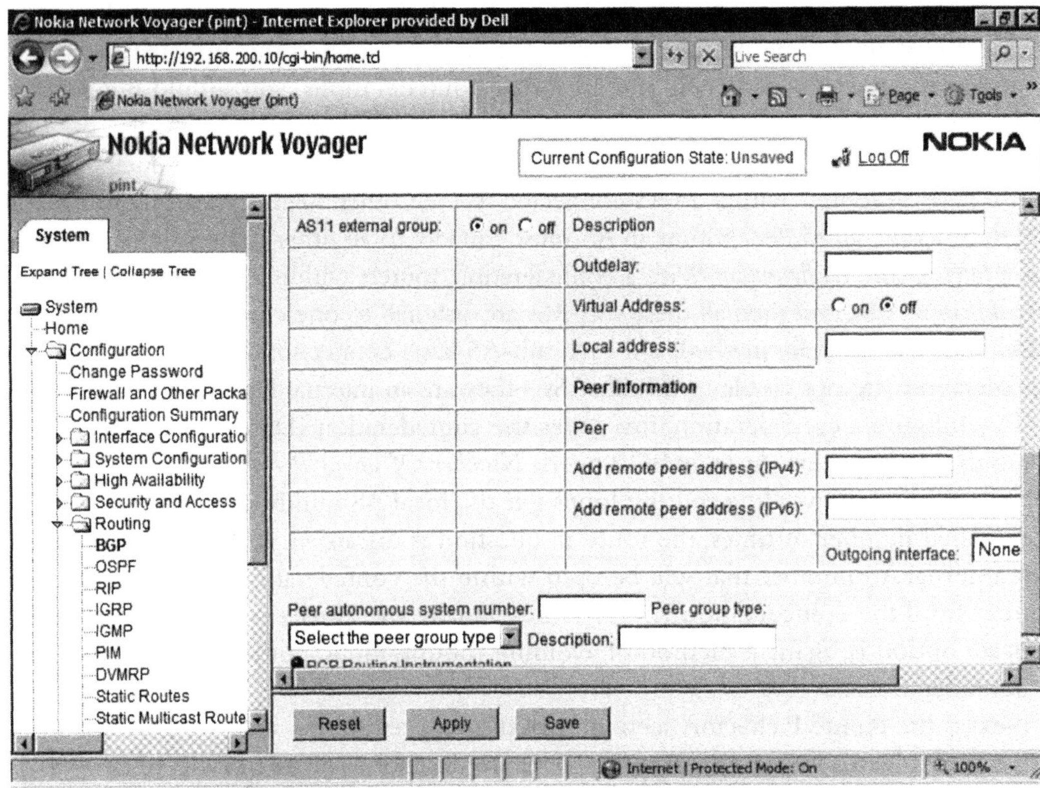

Here, *Outdelay* is the number of seconds a route must remain in the routing table before your BGP router distributes it to its peers. Setting this option to a number higher than 0 is an effective way to prevent flapping routes from being redistributed to other routers.

Local Address is an IP address on your Nokia that is on the same interface that connects to this peer. *Peer IP Prefix To Allow* is how you control what BGP routers within the remote AS can connect to your Nokia. For example, if you set the mask length here to 24, all routers within the subnet you specified will be allowed to establish BGP sessions.

You can also configure peers individually by adding them under *Add Remote Peer IP Address*. Once you do this and click **Apply**, you will see the peer listed, along with its state, and have The ability to turn it off. Click the IP address of the peer, and you will see the peer configuration screen, as shown in Figure 7.8.

Figure 7.8 Peer Options

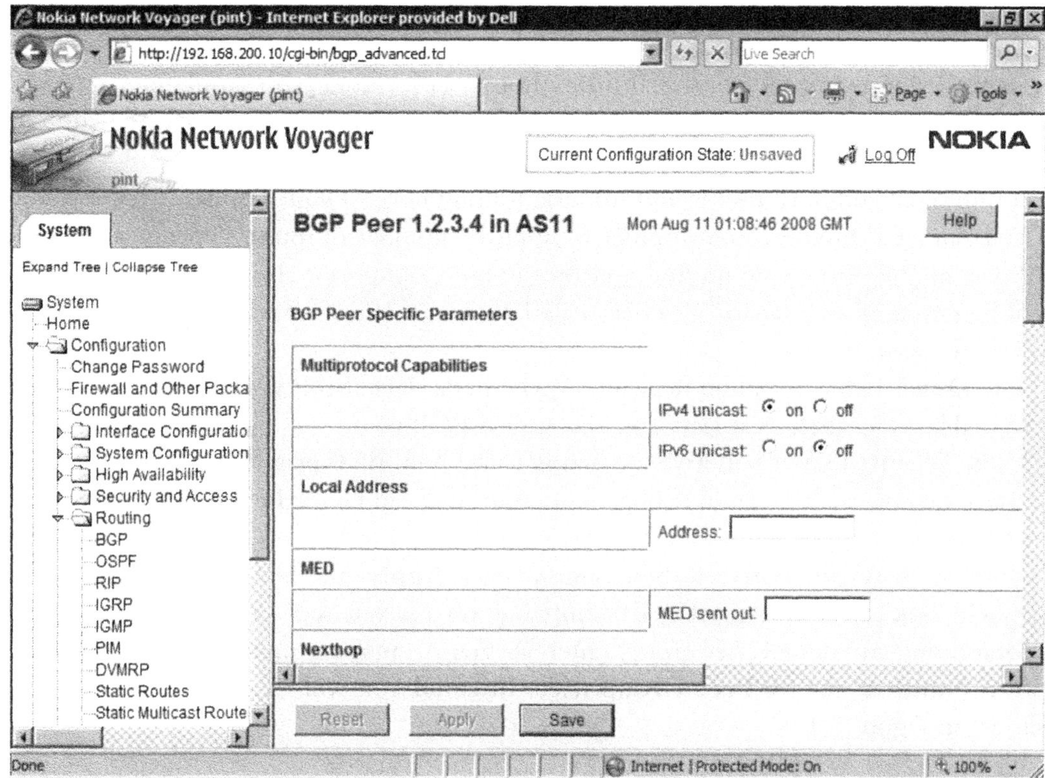

Here, *MED Sent Out* is the metric to be set for all routes sent to this peer. *Accept MED from external peer* determines whether your BGP router will accept metric settings from this peer. *EBPG Multihop* is an option that allows you to establish a peering session with a BGP router that is not directly connected to an interface on your Nokia. *No Aggregator ID* is an option used to prevent aggregate routes with different AS paths.

There are two timers you can configure: Holdtime, which specifies the number of seconds that can elapse with no activity over a BGP session before it is closed; and Keepalive, which sends a keepalive message to BGP peers at the interval you specify, and closes the connection if no response is received.

Ignore First AS Hop instructs the Nokia to discard the first AS number on routes it receives from this peer. This option is not normally used, but it can be useful in cases when your BGP peer is a router that you want to be transparent. *Do Keepalives Always* instructs the Nokia to always send keepalives, even if not required. This option is primarily included for compatibility with devices that always expect keepalives.

In the Routes section, you can set the Nokia to either accept all or none of the incoming routes from this peer by default. Your local routing policy can then further determine what to do with incoming routes.

Setting the Passive option to On causes the Nokia to never try to initiate a BGP session with this peer. In this case, it simply waits for the peer to initiate a BGP session.

AuthType can be set to MD5 in order to enable authentication with this peer, which is recommended if security is an issue. If this option is set to None, you should be confident of the security of network between your Nokia and the BGP peer you will be connecting to. If this network is not secure, someone could maliciously "break in" to your BGP session and inject unwanted and disruptive routes into the routing table of your Nokia.

You can set a throttle count in order to limit the number of routing updates sent to this BGP peer at one time. Since routing updates can use a significant amount of bandwidth, it might be necessary to limit the number of updates sent at once, especially if you have a large number of peers.

The *Default Originate* option determines whether a default route will be added to the routing table when there is at least one operational BGP peer.

In the Logging section, you have the option to log both BGP peer transitions and warnings. The Trace options enable various debugging outputs that can be used to troubleshoot a BGP connection.

After you have configured all these options, click **Apply** and then return to the previous screen. Go back to the Advanced BGP Configuration and you will see the options available for configuring an internal peer group. Enter another AS number under **Peer Autonomous System Number**, and for **Peer Group** select **Internal**. You will see a variety of options, as shown in Figure 7.9.

Figure 7.9 Internal Peer Group Options

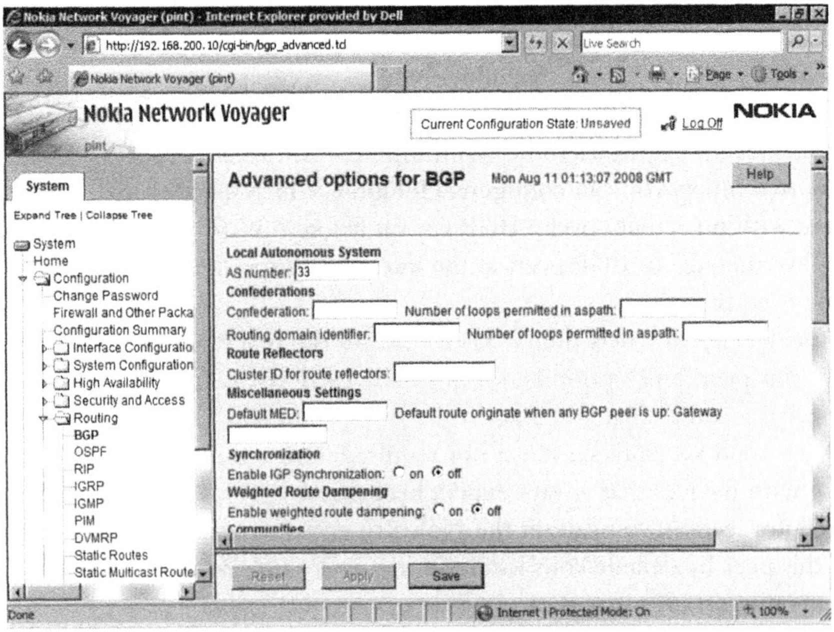

Here you can set the protocols that will be redistributed into BGP, including IGP protocols, BGP, directly learned routes, RIP, static route entries, OSPF, and OSPF ase-type routes. This lets you control exactly how your various routing protocols and manual routes interact.

Next, you can set which interfaces are to be used for this peer group. Restricting the group to only the interfaces on which the BGP peers will connect is recommended and is also a good security precaution.

You can also set the MED, or metric, that is used for routes sent to this peer; the outdelay, the local address; and the allowed peer lists, just as with an external peer. A unique option for internal peers is *Nexthopself*, which transmits the Nokia's own IP address to peers as the gateway to be installed in the routing tables of the peers.

Now that we have gone through all the options available when configuring the Nokia as a BGP router, you can click **Apply** and then **Save**, and you are ready to establish BGP sessions with other routers.

Notes from the Underground...

What Is a BGP Identifier?

The BGP Identifier is a four-octet unsigned, non-zero integer that should be unique within an AS. The value of the BGP Identifier for a BGP speaker is determined on startup and is the same for every local interface and every BGP peer.

If the BGP Identifier field of the OPEN message is zero, or if it is the same as the BGP Identifier of the local BGP speaker, and the message is from an internal peer, then the Error Subcode is set to *Bad BGP Identifier*.

In addition to the OPEN message, the BGP Identifier is currently also used in the following areas:

- In the AGGREGATOR attribute of a route where the combination of a BGP Identifier and an AS number uniquely identifies the BGP speaker that performs the route aggregation.
- In the Route Reflection (in lieu of the Cluster-id) within an AS, where only the BGP Identifier of an internal neighbor may be propagated in the route reflection related attributes.
- In the route selection, where the BGP Identifier is not used in comparing a route from an internal neighbor and a route from an external neighbor. In addition, routes from BGP speakers with identical BGP Identifiers have been dealt with (for example, parallel BGP sessions between two BGP speakers).

Summary

Many organizations have simply not taken the opportunity to implement dynamic routing within their environment. They claim that dynamic routing protocols are insecure by default, or they simply do not have the understanding for such an implementation. In many cases, there is no need to enable dynamic routing on your firewall, but if the need arises, the Nokia IPSO operating system happens to support quite a few of them, including RIP, OSPF, and BGP.

Routing Information Protocol (RIP) is an interior gateway protocol that utilizes distance vectors to calculate the most effective path to a destination. RIPv2 is recommended over RIPv1, unless your environment needs to support legacy equipment that simply does not support RIPv2. RIP is relatively simple to configure and implement in any network, but time and understanding of the protocol is essential to a successful deployment.

Open shortest path first (OSPF) is another interior gateway protocol that utilizes link state to determine the best path to a destination. OSPF is by far the most popular dynamic routing protocol that overcomes many of the limitations of RIP, such as the ability to support variable length subnet masking. The deployment of OSPF should not be taken lightly since a simple configuration issue can cause serious issues.

Unlike RIP and OSPF, border gateway protocol (BGP) is an exterior gateway protocol that uses a patch vector protocol to calculate the best path to the destination. Many are not aware of this, but BGP is the core protocol of the Internet. This should give you a better understanding of the overall effectiveness of this protocol.

Solutions Fast Track

Introducing Dynamic Routing

☑ RIP, which stands for routing information protocol, is a commonly used interior gateway protocol (IGP).

☑ IGPs, as opposed to exterior gateway protocols (EGPs), distribute routing information within one autonomous system, such as your LAN.

☑ OSPF works on the basis of dividing your network into areas. An *area* consists of network nodes and routers that can logically be grouped together.

☑ *Border gateway protocol* (*BGP*) is the most popular exterior gateway protocol (EGP) in use on the Internet today.

Configuring RIP

☑ Enable RIP on the interfaces that will participate in RIP routing.

☑ Use RIPv2. RIPv1 should only be used in conjunction with legacy systems.

☑ Choose to accept RIP updates from other routing equipment on the network.

☑ Set RIP updates via multicast or broadcast. Multicast is the default.

☑ Set RIP authentication if required.

Configuring OSPF

☑ Identify the Nokia by assigning an OSPF router ID to the device.

☑ Assign an interface to the backbone.

☑ Verify that the hello interval, dead interval, and retransmit interval are consistent with policy.

☑ Although not required, it's recommended to set authentication. Enter a passphrase.

Configuring BGP

☑ Identify the Nokia by assigning a Router ID to the device.

☑ Assign the local autonomous system.

☑ Assign a peer IP and whether or not the peer is internal or external.

☑ Configure BGP inbound route filters to accept traffic from BGP neighbors.

Frequently Asked Questions

Q: Do I need a dynamic routing protocol?

A: Dynamic routing protocols are only required when your routing table needs automatic updating based on a number of particular factors. If your routing table always remains the same, you might not need a dynamic routing protocol and can use static routes to direct traffic.

Q: Should I use RIP, OSPF, or BGP on my network?

A: Each has its advantages. RIP is very simple to set up because it does not require much configuration. If your network has a relatively small number of nodes, RIP is a good choice. With a larger number of network nodes, RIP might use up too much bandwidth, and so OSPF is a better choice since you can divide your network into areas and enjoy faster convergence. BGP is used as an external gateway protocol, so you would not usually use it within your local network, although that is also an option in some cases.

Q: With BGP, should I set up my routers in a fully meshed configuration or use confederations or route reflectors?

A: If your network is small enough, the simplest option is to fully mesh. However, as your network grows, you might find it more difficult to do this, so you can move to a confederation or route reflector setup. Confederations are best suited to networks that are easily subdivided into subgroups, whereas route reflectors are more suited to a network that is in a tree type of formation.

Q: Should I use RIP v1 or RIP v2?

A: If all devices on your network that are going to take part in RIP support RIP v2, that is the version you will want to use. The main advantage to RIP v2 over v1 is that v2 transmits subnet mask information with each update, so you are able to advertise networks of varying size.

Q: If I am using OSPF, how many devices should be in each area?

A: There is no set limit or rule as to how many devices should be in each OSPF area. However, it is best to keep areas relatively small to cut down on unnecessary LSA communication between devices, which conserves bandwidth. More than 100 routers in an area are probably too many, and even that number could be a high limit in many cases, especially if bandwidth is at a premium.

We fully acknowledge use of Chapter 09, *"Advanced Routing Configuration," from Nokia Network Security Solutions Handbook, 978-1-931836-70-8*

Chapter 8

Configuring the Check Point NGX Firewall

Solutions in this chapter:

- Preparing for the Firewall Implementation
- Configuring the Check Point NGX Firewall
- Testing the Firewall Configuration
- Upgrading the Firewall

☑ Summary

☑ Solutions Fast Track

☑ Frequently Asked Questions

Introduction

"Now that we have the underlying platform configured, let's dive into the Check Point software portion of the firewall!" exclaimed Shin. "Ming, Marty tells me that you have some experience with Check Point?"

"I used to administer four or five Check Point firewalls at my previous company." replied Ming. "We only had it installed on Windows and Solaris platforms though."

Shin smiled. "I think you'll be pleasantly surprised how easy it is to install and configure the software on IPSO."

Ming rolled her eyes. "That'd be nice for a change. Is it any different once it's installed?"

Shin shook his head. "No, it will look exactly the same from a firewall administration perspective."

Ming gave Marty a thumbs-up. "You know what that means Marty?" Ming asked him.

"What's that?" he said.

Ming smiled. "It means I can use that training budget somewhere else."

Preparing for the Firewall Implementation

Nokia NSP devices run the pre-hardened IPSO operating system, which essentially means there is very little to do from an operating system hardening perspective. However, before installing a firewall on any operating system, it is extremely important to ensure that the operating system is routing packets accordingly, and that you have tested your DNS setup. From a Nokia perspective, you should set up Host Address Assignment, which is essentially the same as a hosts file on a UNIX system. This will ensure that your interfaces are properly named and bound to the correct IP address. In some cases, depending on your Nokia platform and IPSO version, you might need to upgrade the boot manager. However, this is generally done automatically during the upgrade process.

Ensure that you have the following ready before you begin configuring Check Point NGX. How to configure many of the steps outlined here has already been covered throughout the book, so we will briefly look at the Check Point components that have not yet been covered.

- Read the Release Notes available at http://support.nokia.com and www.checkpoint.com. You must have IPSO 3.9 or later installed to run Check Point NGX. Deciding to install NGX on an earlier version of IPSO 3.9 will cause issues, but more importantly, it is not supported by Check Point or Nokia. Should you wish to implement Check Point UTM features, you must install IPSO as a fresh install from boot manager rather than an upgrade. You also need to install the IPSO UTM package prior to the Check Point NGX R65 wrapper.

NOTE

A *wrapper* is an archive file that contains the application installation code for installation on your Nokia appliance.

- Enable your network interface cards and configure the appropriate speed and duplex. Speed and duplex settings have been known to cause serious degradation issues with any device that sits inline on a network. Make sure to triple check the interface settings on the firewall, as well as the switch or router in which they plug into. It is important to note that the Nokia interfaces support auto advertise only and not auto negotiate for speed and duplex.
- Configure the IP address and subnet mask on all network interface cards that will be participating in the implementation. It is important to point out that the default gateway should be set at this stage as well.
- Make sure IP forwarding is enabled (*ipsofwd on admin*). This will ensure that your Nokia NSP is routing traffic. This is enabled by default when Check Point is not installed on the appliance.
- Configure Host Address Assignment.
- At this point, your IP addresses, routes, and DNS settings have been entered into the Nokia NSP. You should now take a few minutes to test routing and DNS.

TIP

Your Nokia appliance should be synchronized to an external NTP server to ensure that it operates and logs any issues encountered correctly.

- Make sure you have at least 512MB of memory and 40MB of free disk space on /opt. Check Point UTM features require 1GB of memory installed on the Nokia NSP and are not supported on Flash or Hybrid systems.
- Verify that your IPSO version is compatible with Check Point NGX (see Table 8.1).
- Obtain Check Point NGX software packages and licenses from Check Point and Nokia support Web sites.

Table 8.1 Nokia Hardware/NGX Compatibility

IPSO Version	NGX Compatibility
IPSO 3.9	NG AI R55, NGX R60, NGX R61, NGX R62, GX NGX, IPv6 Pack
IPSO 3.9	NGX R60
IPSO 3.9.90	VPN-1 VSX NG AI Release 2.2N
IPSO 3.9.91	VPN-1 VSX NG AI Release 2.3N
IPSO 3.9.92	VPN-1 VSX NG AI Release 2.3N
IPSO 4.0	NGX R60, NGX R61, GX NGX, IPv6 Pack
IPSO 4.0.1	NGX R60, NGX R61
IPSO 4.1	NGX R60, NGX R61, NGX R62, NGX R65 (FW Only), FW-1 GX 4.0
IPSO 4.1	NGX R60
IPSO 4.2	NGX R62, NGX R65 (FW & UTM), FW-1 GX 4.0

Obtaining Licenses

If you have already purchased Check Point, an account was created for you at http://usercenter.checkpoint.com. The easiest way to obtain licenses is to visit http://usercenter.checkpoint.com where Check Point would have placed your newly purchased licenses. Check Point licenses and software cannot be provided by Nokia.

You have two options to choose from when you license Check Point: Local and Central. The *Local* method would have you license each individual component of your Check Point infrastructure by the IP address of each specific component. For example, your SmartCenter Server license would be licensed to the IP address of the SmartCenter Server, where the Enforcement Module license would be licensed to the Enforcement Module itself. Although this method is how Check Point historically licensed their products, it is currently not recommended, for a couple for reasons. If you were to change the IP address of an Enforcement Module, you would have to regenerate a license with the new IP address, and it is much more difficult to move a license from one module to another using this method.

The *Central* method of licensing a Check Point firewall would have you bind all licenses to the IP address of the Smart Center Server. The nice thing about using central licenses is that you can change the IP address of an Enforcement Module without needing to replace the license, and you can easily move a license from one module to another.

Although it is recommended to obtain your licenses before you install Check Point, you can always decide to use an evaluation license until you do so. Historically, you would need to contact Check Point or a Check Point Value Added Reseller (VAR) to obtain a 30-day license. Check Point now includes a 15-day evaluation license when installing their products.

Configuring Your Hostname

A previous chapter has already listed the steps on configuring your hostname and host address assignment, but we will briefly cover it here again. If you decided to use the local licensing scheme from Check Point, it is best to know that unless you configure your Hostname and Host Address Assignment properly, your license might fail to install. This can occur if you chose to license your Enforcement Module by its external IP address and generated the local license using the internal IP address.

To add a new hostname or host address assignment, go to Hostname by logging in to Nokia Network Voyager and then navigate to **System | Configuration | System Configuration | Hostname** and **System | Configuration | System Configuration | Host Address**, respectively. In the **Add New Hostname** field, type the fully qualified domain name (FQDN) or the simple hostname. We will use the name *cpngx*. Click **Apply**, and then type in the IP address associated with *cpngx*. Click **Save**.

Configuring the Check Point NGX Firewall

Now we will turn our attention to how we configure a Check Point NGX firewall. After installing the package on your Nokia NSP, you must first enable it through Nokia Network Voyager and run the initial *cpconfig* steps. It is during this initial configuration that you must decide which sort of Check Point implementation you will proceed with. Check Point supports a couple of different installation options: Stand-alone or Distributed. In a stand-alone installation, the Check Point SmartCenter Server and Enforcement Module are installed on the same device. This installation is recommended for small/medium businesses, because having both Check Point components installed on the same NSP can seriously affect firewall performance. If choosing to proceed with a distributed installation, you would install the Enforcement Module on your NSP and the SmartCenter Server on a second Nokia NSP, Solaris system, or Windows server. This section walks you through each step of the initial configuration screens and gives you some tips for disabling the default and initial policies, which might be problematic when you're doing remote maintenance.

Installing the Package

If you have just received a Nokia NSP from a distributor, you will most likely notice that Check Point has already been uploaded and installed on the device. Many times, it is not the latest firewall version, so it is recommended that you uninstall and delete the Check Point package that currently exists and reboot your Nokia NSP.

Continue by uploading the Check Point NGX wrapper to the Nokia NSP in the /opt/packages directory after confirming that there are no existing packages left. The wrapper package is simply a .tgz file that starts off by installing NGX (SVN Foundation and VPN-1 Pro/Express NGX). Here, we guide you through a package installation of NGX on a Nokia using the *newpkg* command.

1. Copy the wrapper file to /opt/packages using Secure Copy (SCP). (The filename will be something like IPSO_wrapper_R61.tgz. There is no need to untar the package.)
2. Navigate to the **/opt/packages** directory and type **newpkg –i**.
3. Select **4** and press **Enter** at the prompt for installation method. This sequence will install the package from the local file system.
4. Next you will be prompted for the pathname to the package. Enter a single period (.) and press **Enter**. A single period or "dot" indicates the current working directory.
5. Now the install program will find the Check Point NGX package and extract the necessary files for installation. You will be prompted with four options—to install, upgrade, skip, or exit. Enter **1** to install. At this time, the packages bundled in the wrapper will be installed. When the process is complete, you will again see the IPSO prompt. You can verify that the packages have been installed by logging in to Voyager and viewing the Manage Installed Packages configuration screen. Please note that it can take between 5 minutes to over 15, depending on the hardware platform you are using. Be patient. It will complete.
6. Now you need to log out and log back in to your IPSO session. This ensures that you get the new environment variables defined during the package installation. Without having these variables set, you cannot run *cpconfig*.
7. Run ***cpconfig***. You can skip to the section on *cpconfig* later in this chapter (titled "Running *cpconfig*") for more help with this configuration tool.
8. Reboot your Nokia after running *cpconfig* by typing **reboot**.

Enabling the Package

Check Point packages are enabled just like any other packages on IPSO. In NGX, you will not have to enable the VPN-1 Pro/Express NGX packages as you had to in the past. If you find you need to enable the packages, you can do so from the Manage Installed Packages configuration screen in Nokia Network Voyager.

Follow these instructions to enable Check Point NGX VPN-1 Pro/Express NGX:

1. Log in to Nokia Network Voyager and click **System Configuration**.
2. Click **Manage Installed Packages**.

3. Toggle the **Check Point VPN-1 Pro/Express NGX** package to **On**.
4. Click **Apply**.
5. Click **Apply** and then click **Save**.

Disabling Check Point NGX is just as easy as enabling it, but in reverse. Simply toggle the **Check Point VPN-1 Pro/Express NGX** package to **Off**.

Understanding Environment and Path

Historically, Check Point commands could not be executed if you did not have the correct environment variables defined on your operating system. Fortunately, with later versions of Check Point including NGX, these are configured for you in the /var/etc/pm_profile file. This profile is called from the .profile in your home directory, so whenever you log in you will always have the necessary environment set to run Check Point commands for installed packages.

Many different environment variables are modified when installing Check Point packages onto an operating system. For example, the CPDIR variable, which informs you of the location of the SVN Foundation, is modified and so is the FWDIR variable, which contains the value of the base VPN-1 Pro/Express NGX installation directory. The FWDIR variable can also be used to easily change directories.

Understanding VPN-1 Pro/Express NGX Directory Structure

Many subdirectories exist within the VPN-1 Pro/Express NGX package directories that are important to know and understand. Here are some of them:

$FWDIR directories:

- **bin** Binary files and scripts such as the firewall binary *fw*, the firewall daemon binary *fwd*, the firewall management binary *fwm*, and the firewall stop and start scripts, *fwstart* and *fwstop*, respectively, are located in this directory.
- **boot** Boot configuration files are stored here, including the compiled default filter file.
- **conf** Configuration files, including objects, rules, and user databases are stored here.
- **database** Database information is stored in this directory.
- **lib** Library files are stored in this directory.
- **log** Log files are stored in this directory. On Nokia devices, this is usually a symbolic link to /var/fw/log.

- **spool** The SMTP Security Server default spool directory is located in this directory.
- **state** State information specific to the firewall is stored here.
- **tmp** The Temporary directory where the daemon pid files are located.

The conf directory stores many of the most important files that make up the configuration of the firewall. Within the conf directory, you will find the objects_5_0.C file, which holds all your FireWall-1 objects and services. Every object including network, host, firewall, and so on are stored in this file. You will also find the rulebases_5_0.fws file contains your rule bases defined on the firewall, and the fwauth.NDB* files, which contain your user database. The objects_5_0.C and rulebases_5_0.fws can be edited in a text editor, although it is not recommended. The fwauth.NDB files are in binary format and cannot be edited.

The files in the lib directory are also important. They are sometimes modified when applying hotfixes or service packs to the firewall. It is very rare that you would ever have to manually edit these files. If you find yourself in this situation, it is extremely important that every file located in the lib directory be backed up.

Firewall log files are just as important as firewall configuration files with regard to applying appropriate maintenance and backup procedures. Within SmartDashboard, there are many ways you can ensure that log files maintain a manageable size, but security server log files such as a httpd.elg, aftpd.elg, and asmtpd.elg will continue to grow in the Nokia $FWDIR/log directory. Most of the files that begin with fw.* will also be part of the active log files.

Firewall state information is contained in the state directory. The information in this directory is updated whenever a policy is installed.

Understanding IP Forwarding as It Pertains to Firewall Policies

To protect the network segment that resides behind the firewall, IP forwarding is disabled when the Nokia NSP is booting up. The Check Point firewall will control IP forwarding by enabling it after its services are started. The firewall also loads a default filter during the boot process, which essentially denies all inbound traffic but allows outbound traffic. This filter is loaded into the kernel before the interfaces of the Nokia are configured. This ensures that there is never a time during the boot process that the machine is unprotected.

Upon initial startup of a Check Point firewall, the initial default policy is applied to ensure that no other traffic can hit the firewall except SmartDashboard GUI traffic. ICMP traffic is also denied, which sometimes confuses first-time users. The only other time the default policy is applied to the firewall is when it cannot fetch a policy from itself. If you find yourself in a position where you cannot connect to the firewall with SmartDashboard, you can run the *fw unloadlocal* command. This command unloads the default policy for you but will not disable IP forwarding. The *fw stat* command is also beneficial since it displays the current policy that is loaded:

```
cpngx[admin]# fw stat
HOST      POLICY        DATE
localhost InitialPolicy 18Jun2008 16:49:19 : [>eth1c0]
```

The difference between running *fwunloadlocal* and *cpstop* is that IP forwarding will be disabled when running *cpstop*. If you wanted to know the current state of IP forwarding, you could simply run the *ipsofwd list* command. If forwarding is disabled, the value of net:ip:forwarding will be 0. A value of 1 would be set if it was enabled. The following are some brief descriptions of commands you can use to control these settings:

- **fwstop –default** Kills all firewall processes and loads the default filter.
- **fwstop –proc** Stops all firewall processes but allows the policy to remain in the kernel for simple accept, drop, and reject inspection.
- **fwstart –f** Starts FireWall-1 services.
- **control_bootsec –r** Removes boot security.
- **control_bootsec –g** Enables boot security.
- **fwboot bootconf** Sets IP forwarding and configures the default filter.
- **comp_init_policy –u** Disables the initial policy.
- **comp_init_policy –g** Enables the initial policy.

Default filters are stored in the $FWDIR.lib directory. Some of the files you may find there are the defaultfilter.boot file, which allows outbound communication originating from the firewall and broadcast traffic. Another example would be the defaultfilter.ipso file, which allows SSH, SSL, and inbound and outbound ICMP traffic originating from the firewall.

There may be an instance where you want to change the default filter your firewall is using. The steps here outline how you can change this behavior so your firewall will use the defaultfilter.ipso file:

1. SSH into your Nokia and navigate to the **$FWDIR/lib** directory.
2. Copy the defaultfilter.ipso file to **$FWDIR/conf/defaultfilter.pf**.
3. Run the ***fw defaultgen*** command. This will compile the defaultfilter.pf file. The output file will be $FWDIR/state/default.bin. The following is an example of what you should see when running the *fw defaultgen* command:

```
cpngx[admin]# fw defaultgen
Generating default filter
defaultfilter:
```

```
Compiled OK.
Backing up default.bin as default.bin.bak
```

4. Lastly, copy the **$FWDIR/state/default.bin** file to the **$FWDIR/boot** directory.

Tools & Traps...

Unload InitialPolicy Script

You must be aware of the *gotchas* that occur when installing a firewall. There really is no difference when installing Check Point. If you run into a situation where you must upgrade a firewall remotely, you must be aware of the InitialPolicy filter that the firewall installs when booting for the first time. This filter blocks all access to the firewall. You can log in to the console and verify that the filter is loaded with the *fw stat* command:

```
cpngx[admin]# fw stat
HOST      POLICY        DATE
localhost InitialPolicy 18Jun2008 16:49:19 : [>eth1c0]
```

Console access to the firewall is recommended so that the following command can be issued if you happen to be caught in this situation:

```
cpngx[admin]# fw unloadlocal
Uninstalling Security Policy from all.all@cpngx
Done.
```

This command unloads the InitialPolicy filter so you can access the firewall.

Running *cpconfig*

Most Nokia NSP devices have a version of VPN-1 Pro/Express NGX installed when you receive it. Although the firewall is installed, it has yet to be configured. In order to configure the installed firewall, you must first run the *cpconfig* command. The cpconfig options that are available to you will permit you to choose a deployment option such as Stand-alone or Distributed. *cpconfig* is also used to apply your license, and configure administrators and GUI clients.

cpconfig can be run from the command line via the console or a remote SSH or Telnet session. The first time you run the *cpconfig* command, you will be prompted to read and accept the license agreement. The configuration options could be a little different depending on your deployment option.

Presented next are the *cpconfig* steps you need to take for a Stand-alone deployment:

1. Log in to your Nokia NSP through a console or remote SSH or Telnet session and run *cpconfig*.
2. Pressing **Enter** will let you read the license agreement. Pressing the **Spacebar** will continue scrolling through the license agreement until you reach the end. You must enter **y** to proceed.
3. It is time to choose your deployment option. In this case, we have chosen option 1, which will install Check Point Enterprise/Pro.
4. Choose option 1.

The Stand-alone option will install the SmartCenter Server and Firewall onto the same Nokia NSP. See Figure 8.1.

Figure 8.1 Initial Configuration

```
cpngx[admin]# cpconfig

Welcome to Check Point Configuration Program
=============================================================================
Please read the following license agreement.
Hit 'ENTER' to continue...

This End-user License Agreement (the "Agreement") is an agreement between
you (both the individual installing the Product and any legal entity on
whose behalf such individual is acting) (hereinafter "You" or "Your") and
Check Point Software Technologies Ltd. (hereinafter "Check Point").

Do you accept all the terms of this license agreement (y/n) ? y

Please select one of the following options:
Check Point Enterprise/Pro - for headquarters and branch offices.
Check Point Express - for medium-sized businesses.
-----------------------------------------------------------------------------

(1) Check Point Enterprise/Pro.
(2) Check Point Express.

Enter your selection (1-2/a-abort) [1]: 1
```

```
Select installation type:
-------------------------

(1) Stand Alone - install VPN-1 Pro Gateway and SmartCenter Enterprise.
(2) Distributed - install VPN-1 Pro Gateway, SmartCenter and/or Log Server.
Enter your selection (1-2/a-abort) [1]: 1
IP forwarding disabled
Hardening OS Security: IP forwarding will be disabled during boot.
Generating default filter
Default Filter installed
Hardening OS Security: Default Filter will be applied during boot.
This program will guide you through several steps where you
will define your Check Point products configuration.
At any later time, you can reconfigure these parameters by running cpconfig
```

Understanding Licenses

Check Point now asks whether you would like to add licenses to the firewall. In this case, we have deployed a Stand-alone Check Point firewall, so our license will be generated using the SmartCenter Server IP address. Follow the steps in Figure 8.2 to add a license during the *cpconfig* process:

1. Enter **y** when prompted to add a license. (In this step, you have the choice to add the license manually or fetch it from a file. Choosing to fetch the license from a file will prompt you for a file name.)
2. To enter it manually, type in **m**. (Figure 8.3 displays how to install the license manually.) The license fields are as follows:
   - **Host** The IP address that was utilized when generating the license.
   - **Date** The date the license expires.
   - **String** The unique license string provided by Check Point to validate the license.
   - **Features** The features included with the license. For example,VPN, QoS, and so on.
3. Carefully enter the license in the fields for **Host**, **Date**, **String**, and **Features** and press **Enter**.

Figure 8.2 Configuring Licenses

```
Configuring Licenses...
======================
Host   Expiration Signature
Features

Note: The recommended way of managing licenses is using SmartUpdate.
cpconfig can be used to manage local licenses only on this machine.

Do you want to add licenses (y/n) [y] ? y

Do you want to add licenses [M]anually or [F]etch from file: m
IP Address: 192.168.70.1
Expiration Date: 18Jul2008
Signature Key: W2K7hu9g-cCrsCsVhp-GturZobaj-oVHiK8mYv
SKU/Features: CPMP-EVAL-1-NGX CK-CP

License was added successfully
```

Figure 8.3 Adding an Administrator

```
Configuring Administrator...
===========================
No Check Point products Administrator is currently
defined for this SmartCenter Server.

Do you want to add an administrator (y/n) [y] ?
Administrator name: peter
Password:
Verify Password:

Administrator peter was added successfully and has
Read/Write Permission for all products with Permission to Manage Administrators
```

The next step in the *cpconfig* process is to add an administrator. A single administrator must be added at this point, but more administrators can be added at a later date. Figure 8.3 displays the steps involved to add your administrator.

NOTE

If you chose a Distributed deployment and your Nokia has a single Enforcement Module installed, you will not be required to add an administrator. The administrator is used to access the SmartCenter Server.

Many organizations tend to use the username *fwadmin*. Although this is easy to remember, it can become an issue when multiple members of a security team begin managing the firewall. Using the same username denies the organization the ability to audit the tasks of the firewall administrators. It is important to know what the last changes were made to a firewall and who performed them. This becomes more and more important when several people are administering a firewall system. The following steps must be performed to configure an administrator.

- **Administrator Name** The name must be unique and is case-sensitive.
- **Password** Passwords must be a minimum of four characters and are also case-sensitive.
- **Verify Password** Repeat the same password just entered.
- **Permissions for all Management Clients (Read/[W]rite All, [R]ead Only All, [C]ustomized)** The Customized option lets you create granular controls for specific administrators of the firewall
- **Permission to manage administrators (Yes or No)** Some users may need a higher level access than others. This option lets you permit specific users to create other firewall administrator accounts.

If you select Read/[W]rite All or [R]ead Only All, your firewall administrator will have access to all the available GUI client features, with the ability to make changes and updates or view the configuration and logs only. Customized access will allow you to specify firewall administrator access on a much more granular level. To do this, select **Customized** and configure each of these options. Listed next are descriptions of some of the options you are presented with if you choose to set granular permissions on your firewall administrators.

- **SmartUpdate** This GUI tool lets you manage licenses and update remote modules.
- **Check Point Users Database** Allows you to manage users through the SmartDashboard.

- **LDAP Users Database** Lets you manage LDAP users through SmartDashboard.
- **Security Policy** Allows you to manage the Security Policy tab in the SmartDashboard.
- **QoS Policy** Allows you to manage the QoS (FloodGate-1) bandwidth management policy in the SmartDashboard.
- **Monitoring** Enables access to the LogViewer, System Status, and Traffic Monitoring GUI clients.

Management Clients

Management clients, otherwise known as GUI clients, are configured on the firewall so an administrator who installs the SmartConsole application on their desktop will be permitted to connect to the firewall to make changes or view the current firewall configuration.

NOTE

The SmartConsole application is a group of GUIs that includes SmartDashboard, SmartView Tracker, SmartView Monitor, SmartUpdate, SmartLSM, and many others.

SmartConsole is installed on Windows, Solaris (X-Motif), or Linux. These clients can be installed on as many desktops as you like, but they cannot connect to the SmartCenter Server until you enter the desktop IP address into *cpconfig* (see Figure 8.4). A single IP address, network range, or the keyword *Any* can be entered, but when first running *cpconfig* you are not required to enter any GUI client IP addresses. This can be configured at a later time.

Figure 8.4 Configuring Management Clients

```
Configuring GUI Clients...
==========================
GUI Clients are trusted hosts from which
Administrators are allowed to log on to this SmartCenter Server using Windows/
X-Motif GUI.
No GUI Clients defined
Do you want to add a GUI Client (y/n) [y] ?
You can add GUI Clients using any of the following formats:
```

```
1. IP address.
2. Machine name.
3. "Any" - Any IP without restriction.
4. IP/Netmask - A range of addresses, for example 192.168.10.0/255.255.255.0
5. A range of addresses - for example 192.168.10.8-192.168.10.16
6. Wild cards (IP only) - for example 192.168.10.*
Please enter the list of hosts that will be GUI Clients.
Enter GUI Client one per line, terminating with CTRL-D or your EOF
character.
Any
10.1.1.0/255.255.255.0
Warning: Every gui client can connect to this SmartCenter Server.
Is this correct (y/n) [y] ? y
```

NOTE

If you chose a Distributed deployment and your Nokia has a single Enforcement Module installed, you will not be required to add a management client. The management client is used to access the SmartCenter Server.

GUI client information entered into *cpconfig* must be on a one-per-line basis. You must press **Enter** at the end of each. When you have finished entering the information, press **Ctrl** + **D** to send an end-of-file (EOF) control character to the program to continue.

You are allowed to use wildcards in each GUI client host specification as follows:

- **Any** If you type in the word Any, you will allow anyone to connect without restriction. This practice is not recommended.
- **Asterisks** You may use asterisks in the hostname, such as 10.10.20.*, which means any host in the 10.10.20.0/24 network; *.domainname.com means any hostname within the domainname.com domain. Unless this is a secured network, this practice is not recommended either.
- **Ranges** You may use a dash (-) to represent a range of IP addresses, such as 10.1.1.100-10.1.1.1110.

Figure 8.5 presents an example of how management clients can be configured using *cpconfig*. Configuring a hostname of domain name is not recommended. This would require you to set up DNS on the firewall. Utilizing IP addresses does not rely on resolution and is currently recommended.

Figure 8.5 Management Client Wildcards

```
Please enter the list hosts that will be Management clients.
Enter hostname or IP address, one per line, terminating with CTRL-D or
  your EOF character.
10.1.1.100-10.1.1.110
10.1.1.115
10.10.10.*
theacademy.ca
Is this correct (y/n) [y] ? y
```

Figure 8.6 is a step that permits you to configure group permissions for superuser individuals of the firewall. In many cases, you should choose not to create a group and leave the defaults intact.

Figure 8.6 Configuring Group Permissions

```
Configuring Group Permissions...
================================
Please specify group name [<RET> for super-user group]:
No group permissions will be granted. Is this ok (y/n) [y] ?
```

Understanding Certificate Authority Initialization

Check Point includes its own Internal Certificate Authority (ICA), which can be used to issue certificates to trusted components within your firewall architecture. You can choose to issue certificates to remote access VPN users and remote gateways where you want to establish a site-to-site VPN tunnel. The ICA is also used for Secure Internal Communication (SIC).

At this point, you are presented with the Random Pool configuration option. You are now asked to input random text until you hear a beep. The timing latency between your key presses will be used to generate cryptographic data, so it is recommended you enter the data at a random pace so some keystrokes are close together and others have a longer pause between them. The more random the key-press intervals, the more unlikely the input can be duplicated.

NOTE

The Random Pool configuration screen is presented to you when an Enforcement Module has been installed. This way you can generate an internal certificate for SIC.

Figure 8.7 displays what you will see during the Random Pool configuration. Upon completion, the internal CA must be initialized. This could take a minute depending on the processing power of your server. Figure 8.8 displays the messages you will receive on the console while configuring the CA. Press **Enter** to initialize the CA.

Figure 8.7 Random Pool

```
Configuring Random Pool...
==========================
You are now asked to perform a short random keystroke session.
The random data collected in this session will be used in
various cryptographic operations.
Please enter random text containing at least six different
characters. You will see the '*' symbol after keystrokes that
are too fast or too similar to preceding keystrokes. These
keystrokes will be ignored.
Please keep typing until you hear the beep and the bar is full.
  [.......................]
Thank you.
```

Figure 8.8 Configuring Certificate Authority

```
Configuring Certificate Authority...
====================================
The Internal CA will now be initialized
with the following name: cpngx
Initializing the Internal CA...(may take several minutes)
Internal Certificate Authority created successfully
Certificate was created successfully
Certificate Authority initialization ended successfully
Trying to contact Certificate Authority. It might take a while...
cpngx was successfully set to the Internal CA
Done
```

WARNING

Please make sure you choose the name carefully. Changing it shortly after the fact is simple enough to accomplish using the *fwm sic_reset* command, but it can become a nightmare if you decide to change it after a full VPN deployment.

The last step in the *cpconfig* process is the presentation of the SmartCenter Server fingerprint. This unique fingerprint is displayed to you when you first log in to Check Point SmartDashboard. It is an easy verification to ensure that the fingerprint being presented to you is the same as the fingerprint that was generated by the system when running *cpconfig*. If the fingerprint presented when you first connect to the SmartCenter Server is different, you will receive a warning message and may choose to log in since something is amiss. The steps outlined are also displayed in Figure 8.9:

You will be prompted on whether or not you would like to save the fingerprint to a file by *cpconfig*, "Do you want to save it to a file?"

1. Type **y** and press **Enter**.
2. Type a filename and press **Enter**. The file will be saved in the /opt/CPsuite-R61/svn/conf directory.
3. Enter **y** to confirm.

Figure 8.9 Saving the Certificate Fingerprint

```
Configuring Certificate's Fingerprint...
========================================
The following text is the fingerprint of this SmartCenter Server:
GONG HERS LIKE WACK JAIL YOKE SIGH LOSE RAID DART MUFF FUME
Do you want to save it to a file? (y/n) [n] ? y
Please enter the file name [/opt/CPsuite-R61/svn/conf]: fingerprint.txt
The fingerprint will be saved as /opt/CPsuite-R61/svn/conf/fingerprint.txt.
Are you sure? (y/n) [n] ? y
The fingerprint was successfully saved.
generating INSPECT code for GUI Clients
initial_management:
Compiled OK.
Hardening OS Security: Initial policy will be applied until the first policy is
installed
```

Completing an Installation

When the configuration program ends, you are prompted to reboot the firewall, as shown in Figure 8.10. If you elect not to reboot, you will exit the installation and go back to a shell prompt. If you choose to reboot, the system is restarted immediately.

Figure 8.10 Installation Complete

```
generating INSPECT code for GUI Clients
initial_management:
Compiled OK.
Hardening OS Security: Initial policy will be applied
until the first policy is installed
In order to complete the installation
you must reboot the machine.
Do you want to reboot? (y/n) [y] ? y
```

WARNING

If you are remotely connected to this firewall, you will not have access after rebooting. The firewall loads a policy named InitialPolicy, which prevents all access after an install. See the sidebar "Unload InitialPolicy Script" for a workaround.

Getting Back to Configuration

All the steps we have so far taken to configure the firewall using *cpconfig* can be reinitialized after rebooting the firewall by running the *cpconfig* command. For example, if you chose not to add a license when first running *cpconfig*, you can easily add it later. The same applies for adding GUI clients, additional administrators, group permissions and many more. Each screen you ran through during the initial configuration will now be listed as a menu item, as shown in Figure 8.11.

Figure 8.11 *cpconfig*

```
cpngx[admin]# cpconfig
This program will let you re-configure
your Check Point products configuration.
```

```
Configuration Options:
----------------------
(1) Licenses
(2) Administrator
(3) GUI Clients
(4) SNMP Extension
(5) Group Permissions
(6) PKCS#11 Token
(7) Random Pool
(8) Certificate Authority
(9) Certificate's Fingerprint
(10) Enable Check Point SecureXL
(11) Automatic start of Check Point Products
(12) Exit
Enter your choice (1-12):
```

You might notice some options in the menu that were not presented to you when *cpconfig* was first initialized. The SNMP Extension option configures the SNMP Extension. By default, the Check Point module SNMP daemon is disabled, but if you want to export SNMP MIBS to network monitors, you can use this option to enable SNMP. The PKCS#11 token lets you install an add-on card such as an accelerator card. Option 10 allows you to enable SecureXL, while option 11 gives you the ability to automatically start upon a reboot.

NOTE

This menu will be slightly different if you decided to perform a distributed installation of the firewall.

When running *cpconfig* on an Enforcement Module, you will notice two different options:

- **Secure Internal Communication** (SIC) Enables a one-time password that will be used for authentication between this enforcement module and the SmartCenter Server, as well as any other remote modules it might communicate with.
- **High Availability** Lets you enable this enforcement module to participate in a Check Point High Availability (CPHA) configuration with one or more other enforcement modules.

Testing the Firewall Configuration

Now that the firewall has been installed and configured, we can proceed in testing our deployment. In order to do so, we need to test basic administrative tasks. This is particularly important after we have performed an upgrade and the firewall continues to be active on the network. We will now test SmartDashboard access, as well as defining and installing a basic policy.

Testing SmartDashboard access

To configure a policy on a Check Point firewall, you must connect to the SmartCenter Server with SmartDashboard. Although the InitialPolicy is loaded, you should be able to connect to the firewall with SmartDashboard. If you cannot connect, you need to issue the *fw unloadlocal* command using the command line. You can run the management clients on the following operating systems:

- Windows XP (Home or Professional)
- Windows 2000 SP1-SP4 (Professional, Server, or Advanced Server)
- Windows 2003 Server SP1 and SP2
- Solaris 8, 9, and 10 (32 or 64 bit—note that running the GUI on Solaris requires a Motif license)

If you are using Windows, you can begin by clicking **Start** | **Programs** | **Check Point SmartConsole NGX R61** | **SmartDashboard**. You will be presented with a login prompt like the one in Figure 8.12.

Figure 8.12 SmartDashboard Login

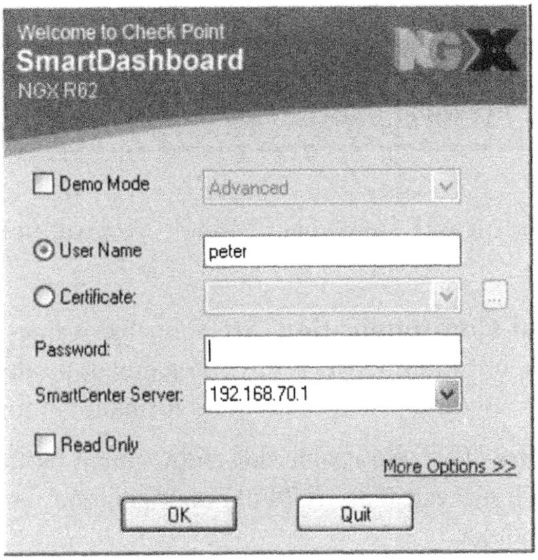

Unless you have configured your user with the ability to use a certificate when logging in to the firewall, you will need your username, password, and the IP address of the SmartCenter Server to log in to the firewall. We have chosen to install a Stand-alone deployment of the Check Point firewall so the IP address to enter would most likely be the internal IP address of the Nokia NSP. If this is your first attempt at connecting to the firewall you will be presented with the SmartCenter Server fingerprint. This should be the same fingerprint that was presented to you when running *cpconfig*. It is recommended you download the fingerprint.txt file you saved during the initial *cpconfig* procedure and compare it to the fingerprint that the firewall is presenting to you. If it matches, click **Approve** to continue logging in to the SmartCenter Server.

NOTE

Notice that you have the ability to check Demo Mode on the initial login screen. This gives the junior firewall administrator the ability to launch SmartDashboard and learn how to navigate the GUI and create objects without affecting the production firewall.

It is a rare occurrence that your SmartCenter Server fingerprint would change. Unless you reinstall the SmartCenter Server, you should never have to deal with it. As long as the fingerprint remains the same, you will not get a message after the first acceptance. After successfully authenticating to the firewall and accepting the fingerprint, you will be presented with the window in Figure 8.13. Historically, you would need to request an evaluation license from Check Point or a Check Point VAR before being permitted to log in to the firewall. With later versions of Check Point, you are entitled to a 15-day evaluation license.

Figure 8.13 Check Point SmartDashboard

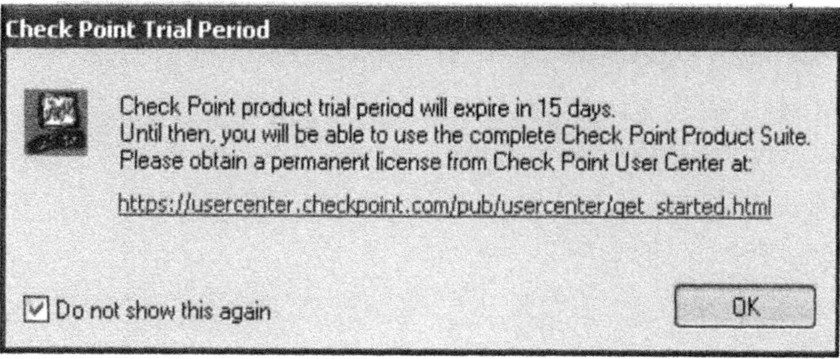

Initially, you will have a single object configured to represent your firewall, which NGX creates for you during installation. See Figure 8.14.

Figure 8.14 Check Point SmartDashboard

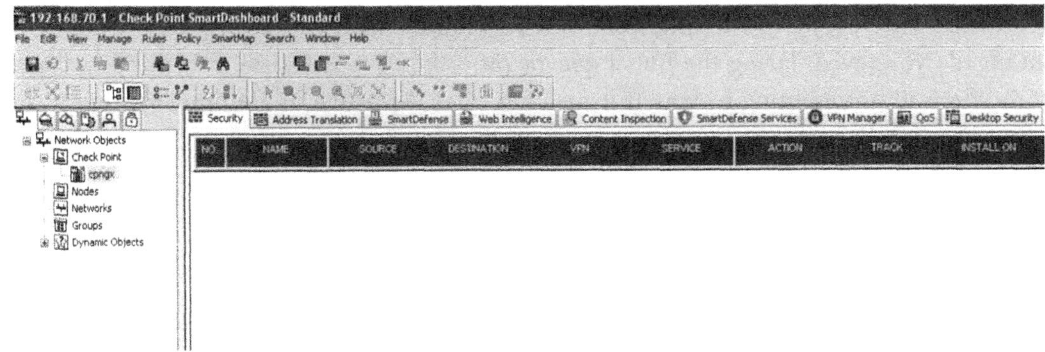

Before creating rules and objects it is recommended you take a few minutes and review the settings on your Check Point Security Gateway object. To edit the firewall object, you can simply double-click it or click **Manage** in the main menu and select **Network Objects**. Highlight the firewall object and click **Edit**. Check to ensure that the IP address defined on the object is correct. You might also want to modify the Check Point products installed to include product options that the installation did not select for you. For example, you can select Anti-Virus, SmartView Monitor, and many others. See Figure 8.15.

Figure 8.15 Check Point Gateway Object

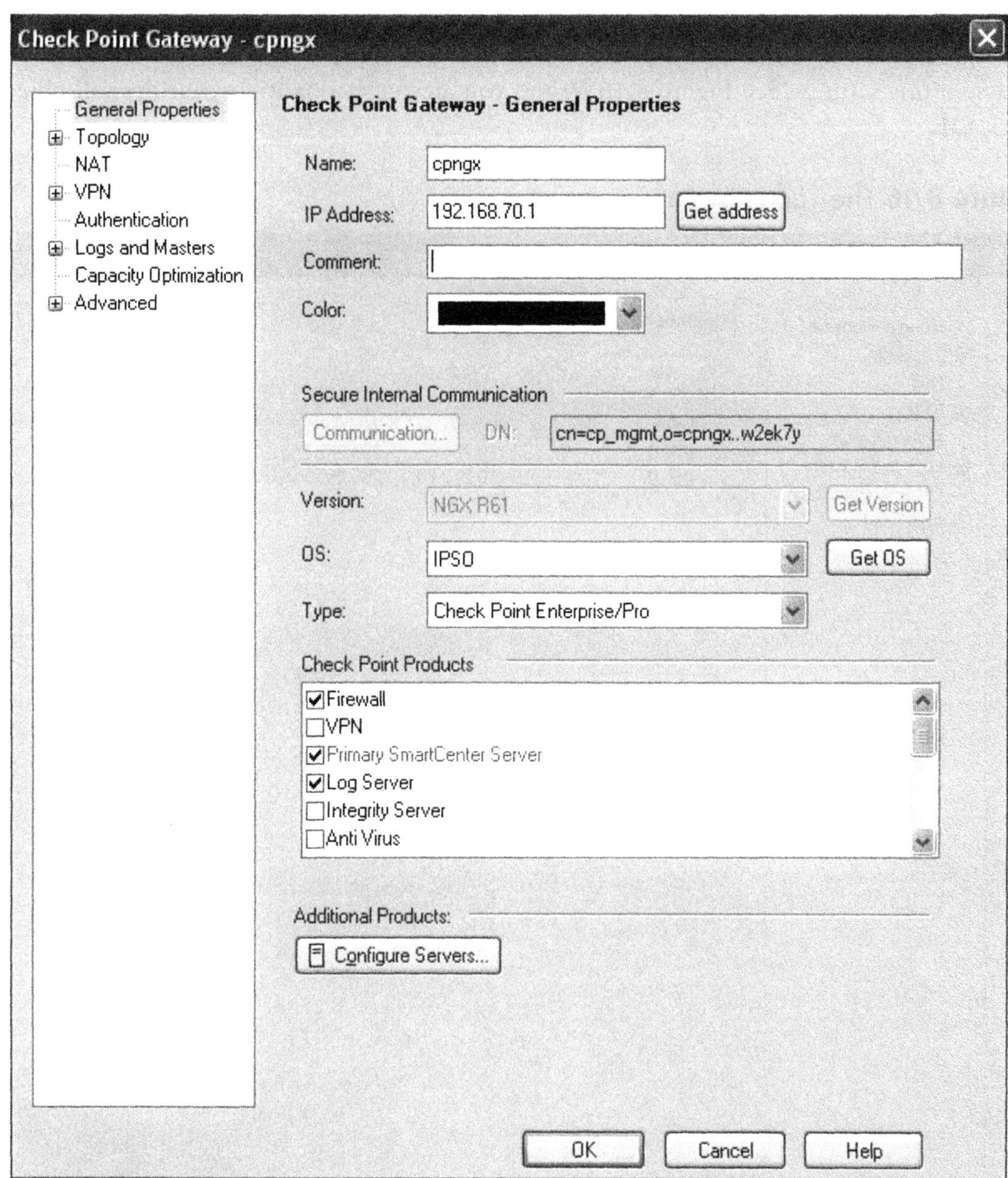

NOTE

If you have a distributed installation, you must create the firewall object for your Nokia. It will not be created for you as it was in our previous example.

You also want to verify that the Topology is configured with the correct information about your firewall. The Topology is where you define which interface the firewall should consider, external versus internal. It is here that you would also specify your anti-spoofing settings. See Figure 8.16. When you are finished editing your firewall object, click **OK**.

Figure 8.16 The Topology Page

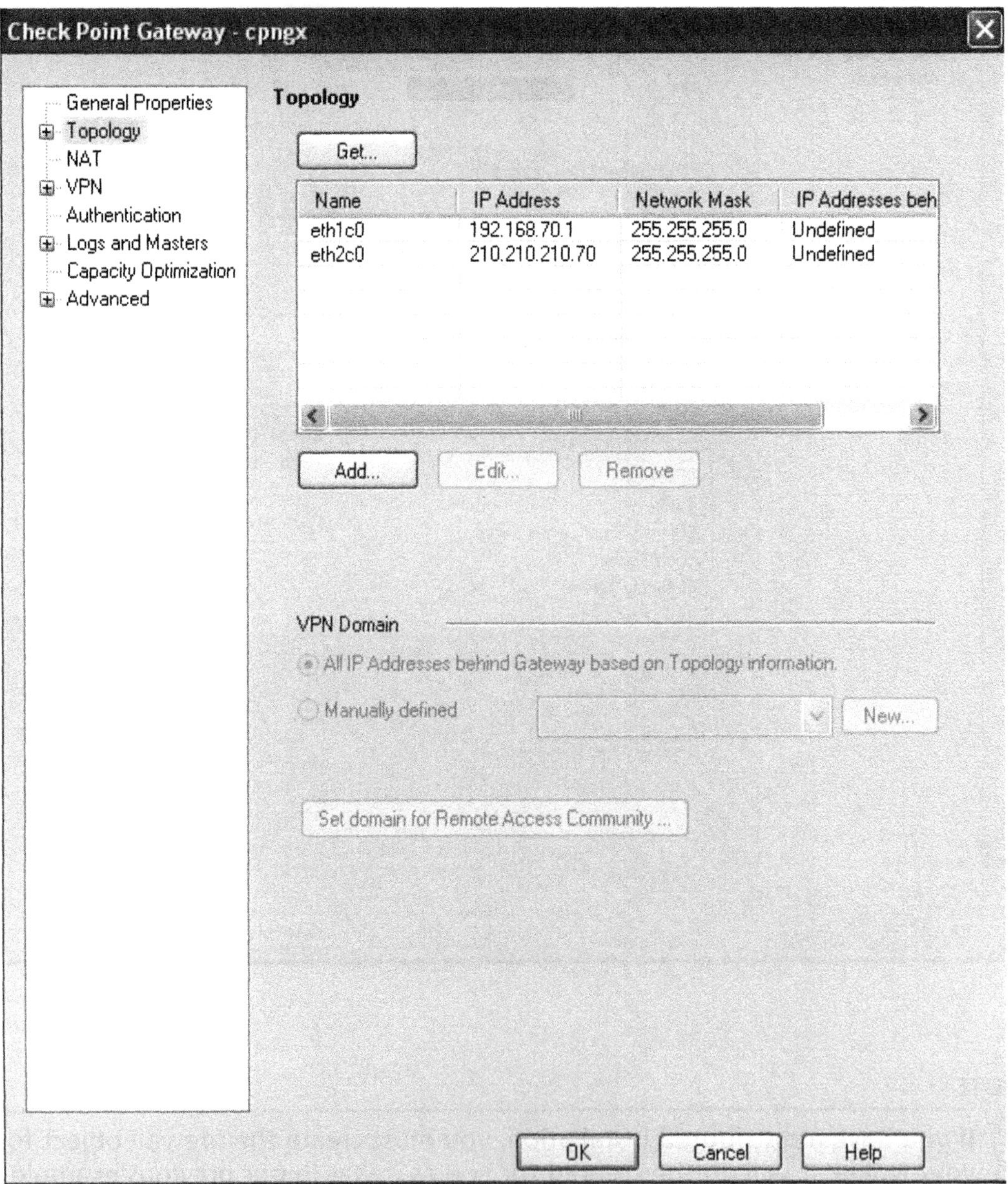

After confirming that your Check Point Gateway object is configured correctly, you can move forward and begin creating network objects, users, and node objects that you will use in your Security Policy. In Figure 8.17, we have created a simple "any, any, accept" rule to illustrate how a rule is created. It is not recommended you have this type of rule present on your firewall because it would not provide your network with any protection.

Figure 8.17 Check Point Rulebase

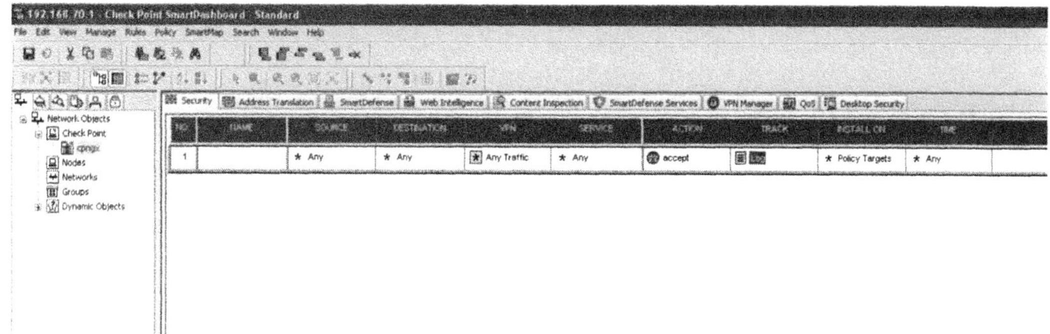

Click the **Rules** menu option and select **Add Rule | Top**. This will enter the default rule, any source, destination, or service to drop without logging. Right-click the **Action** cell and select **Accept**. Then, right-click the Track cell and select **Log**.

Now choose the **File** menu and **Save** the policy. The policy is named *Standard* by default and is defined in Figure 8.17.

Pushing and Fetching Policy

Pushing a policy to Check Point is an easy task. Click the **Policy** menu and choose **Install**. Your objects, rules, and users will be saved at this time. The first time you install a policy you will receive a warning message. See Figure 8.18. Selecting the Don't Show This Message Again box will ensure that the message is not presented to you every time you push a policy.

Figure 8.18 The Initial Policy Push Warning

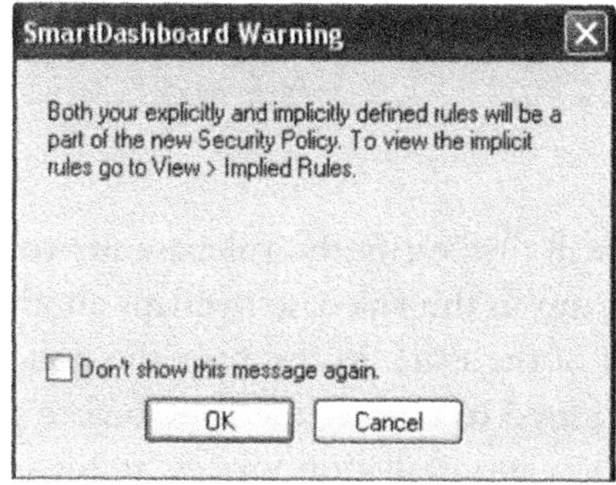

This message simply informs you that there are Implicit rules that are defined through the Global Properties that cannot be configured through the rulebase. Implicit rules are not visible in your Security Policy window. You can make these rules visible by selecting **Implied Rules** from the **View** menu.

Next, you will receive a policy installation targets window where you need to select the firewall that will receive the policy (see Figure 8.19). If you manage multiple firewalls from the same SmartCenter Server they are all displayed in this window. Accept the default values and click **OK** to begin the installation process.

Figure 8.19 Policy Installation Targets

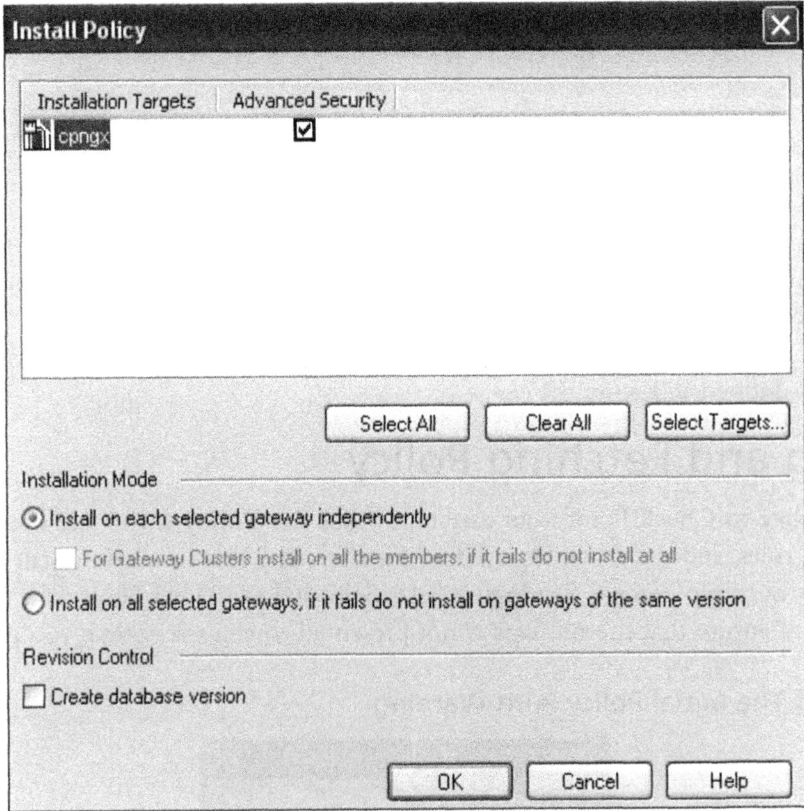

The SmartCenter Server will first verify the rulebase for you. If you happened to create a rulebase where a rule higher up in the rulebase overlaps another, the SmartCenter Server returns an error notifying you of the issue. In this case, the policy is not installed on the firewall object and you are required to correct the issue before proceeding. If your rulebase is verified with no discrepancies, an installation process status window will be displayed similar to the one in Figure 8.20. When the installation is done, the Close button will light up, and if the install was successful, the status changes to a green check mark. A red X indicates there were errors when pushing the policy.

Figure 8.20 Installation Process

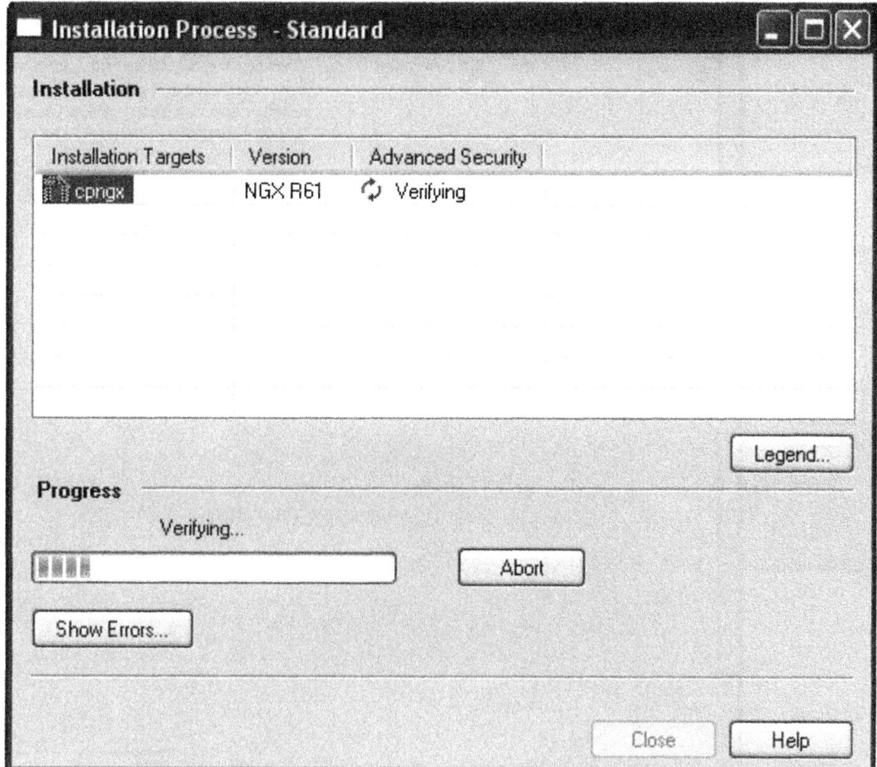

If you receive warnings or errors on the installation, you can view these messages by clicking **Show Warnings**, as displayed in Figure 8.21. In Figure 8.21, notice that we received a warning that anti-spoofing settings have not been clearly defined on the firewall object. Although the policy was successfully pushed to the Enforcement Module, we need to ensure that we revisit our firewall object and complete the configuration.

Figure 8.21 Installation Succeeded, but with Warnings

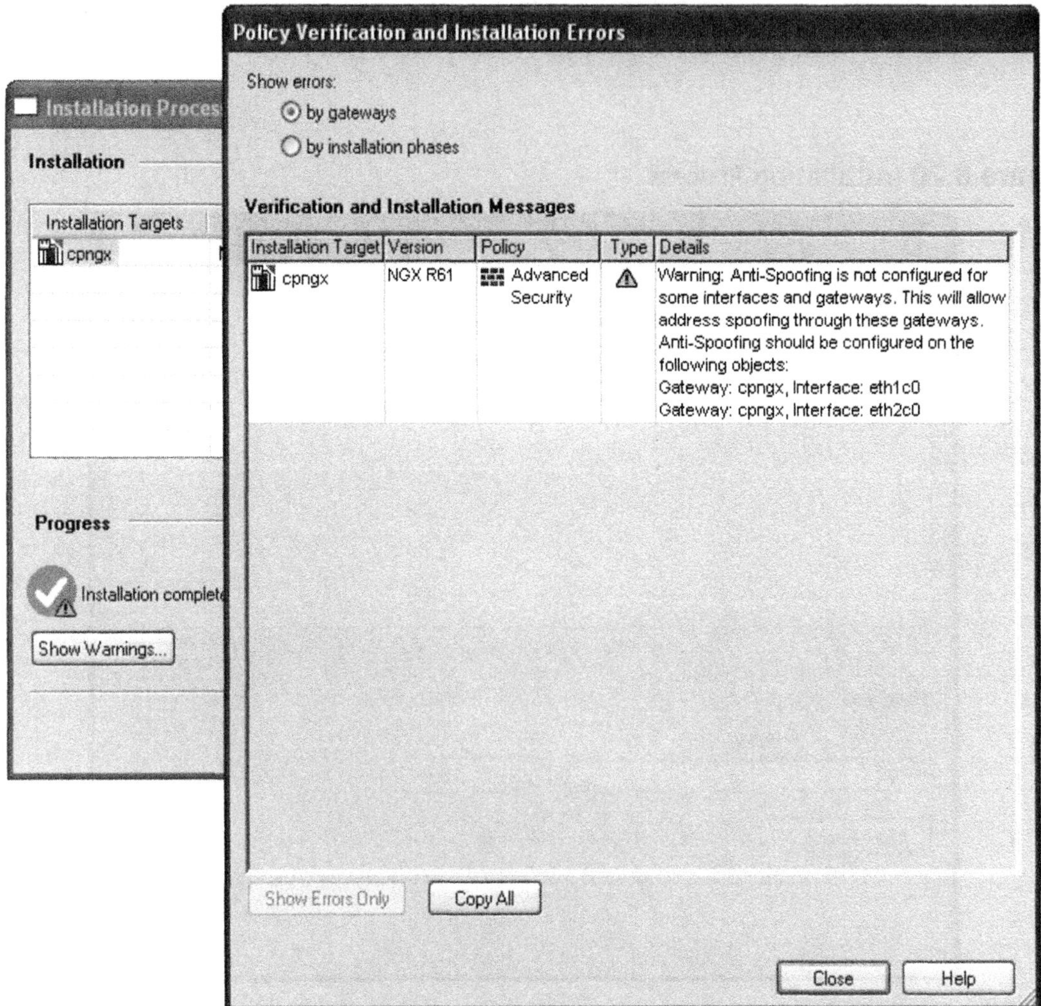

A green checkmark indicates that the policy was pushed successfully. You can now continue to modify the rulebase as you wish. The following are a few different troubleshooting steps that can be utilized if your policy installation fails:

- You first want to verify that the firewall process is up and running. From the command line type *ps –auxw | grep fw*. If you receive a result, you can be sure that the firewall process is running.
- Unloading the policy with the *fw unloadlocal* and reinstalling will sometimes do the trick.
- Test connectivity by pinging the firewall from the SmartCenter Server.

By default, when a Nokia NSP is rebooted, it automatically attempts to fetch a policy from the SmartCenter Server. If the SmartCenter cannot be reached, the Nokia NSP loads the last policy that was pushed to it. You can also have the Nokia NSP manually fetch a policy from the SmartCenter Server. To force this behavior, you must use the *fw fetch* command. Table 8.2 outlines the available switches for this command. The *fw fetch localhost* command manually loads the last policy installed on the Enforcement Module, while the *fw fetch SmartCenterServer* command instructs the Enforcement Module to fetch a policy from the SmartCenter Server. The SmartCenterServer keyword mentioned earlier is the name of the SmartCenter Server system, which is defined in the $FWDIR/conf/masters file.

Table 8.2 *fw fetch* Switches

Switch	Description
-n	Fetches a policy from the SmartCenter Server and only loads the policy if it is different from the current policy loaded.
-f <filename>	Fetches a policy from the SmartCenter Server listed in *<filename>*. If no filename is specified, it uses the $FWDIR/conf/masters file.
-i	Ignores the SIC information, such as SIC names.

Configuring & Implementing...

Check Point NGX CLI Reference

A Check Point Technical Reference Guide is available from the Check Point Web site. It is roughly 500 pages in length and outlines all of the different commands available on the firewall. The following are some of the commands you will frequently use when managing a Check Point NGX firewall:

- **cpstop** Stops all Check Point products and the SVN Foundation.
- **cpstart** Starts the SVN Foundation and all Check Point products.
- **cplic print** Prints the currently installed licenses to the console.

Continued

- **cplic put** This command will add a license to the firewall.
- **fw tab –t connections –s** Lists the number of connections in the Check Point firewall connections table.
- **fw ver** Displays the version of Check Point firewall. The *–k* switch will display the kernel version.
- **fw stat** Lists the currently loaded policy, the date the policy was last installed, and the interface and direction the security policy is enforcing.
- **fw unloadlocal** Unloads the current security policy so no policy is loaded. This command is very useful if you have lost access to the firewall or if you wish to troubleshoot.
- **fw load** This can push a policy from command line to a remote module when run on a SmartCenter Server.

Upgrading the Firewall

In this section, we are going to briefly outline how you can upgrade a Check Point firewall installed on a Nokia NSP. The first recommended step is to research your current Nokia IPSO version to ensure that the version of Check Point firewall you are upgrading to will be supported. Although many newer Check Point firewall versions will run on an older version of Nokia IPSO, it is simply not supported by Nokia or Check Point. So, before you get yourself into this situation, take a minute and download the latest IPSO/Check Point compatibility matrix from the Nokia support Web site. In most cases, you need to upgrade your version of IPSO to support the latest version of Check Point firewall. Before you do, take another minute to ensure that the Nokia hardware you own supports the latest IPSO/ Check Point firewall.

After your research is complete, you can begin the actual upgrade. To ensure a successful upgrade with minimal complications, it is recommended you use the freely available pre-upgrade verifier tool from Check Point. The pre-upgrade verifier will analyze the current configuration in the SmartCenter Server $FWDIR/conf directory to ensure it is compatible with the latest release of Check Point firewall. This tool is available as a download from the Check Point Web site, but it should be included in the latest media shipped by Check Point.

1. Place the pre-upgrade verifier package into the /var/admin directory.
2. Run **gunzip** * to uncompress the file.
3. Extract the file with the command **tar –xvf upgrade***.

4. Run the pre_upgrade_verifier with the following syntax:

   pre_upgrade_verifier –p SmartCenterPath –c CurrentVersion –t TargetVersion –f filename.txt

5. Look in the filename.txt file to determine what you might need to change before beginning the upgrade process.

Upgrading from NG AI R55 to NGX R62

The steps you take to upgrade your firewall will be slightly different depending on the deployment option you chose. If you are running a distributed deployment, you must upgrade the SmartCenter Server first. The reason is because if you upgrade the Enforcement Module first, you will not be able to manage it with a SmartCenter Server on a lower version. We will provide the instructions to upgrade a Stand-alone deployment where the SmartCenter Server and Enforcement Point are running on the same Nokia NSP. The first thing you want to do is download a Nokia IPSO version that supports Check Point NGX. In this case, IPSO 3.9 or 4.1 will do for NGX R60-R62. If you decide to upgrade to NGX R65, you need to install IPSO 4.2 Build HF002.

1. Follow the steps in previous chapters with regard to upgrading an IPSO image.
2. Upload the NGX_R62_Wrapper.tgz package to the /opt/packages directory.
3. Run **newpkg –i** from the **/opt/packages directory**.
4. Option 4 installs the package from the local filesystem. Choose option 4 and press **Enter**.
5. Enter a single dot (.) when asked to type the path to the file, and then press **Enter**.
6. Choose option 2 and press **Enter**. This will upgrade the current Check Point firewall.
7. Select the correct displayed package, choose **1**, and press **Enter** to continue.
8. Enter **y** to confirm that you want to upgrade the current package, then and press **Enter** to continue. You can follow the upgrade process by typing **tail –f /var/log/messages**.
9. When you arrive at a shell prompt, the upgrade has completed. You need to log out and log back in to the Nokia to obtain the latest environment variables.
10. Type **exit** and then log in again.
11. Run ***cpconfig*** so you can apply your new licenses. (Licenses can also be added later from SmartUpdate.)
12. Type **reboot**. The system installs the defaultfilter policy. You need to push the policy to the firewall the first time after the upgrade.

13. Install the Check Point NGX R62 SmartConsole onto your desktop and log in to your SmartCenter Server.
14. Accept the fingerprint and verify that your policy appears to be intact after the upgrade.
15. Select **Install** from the **Policy** menu to push a policy.
16. Test your firewall. Is it passing traffic inbound and outbound? Are your NATs working?

NOTE

One of the most important steps to take when upgrading from NG AI to NGX is the upgrade of your licenses. Visit http://usercenter.checkpoint.com and regenerate your licenses as NGX. If your licenses are not properly generated, you will not be able to access your SmartCenter Server.

Upgrading from NGX R62 to NGX R65

Although there are some major enhancements to NGX in version R65, the upgrade procedure from NGX R62 is very simple. Begin the same way you started out with the NGX R62 upgrade—by running the pre-upgrade "verifier." This ensures that you address any issues before performing the upgrade. After this is complete you can upgrade the firewall the same way as we described earlier—run the ***newpkg –i*** command and select option **2**.

When the upgrade has completed, log out, and then log back in to the Nokia NSP CLI and run ***cpconfig***. Make any necessary changes and reboot the Nokia NSP. Install the latest SmartConsole on your desktop and connect to the SmartCenter Server. Proceed to push a policy.

Summary

It cannot be stressed enough that firewall administrators have the basic skills required to install, maintain, and upgrade your Nokia Check Point firewall environment. Having these skills will ensure that your Nokia Check Point firewall environment is properly configured to thwart off any attacks targeted at your organization network. This chapter has provided the tools necessary to complete these tasks.

When upgrading your Check Point Nokia firewall environment, research and preparation is the key. The steps required are simple enough to accomplish, but you must be aware of the compatibility issues that may arise from installing a Check Point version with a version of IPSO that is not supported. You need to first obtain licenses, configure a host's entry, and possibly upgrade the IPSO image on your Nokia before you can begin installing or upgrading Check Point.

Upon completion, you will need to run *cpconfig*. *cpconfig* is used to essentially initialize the Check Point firewall. After this step is done, you should log in to your SmartDashboard and push a policy to ensure that connectivity is established. If a policy push fails, you need to troubleshoot. Verify that the firewall is running. If it is running you can always try unloading the current policy from the firewall. This usually does the trick.

Upgrading the firewall is an easy task, but many times you will need to upgrade Nokia IPSO to ensure that the latest version of Check Point can function on it. Begin by downloading the latest versions or IPSO and Check Point. Upgrade the IPSO first and be sure to test your environment before proceeding with the Check Point upgrade. If all is well, proceed by upgrading Check Point and testing your environment again. It is recommended that a test script be written before you upgrade your environment. A test script is a list of steps you are going to take to ensure that your environment is functional. For example, does outbound connectivity work? What about inbound connectivity for publicly available servers such as e-mail, the Web, and ftp? Are remote access and site-to-site VPNs working? The importance of such a script should be stressed. Do not try and remember all that your environment offers. There will come a time that you forget your script only to discover on a Monday morning that e-mail is not working. Do not let yourself get caught in this situation.

Solutions Fast Track

Preparing for the Firewall Implementation

☑ Read the release notes.

☑ Enable the Nokia NSP network cards, and configure IP addresses and routing.

☑ Configure Host Address Assignment and proceed to test routing and DNS.

- ☑ Verify Nokia IPSO and Check Point compatibility.
- ☑ Obtain Nokia IPSO and Check Point software packages and licenses.

Configuring the Check Point NGX Firewall

- ☑ Install or upgrade the Nokia IPSO image.
- ☑ Install or upgrade the Check Point NGX package with *newpkg –i*.
- ☑ Enable the Check Point packages. In most cases, this is done for you by default.
- ☑ Run *cpconfig* to finish the Check Point FireWall-1 configuration.
- ☑ Reboot your Nokia NSP afterwards.

Testing the Firewall Configuration

- ☑ Install the appropriate SmartConsole package and log in to the SmartCenter Server via SmartDashboard.
- ☑ Push a policy to your Enforcement Module.
- ☑ Fetch a policy from your SmartCenter Server.

Upgrading the Firewall

- ☑ Use the pre-upgrade verifier tools from the Check Point Web site to ensure that any issues that may arise from the upgrade are mitigated before the upgrade.
- ☑ Upgrade the Nokia IPSO image and test your environment.
- ☑ Upgrade the Check Point firewall and test your environment.

Frequently Asked Questions

Q: After upgrading my firewall from NG AI R55 to NGX R62 I am no longer able to log in to SmartCenter Server. What could possibly be wrong?

A: Make sure you uninstalled your NG AI R55 GUI client from your desktop. Install the NGX R62 client and try again. You can also try issuing the *fw unloadlocal* command on the Enforcement Module.

Q: I just upgraded one of my Check Point NG AI R55 firewalls to NGX R62 running on IPSO 3.7. I am having intermittent issues with the firewall. What could possibly be wrong?

A: There is one glaring issue with your deployment. Check Point NGX is only supported on IPSO 3.9 and later.

Q: I am currently having issues connecting SmartDashboard to my NGX R62 firewall. Do you know why?

A: It's recommended that you check to ensure that the fw process is up and running. Running *cpstart* will tell you whether or not the firewall was stopped. Also check to see if you are defined as a GUI client using *cpconfig*.

Q: I have installed Check Point in a distributed deployment, but I am not able to push a policy to the Enforcement Module. Why?

A: I would definitely check connectivity by issuing a ping to the Enforcement Module. If this doesn't work, you may want to check to ensure that Secure Internal Communications (SIC) is established. If not, this needs to be completed before you can push a policy to the Enforcement Module. If you have checked these settings, you can try to issue the *fw unloadlocal* command on the Enforcement Module and try again.

Q: What command can I use to quickly discover whether or not my Enforcement Module is enforcing the InitialPolicy?

A: I would run the *fw stat* command from the Enforcement Module CLI. This will display the currently installed policy on the firewall.

Frequently Asked Questions

Chapter 9

System Monitoring

Solutions in this chapter:

- Monitoring System Utilization
- Monitoring Protocols
- Monitoring System Health
- Using the iclid Tool

☑ Summary

☑ Solutions Fast Track

☑ Frequently Asked Questions

Introduction

"How easy is it to diagnose process utilization and system health on the Nokia appliance?" asked Ming.

"Good question," Marty replied. "We've had issues in the past where our routing devices were less than willing to point us in the right direction for troubleshooting."

Shin clicked through the Nokia Network Voyager interface and ended up in the Monitor section. "From the Monitor section of the Nokia Network Voyager we can look at system utilization, health, logs, and even detailed routing protocol information," explained Shin. "The Hardware Monitoring section will also give you information about the slots on the platform. In addition, you can use the *iclid* tool to obtain routing diagnostic information from the command line. *iclid* has been around for a while but it continues to be a great source of routing diagnostic information when you're having issues."

Mark wrote furiously as Shin continued to explain the system monitoring features, but every time he was about to ask a question, Marty or Ming beat him to it. "I'm just going to sit here and let you guys hash it all out," said Mark. "We're obviously all on the same page when it comes to monitoring this appliance."

Monitoring System Utilization

You can use Nokia Network Voyager to monitor several aspects of your IP security platform to better maintain performance and security. For example, you can monitor state information for each interface, view the contents of IP routing tables, and generate reports on events such as throughput, bandwidth utilization, and link states over specific periods of time.

Viewing System Utilization Statistics

Use the system utilization statistics to monitor and tune the allocation of your system re-sources. For example, if the file system capacity percentage increases, you should take action, such as deleting old IPSO images and packages or moving your log files to a remote system. To view statistical information on system utilization, click CPU-Memory Live Utilization, Disk and Swap Space Utilization, or Process Utilization under System Utilization of the Monitor folder in the tree view.

The CPU-Memory Live Utilization page shows system resources usage, including CPU and memory usage. This page retrieves the updated CPU and memory usage every 20 seconds. Figure 9.1 shows the CPU And Memory Utilization page in Nokia Network Voyager.

Figure 9.1 The CPU and Memory Utilization Page

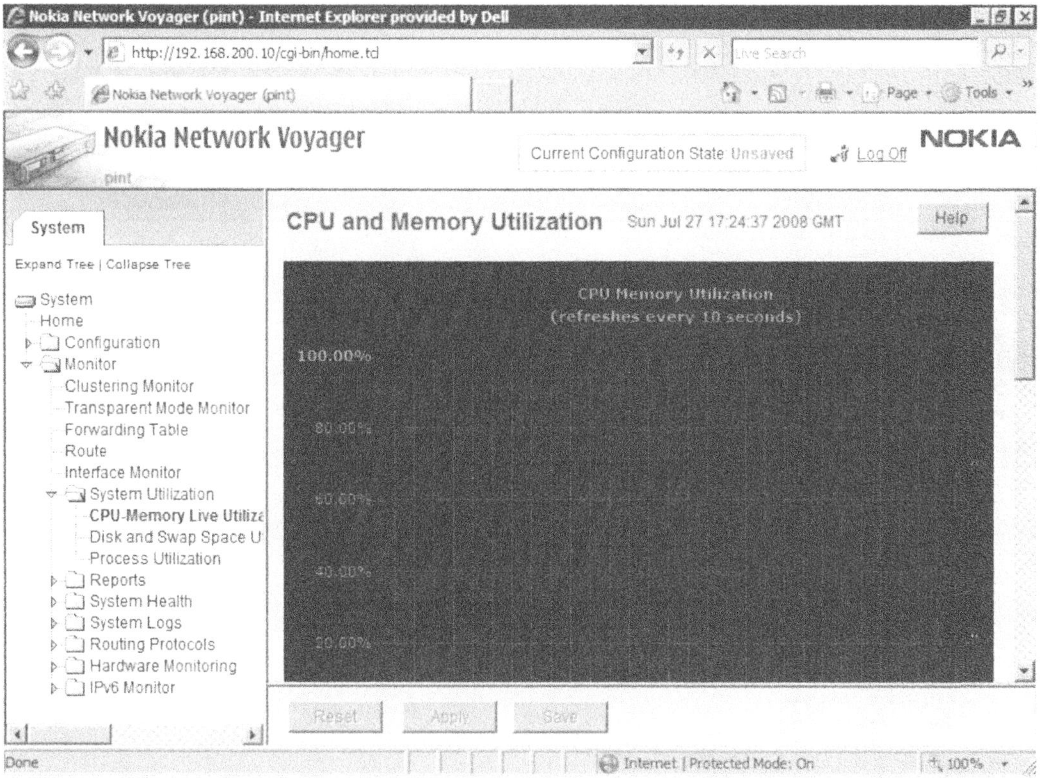

The CPU and Memory Utilization table summarizes your CPU usage (in KBs) and the System Load Average table summarizes the load averages, which are the number of processes in the system run queue averaged over the last 1, 5, and 15 minutes, respectively. Load averages that are high, such as over two in all three fields, indicate that the system is under continuous heavy load.

NOTE

Free memory, which is memory available to the operating system, is defined as free and cache pages. The remainder is active memory, which is memory currently in use by the operating system.

The Disk And Swap Space Utilization page, shown in Figure 9.2, shows system resources use, including disk and swap space use. This page retrieves the updated disk and swap space use every 20 seconds.

Figure 9.2 The Disk and Swap Space Utilization Page

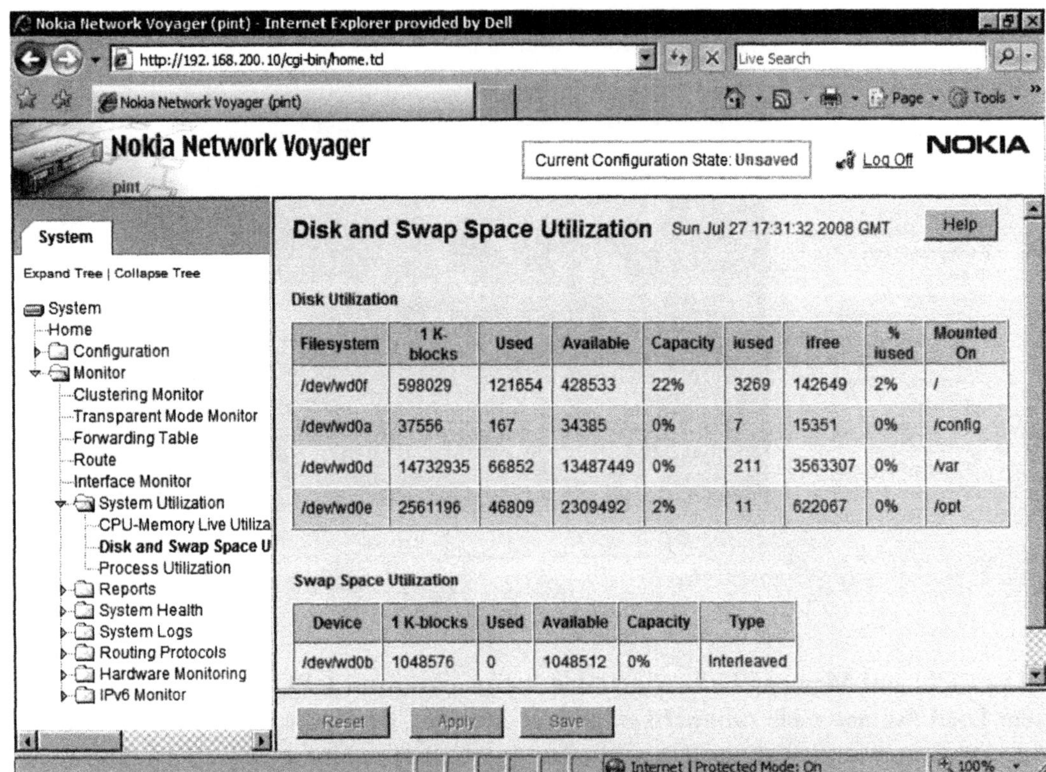

For each file system, you can monitor the number of kilobytes used and available, the percentage of disk space being used, the number of inodes used and free, and the location where it is mounted. The inode is the internal identifier for a file, and a limited number are available in a partition. A system can run out of inodes before it runs out of disk space.

For swap space, you can monitor the name of the device, total number of swap data blocks on the device, the number of used and free swap data blocks on the device, and the type of device.

NOTE

You should monitor the /config, /var, and /opt partitions because these store the configuration files, logs, and optional user software. Unlike read-only partitions, these can grow dynamically.

The Process Utilization page shows the status of processes. You must monitor and control processes to manage CPU and memory resources. Figure 9.3 shows the Process Utilization page.

Figure 9.3 The Process Utilization Page

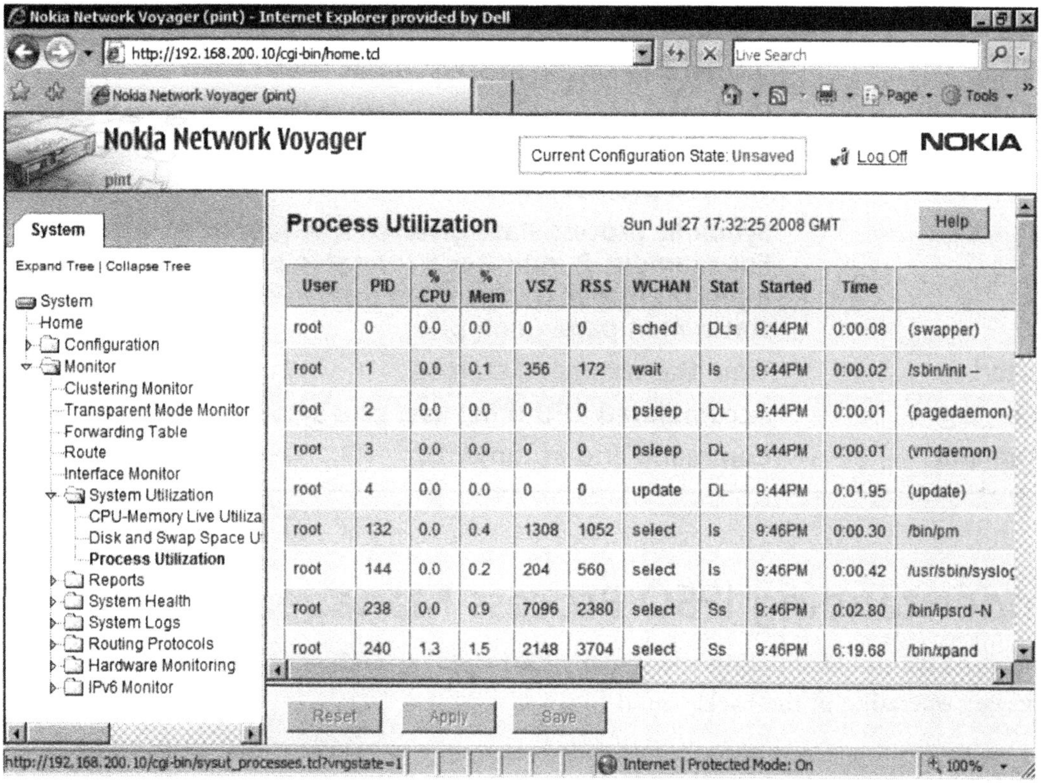

This page retrieves the updated process status every 30 seconds. When you access this page, a table displays the fields described in Table 9.1 for each process.

Table 9.1 Process Utilization Fields

Field	Description
User	User who initiated or executed the process.
PID	Identifier used by the kernel to uniquely identify the process.
%CPU	Percentage of CPU used by the process while active. This is a decaying average taken over a time period of up to the previous minute. Because the time base over which CPU utilization of the process is computed varies (processes might be very young), the sum of all CPU fields can exceed 100 percent.
%Mem	Percentage of real memory used by the process while active.
VSZ	Virtual size of the process in KBs (also called vsize).
RSS	Real memory (resident set) size of the process in KBs.
WCHAN	Wait channel (as a symbolic name). This is the event on which a process waits.
Stat	Symbolic process state given as a sequence of letters. For example, R indicates a runnable process (R) that is a session leader (s). For more information, see the process status man page (man ps).
Started	Time the command started.
Time	Accumulated CPU time: user plus system (alias, cputime).
Command	Command and arguments.

Understanding IPSO Process Management

When you are troubleshooting any system, it is helpful to understand the daemons, or system processes, operating in the background.

Tools & Traps...

Process Monitor

The process monitor (PM) monitors critical Nokia IPSO processes. The PM is responsible for:

- Starting and stopping the processes under its control
- Automatically restarting the processes if they terminate abnormally

The Nokia IPSO processes that the PM monitors are listed in Table 9.2. Additionally, the PM might monitor application package processes, such as IFWD, FWD, and CPRID.

Table 9.2 Nokia IPSO Monitored Processes

Process	Description
inetd	Internet daemon. This daemon helps manage Internet services on IPSO by monitoring port numbers and handling all requests for services.
ipsrd	Routing daemon. This daemon is a user-level process that constructs a routing table for the associated kernel to use for packet forwarding. With a few exceptions, IPSRD completely controls the contents of the kernel forwarding table. This daemon factors out (and separately provides) functionality common to most protocol implementations. This daemon maintains and implements the routing policy through a database.
ifm	Interface management daemon. This daemon sends and receives information to and from the kernel to verify the integrity of the interface configuration.
xntpd	Network time protocol daemon. This daemon sets and maintains a UNIX system time-of-day in compliance with Internet standard time servers.
monitord	System monitor daemon. This daemon monitors system health, collects and stores statistical information, and displays the data on request.

Continued

Table 9.2 Continued. Nokia IPSO Monitored Processes

Process	Description
httpd	Web server daemon.
sshd	Secure shell daemon.
xpand	Configuration daemon (also called configd). This daemon processes and validates all user configuration requests, updates the system configuration database, and calls other utilities to carry out the request.
snmpd	SNMP agent. Responds to queries via SNMP.

The PM frequently checks the status of the processes it monitors and typically takes less than a second to notice if a process has abnormally terminated. If a process has terminated abnormally, the PM attempts to restart the process. If the process fails to start, the PM continues to attempt a restart at regular intervals, with each interval increasing by a factor of two (for example, 2 seconds, 4 seconds, 8 seconds, 16 seconds, and so on). If the PM fails to start the process after 900 seconds, it stops trying. Each unsuccessful attempt is logged in the system message log. The process monitoring behavior of the PM is not user configurable.

Generating Monitor Reports

You can generate reports of data collection events by clicking the link for the appropriate report under Monitor Reports in the tree view. The administrator can configure how often the data is collected, whether each data collection event is enabled or disabled, and how many hours worth of collected data are stored on the system. Figure 9.4 here shows the Rate Shaping Report, and Table 9.3 describes the various monitoring reports available.

Figure 9.4 The Rate Shaping Report Page

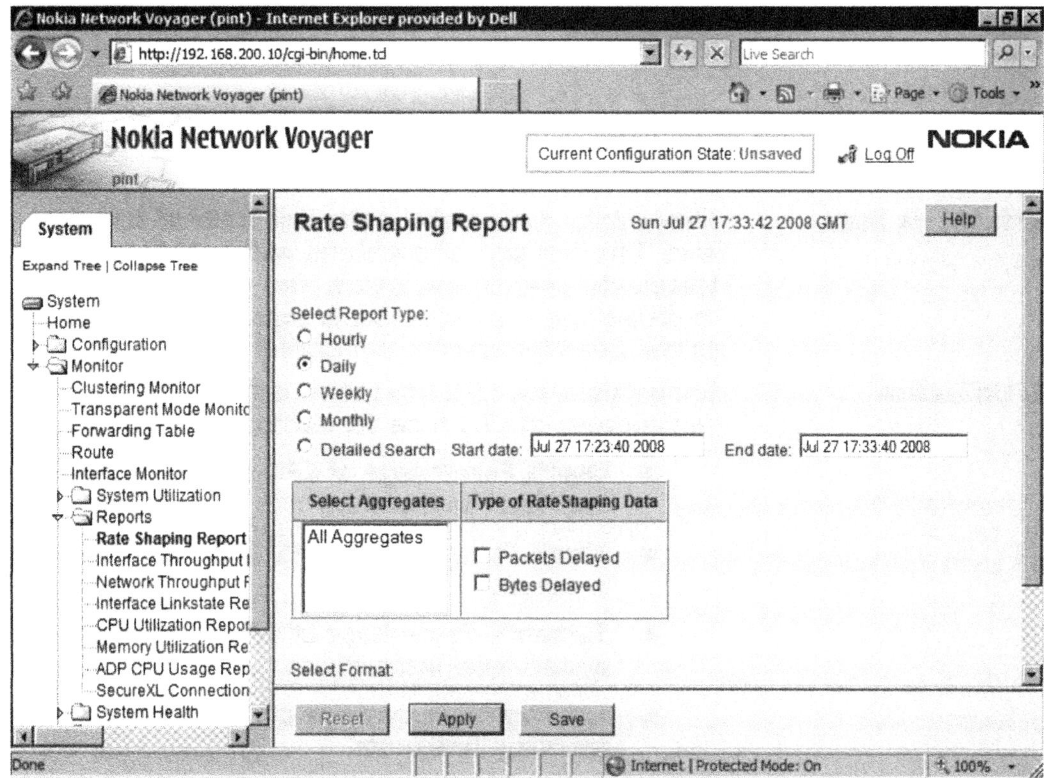

Table 9.3 Monitoring Reports

Report	Description
Rate-Shaping	Shows specific bandwidth utilization. You can use traffic shaping to implement a specific policy that controls the way data is queued for transmission. Inclusion of number of packets delayed and bytes delayed is configurable by the administrator. By default, both are included.
Interface Throughput	Shows historical throughput for each interface. You can often use this information to optimize network performance or troubleshoot issues of network traffic congestion. Inclusion of packet throughput, byte throughput, broadcast packets, and multicast packets for each interface is configurable by the administrator. By default, all are included.

Continued

Table 9.3 Continued. Monitoring Reports

Report	Description
Network Throughput	Similar to the interface throughput report, except that the query is based on the network address rather than the interface name.
Interface Link State	Shows information about the link state of each interface. The first sign of problems with interfaces is frequently seen in link errors. You can use this report to determine if an interface is experiencing problems or has been incorrectly configured.
CPU Utilization	Shows historical CPU utilization data, including percentages of CPU time for each of the following: ■ **User%** Percentage of CPU time spent in user-level instructions ■ **Nice%** Percentage of CPU time spent in "Nice" processes ■ **System%** Percentage of CPU time spent in system-level instructions ■ **Interrupt%** Percentage of CPU time spent in servicing interrupts ■ **Idle%** Percentage of time CPU was idle
Memory Utilization	Shows historical memory utilization, including: ■ **Active Real Memory** Kilobytes of real memory being used in a given time interval. ■ **Free Real Memory** Kilobytes of real memory free in a given time interval.

1. In the system tree, under **Monitor | Reports**, click the report type.
2. Under **Select Report Type**, select one of the following:

- **Hourly** Hourly report with a one-hour display interval up to a maximum of seven days.
- **Daily** Daily report with a one-day display interval up to a maximum of 35 days.

- **Weekly** Weekly report with seven-day display interval up to a maximum of 52 weeks.
- **Monthly** Monthly report with a one-month display interval up to a maximum of 60 months.
- **Detailed Search** Select a specific time period. These reports have a default data interval of one minute. The number of hours' worth of data stored for detailed searches is configured by the administrator.

3. For the **Rate-Shaping Bandwidth** report, select an aggregation class for which you want to display a report or select **All Aggregates** to display data for all configured aggregation classes.

NOTE

You must configure an aggregation class and associate it with an Access Control List for the name to appear as a choice in the Aggregation Class list.

4. For the **Interface Throughput**, **Network Throughput**, or **Interface Link State** reports, select **All Logical** or a specific interface name from the **Select Interface** drop-down list.
5. Under **Select Format**, select **Graphical View** or **Delimited Text**. If you select **Delimited Text**, choose **Semi-Colon(;)**, **Comma(,)**, or **Tab** from the **Delimiter** list. The Graphical View option displays pie and graph charts, as well as those in table format. The Delimited Text option displays the report in a new page from which you can download the information.
6. Click **Apply**.

Monitoring System Logs

The system logs links allow you to display updated system logs. The system logs are available under Monitor | System Logs in the tree view. To refresh the information in a log, reload the Web page. Figure 9.5 shows the System Message Log page under the System Logs folder.

Figure 9.5 The System Message Log

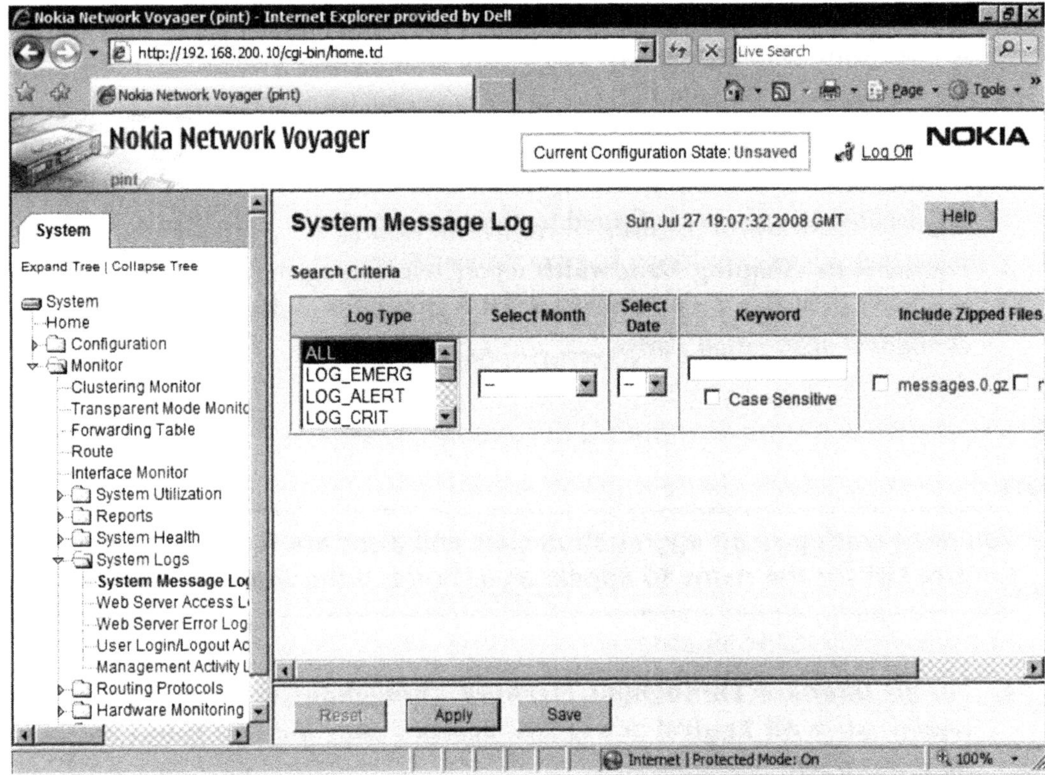

System logs include the following:

- **System Message Log** You can view the message log file in its entirety or select search criteria to view specific system log activity. Search criteria include:
  - **Types of log activity** Select one or more from All, Emergency, Alerts, Critical, Errors, Warnings, Notifications, Informational, or Debug Messages.
  - **Month**
  - **Particular date** You must also select a month to activate this option.
  - **Keyword** To make the keyword search case-sensitive, select Case Sensitive.
  - You can include certain zipped files in your search by clicking the appropriate check box in the Include Zipped Files In Search section.
  - The system log also displays messages generated by the system configuration audit log.
- **Web Server Access Log** Shows information about accesses to the Nokia Network Voyager interface using HTTP or HTTPS. The messages include the IP address from which the local host did an http access to the system, user, date, time, and HTTP access command.

- **Web Server Error Log** Shows error messages from the HTTPD Error Log File, including the date and time when the error occurred, transaction (the type of log message), location, and the contents of the log message.
- **User Login/Logout Activity** Shows the login and logout activity for users. By default, the activity for all users is displayed. You can view activity for a particular user by selecting the username from the list.
- **Management Activity Log** Shows the user login activity and details about changes made to the IPSO configuration. The log includes a timestamp, the hostname or IP address from which the user logged in, and the config entry, which displays the entry changed in the configuration database.

NOTE

You do not need to configure the Web Server Access log or the Web Server Error log.

Preventing Full Log Buffers and Related Console Messages

When a significant amount of your traffic is using fast path for delay-critical real-time routing through the firewall, the console might display one of the following error messages:

```
[LOG-CRIT] kernel: FW-1: Log Buffer is full
[LOG-CRIT] kernel: FW-1: lost 500 log/trap messages
```

Tools & Traps...

Kernel Module

The kernel module maintains a buffer of waiting log messages that it forwards through **fwd** rough **fwd** to the management module. The buffer is circular, so that high logging volumes can cause buffer entries to be overwritten before they are sent to fwd. When this happens, the system log displays the following message:

```
log records lost
```

The lost records should have been recorded in the FW-1 log message file (typically located in the $FWDIR/log directory). You can use one or both of the following solutions to resolve this issue:

- Reducing the number of rules that are logged by:
  - Disabling as many accounting rules as possible
  - Changing as many long logging rules to short logging as possible
  - Eliminating logging entirely if it is practical to do so
- Increasing the size of the kernel module buffer

Perform the following procedures using the modzap utility. The modzap utility provides a way to modify some variable values upon bootup.

1. Set the execute permissions by issuing a ***cpstop*** command.
2. To confirm you have sufficient resources to increase the buffer size, issue the following command:

   ```
   modzap -n _fw_log_bufsize $FWDIR/boot/modules/fwmod.o 0x200000
   ```

   Where *0x200000* indicates a buffer size of 2MB, and the -n option causes *modzap* to check the value at the symbol reported.

   A console message is displayed confirming the change that will take place when you issue the *modzap* command in the next step.

   You can safely ignore this message.

NOTE

If the message indicates that you have insufficient resources to accommodate a larger buffer size, take appropriate actions and try this procedure again.

3. After you verify that the change is appropriate, issue the same command without the *-n* option:

   ```
   modzap _fw_log_bufsize $FWDIR/boot/modules/fwmod.o 0x200000
   ```

   A confirmation message is displayed, which you can safely ignore.
4. Reboot the system.

Because these console messages are also written to the FW-1 log message file, Nokia recommends that you do the following to prevent depleting the disk space allocated for the FW-1 log message file:

1. Move your log files from the system hard drive to a server.
2. Configure the relocated files by using the Check Point management client GUI (SmartDashboard) as follows:
    1. Select the Check Point gateway object you are configuring.
    2. Under **Gateway Object Configuration**, select the **Logs And Masters** section and do the following:
        - Specify the amount of free disk space required for local logging.
        - Specify to stop logging when the free disk space drops below x MB and to start logging to a new file.

When a new file is being used, the previously used log files are deleted until the required free disk space is restored.

Monitoring Protocols

In Nokia Network Voyager, you can view cluster status and members as well as routing protocol information.

Viewing Cluster Status and Members

You can view information about cluster status and members by clicking Clustering Monitor under Monitor in the tree view. This page summarizes information about a configured IPSO cluster, including information about cluster status and load sharing among members of the cluster. The information summary is refreshed every 30 seconds. The Cluster Status table contains the information described in Table 9.4, and the Cluster Member table contains the information described in Table 9.5.

Table 9.4 The Cluster Status Table

Field	Description
Cluster ID	ID number of the cluster
Cluster Uptime	Time since the cluster was formed
Number of Members	Current number of members in the cluster
Number of Interfaces	Number of interfaces where clustering is enabled
Network	Networks where clustering is enabled
Cluster IP Address	Cluster IP address on each network

Table 9.5 Member Status Table

Field	Description
Member ID	Node ID in the cluster
IP Addr	Primary IP address of the member
Hostname	Node hostname
Platform	Type of platform
OS Release	Operating system version that the node is running
Rating	Node performance rating
Time Since Join	Time since the node joined the cluster
Work Assigned (%)	Percentage of work load assigned to this node

NOTE

If your cluster is not initialized, the Cluster Monitor page contains a link to the Cluster Configuration page, which enables you to configure cluster parameters for this node. Figure 9.6 shows the Cluster Monitoring page when clustering has not been configured.

Figure 9.6 The Cluster Monitoring Page

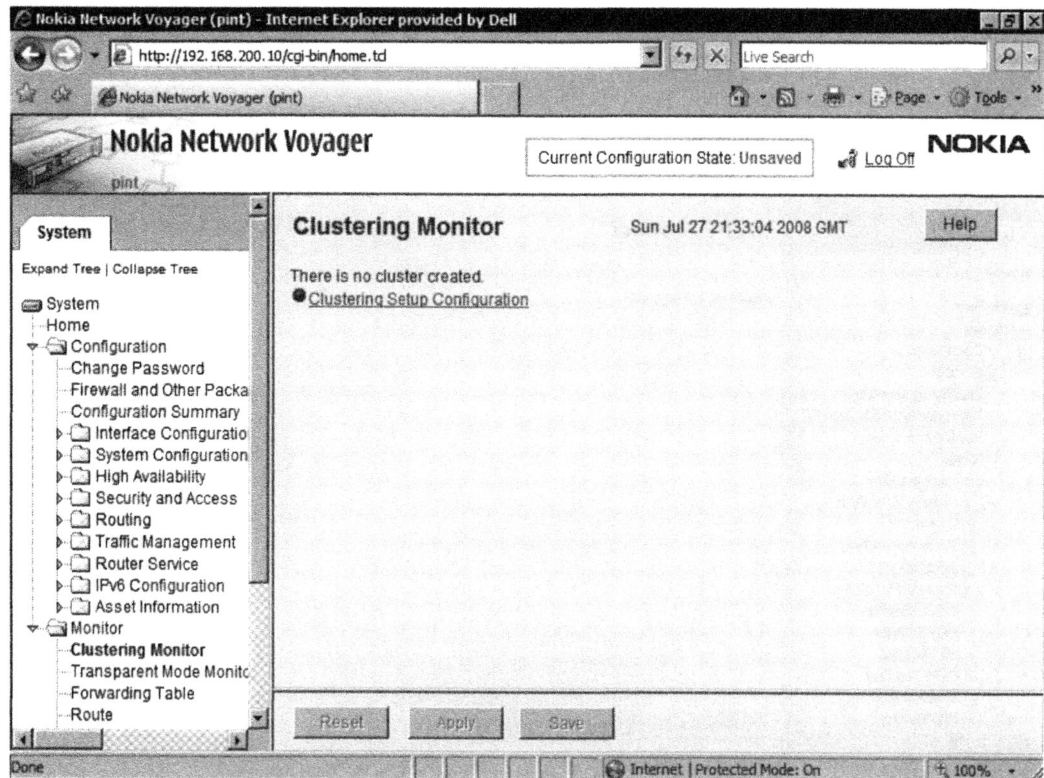

Viewing Routing Protocol Information

You can view statistical information about routing protocols by clicking the appropriate link under Monitor | Routing Protocols. Figure 9.7 here shows the routing protocols available in Nokia Network Voyager.

Figure 9.7 Routing Protocols

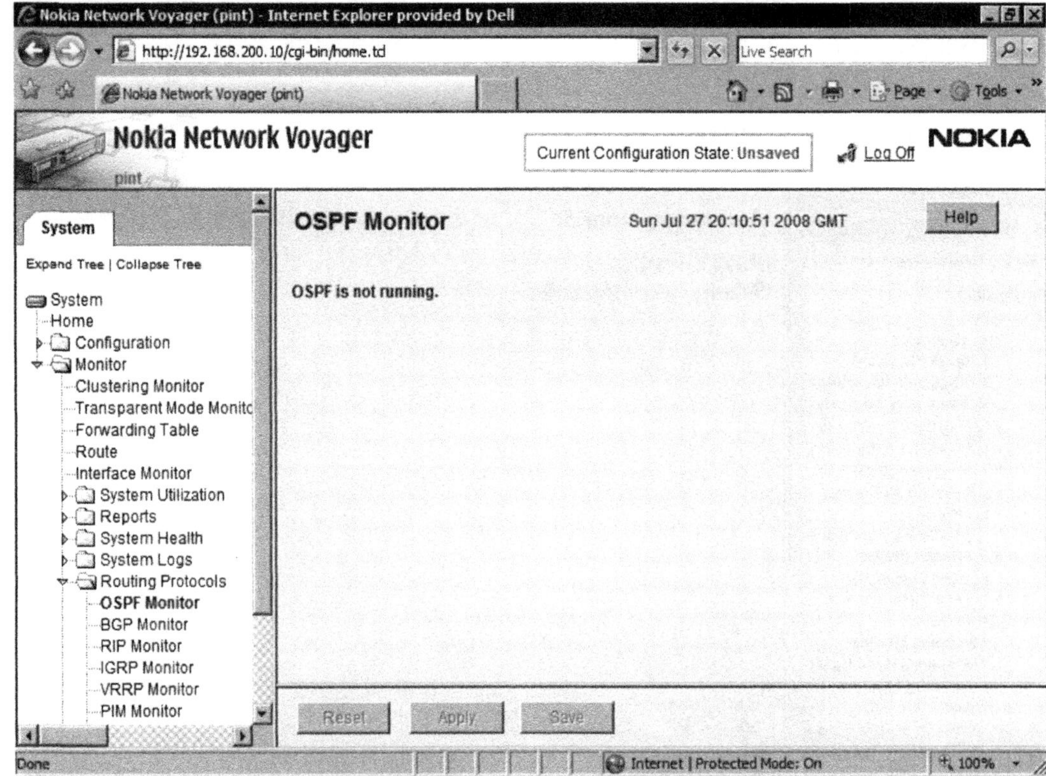

You can select from the following links:

- OSPF Monitor
- BGP Monitor
- RIP Monitor
- IGRP Monitor
- VRRP Monitor
- PIM Monitor
- DVMRP Monitor
- IGMP Monitor

To monitor routing protocol information for IPv6, you can select from the following links under Monitor | IPv6 Monitor:

- OSPFv3 Monitor
- RIPng Monitor
- IPv6 VRRP Monitor
- IPv6 Router Discovery Monitor
- IPv6 Route Monitor
- IPv6 Forwarding Table

Figure 9.8 shows the IPv6 monitoring options in Nokia Network Voyager.

Figure: 9.8 IPv6 Monitors

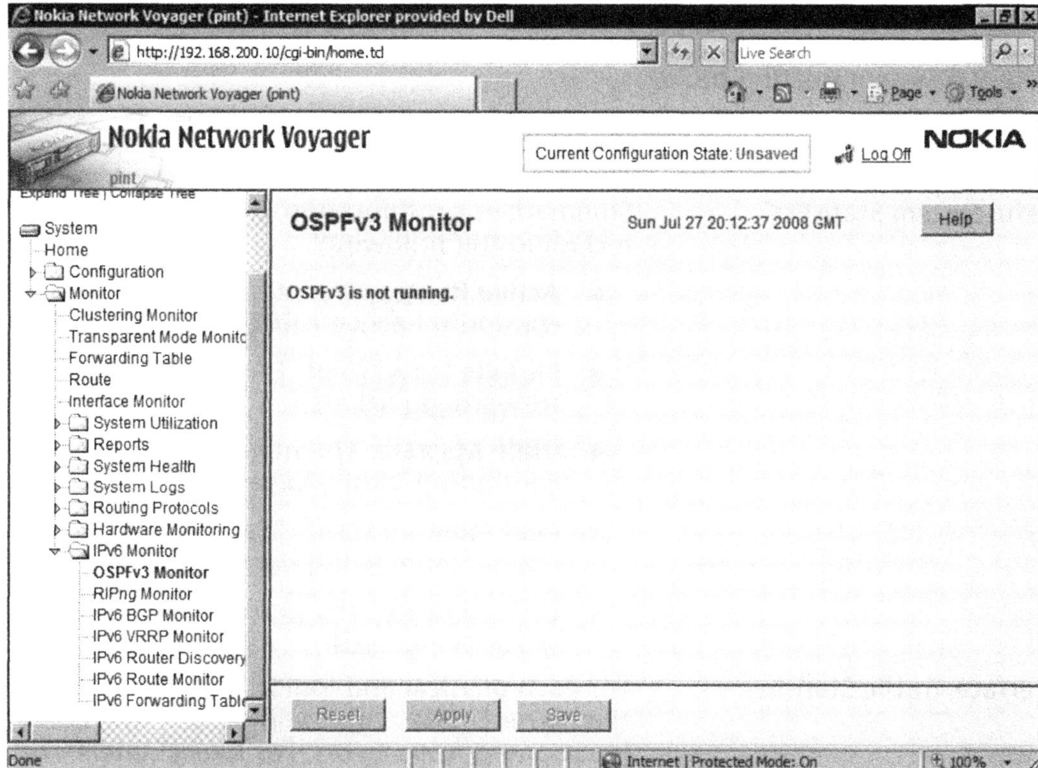

You can also view the following:

- **Kernal Forwarding Table** To view the IP forwarding table that the kernel is using to make its forwarding decisions, click **Forwarding Table** under **Monitor** | **Routing Protocols** in the tree view.
  - For IPv6, click **IPv6 Forwarding Table** under **Monitor** | **IPv6 Monitor**.

- **Route Settings** To view the route settings for your system, click **Route** under **Monitor** | **Routing Protocols** in the tree view.
- For IPv6, click **IPv6 Route Monitor** under **Monitor** | **IPv6 Monitor**.

- **Interface Settings** To view the interface settings for your system, click **Route** under **Monitor** | **Routing Protocols** in the tree view.

Monitoring System Health

The system health links let you display statistics to help you monitor the status of your IP security platform. To view this information, click the appropriate link under Monitor | System Health in the tree view. Table 9.6 describes the various system health checks, and Figure 9.9 shows the Useful System Statistics page in Nokia Network Voyager.

Table 9.6 System Health Checks

System Health	Description
Useful System Statistics	Summarizes configuration information, including the following: ■ **Active Routes** The number of configured active routes. ■ **Packets Forwarded** The number of forwarded packets. ■ **VRRP Masters** The number of configured VRRP masters. ■ **Real Memory Used** The percentage of the real memory being used. ■ **Disk Capacity** The percentage of the disk space being used.
Interface Traffic Statistics	For each physical and logical interface, it shows the current state, input and output bytes, and input and output errors. For logical interfaces, it also shows the type of device or virtual circuit accessed through the logical interface (for example, Ethernet, ATM, or FDDI). This page includes a link to the Link Aggregation Statistics page, which displays information about link aggregation groups and the individual interfaces in the groups.

Continued

Table 9.6 Continued. System Health Checks

System Health	Description
Interface Queue Statistics	Shows the current information for interface queues, including the following: ■ **Logical Name** The configured name of the queue. ■ **Maximum Packets** The configured maximum number of packets that can be buffered by this queue. ■ **Packets Passed** The number of packets sent from this queue to the physical interface. ■ **Bytes Passed** The number of bytes sent from this queue to the physical interface. ■ **Packets Dropped** The number of packets dropped at this queue due to lack of buffer space. ■ **Bytes Dropped** The number of bytes dropped at this queue due to lack of buffer space.
SecureXL Connection Statistics	Use this page to monitor SecureXL connections. This page retrieves the updated system statistics information every 15 seconds. The SecureXL Connection Statistics table summarizes information about connections, such as existing, added, and deleted connections handled by IPSO's SecureXL and ADP, if present in the system. ■ **Existing** The number of active connections. ■ **Added** The number of connections created in the last interval. ■ **Deleted** The number of connections torn down in the last interval.

Figure 9.9 The Useful System Statistics Page

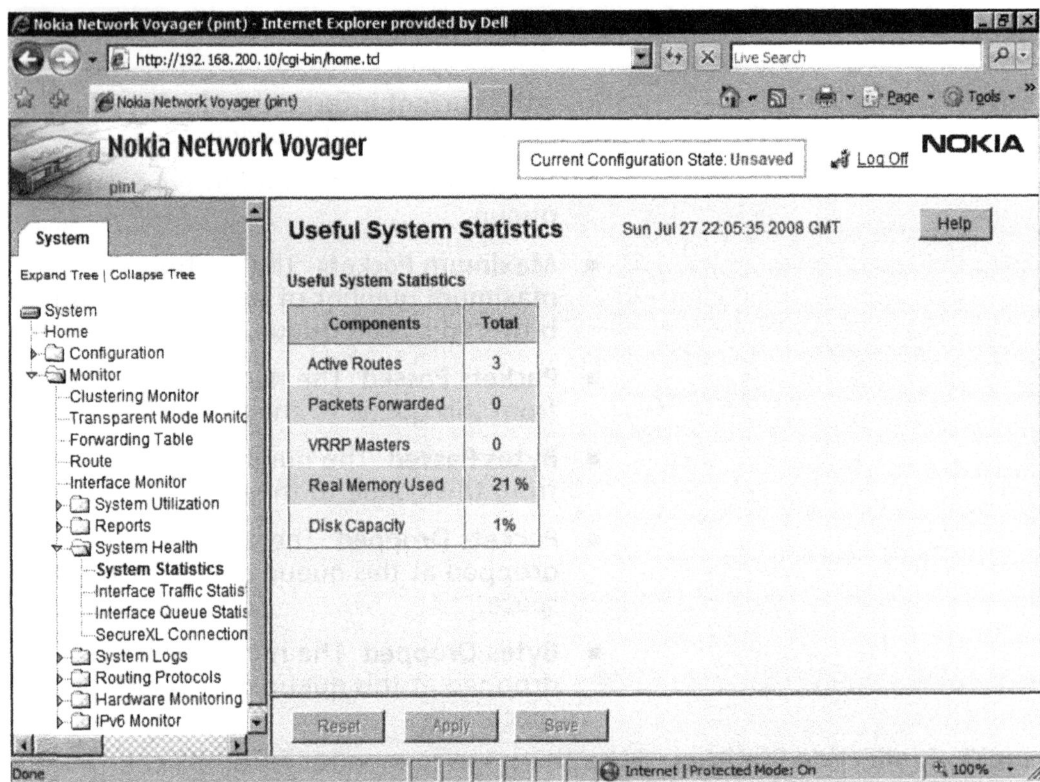

Monitoring Hardware

Located under Monitor | Hardware Monitoring, you can monitor system statuses, slot status, ADP status, and cryptographic accelerator statistics. You can use the System Status page to monitor system characteristics such as temperature fan power and watchdog timer, as well as to retrieve information about power supplies. Status appears only for elements that are present in your system. Figure 9.10 shows the System Status page.

Figure 9.10 The System Status Page

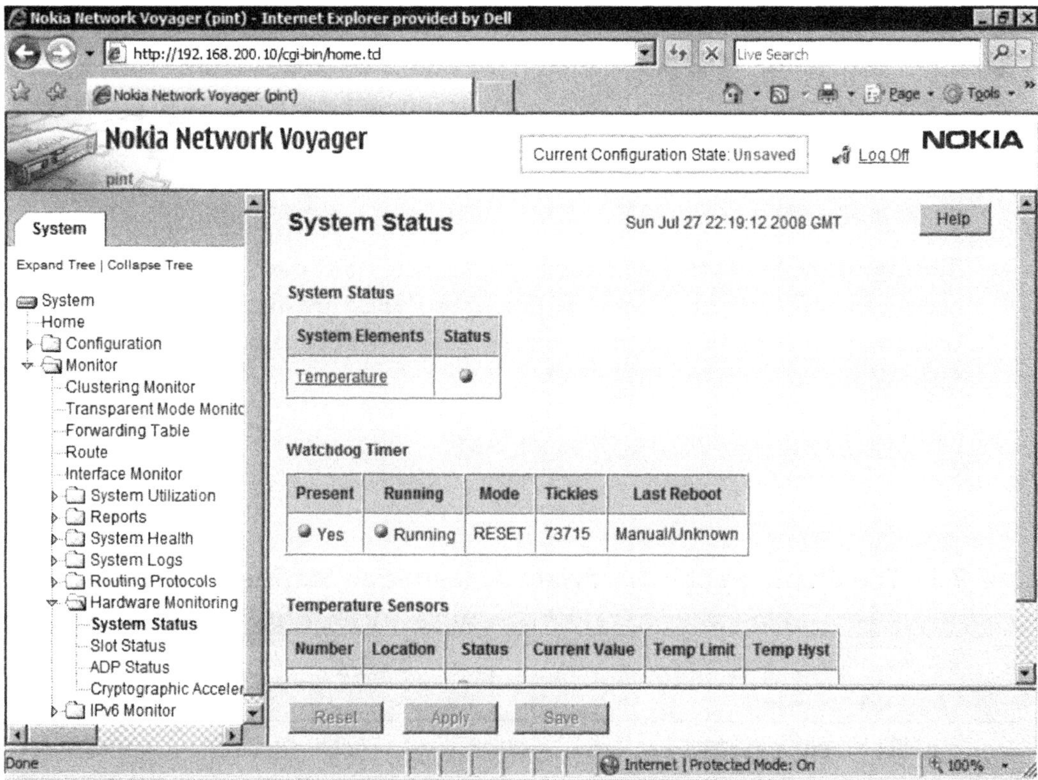

- **System Elements** This table summarizes the status of the various sensors. The status will be green if no sensor indicates a fault, and red otherwise.
- **Watchdog Timer** This table shows the state and activity of the watchdog timer.
- **Mode** Specifies the action taken when the watchdog timer expires. If RESET, then a system wide reset will be issued. If NMI, an NMI is generated.
- **Tickles** The System column shows the number of times the system tickled the watchdog timer.
- **Last Reboot** This message identifies the last cause of machine reboot.
- **Temperature Sensors** This table shows the state and activity of the temperature sensors. The columns specify the temperature sensor ID Number, Location, Status, Current Value, Temp Limit, and Temp Hyst, respectively, for each temperature sensor.

Use the Slot Status page to monitor the status of the I/O slots (PCI, CPCI, and so on) in your system.

Use the ADP Status page to monitor ADP card status. This status information is updated every 30 seconds.

- **CPU Utilization** The graph displays the utilization percentage for each processor core in the ADP subsystem. If multiple cores are utilized at the same percentage, only one indicator is shown for these cores. For example, if all the cores are utilized at 20 percent at a given time, the graph shows only one indicator at that time (at 20 percent).
- **Temperature Sensors** The temperatures of the ADP card (indicated by the onboard sensor) and ADP network processor (NPU) are indicated by the arrows in each graph. Temperatures in the green range are normal, while red indicates the fault range.

The Cryptographic Hardware Acceleration Statistics page (shown in Figure 9.11) shows status information for the cryptographic hardware accelerator.

Figure 9.11 The Cryptographic Hardware Acceleration Statistics Page

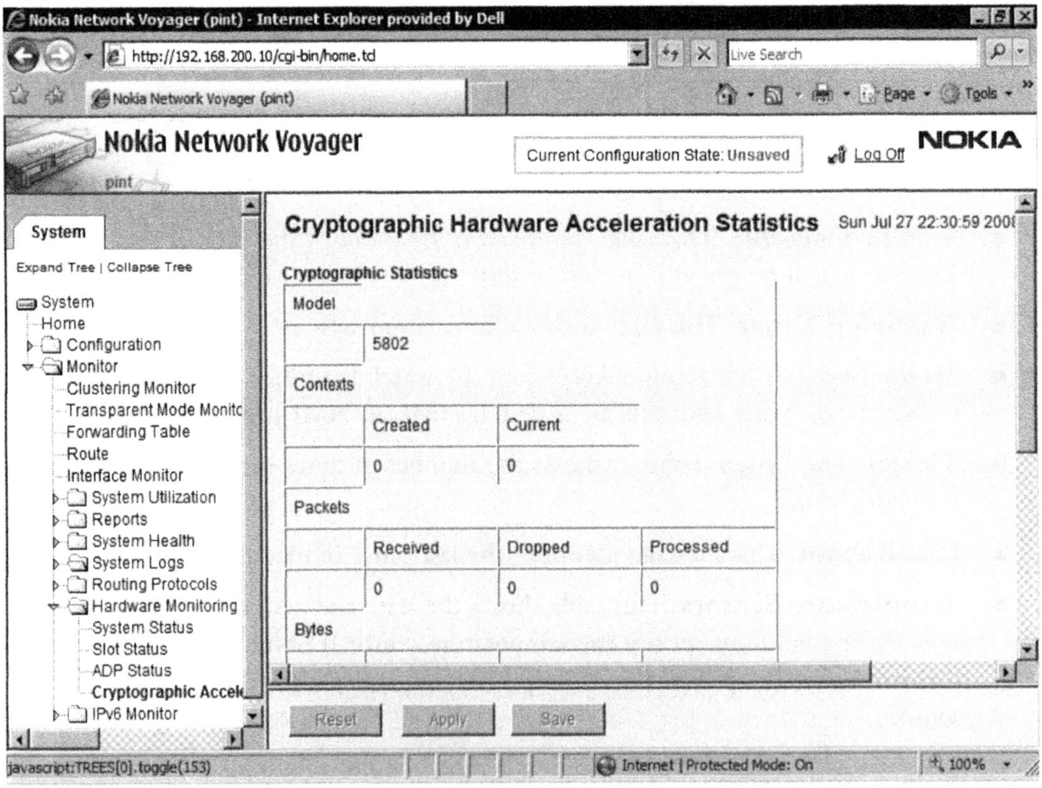

- **Contexts** A context is a Security Association. This provides a context for encrypting or decrypting data. There are generally two contexts created for one communications channel (one for each end of the channel).
    - *Created* context is a count of the contexts created since the last reboot.
    - *Current* context is a count of the contexts currently active on the device.
- **Packets** The packet statistics keep a count of the data packets passing through the device.
    - *Received* is a count of the packets passed to the driver for processing.
    - *Dropped* is a count of the number of packets that could not be processed by the device.
    - *Processed* is a count of the packets successfully processed by the device.
- **Bytes** The byte statistics keep a count of the data bytes passing through the device.
    - *Received* is a count of the number of data bytes received by the driver for processing.
    - *Dropped* is a count of the number of data bytes that could not be processed by the device.
    - *Processed* is a count of the number of data bytes successfully processed by the device.

NOTE

Byte statistics may overflow quickly on a heavily utilized encrypted channel.

- **Errors** The error statistics provide counts of errors associated with the device.
    - *Received Digest* errors are a count of the number of times that an invalid digest was encountered when a received message was processed.
    - *Random Number* errors are a count of the number of times a random number could not be generated.
    - *Buffer Alignment* errors are a count of the number of buffers passed to the device that were incorrectly aligned.

- *Device* errors are a count of the number of times that a device was not available to process a data message.
- *Memory* errors are a count of the number of times that memory could not be allocated to process a data message.
- *Context* errors are a count of the number of times that an invalid context was specified to process a data message.
- *Packet Header* errors are a count of the number of times that an mbuf did not have a valid header.

Using the iclid Tool

You can obtain routing diagnostic information by establishing a remote access session on the IP security platform and running *iclid* (IPSRD command-line interface daemon). To display routing daemon status using iclid:

1. Create a Telnet session and log in to the firewall.
2. Enter **iclid**. The prompt changes (to <node-name>) to indicate that you can now enter iclid commands.

Table 9.7 describes the iclid commands.

Table 9.7 iclid Commands

Command	Description
? or *<tab>*	Shows all possible command completions
help	Displays help information
quit or *exit*	Quits iclid and returns to the firewall shell
show	Shows formatted, categorized system information

Some commands might produce more output than can fit on a single screen. iclid pages the output of such commands for you—meaning it stops the output after one screen and adds a MORE prompt to indicate there is more output. You can see the next screen of output by pressing any key except the **q** key. You can abort the command and any further output by typing **q** at the MORE prompt. If you do not enter anything after approximately 30 seconds, the system automatically pages to the next screen of information. You can temporarily suspend this automatic paging by pressing **ctrl** + **S**. However, when you resume scrolling (by pressing any key) you might lose a page of information.

At any point in iclid, you can type **?** to display possible command completions. You can also abbreviate commands when an abbreviation is not ambiguous.

The *help* command takes as arguments iclid commands and top-level iclid categories. It displays a brief summary of what the specified command displays.

The *show* command provides many kinds of information, displayed in useful formats. Table 9.8 shows examples of the top-level iclid element that can be displayed by the *show* command as applied to each parameter, along with any selected categories and subcategories, and a description of the information the command displays.

Table 9.8 Top-Level iclid Elements

Element	Category	Subcategory	Description
Bgp			Provides a BGP summary
	Errors		A table of BGP errors
	Groups		A table of parameters and data for each BGP group
		Detailed	Detailed statistics on BGP groups
		Summary	A summary of statistics on BGP groups
	Memory		Lists BGP memory parameters and statistics
	Neighbor	<peerid> advertise	Shows BGP neighbor statistics
		detailed	Provides detailed information about BGP neighbors and is organized by neighbor address
	Paths		List of BGP paths
	Peers		Summary of information about peer firewalls
		detailed	Detailed information about each peer firewall
		summary	Summary table about peer firewalls

Continued

Table 9.8 Continued. Top-Level iclid Elements

Element	Category	Subcategory	Description
	redistribution	to AS <as number>	Shows detailed redistribution data from BGP to the designated AS
		to AS <as number> from <proto>	Shows detailed redistribution data to the designated AS from the specified protocol
	Statistics		A table of peer parameters and statistics
	Summary		BGP summary
bootpgw	Interface		BOOTP relay state of interfaces enabled for BOOT protocols
		<interface>	BOOTP relay state of specified interface
	Stats		Summary of BOOTP relay requests, and replies received and made
		rec	Summary of BOOTP relay requests received
		req	Summary of BOOTP relay requests made
		rep	Summary of BOOTP relay replies made
dvmrp			Summary of DVMRP state
	Interface		Interface-specific state of DVMRP for each DVMRP-enabled interface
	neighbor routes		State of DVMRP neighbor route
	Neighbors		Interface state of DVMRP neighbor parameters
	Route		Shows state of DVMRP route parameters

Continued

Table 9.8 Continued. Top-Level iclid Elements

Element	Category	Subcategory	Description
	Stats		Statistical information about DVMRP packets sent and received, including an error summary
		receive	A summary of statistical information about received DVMRP packets
		transmit	A summary of statistical information about transmitted DVMRP packets
		error	A summary of DVMRP packets with errors
igmp			State of IGMP
	Groups		State of the IGMP groups maintained for each network interface
	if stats		Summary of information about IGMP interface packets transmitted and received for each network interface
	Interface		IGMP settings for each network interface
	Stats		Statistical information about IGMP packets sent and received, as well as an error summary
inbound filter			Lists inbound filters and data for all protocols
interface			Status and addresses of all configured interfaces
krt			Displays IPSRD core information
memory			Total memory usage in kilobytes

Continued

Table 9.8 Continued. Top-Level iclid Elements

Element	Category	Subcategory	Description
	Detailed		Total memory use as well as memory use by each routing protocol
ospf	border routers		Lists OSPF border routers and associated codes
	Database	area	Provides statistical data on OSPF database area
		database summary	A database summary of the OSPF firewall
		router	Statistical data on fire-wall link states and link connections
		asbr summary	A summary of the OSPF firewall
		external	Information on the OSPF external database
		summary	Summary of the OSPF database
		checksum	Statistical data on the OSPF checksum database
		network	Data on the OSPF database network
		type	Data on the state of fire-wall link parameters
	Errors	brief	Provides basic data on OSPF errors
		Dd	OSPF dd errors
		hello	OSPF hello errors
		Ip	OSPF interface protocol errors
		lsack	OSPF ls acknowledge errors
		Lsr	OSPF lsr errors
		Lsu	OSPF lsu errors

Continued

Table 9.8 Continued. Top-Level iclid Elements

Element	Category	Subcategory	Description
		proto	OSPF protocol errors
	Events		OSPF events and event occurrences
	Interface	detail	Comprehensive presentation of detailed OSPF interface data
		stats	Comprehensive list of OSPF interface statistics
	Neighbor		Lists OSPF neighbors and associated parameters
	Packets		Lists received and transmitted OSPF packets
<proto>	inbound filter		Lists inbound filter data for the specified protocol
	redistribution		Lists redistributions from all sources to the designated protocol
	redistribution from <proto>		Lists redistributions from a specified protocol to another specified protocol
redistribution			Comprehensive list of redistributions to various protocols and autonomous systems, and includes detailed distribution data
resource			Comprehensive list of resource statistics
rip			Summary of information on the RIP routing process
	Errors		List of various RIP errors
	Packets		Statistics on various RIP packets transmitted and received
route			Lists data on static and directly connected routes

Continued

Table 9.8 Continued. Top-Level iclid Elements

Element	Category	Subcategory	Description
	Aggregate		Data on aggregate routes by code letter
	All		List of all routes and status data
		aggregate	Data on all aggregate routes by code letter
		bgp	Data on BGP routes
		direct	Data on direct routes
		igrp	Data on IGRP routes
		ospf	Data on OSPF routes
		Rip	Data on RIP routes
		static	Data on static routes
	bgp		Statistics on BGP routes
		aspath	List of parameters and status of BGP AS path
		communities	Status of BGP communities
		detailed	Details of BGP routes
		metrics	Status of BGP metrics
		suppressed	List and status of suppressed BGP routes
	direct		Directly connected routes and their status
	igrp		Displays IGRP routes
	inactive		Inactive routes
		aggregate	Inactive aggregate routes
		bgp	Inactive BGP routes
		direct	Inactive direct routes
		igrp	Inactive IGRP routes
		ospf	Inactive OSPF routes
		rip	Inactive RIP routes
		static	Inactive static routes

Continued

Table 9.8 Continued. Top-Level iclid Elements

Element	Category	Subcategory	Description
	ospf		OSPF route data
	rip		Static route data
	static		Displays the number of routes for each protocol
	summary		Displays the number of routes for each protocol
version			Operating system version information
vrrp			VRRP state information
	interface		VRRP interfaces and associated information
	stats		VRRP transmission and reception statistics

Table 9.9 shows examples of the iclid *show* command.

Table 9.9 The iclid *show Command*

iclid show command	Shows
show ospf	OSPF summary information
show ospf neighbor (s o n)	OSPF neighbor information
show route	All routes
show route bgp 127	Only BGP routes that start with 127
show b?	All possible command completions for show b

Summary

Using Nokia Network Voyager, you can monitor several aspects of your IP security platform to better maintain performance and security. For example, you can monitor state information for each interface, view the contents of IP routing tables, and generate reports on events such as throughput, bandwidth utilization, and link states over specific periods of time.

You can use the system utilization statistics to monitor and tune the allocation of your system resources. For example, if the file system capacity percentage increases, you should take action, such as deleting old IPSO images and packages or moving your log files to a remote system. To view statistical information on system utilization, click CPU-Memory Live Utilization, Disk and Swap Space Utilization, or Process Utilization under System Utilization of the Monitor folder in the tree view.

By clicking the link for the appropriate report under Monitor | Reports in the tree view, you can generate reports of data collection events. The administrator can configure how often the data is collected, whether each data collection event is enabled or disabled, and how many hours worth of collected data are stored on the system.

You can view information about cluster status and members, by clicking Clustering Monitor under Monitor in the tree view. This page summarizes information about a configured IPSO cluster, including information about cluster status and load sharing among members of the cluster. You can also view statistical information about routing protocols by clicking the appropriate link under Monitor | Routing Protocols.

The system health links let you display statistics to help you monitor the status of your IP security platform. To view this information, click the appropriate link under Monitor | System Health in the tree view. You can view the system health for Useful System Statistics, Interface Traffic Statistics, Interface Queue Statistics, and SecureXL Connection Statistics. Located under Monitor | Hardware Monitoring, you can monitor system statuses, slot status, ADP status, and cryptographic accelerator statistics.

You can obtain routing diagnostic information by creating a telnet session on the IP security platform and running iclid. Some commands might produce more output than can fit on a single screen; iclid pages the output of such commands for you—meaning it stops the output after one screen and adds a MORE prompt to indicate there is more output. You can see the next screen of output by pressing any key except the **q** key. You can abort the command and any further output by typing **q** at the MORE prompt. If you do not enter anything after approximately 30 seconds, the system automatically pages to the next screen of information.

Solutions Fast Track

Monitoring System Utilization

☑ Using Nokia Network Voyager, you can monitor several aspects of your IP security platform to better maintain performance and security.

☑ Use the system utilization statistics to monitor and tune the allocation of your system resources.

☑ The administrator can configure how often the data is collected, whether each data collection event is enabled or disabled, and how many hours' worth of collected data are stored on the system.

Monitoring Protocols

☑ You can view information about cluster status and members by clicking Clustering Monitor under Monitor in the tree view.

☑ If your cluster is not initialized, the Cluster Monitor page contains a link to the Cluster Configuration page, which enables you to configure cluster parameters for this node.

☑ You can also view statistical information about routing protocols by clicking the appropriate link under Monitor | Routing Protocols.

Monitoring System Health

☑ The system health links allow you to display statistics to help you monitor the status of your IP security platform.

☑ You can view the system health for Useful System Statistics, Interface Traffic Statistics, Interface Queue Statistics, and SecureXL Connection Statistics.

☑ Located under Monitor | Hardware Monitoring, you can monitor system statuses, slot status, ADP status, and cryptographic accelerator statistics.

Using the iclid Tool

☑ You can obtain routing diagnostic information by creating a telnet session on the IP security platform and running iclid.

☑ The *help* command takes as arguments iclid commands and top-level iclid categories. It displays a brief summary of what the specified command displays.

☑ The *show* command provides many kinds of information, displayed in useful formats.

Frequently Asked Questions

Q: Where can I view statistical information on system use?

A: To view statistical information on system utilization, click CPU-Memory Live Utilization, Disk and Swap Space Utilization, or Process Utilization under System Utilization of the Monitor folder in the tree view.

Q: How do I read the values in the System Load table?

A: The System Load Average table summarizes the load averages, which are the number of processes in the system run queue averaged over the last 1, 5, and 15 minutes, respectively. Load averages that are high, such as over 2 in all three fields, indicate that the system is under continuous heavy load.

Q: Can I view specific bandwidth utilization?

A: Yes, by using the Rate-Shaping report. You can use traffic shaping to implement a specific policy that controls the way data is queued for transmission.

Q: How can I view the IP forwarding table that the kernel is using to make its forwarding decisions?

A: Click Forwarding Table under Monitor | Routing Protocols in the tree view.

Q: Can I monitor clusters?

A: Yes. You must initialize the cluster first, however. If your cluster is not initialized, the Cluster Monitor page contains a link to the Cluster Configuration page that enables you to configure cluster parameters for this node.

Q: How can I view the route settings for my system?

A: To view the route settings for your system, click Route under Monitor | Routing Protocols in the tree view.

Q: How do I read the information on the SecureXL table?

A: This page retrieves the updated system statistics information every 15 seconds. The SecureXL Connection Statistics table summarizes information about connections, such as existing, added, and deleted connections handled by IPSO's SecureXL and ADP, if present in the system. The number of active connections is represented by *Existing*, while the number of connections created in the last interval is represented by *Added*, and the number of connections torn down in the last interval is represented by *Deleted*.

Q: What type of information is reported on interface traffic?

A: For each physical and logical interface, it shows the current state, input and output bytes, and input and output errors. For logical interfaces, it also shows the type of device or virtual circuit accessed through the logical interface (for example, Ethernet, ATM, or FDDI).

Q: What hardware information can I monitor?

A: You can monitor system statuses, slot status, ADP status, and cryptographic accelerator statistics. You can also use the System Status page to monitor system characteristics such as temperature fan power and watchdog timer as well as to retrieve information about power supplies.

Q: What is iclid?

A: You can use iclid to obtain routing diagnostic information in a telnet session on the IP security platform.

Q: Is there a man page for iclid?

A: No. See Tables 9.7, 9.8, and 9.9 for iclid commands and elements.

Q: The resulting output advanced a screen before I could finish reading the results. Can I go back?

A: No. You need to re-run the command. If you do not enter anything after approximately 30 seconds, the system automatically pages to the next screen of information. You can temporarily suspend this automatic paging by pressing **ctrl** + **S**, although when you resume scrolling (by pressing any key) you might lose a page of information.

Chapter 10

High Availability

Solutions in this chapter:

- Understanding Check Point High Availability
- Configuring the Nokia VRRP Implementation
- Configuring the Nokia VRRP Monitored Circuit
- Configuring Check Point Gateway Clusters to Use the Nokia VRRP

☑ Summary

☑ Solutions Fast Track

☑ Frequently Asked Questions

Introduction

"What about high availability?" asked Mark. "We're going to want to have these firewalls deployed using an active-standby architecture in case of failure."

Shin moved to the High Availability section of the Configuration menu. "From the High Availability section, you can configure VRRP for active standby, or Nokia IP Clustering where both Nokia appliances share the load across multiple platforms," replied Shin. "Since your requirement is for active-standby, we'll walk through the configuration of VRRP."

Mark and Ming took notes as Shin explained how to configure the two Nokia appliances to interoperate using the VRRP protocol. Shin defined one system as the primary and the other as the backup. "This will ensure that if the primary Nokia appliance fails, the other Nokia appliance will take over as master and continue to pass the traffic," explained Shin.

"You know what this means, Mark?" Marty asked him.

"What?" Mark said.

"Not only has Ming saved me money on training but I may have just saved a bundle on overtime pay for you."

Ming laughed as Mark shot her an uneasy look.

"Trust me, Mark," Marty said with a smile. "Your wife and kids will appreciate having you home instead of running into the office at 2 A.M. to swap out a border firewall."

Mark smiled. "I guess I'll have to get used to this sleep thing I've been hearing so much about."

Understanding Check Point High Availability

The major components of the high-availability solutions from Nokia are firewall synchronization and the handling of IP address failover. We will first discuss the synchronization process of the firewall.

As connections pass through a Check Point, the firewall is building a connections table of information to track the traffic. The connections table is what Check Point uses in their patented stateful inspection technology. If a session is permitted by the inspection engine of the kernel, all packets associated with the session are permitted through the firewall. This method of analyzing traffic is advantageous from a performance and scalability perspective, but can produce issues when dealing with a high-availability implementation.

In this example, we assume that Peter connects to the Internet through the Check Point firewall from his corporate network, shown in Figure 10.1.

1. Check Point firewall A will inspect the outgoing packets.
2. It will log these connections into the connections table. If Check Point firewall A fails, then Check Point firewall B will take over.

3. The Web server that we connect to will return the response to Peter's initial connection to Check Point firewall A. When Check Point firewall B examines this connection, it will drop the packet because it has no prior record of the connection.

Figure 10.1 Dual Firewalls Without State Synchronization

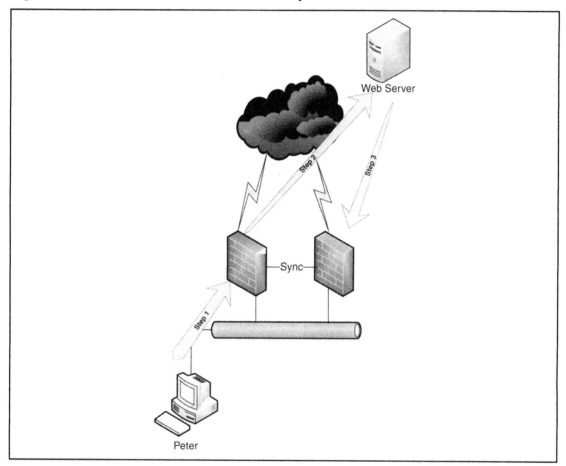

Although in our first example we had a failover firewall for any new connections, existing connections were dropped. This could cause serious repercussions in an environment where existing connections must be kept to transfer data. To accomplish this, we need to ensure that the firewalls share their connections table. Check Point accomplishes this with the state-synchronization protocol. We will perform the same test again, but this time using the state-synchronization protocol, shown in Figure 10.2.

1. Check Point A will inspect the outgoing packets.
2. It will log these connections into the connections table.

3. Check Point firewall A will copy the new connection table entry to the Check Point firewall B connection table via the Check Point Synchronization protocol.
4. If Check Point firewall A fails, then Check Point firewall B will assume control over the existing connections from the Web server and forward them to user Peter.

Figure 10.2 Dual Firewalls With State Synchronization

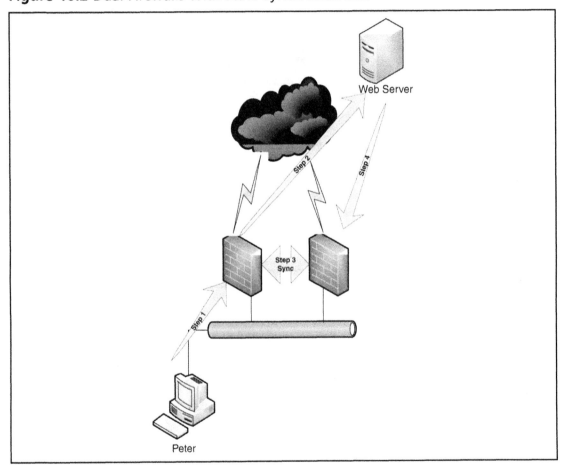

The second major component of a Nokia high-availability solution is IP failover. In our previous example, we discussed how Check Point firewall B would take over all existing and new connections if Check Point firewall A were to go offline for some reason. For this to transparently and seamlessly take place, the IP address of the primary firewall would have to be passed to the backup firewall. See Figure 10.3.

Figure 10.3 High Availability and IP Address Failover

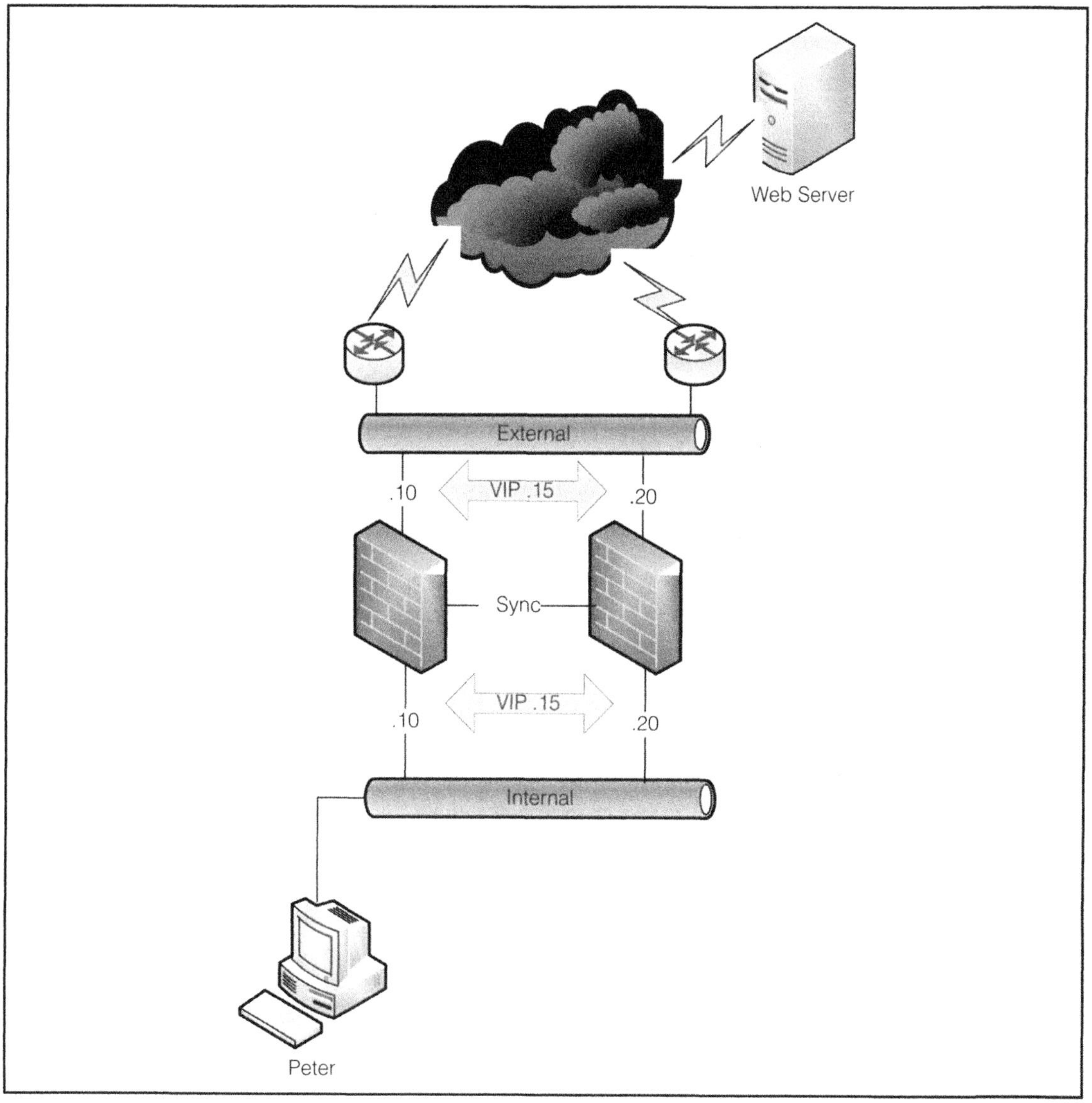

Figure 10.3 shows the firewalls having two sets of addresses: one external IP address, typically allocated by your ISP, and an internal IP address. Check Point firewall A has been implemented with a .10 address, while Check Point B has a .20. The .15 address is a virtual IP address (VIP) and is shared by the two firewalls. For example, if Peter wanted to connect to Check Point firewall A, he could use the .10 IP address or the VIP, but only if Check Point firewall A was the master.

VIPs are handled a little differently depending on whether you decide to implement Nokia VRRP or IP Clustering. The virtual address of the internal interfaces of the firewalls would be used as the default gateway for your user systems on the network, and the real IP addresses of the firewalls are mostly used for administration and maintenance.

Tools & Traps...

Synchronization Networks

When designing your network for highly available firewalls, you should use a separate network to handle the firewall synchronization traffic. This network should not be used on your existing network.

It is also recommended that no other device be connected to the synchronization network. There simply is no need to have any additional traffic load on this network.

Configuring the Nokia VRRP Implementation

Nokia currently supports two solutions to provide a highly available firewall: VRRP Monitored Circuit and IP Clustering. Both features are built into the IPSO operating system and take a minimal amount of time to configure. First, we are going to discuss the more popular and widely used VRRP Monitored Circuit.

Understanding the VRRP Configuration

When configuring a Nokia for VRRP, you must designate a primary router and backup routers. The master router will be responsible for passing packets sent to the VIPs.

Tools & Traps...

Master Router

The master router will pass packets that are sent to its VIP addresses, but by default, you will not be able to connect to the VIP addresses themselves. You must specifically permit these connections if you must connect to the firewall using the VIP address.

If you are going to be configuring Nokia VRRP with VPNs, you need to enable the Accept Connections To VRRP IP option in Voyager. This step facilitates IKE key exchange between VPN endpoints.

If Check Point firewall A fails, then Check Point firewall B assumes the VIPs of the primary firewall and takes over any existing and new connections with no interruption to the users. Essentially, VRRP provides router resiliency in a statically routed environment without requiring configuration of dynamic routing or router discovery protocols.

Understanding the VRRP Protocol

To fully understand the VRRP protocol and how it handles failover, it is essential that we look at a few of the parameters within the protocol. Figure 10.4 presents the different fields in the VRRP Packet Header.

Figure 10.4 VRRP Packet Header

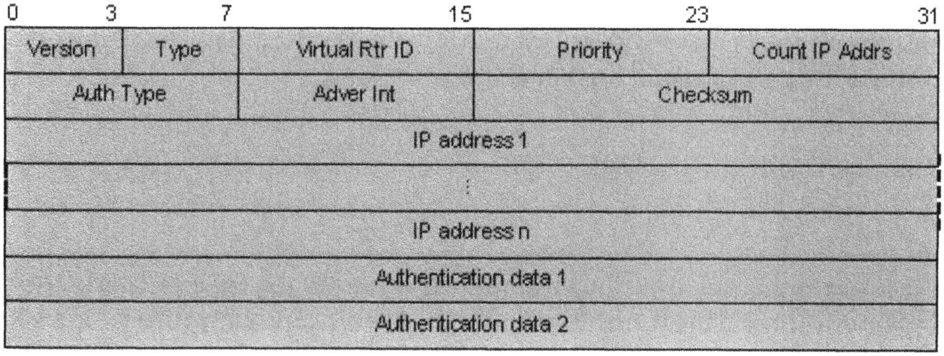

0 3 7 15 23 31

Version	Type	Virtual Rtr ID	Priority	Count IP Addrs
Auth Type		Adver Int	Checksum	
IP address 1				
⋮				
IP address n				
Authentication data 1				
Authentication data 2				

- **Version** This field specifies the VRRP protocol version that is being used. It cannot be altered within the IPSO operating system.

- **Type** A message type of 1 is used in this field to designate the message type. This cannot be altered within the IPSO operating system.
- **Priority** This field is crucial during the election process to determine the state of a master and backup. The router with the highest priority configured will be master.
- **IP Address Count** Denotes the number of IP addresses contained in this VRRP advertisement. The IP address count field is limited to 8 bits. This allows us to calculate the total number of virtual routers supported on one segment to 255. Considering this is calculated on a segment-by-segment basis, this should be adequate for any environment size.
- **Authentication Type** VRRP supports three different authentication types, which are identified in this field, but Nokia currently only recognizes two of them.
- **Advertisement Interval** This field presents the time, in seconds, between VRRP advertisements. It only takes three missed advertisements for the backup to assume that the primary router is down and unavailable.
- **Checksum** The checksum field is a simple error checking mechanism.
- **IP addresses** This field will list all of the VIPs the master is currently using.
- **Authentication Data** This field is variable in length and may contain up to an eight-character alphanumeric string. If a VRRP advertisement is received with the incorrect authentication string, it is discarded and the incident logged in the /varlog/messages file.

Implementing VRRP for XYZ Inc.

Now that we understand how Nokia VRRP works, let's run through how to implement it for an organization. As shown in Figure 10.3, XYZ has decided to implement Nokia VRRP to ensure that inbound and outbound connections are reliable at all times.

Both firewalls are identical with regard to hardware specifications. The settings shown in Table 10.1 and 10.2 are made on each interface.

NOTE

In this example, we are using the identical hardware for our Nokia VRRP implementation. This is not a requirement. You can configure Nokia VRRP with an IP380 and an IP150.

Be advised that if your backup firewall cannot handle your traffic load and your primary fails, you might have problems. Investing in two firewalls that can handle your traffic load is recommended.

Table 10.1 Internal Interfaces

VRRP Settings	Nokia A	Nokia B
VRID	10	10
Virtual Address	10.1.1.225	10.1.1.225
Priority	100	95
Hello Interval	1	1

Table 10.2 External Interfaces

VRRP Settings	Nokia A	Nokia B
VRID	20	20
Virtual Address	222.222.222.1	222.222.222.1
Priority	100	95
Hello Interval	1	1

These settings successfully satisfy the stated requirements. Two networks are running VRRP, one on the internal network and the other on the external network. Nokia A begins as the master because it has the higher priority. If Nokia B does not receive three consecutive advertisements, it thinks that the primary is down and assumes the position of master.

NOTE

Nokia A assumes primary control when it comes back online, but this can now be preconfigured in Check Point SmartDashboard so that the firewall currently online resumes control even if the primary comes back online.

Although not a requirement, most organizations implement their highly available firewalls to always switch control back to the primary firewall.

Understanding VRRP Monitored Circuits

You might be wondering what happens when only an interface on the primary VRRP router goes down, but all other interfaces continue to be active. This would cause a problem because the backup router would assume control for the failed interface, but not for any other interface.

To get around this issue, Nokia introduced the Monitored Circuits feature. This feature allows a firewall to monitor the link state of its interfaces so that if an interface fails, the priority in the advertisements of its other interfaces is degraded.

In the previous example, if we were configuring the internal interface of Nokia A, we would have it monitor the link status of its external interface. If the external interface goes down, the internal priority is affected. The external interface delta value is subtracted from the overall priority to yield a new priority.

If you are still confused, we will look at the same example for XYZ Inc., but this time include some additional configuration options such as delta values, which are an option with monitored circuits. It is extremely important to pay close attention to the delta values you choose when configuring monitored circuits. The value you choose must degrade the primary router.

For this example, we have two Nokia devices. Nokia A is the master for all three VRRP circuits, as outlined in Tables 10.3, 10.4, and 10.5. For each interface that the Nokia devices share, they must have the same backup IP address and VRID.

Table 10.3 VRRP Monitored Interface eth-s1p1c0 Settings

eth-s1p1c0	Nokia A	Nokia B
VRID	10	10
Virtual Address	10.1.1.225	10.1.1.225
Priority	100	95
Hello Interval	1	1
Monitored Interfaces	eth-s1p2	eth-s1p2
	eth-s1p3	eth-s1p3
Delta	20	20

Table 10.4 VRRP Monitored Interface eth-s1p3c0 Settings

eth-s1p2c0	Nokia A	Nokia B
VRID	20	20
Virtual Address	222.222.222.1	222.222.222.1
Priority	100	95
Hello Interval	1	1
Monitored Interfaces	eth-s1p1	eth-s1p1
	eth-s1p3	eth-s1p3
Delta	20	20

Table 10.5 VRRP Monitored Interface eth-s1p3c0 Settings

eth-s1p3c0	Nokia A	Nokia B
VRID	30	30
Virtual Address	10.10.10.1	10.10.10.1
Priority	100	95
Hello Interval	1	1
Monitored Interfaces	eth-s1p1	eth-s1p1
	eth-s1p2	eth-s1p2
Delta	20	20

NOTE

This configuration is classified as an active/passive or HA configuration. The only time that the backup firewall handles traffic in any direction is if the primary firewall goes down. This type of configuration is most common with organizations today.

Nokia also supports IPSO Clustering, which checks if all of the highly available firewalls handle traffic and maintain a consistent load amongst them. This is a great feature but is not as common as an active/passive implementation.

With regard to priorities, you can essentially choose the value you like. Most implementations begin with priority 100 for the master. All other firewall priority settings should obviously be somewhere below the priority set for the master.

The priority settings are set up so Nokia A is the master of all three addresses, but if any of the Nokia A interfaces fail, Nokia A fails over to Nokia B. In our example, the Nokia A base priority is 100, which is lowered to 80 if an interface goes down (100 – 20 = 80). Nokia B would then take over because it has a priority of 95, which is higher than the priority of 80.

Comparing VRRP v2 to Monitored Circuits

Version 2 of VRRP is an older and less functional way of implementing VRRP. VRRPv2 does not use virtual addresses to provide failover capabilities. Instead, it uses dynamic routing protocols to advertise alternate routes to networks.

The biggest disadvantage to using VRRPv2 is that, unless your firewall completely crashes and goes offline, you stand to have serious issues with a complete failover. For example, if one network interface goes offline when using VRRPv2, the other interfaces continue to advertise as master. This causes asymmetric routing issues that most firewalls do not like.

Due to this issue with firewalls, specifically Check Point firewalls, Nokia no longer recommends VRRPv2 for customers who want to implement VRRP solutions. Using Monitored Circuits eliminates the asymmetric routing conditions.

Configuring the Nokia VRRP Monitored Circuit

We have covered how to implement Nokia VRRP from a theoretical standpoint. We will now demonstrate how to implement this solution using the Nokia CLI and Network Voyager interface using the same example network from the previous section. We will work with two Nokia firewalls that are configured with internal, external, and synchronization interfaces, respectively.

The first thing we need to do is configure the Nokia firewalls individually. For example, network interfaces, DNS settings, routing, and so on. After this has been completed, we can configure VRRP and then add both Nokia firewalls to a Check Point gateway cluster object.

Here is a list of steps to follow:

1. Configure all interfaces.
2. Synchronize the system time.
3. Add entries to the Host tables.
4. Configure VRRP settings.
5. Configure a Check Point gateway cluster.

Configuring All Interfaces

Using Tables 10.3 and 10.4, we configure our interfaces as shown in Figures 10.5 and 10.6.

Figure 10.5 The Nokia A Interface Configuration

Interface Configuration Mon Jul 21 18:27:13 2008 GMT

Maximum number of VLANs allowed (0 - 1015):

Physical	Up	Logical	VLAN ID	Active	Up	Type	IP Address	Destination	Comments
eth1		eth1c0		On Off		Fast Ethernet	10.1.1.222	10.1.1.0/24	Internal
eth2		eth2c0		On Off		Fast Ethernet	222.222.222.11	222.222.222.0/24	External
eth3		eth3c0		On Off		Ethernet	172.16.1.1	172.16.1.0/24	Sync
eth4		eth4c0		On Off		Ethernet			
loop0		loop0c0				Loopback	127.0.0.1		
pppoe0						PPP-over-Ethernet			
Tunnels						Tunnel			

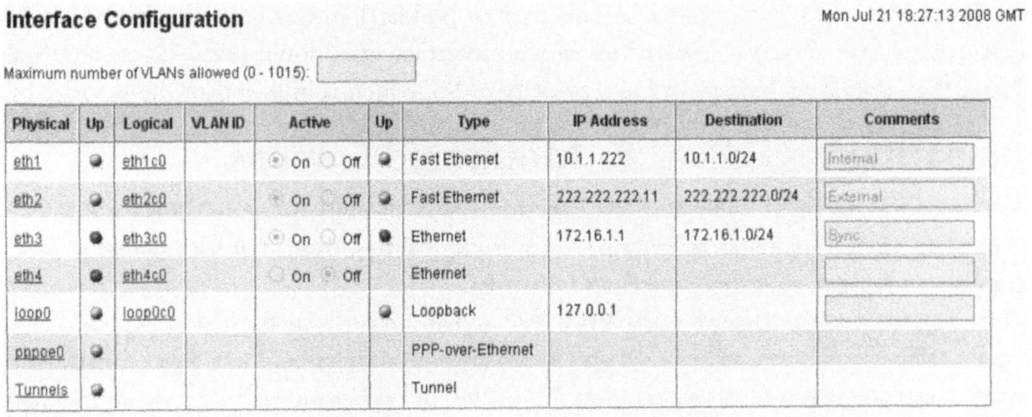

Figure 10.6 The Nokia B Interface Configuration

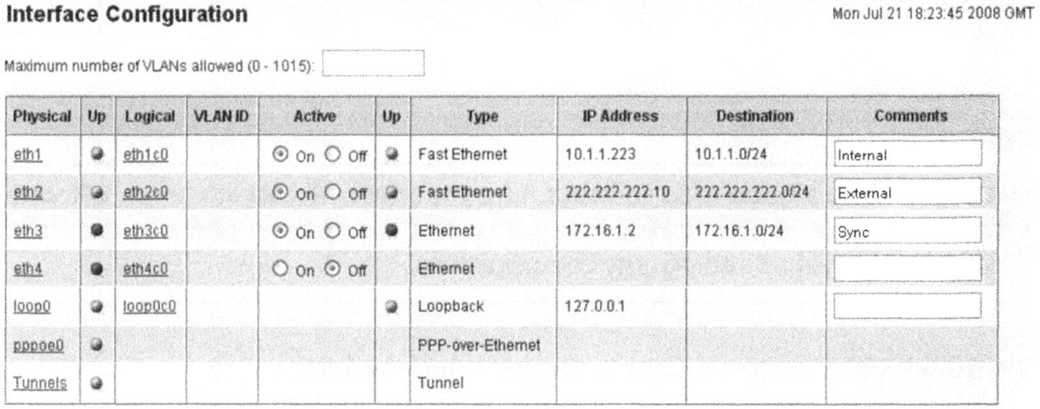

Interface Configuration Mon Jul 21 18:23:45 2008 GMT

Maximum number of VLANs allowed (0 - 1015):

Physical	Up	Logical	VLAN ID	Active	Up	Type	IP Address	Destination	Comments
eth1		eth1c0		(•) On ( ) Off		Fast Ethernet	10.1.1.223	10.1.1.0/24	Internal
eth2		eth2c0		(•) On ( ) Off		Fast Ethernet	222.222.222.10	222.222.222.0/24	External
eth3		eth3c0		(•) On ( ) Off		Ethernet	172.16.1.2	172.16.1.0/24	Sync
eth4		eth4c0		( ) On (•) Off		Ethernet			
loop0		loop0c0				Loopback	127.0.0.1		
pppoe0						PPP-over-Ethernet			
Tunnels						Tunnel			

Synchronizing the Time

Synchronizing the time is the most important step to remember when configuring your highly available firewalls to properly failover. The Check Point synchronization protocol demands that the firewalls used in a gateway cluster object be no more than a few seconds in sync with each other. It is best to use a time server (NTP) for consistency.

NOTE

The Nokia Security Platform (NSP) has an internal CMOS clock that can also be used. Considering that most hardware clocks tend to lag over time, this is not always a recommended solution.

To ensure that the time on your firewalls is always maintained, it is recommended that NTP be configured. This way you can be sure that a proper failover will occur if the primary firewall crashes.

Configuring the Host Table

Configuring the host table is not required, but it is recommended by Nokia, which prefers that you configure the hostname and IP address pair of each cluster member into the other host table. Configuring the host table is simple and was covered earlier in the book.

Configuring VRRP Settings Using Voyager

Setting the Voyager VRRP settings takes some getting used to. Like other parts of Nokia Network Voyager, the configuration form changes dynamically as you fill in and apply settings.

Before we start, we should make a table for our VRRP settings. We will use this table as a reference when we go into the configuration pages (see Tables 10.6 and 10.7).

NOTE

It is generally a good idea to make sure that firewall monitoring is off when configuring VRRP. This makes it easier to test the failover without the firewall configuration adding any complications.

Table 10.6 VRRP Monitored Circuit Internal Interface Settings

Internal	Nokia A	Nokia B
VRID	10	10
Virtual Address	10.1.1.225	10.1.1.225
Priority	100	95
Hello Interval	1	1
Monitored Interfaces	eth-s2p1	eth-s2p1
Delta	20	20

Table 10.7 VRRP Monitored Circuit External Interface Settings

External	Nokia A	Nokia B
VRID	20	20
Virtual Address	222.222.222.1	222.222.222.1
Priority	100	95
Hello Interval	1	1
Monitored Interfaces	eth-s1p1	eth-s1p1
Deltas	20	20

We will configure Nokia A first:

1. In Nokia Network Voyager, go to **Configuration** | **High Availability** | **VRRP**.
2. Select **Legacy VRRP Configuration** and **Monitored Circuit** for the internal and external interfaces, as shown in Figure 10.7.

Figure 10.7 Enabling Monitored Circuits

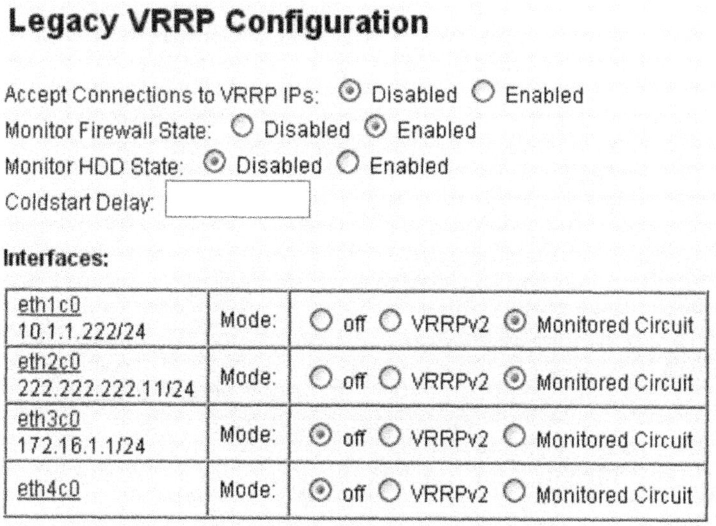

Legacy VRRP Configuration

Accept Connections to VRRP IPs: ⦿ Disabled ○ Enabled
Monitor Firewall State: ○ Disabled ⦿ Enabled
Monitor HDD State: ⦿ Disabled ○ Enabled
Coldstart Delay:

Interfaces:

eth1c0 10.1.1.222/24	Mode:	○ off ○ VRRPv2 ⦿ Monitored Circuit
eth2c0 222.222.222.11/24	Mode:	○ off ○ VRRPv2 ⦿ Monitored Circuit
eth3c0 172.16.1.1/24	Mode:	⦿ off ○ VRRPv2 ○ Monitored Circuit
eth4c0	Mode:	⦿ off ○ VRRPv2 ○ Monitored Circuit

3. Click **Apply**. The Virtual Router field will appear, as shown in Figure 10.8.

Figure 10.8 Creating a Virtual Router

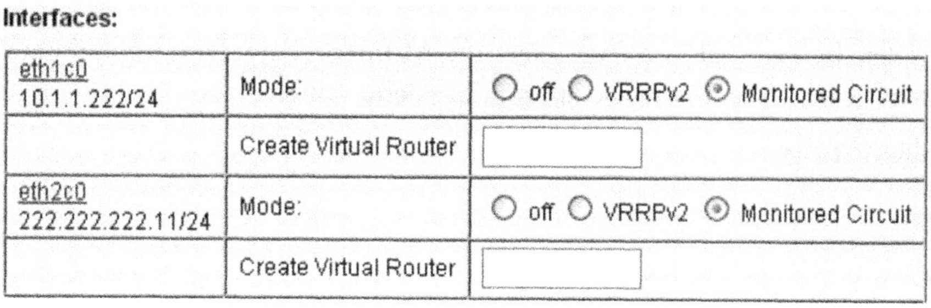

Interfaces:

eth1c0 10.1.1.222/24	Mode:	○ off ○ VRRPv2 ⦿ Monitored Circuit
	Create Virtual Router	
eth2c0 222.222.222.11/24	Mode:	○ off ○ VRRPv2 ⦿ Monitored Circuit
	Create Virtual Router	

4. Create the virtual router by entering the VRID field (from Figure10.8) in the interface, and then click **Apply**.
5. Set the **Backup Addresses**, **Priorities**, and **Hello Intervals** for both interfaces, using the data from Figures 10.8 and 10.9, and apply your changes.

Figure 10.9 Building a Nokia A VRRP Configuration

Interfaces:

eth1c0 10.1.1.222/24	Mode:	○ off ○ VRRPv2 ⦿ Monitored Circuit				
	Virtual Router: 10	⦿ on ○ off	Priority:		Hello Interval:	
			VMAC Mode:	VRRP	Static VMAC:	
		Preempt Mode:	⦿ Enabled ○ Disabled			
		Backup Address:				
		Monitor Interface	None	Priority Delta:		
		Auto-deactivation	⦿ Disabled ○ Enabled			
	Create Virtual Router					
	Authentication	⦿ None ○ Simple				
eth2c0 222.222.222.11/24	Mode:	○ off ○ VRRPv2 ⦿ Monitored Circuit				
	Virtual Router: 20	⦿ on ○ off	Priority:		Hello Interval:	
			VMAC Mode:	VRRP	Static VMAC:	
		Preempt Mode:	⦿ Enabled ○ Disabled			
		Backup Address:				
		Monitor Interface	None	Priority Delta:		
		Auto-deactivation	⦿ Disabled ○ Enabled			
	Create Virtual Router					
	Authentication	⦿ None ○ Simple				
eth3c0 172.16.1.1/24	Mode:	⦿ off ○ VRRPv2 ○ Monitored Circuit				

6. Under the internal interface, select the **Monitor Interface** list and choose the external interface. Insert the appropriate delta value.
7. Under the external interface, select the **Monitor Interface** list and choose the internal interface. Insert the appropriate delta value.
8. Click **Apply**.

Figure 10.10 A Nokia A VRRP Configuration

Interfaces:

eth1c0 10.1.1.222/24	Mode:	( ) off ( ) VRRPv2 (•) Monitored Circuit				
	Virtual Router: 10	(•) on ( ) off	Priority:	100	Hello Interval:	1
			VMAC Mode:	VRRP	Static VMAC:	
		10.1.1.225	(•) on ( ) off			
		Preempt Mode:	(•) Enabled ( ) Disabled			
		Backup Address:				
		eth2c0	(•) on ( ) off	Priority Delta:	20	
		Monitor Interface	None	Priority Delta:		
		Auto-deactivation	(•) Disabled ( ) Enabled			
	Create Virtual Router					
	Authentication	(•) None ( ) Simple				
eth2c0 222.222.222.11/24	Mode:	( ) off ( ) VRRPv2 (•) Monitored Circuit				
	Virtual Router: 20	(•) on ( ) off	Priority:	95	Hello Interval:	1
			VMAC Mode:	VRRP	Static VMAC:	
		222.222.222.1	(•) on ( ) off			
		Preempt Mode:	(•) Enabled ( ) Disabled			
		Backup Address:				
		eth1c0	(•) on ( ) off	Priority Delta:	20	
		Monitor Interface	None	Priority Delta:		
		Auto-deactivation	(•) Disabled ( ) Enabled			
	Create Virtual Router					
	Authentication	(•) None ( ) Simple				
eth3c0 172.16.1.1/24	Mode:	(•) off ( ) VRRPv2 ( ) Monitored Circuit				

NOTE

Each interface can only be configured to monitor one interface at a time. You must select an interface from the list and click **Apply**. After the changes are applied, you can choose another interface to monitor.

It is important to note that Nokia Network Voyager is dynamic, so you should not use the back button in the browser to retrace your steps. If you have misconfigured a setting, go back into the configuration screen by using the menu on the left.

The exact same steps must be followed to configure Nokia B. When both firewalls are properly configured, you can proceed to check the configuration using the VRRP Monitor tab in Nokia Network Voyager.

Tools and Traps...

Additional VRRP Settings

- **Coldstart Delay** This setting is used to ensure that a Nokia device does not automatically make itself master before the Check Point firewall has finished loading. Typically, 90 seconds is recommended in this field. This will give the Check Point firewall enough time to boot up.
- **Accept Connections To VRRP IPs** This feature allows the Nokia to respond to packets directed to the VIP addresses.

Configuring Check Point Gateway Clusters to Use the Nokia VRRP

Now that we have set up the Nokia for VRRP within the Nokia device, we need to turn our attention toward how to configure the Check Point firewall for Nokia VRRP. Check Point currently supports its own high availability solution named Cluster XL. This feature must be disabled within Check Point if you plan on using Nokia VRRP.

When implementing a solution such as this, you must ensure that Check Point is installed in a distributed fashion. For example, the gateways should be installed as enforcement points, and the SmartCenter Server must be installed on a separate server. When installing the enforcement points, you must run *cpconfig* from the command line and choose option 7: Enable Cluster Membership For This Gateway.

In this section, we assume that the enforcement points are created within SmartDashboard and that SIC has been established. We must create a Gateway Cluster object to finalize the configuration of Nokia VRRP.

Configuring a Gateway Cluster

We must first ensure that cluster membership has been enabled on both enforcement points by using the command line and typing **cpconfig**. This will present you with the menu shown in Figure 10.11. You must choose option 7. This will enable the cluster membership which is required.

Figure 10.11 Enabling Cluster Membership

```
This program will let you re-configure
your Check Point products configuration.


Configuration Options:
----------------------
(1)  Licenses
(2)  SNMP Extension
(3)  Group Permissions
(4)  PKCS#11 Token
(5)  Random Pool
(6)  Secure Internal Communication
(7)  Disable cluster membership for this gateway
(8)  Disable Check Point SecureXL
(9)  Automatic start of Check Point Products

(10) Exit

Enter your choice (1-10) :
```

You can then proceed to create a gateway cluster with one of the VIPs you are assigning to the cluster. You must be sure to disable the ClusterXL option from the Check Point Products pane of the Gateway Cluster Properties (see Figure 10.12).

Figure 10.12 Creating a Gateway Cluster Object

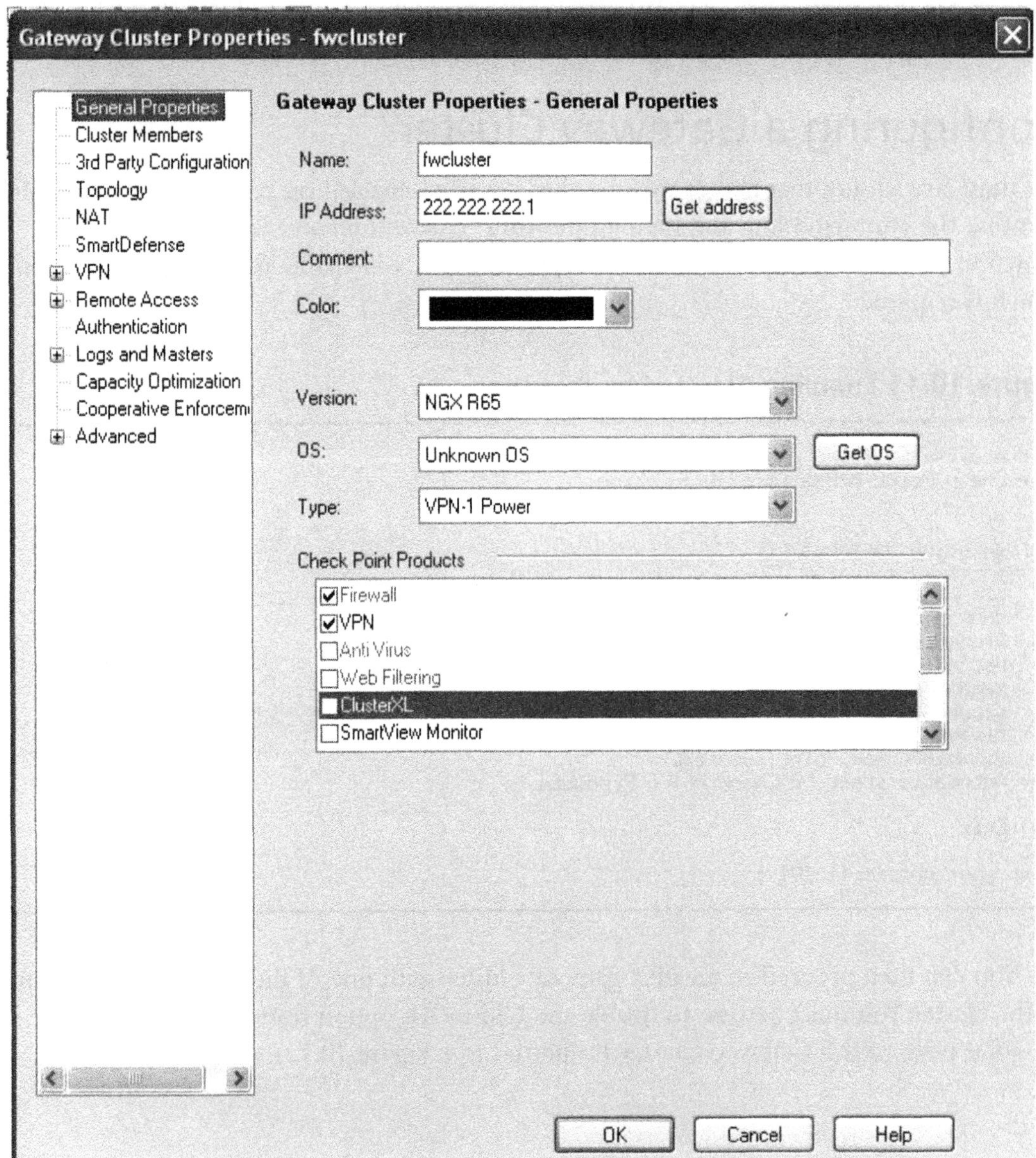

The next step is to configure the Gateway Cluster to support Nokia VRRP, as shown in Figure 10.13. You have the option to select High Availability or Load Sharing. The primary difference is that Load Sharing enables both firewalls at the same time to share the load. The Use State Synchronization option must also be selected.

Figure 10.13 Enabling Nokia VRRP

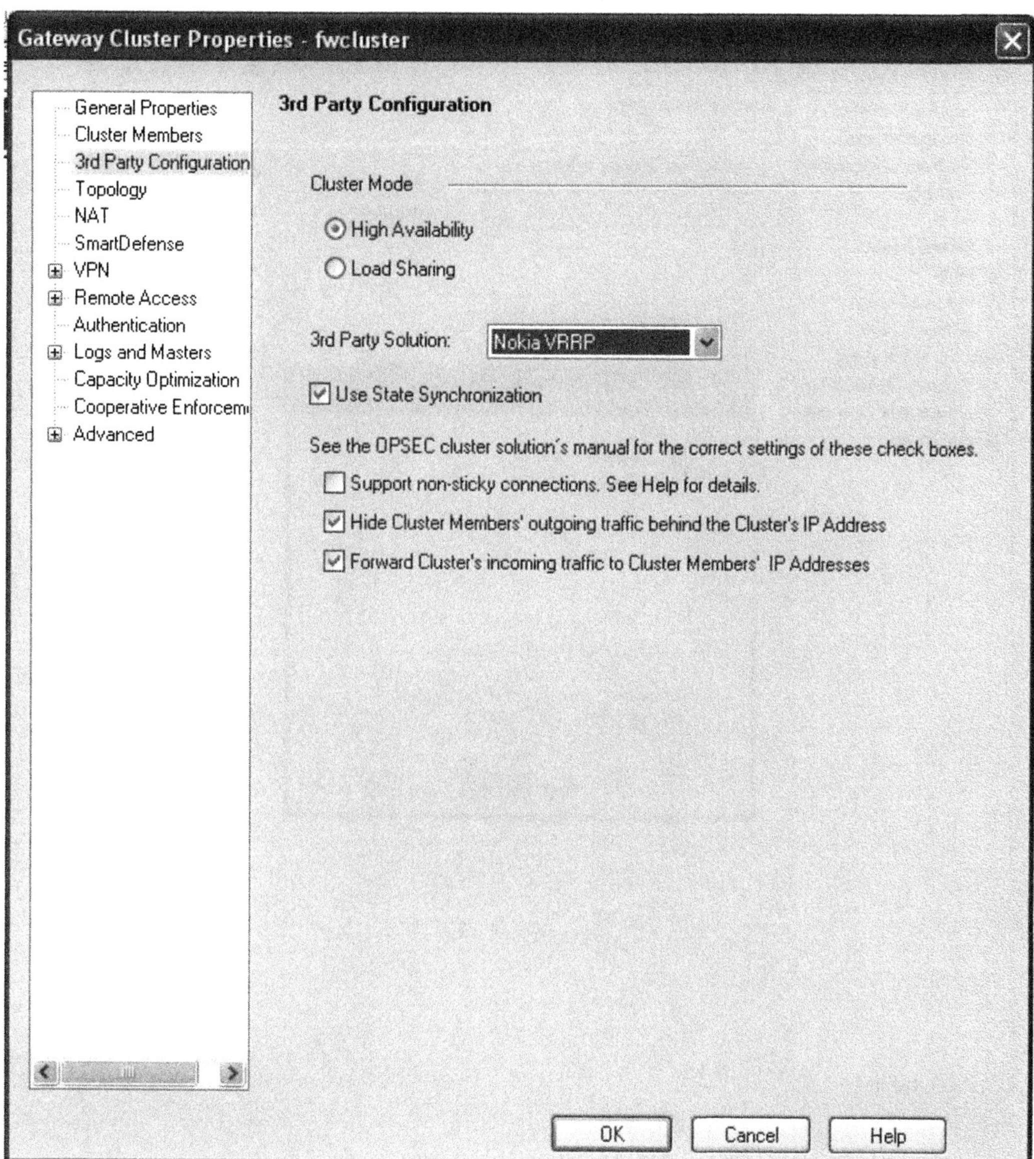

You can now add the individual enforcement points to the Gateway Cluster object. Go to **Cluster Members** and click **Add**. From here, both enforcement points will be added (see Figure 10.14).

Figure 10.14 Adding Gateways to the Cluster Object

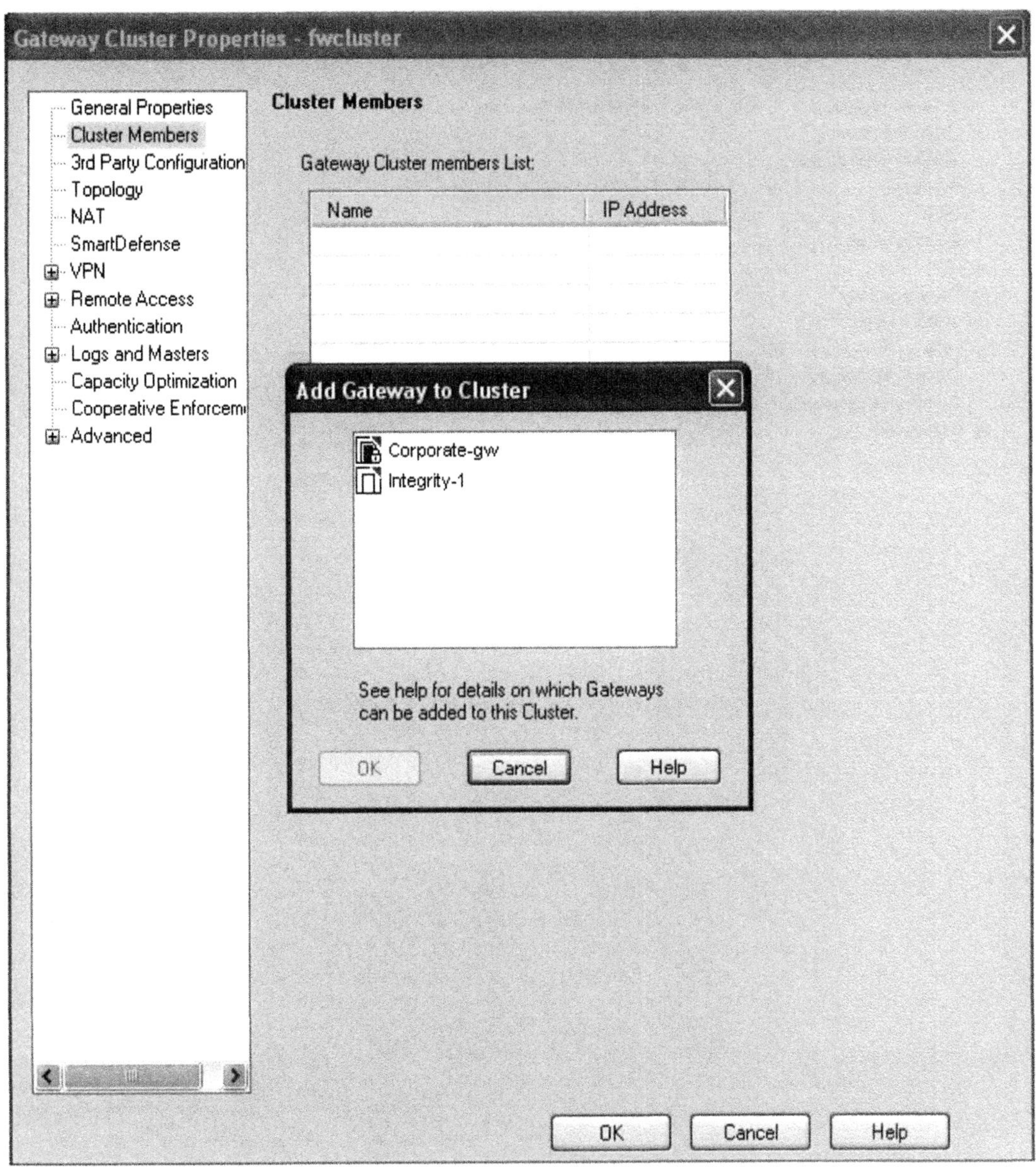

The last step in configuring your gateway cluster is to ensure that all of the VIPs are defined in the Topology of the Gateway Cluster object and to add a Synchronization network to the Topology. Select **Topology** and click **Edit**. As shown in Figure 10.15, you can add your VIPs and synchronization networks from here. When you have completed entering all of your settings, click **OK**.

Figure 10.15 Gateway Cluster Topology

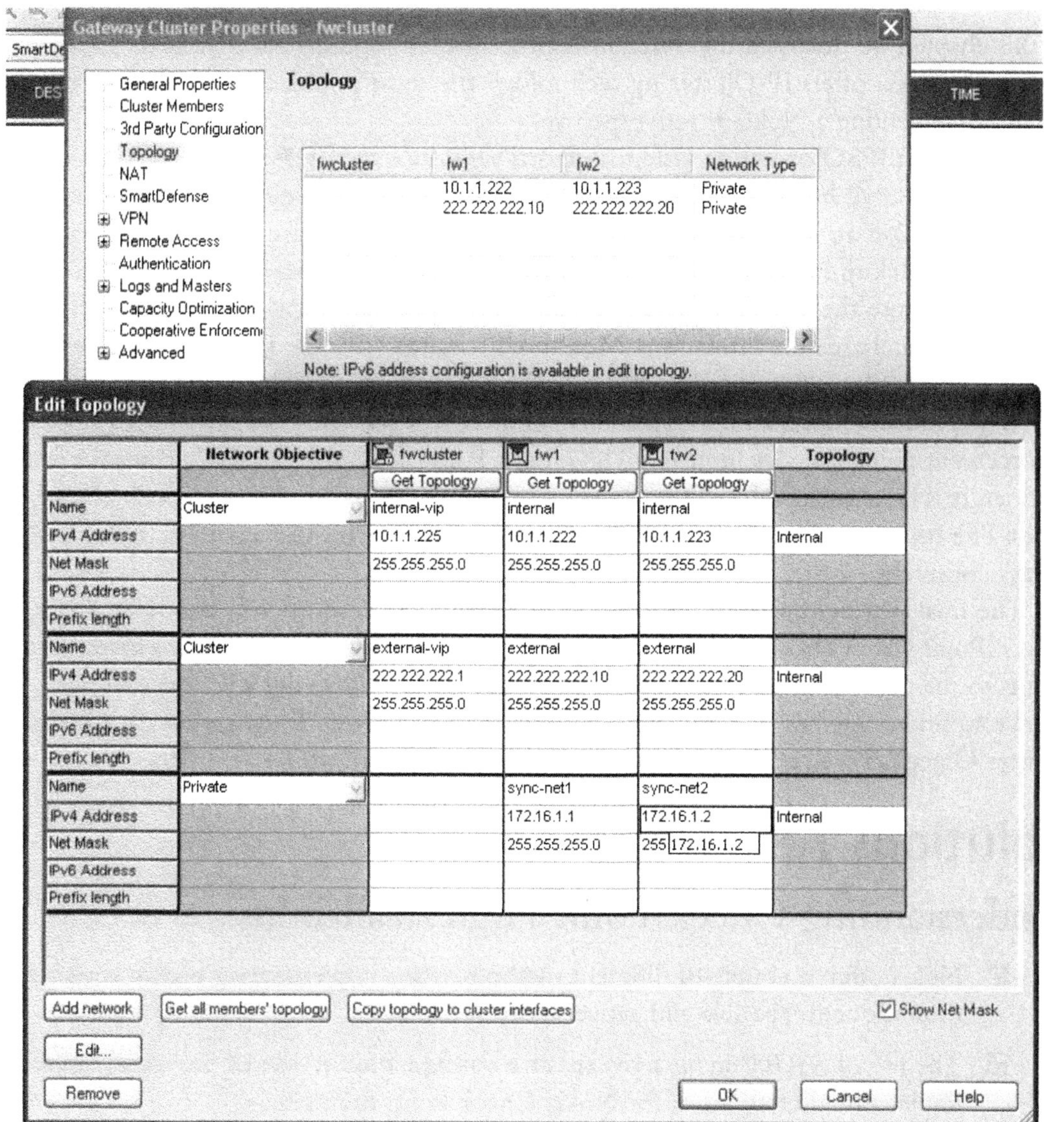

You have now successfully implemented a Nokia Check Point high-availability solution. To test your configuration, you can use *tcpdump* to verify the traffic flow across your synchronization network. It is also recommended to log in to the Check Point SmartView Tracker to verify that traffic between the cluster members is permitted.

Summary

In this chapter, we discussed the different high-availability options available with a Nokia. Although Nokia offers IP Clustering technology, the most popular high-availability mode when implementing a Nokia is active/passive.

The Nokia IPSO operating system supports VRRPv2 and VRRP Monitored Circuits. Although VRRPv2 has its advantages, it is recommended that Monitored Circuits be used. With VRRPv2, if an interface on the firewall was to go down, there would be no way of sending the backup Nokia device a message stating the current status of the interface. This would cause the backup device to assume the master role for the fallen interface only. You can definitely see the limitations. Monitored Circuits offer the feature of not only monitoring whether the firewall itself has crashed, but also if a network card has gone done.

When implementing a high-availability solution, it is vital that the system clocks of both enforcement points are synchronized. The Check Point firewall is extremely sensitive in this manner. It is recommended that the enforcement points be within three seconds of each other. The best way to synchronize the time is to use NTP. This will ensure that the time is always consistent.

The final step in implementing a highly available firewall solution is to configure the Check Point Gateway Cluster Object. Not only must you add the individual enforcement points to the object, but you must configure the Topology with your VIP addresses and synchronization network. Do not forget to deselect the ClusterXL option on the Gateway Cluster Object, as well as enable Nokia VRRP as the high-availability method.

Solutions Fast Track

Understanding Check Point High Availability

☑ Nokia offers a couple of different methods when implementing highly available firewalls: active/passive and active/active.

☑ The use of VRRP in an active/passive configuration is one of the most commonly implemented methods of for Nokia Check Point firewalls.

☑ State synchronization ensures that an organization does not have asymmetric routing problems with their highly available firewall implementation.

Configuring the Nokia VRRP Implementation

☑ VRRP implementations have one master and a minimum of one backup router.

☑ The VRRP protocol is outlined in RFC proposed standard number 2338.

- ☑ VRRP implementation chooses the router with the highest effective priority to be the master.
- ☑ Monitored Circuits is an extension to VRRPv2 that allows an interface to monitor other interfaces and effectively respond when an interface goes down.
- ☑ VRRPv2 is supported by Nokia but is no longer recommended.

Configuring the Nokia VRRP Monitored Circuit

- ☑ Nokia Monitored Circuits can be configured and monitored entirely through Nokia Network Voyager.
- ☑ System clocks need to be synchronized for a successful implementation.
- ☑ Members can be entered into each other's host tables, but it is not required.

Configuring Check Point Gateway Clusters to Use the Nokia VRRP

- ☑ Clustering must be enabled on each enforcement point through the command line using *cpconfig*.
- ☑ You must create a Gateway Cluster Object.
- ☑ The cluster object must contain all VIPs defined on the Nokia devices.
- ☑ You can add predefined enforcement points to the Gateway Cluster Object, or create them at the same time you create the Gateway Cluster Object.

Frequently Asked Questions

Q: Can I configure VRRP through Nokia CLISH?

A: Yes. The *set vrrp* and *set vrrp interface* commands can be used to accomplish this task. CLISH also has the *show vrrp summary* or *show vrrp interfaces* commands that provide a wealth of information about the current status of your VRRP setup.

Q: Should I enable the ClusterXL option on my Gateway Cluster Object if I am using Nokia VRRP?

A: No. ClusterXL is a proprietary Check Point technology that interferes with a Nokia VRRP implementation.

Q: How many virtual routers does VRRP support on a network segment?

A: VRRP currently supports up to 255 virtual routers on a network segment.

Q: Should I use the VRRPv2 or Monitored Circuits option?

A: Although Nokia supports VRRPv2, it is recommended that the Monitored Circuits option be used instead. VRRPv2 is a good solution only if the primary firewall crashes. If you were to lose a network card in your firewall, the backup firewall would assume master for that network card, but not the others.

Q: Which high-availability options does Nokia support?

A: The Nokia supports VRRP and IPSO Clustering. VRRP is implemented as active/passive, while IPSO Clustering is implemented as active/active.

Q: Which Check Point option assists organizations with asymmetric routing issues?

A: The Check Point state synchronization ensures that asymmetric routing issues do not occur.

Q: Which IP address should I connect to in order to administer my Nokia VRRP implementation?

A: Considering that VIPs are virtual, it is best to connect to the real IP address of the firewalls in your high-availability implementation.

Q: Will a Nokia Check Point VRRP implementation successfully failover existing connections?

A: Yes. The Check Point state synchronization ensures that the connections table is copied to the backup firewall.

Q: Does the priority set within the VRRP configuration of a Nokia need to be 255?

A: No. Although many would recommend that the value be set to 255, the priority can be any number you want.

Q: How do I enable cluster membership on my enforcement points?

A: This setting is enabled on the command line by issuing *cpconfig* and choosing option 7.

Q: Am I required to configure each enforcement point's host table?

A: No. Although this is not a requirement, it makes administration a little easier because you can connect to the devices through the name and not the IP address.

Q: What is the reason for the Coldstart Delay VRRP setting?

A: This setting is used to ensure that a Nokia device does not automatically make itself master before the Check Point firewall has finished loading.

Chapter 11

IPSO Command Interface Line Shell (CLISH)

Solutions in this chapter:

- Configuring Interfaces
- Applying Security Tuning
- Configuring System Options
- Configuring Network Security and Access
- Configuring Routing

☑ Summary

☑ Solutions Fast Track

☑ Frequently Asked Questions

Introduction

Marty walked over with a huge printout of a network diagram that detailed the current site architecture and the remote site locations.

"One problem we'll have," explained Marty, "is that we'll need to deploy some of these Nokia firewalls at our remote sites. Our current information security policy doesn't allow us to connect over the public Internet using standard Web protocols for administration of border devices."

Mark rolled his eyes and Marty caught it out of the corner of his eye.

"And," Marty continued. "Even though some people, like Mark here, think we *should* be able to do this, our policy states we can't."

Mark's eyes went wide. He looked at Marty and felt his face go red.

"What Marty is getting at," said Ming, "is that we need an easy way to administer these systems remotely without using the Nokia Network Voyager interface."

"Can SSH be used?" asked Shin.

"Sure can." Marty replied.

"Well," continued Shin, "in that case, we can use the IPSO Command Line Interface Shell, more commonly known as CLISH, to configure, monitor, and administer the system."

Mark's eyes returned to the screen as Shin opened a SSH terminal session to the Nokia appliance.

"Will SSH work for you, Mark?" Marty asked jokingly.

"Sure will boss," replied Mark. "You know I prefer the command line anyway."

This chapter will review some of the most important, and most commonly used IPSO command line interface (CLISH) commands. We will not cover every command and its associated switches, because this would be a book in itself. The *CLI Reference Guide for Nokia IPSO 4.2*, which is available for download from the Nokia support site, provides a thorough walkthrough of every possible CLISH command available and should be referenced if there is a configuration option not explained in this chapter.

Configuring Interfaces

When configuring interfaces, you must know the IP address and netmask of each interface you plan to use. Physical interfaces exist for each physical port on a NIC installed on the appliance. The interface names have the following form:

```
<type>-s<slot>p<port>
```

- **<type>** The prefix for the device type.
- **<slot>** The slot number for the device on the appliance.
- **<port>** The NIC port number. The first port on a NIC is port one. A two-port Ethernet NIC in slot two is represented by two physical interfaces: eth-s2p1 and eth-s2p2.

The various interface names are explained in Table 4.4 in Chapter 4.

Configuring Ethernet Interfaces

You can configure several parameters for each Ethernet interface, including:

- Enable or disable the interface
- Change the IP address of the interface
- Change the speed and duplex mode

Before you assign IP address and subnet information to an interface, you must configure the physical interface.

Configuring the Physical Interface

Use the following commands to configure the settings for your physical Ethernet interfaces:

```
set interface phys_if_name
        speed <10M | 100M | 1000M>
        duplex <full | half>
        auto-advertise <on | off>
        link-recog-delay <1-255>
        active <on | off>
        flow-control <on | off>
        udld-enable <on | off>
        descriptor_size <128-512>
```

The physical interface configuration parameters are explained in Table 11.1.

Table 11.1 Physical Interface Configuration Parameters

Physical Interface Parameters	Description
speed <10M | 100M | 1000M>	Specifies the speed, in megabits per second, at which your interface will operate. Default: 10M
duplex <full | half>	Specifies the duplex mode in which your interface will operate. Default: half
auto-advertise <on | off>	Specifies whether your interface will advertise its speed and duplex setting using Ethernet autonegotiation. Default: on

Continued

Table 11.1 Continued. Physical Interface Configuration Parameters

Physical Interface Parameters	Description
link-recog-delay <1–255>	Specifies how many seconds a link must be active before the system declares the interface is up. Default: 6
flow-control <on | off>	Specifies whether flow control is on. Default: on
active <on | off>	Specifies whether your physical interface is active. Default: on
status	Shows whether your physical interface is active.
udld-enable <on | off>	Specifies whether to use the Cisco Unidirectional Link Detection (UDLD) protocol to improve detection of partial failures in fiber links. Default: off
descriptor_size <128–512>	Specifies the number of descriptors available for Gigabit Ethernet interfaces. Default: 128

If you wanted to configure and enable the eth-s3p1 interface to be 100M full duplex with auto-advertise enabled, you could use the following command:

```
pint[admin]# clish
NokiaIP130:15> set interface eth-s3p1 speed 100M duplex full auto-advertise on
active on
```

Some parameters have special rules associated with them. For example, Gigabit Ethernet Interfaces cannot use the *auto-advertise* parameter, whereas the *flow-control* parameter is only valid for Gigabit Ethernet interfaces. Also, increasing the *descriptor_size* parameter allows the system to temporarily store more packets while waiting for the CPU to service them. The system uses one descriptor per packet unless it receives jumbo frames, in which case it uses multiple descriptors per packet. The acceptable values for the *descriptor_size* parameter are 128, 256, and 512.

NOTE

An Ethernet frame larger than 1518 bytes is known as a "jumbo frame."

Configuring the Logical Interface

When a physical interface is installed, the system automatically creates a corresponding logical interface. Use the following commands to create and configure your logical Ethernet interfaces:

```
add interface <log_if_name | phys_if_name> [vlanid <2-4094>] address ip_
address/<0-31>
      comments comments
      logical-name new_log_if_name
      unit <1-4094>
      enable | disable

set interface log_if_name
      arp-mirroring <on | off>
      comments comments
      vlanid <2-4094>
      logical-name new_log_if_name
      enable | disable
      MTU <1500-16000>
```

The logical interface configuration parameters are explained in Table 11.2.

Table 11.2 Logical Interface Configuration Parameters

Logical Interface Parameters	Description
log_if_name | phys_if_name	If you want to configure the default logical interface, then specify the logical name associated with the physical interface. For example, the default logical interface name of eth-s3p1 would be eth-s3p1c0. If you want to add more logical interfaces, then specify the physical interface.
unit <1-4094>	Specifies the final digit of the logical name (for example, eth-s3p1c0). If you do not specify this parameter, then IPSO will use the next available number for the logical interface.
arp-mirroring <on | off>	If you are using VRRP on this interface, the arp-mirroring parameter, if enabled, tells the interface to learn the same ARP information as its master if it is on a backup router. This can speed up VRRP failovers because the newly promoted master would not need to learn the MAC address information for the next hop IP address.

Continued

Table 11.2 Continued. Logical Interface Configuration Parameters

Logical Interface Parameters	Description
comments comments	Specifies comments pertaining to the interface.
vlanid <2-4094>	Specifies the virtual LAN that the logical interface is assigned to. You cannot assign a virtual LAN ID to the first logical interface for a given physical interface.
address ip_address/<0-31>	Specifies the IP address and subnet mask length for the logical interface.
logical-name new_log_if_name	Specifies a new logical name for the interface.
enable | disable	Enables or disables the logical interface.
MTU <1500-16000>	Specifies the MTU for the interface. The value must be an integer. Default: 1500

NOTE

When adding a logical interface, you must specify a VLAN ID.

Perhaps you want to assign an IP address to your default logical interface on the eth-s3p1 physical interface. Using your 192.168.20.1 IP address and 255.255.255.0 subnet information, you could use the following command to configure, and then enable, the interface:

```
NokiaIP130:26> add interface eth-s3p1c0 address 192.168.20.1/24 enable
```

Maybe you want to add another logical interface on the same physical interface (eth-s3p1) with a new IP address and subnet (192.168.25.1/24) to participate in a VLAN defined on the connecting switch (VLAN 55). You could use the following command to add your additional interface (eth-s3p1c1):

```
NokiaIP130:28> add interface eth-s3p1 vlanid 55 address 192.168.25.1/24 enable
```

If, for some reason, you discover you have added the interface to the wrong VLAN, you could use the following command to change the VLAN it is associated with:

```
NokiaIP130:31> set interface eth-s3p1c1 vlanid 56 enable
```

Showing Interface Configurations

Using the *show interface* command, you can view the interface configurations on the appliance. The show commands work for the physical and logical interface configurations. You can use the following parameters, which were described in Table 11.1, to determine physical interface related information:

```
show interface phys_if_name
        speed
        duplex
        auto-advertise
        link-recog-delay
        flow-control
        status
        udld-enable
```

For example, to see the current status of the eth-s3p1 interface, the following command would be used:

```
NokiaIP130:40> show interface eth-s3p1 status
Interface NameStatus
eth-s3p1on
```

To see the speed of the interface, the following command would be used:

```
NokiaIP130:39> show interface eth-s3p1 speed
Name                    Value
Speed                   100M
```

NOTE

You will not see the interface name listed as a result of the *show interface phys_if_name speed* command even though the results indicate you should. The speed listed is the speed of the interface that you specified in the command.

The following parameters, which were described in Table 11.2, can be used to determine logical interface related information:

```
show interface log_if_name
        arp-mirroring
        comments
        vlanid
        logical-name
        MTU
```

For example, to see the current VLAN information for the eth-s3p1c1 interface, the following command would be used:

```
NokiaIP130:46> show interface eth-s3p1c1 vlanid
Vlanid:  56
```

To see the MTU associated with the interface, the following command would be used:

```
NokiaIP130:47> show interface eth-s3p1c0 MTU
MTU: 1500
```

You can also use the *show interfaces* command to list information about all interfaces on the platform. The show interfaces command displays the physical and logical names of all the installed interfaces (as well as other information). The following is a sample output from a Nokia IP130 appliance:

```
NokiaIP130:49> show interfaces
Physical Interface                  eth-s1p1
        Up
        Logical Interface               eth-s1p1c0
                Active                      On
                link_avail                  Up
                Type                        Fast Ethernet
                IP Address                          Destination
                192.168.200.10                      192.168.200.0/24
Physical Interface                  eth-s3p1
        Down
        Logical Interface               eth-s3p1c0
                Active                      On
                link_avail                  Down
                Type                        Fast Ethernet
                IP Address                          Destination
                192.168.20.1                        192.168.20.0/24
        Logical Interface eth-s3p1c1
                VlanId 56
                Active On
                link_avail Down
                Type Fast Ethernet
                IP Address                  Destination
                192.168.25.1                192.168.25.0/24
```

```
Physical Interface          loop0
       Up
       Logical Interface       loop0c0
              Up                   Up
              Type                 loopback
              IP Address           Destination
              127.0.0.1
Physical Interface          eth-s2p1
       Down
       Logical Interface       eth-s2p1c0
              Active               Off
              Type                 Ethernet
              IP Address           Destination
Physical Interface          pppoe0
       Up
       Type                    pppoe
Physical Interface          Tunnels
       Up
       Type                    tunnel
```

Deleting a Logical Interface

If you want to delete a logical interface, you can use the *delete interface* command to remove it from your IPSO configuration. To delete a logical interface, use the following command:

```
delete interface log_if_name
```

For example, to delete the eth-s3p1c1 interface, use the following:

```
NokiaIP130:50> delete interface eth-s3p1c1
```

If you simply want to delete an IP address from the logical interface, the *address* parameter can be used. To delete the IP address of a logical interface (without deleting the logical interface itself), use the following command:

```
delete interface log_if_name address ip_address
```

For example, to delete the IP address associated with eth-s3p1c0, use the following:

```
NokiaIP130:51> delete interface eth-s3p1c0 address 192.168.20.1
```

If you delete all logical interfaces or all the IP addresses for an interface, the interface is no longer accessible over the network. If you delete all logical interfaces or all the IP addresses for all the connected interfaces, the IP system is no longer accessible over the network. If this occurs, restore network access to the system by connecting to it using a console connection and creating a logical interface for one of the connected physical interfaces.

Applying Security Tuning

The outlined configurations are for specific tuning purposes. In most circumstances, you should not change any default settings.

Controlling Sequence Validation

Use the following command to enable and disable sequence validation:

```
set advanced-tuning tcp-options sequence-validation <on | off>
```

Use the following command to view whether sequence validation is enabled or disabled:

```
show advanced-tuning tcp-options sequence-validation
```

Example:

```
NokiaIP130:55> show advanced-tuning tcp-options sequence-validation
Sequence Validation Off
```

Tuning the TCP/IP Stack

Use the following command to set the TCP maximum segment size (MSS) for segments received by your local system:

```
set advanced-tuning tcp-ip tcp-mss <512-1500>
```

NOTE

The default value is 1024.

Use the following command to view the configured TCP MSS value:

```
show advanced-tuning tcp-ip tcp-mss
```

Example:

```
NokiaIP130:56> show advanced-tuning tcp-ip tcp-mss
TcpMSS 1024
```

Using the Router Alert IP Option

Use the following command to specify if IPSO should strip the router alert IP option before passing packets to the firewall:

```
set advanced-tuning ip-options stripra <1 | 0>
```

NOTE

The router alert IP option is commonly enabled in IGMP packets.

Use the following command to view the configured setting:

```
show advanced-tuning ip-options stripra
```

Optimizing IP1260 Ports

You can use the following command to optimize the performance of the interfaces of two-port Gigabit Ethernet NICs in IP1260 platforms when the interfaces forward unidirectional UDP traffic:

```
set advanced-tuning ethernet-options <on | off>
```

Enabling this option does not optimize throughput for other types of traffic or other interfaces. This command is not available on the IP1220.

WARNING

Do not enable this option if more than two Gigabit Ethernet interfaces are installed in the system. Doing so can impair system performance.

Configuring System Options

Various system configuration options can be managed from the CLI using CLISH. Before starting your configuration of system services, it might be a good idea to take a look at what is currently configured. Using the *show summary* command provides a detailed list of the current system configuration options on your Nokia appliance. The configuration summary provides details for the following sections:

- IP interfaces
- ARP
- Traffic Management
- Router Services
- System

- Security and Access
- IPSec
- SNMP
- Monitoring
- Licenses

Are You Owned?

Auditing Security and Access Configurations

If you are tasked with performing an audit of an IPSO-based appliance, perhaps the best place to start is to see what the administrator has configured in the Configuration Security And Access section of the *Configuration Summary* output.

Important information, such as password settings, configured users, AAA settings, and which basic services are enabled, are all contained within this section. A sample of some of this information is shown next:

```
Configuration Security and Access
    User       Mode       Sequence No.    Seed
    admin      admin      n/a             n/a
    monitor    monitor    n/a             n/a
    User  Uid  Gid  Home Dir.  Shell  Default Page  Info  Notes
    admin  0  10  /var/emhome/admin  /bin/csh  home  Admin
    monitor  102  10  /var/emhome/monitor  /etc/cli.sh  home  Monitor
```

Configuring the DHCP Server

The first thing you must do, before configuring your DHCP server information, is enable the DHCP server service using the *set dhcp service server* command. This specifies that the server process will be configured on your Nokia appliance.

You must then set DHCP-related information, such as lease time, DNS information, and so on, that your Nokia appliance will use in its leased DHCP IP addresses. Using the *add dhcp server* command, you can configure these options:

```
add dhcp server subnet ip_address netmask <1-32>
router ip_address
default-lease <0-4294967295>
```

```
max-lease <0-4294967295>
domain name
dns ip_address
ntp ip_address
tftp name | ip_address
wins ip_address
ddserver ip_address
note-type <B-node, P-node, M-node, H-node>
scope name
zone name
     swap name | ip_address
```

Table 11.3 explains the arguments that can be configured using the *add dhcp server* command.

Table 11.3 DHCP Server Configuration Arguments

Argument	Description
add dhcp server subnet *ip_address* netmask *<1-32>*	Specifies the subnet where the server will listen for DHCP messages from clients.
router *ip_address*	Specifies the default route clients will use.
default-lease *<0-4294967295>*	Specifies the IP address lease time, in seconds, that clients will be given if clients do not request a specific lease time. The default is 43200 seconds.
max-lease *<0-4294967295>*	Specifies the maximum IP address lease time, in seconds, that clients will be given regardless of client requests. The default is 43200 seconds.
domain *name*	Specifies the domain name clients will be given—for example, bob.theacademy.ca.
dns *ip_address*	Specifies, in order of precedents, the DNS servers for clients. Use commas to separate addresses.
ntp *ip_address*	Specifies, in order of precedents, the NTP servers for clients. Use commas to separate addresses.
tftp *name* | *ip_address*	Specifies the TFTP servers for clients. Use a valid IP address or a valid hostname.
wins *ip_address*	When configuring NetBIOS, specifies, in order of precedents, the WINS servers for clients. Use commas to separate addresses.

Continued

Table 11.3 Continued. DHCP Server Configuration Arguments

Argument	Description
ddserver *ip_address*	When configuring NetBIOS, specifies, in order of precedents, the Datagram Distribution (DD) servers for clients. Use commas to separate addresses.
node-type <B-node, H-node, M-node, P-node>	When configuring NetBIOS, specifies the node type the client should use to designate itself. ■ **`B-node`** Only broadcast on the local network for NetBIOS resolution and advertising. ■ **`H-node`** Unicast to WINS servers. If this fails, broadcast. ■ **`M-node`** Broadcast on local network; unicast to WINS server. ■ **`P-node`** Only unicast to WINS server for NetBIOS resolution and advertising.
scope *name*	When configuring NetBIOS, specifies the scope for the client.
zone *name*	When configuring NetBIOS, specifies the zone for the client.
swap name | ip_address	Specifies the server that provides a swap space for clients. Use a valid IP address or valid hostname.

With the DHCP server settings configured, the final step is to configure the DHCP IP address scope. This defines the start and end IP address to be used for your DHCP IP address pool. Use the following commands to configure the pool information:

```
add dhcp server subnet ip_address
    pool start ip_address end ip_address
```

NOTE

The start and end addresses of the pool must belong to the subnet being configured.

Configuring DNS

To configure the DNS server you wish your Nokia appliance to use, you must use the *set dns* command. This command, whose arguments are explained in Table 11.4, is invoked as follows:

```
set dns
      domainname name
      primary ip_address
      secondary ip_address
      tertiary ip_address
```

Table 11.4 DNS Configuration Arguments

Argument	Description
domainname name	Specifies the name that is put at the end of all DNS searches if they fail. This name should be your local domain name and should begin with an alphabetic letter and may consist only of alphanumeric characters and hyphens. Example: theacademy.ca.
primary ip_address	Specifies the IP address of the first server to use when resolving hostnames.
secondary ip_address	Specifies the IP address of the second server to use when resolving hostnames.
tertiary ip_address	Specifies the IP address of the server to use when resolving hostnames if the primary and secondary servers do not respond.

For example, if you wanted to configure your Nokia appliance that is part of the acme.com domain to use 172.16.22.55 as its primary DNS server, you would use the following commands:

```
NokiaIP130:4> set dns domainname acme.com
NokiaIP130:5> set dns primary 172.16.22.55
```

Configuring Date and Time

There are three ways to set the date and time on your Nokia appliance using CLISH. The first is by using the *set clock* command. You can use one of the following two *set clock* commands to manually set the date and time:

```
set clock time month date year
set clock time date month year
```

Table 11.5 describes the arguments for the *set clock* command.

Table 11.5 *set clock* Configuration Arguments

Argument	Description
Time	Specifies the time. Use the following format: hh:mm:ss. For example, 15:58:46.
Month	Specifies the month of the year. Enter one of the following: jan, feb, mar, apr, may, jun, jul, aug, sep, oct, nov, or dec.
Day	Specifies the date. Enter 1-31.
Year	Specifies the year. Enter a four-digit value.

The second, and perhaps more reliable method, is to perform a one-time synchronization with a NTP server. You can use the *set date* command, with the following arguments, to synchronize your Nokia appliance with a NTP server:

```
set date
      once-from-ntpserver <ip_address Ð fully qualified domain name>
      timezone-city value
day <1-31>
hour <0-23>
minute <0-59>
second <0-59>
month <1-12>
year <yyyy>
```

NOTE

To display a complete list of timezone values, press **Tab** after *timezone-city*. The default value is Greenwich(GMT).

Table 11.6 describes the arguments for the *set date* command.

Table 11.6 *set date* Configuration Arguments

Argument	Description
once-from ntpserver <ip_address | fully qualified domain name>	Specifies to set the local time by contacting the NTP server. Enter either the NTP server IP address or fully qualified domain name.
timezone-city value	Specifies a time based on the time zone of a particular place. The default is Greenwich Mean Time (GMT).
day <1-31>	Specifies which day of the month to use to set the initial time.
hour <0-23>	Specifies which hour of the day to use to set the initial time.
minute <0-59>	Specifies which minute of the hour to use to set the initial time.
Second <0-59>	Specifies which second of the minute to use to set the initial time.
month <1-12>	Specifies which month of the year to use to set the initial time.
year <yyyy>	Specifies which year to use to set the initial time. For example, enter 2008. The valid range is 1970–2037.

The third and most advisable method is to constantly synchronize your Nokia appliance with a NTP server. Use the following commands to specify other systems as network time protocol servers for your Nokia appliance:

```
add ntp server ip_address version <1-3> [prefer <yes | no>]
```

Table 11.7 describes the arguments for the *add ntp server* command.

Table 11.7 *add ntp server* Configuration Arguments

Argument	Description
server ip_address	Specifies the address of a time server from which this machine synchronizes its clock. The specified server does not synchronize its clock to the local clock of this system.
version <1–3>	Specifies which version of NTP to use when synchronizing with the specified system. Nokia recommends this be set to version 3, the most recent version.
prefer <yes | no>	Specifies whether to select this system as the time source if more than one server or peer is available to another system that requests a time source. This setting is used as a tiebreaker. Default: no

WARNING

You can configure your Nokia appliance as a DHCP server, but it is not recommended. We suggest you use a dedicated server to perform this function to ensure your Nokia appliance resources are free to perform more important tasks.

Backing Up and Restoring Files

Just because you have your Nokia appliance in a remote location does not mean it cannot be part of your enterprise backup and restore plans. Using CLISH, you can manually back up your files when needed, schedule backups to occur at regular intervals, and transfer the files off of the appliance.

By default, the backup file contains all the configuration (/config), cron (/var/cron), etc (/var/etc), and IPSec files (/var/etc/ipsec).

WARNING

Versions of IPSO for export do not include IPSec files in the backup.

Manually Backing Up

Sometimes you need to make a backup of your Nokia appliance at a time outside of your regular backup schedule. You can initiate a manual backup of your appliance at any time using the following CLISH commands:

```
set backup manual
on
filename name
homedirs <on | off>
logfiles <on | off>
   package name <on | off>
```

Table 11.8 describes the arguments for the *set backup manual* command.

Table 11.8 *set backup manual* Configuration Arguments

<table>
<tr><th>Argument</th><th>Description</th></tr>
<tr><td>On</td><td>Specifies to perform a manual backup.</td></tr>
<tr><td>Filename name</td><td>Specifies the name of the file that includes all the backed-up files. You must specify this name to configure a manual backup.</td></tr>
<tr><td>homedirs <on | off></td><td>Specifies whether to include all home directories in the backup file.
Default: off</td></tr>
<tr><td>logfiles <on | off></td><td>Specifies whether to include all log files in the backup file.
Default: off</td></tr>
<tr><td>gplcfiles <on | off></td><td>Specifies whether to include all GPLC files in the backup file.</td></tr>
<tr><td>package name <on | off></td><td>Specifies whether to include a specific package file in the backup file. Package files are not automatically included in a backup file. Enter the filename for the package you want to include in the backup.</td></tr>
</table>

NOTE

The GNU Perl Compiler (GPLC) files are Perl files used by the Nokia Network Voyager backend. Unless you have changed these files, there is no reason to back them up.

For example, to back up your system to a Nokia appliance to a file named *nokia_backup* you would use the following commands:

```
NokiaIP130:7> set backup manual filename nokia_backup
NokiaIP130:9> set backup manual on
backup successful
NokiaIP130:10> quit
```

If the backup completes successfully, you will see a *backup successful* message, as shown in the output. All backups are stored in */var/backup/* by default. You can verify this by using the *ls* command:

```
pint[admin]# ls -al /var/backup/
total 46
drwxrwxr-x  4 root wheel  512 Aug 5 21:48 .
drwxr-xr-x 14 root wheel  512 Aug 5 21:48 ..
-rw-r--r--  1 root wheel  181 Aug 5 21:48 .htaccess
-rw-rw-r--  1 root wheel 41441 Aug 5 21:48 nokia_backup_20080805.tgz
drwxrwxr-x  2 root wheel  512 Aug 5 21:48 pkg
drwxrwxr-x  2 root wheel  512 Aug 5 21:48 sched
```

Note that the archive name starts with the name we specified earlier and ends with a timestamp in the format *YYYMMDD.tgz*. This lets you differentiate between backup archives files.

WARNING

If you run two manual backups using the same *name* value, the second backup will overwrite the previously compiled backup.

Scheduling Backups

You can also schedule backups to be run on a regular schedule using the *add backup scheduled* command. The archives produced by scheduled backups reside in the */var/backup/sched/* directory and are timestamped.

```
add backup scheduled
filename name
dayofmonth <1-31>
minute <0-59>
dayofweek <1-7>
hour <0-23>
       minute <0-59>
```

Table 11.9 describes the arguments for the *add backup scheduled* command.

Table 11.9 *add backup scheduled* Configuration Arguments

Argument	Description
filename name	Specifies the name of the file that includes all the backed up files. You must specify this name to configure a manual backup.
dayofmonth <1-31>	Specifies which day of the month to schedule the backup. This option applies only to monthly scheduled backups.
dayofweek <1-7>	Specifies which day of the week to schedule the backup. This option applies only to weekly scheduled backups.
hour <0-23>	Specifies which hour of the day to schedule the backup.
minute <0-59>	Specifies which minute of the day to schedule the backup.

For example, to schedule your *nokia_backup* to occur on the 15th of every month at 1:00 A.M., use the following command:

```
NokiaIP130:28> add backup scheduled filename nokia_andrew dayofmonth 13 hour 1
```

If you need to change the scheduled backup, you must delete the existing scheduled backup and use the *set backup scheduled* command to configure a new regularly scheduled backup.

NOTE

Use the *delete scheduled backup* command to remove the scheduled backups on your Nokia appliance.

```
set backup scheduled
on
filename name
hour <0-23>
minute <0-59>
homedirs <on | off>
logfiles <on | off>
package name <on | off>
```

Tools & Traps...

Transferring Backup Files

You can transfer backup files to a remote server manually or in an automated manner, but the automated mechanism is far more useful. To use the automated approach, configure a scheduled backup and then use the *set backup auto-transfer* command to automatically transfer the file off of your Nokia appliance.

```
The set backup auto-transfer command has the following arguments:
set backup auto-transfer
ipaddr ip_address
protocol
ftp ftp-dir path_name
tftp
```

You must specify an IP address (*ip_address*) and a transfer protocol (*ftp* or *tftp*). If using FTP, you can specify a remote directory using the ftp-dir argument. Example:

```
NokiaIP130:7> set backup auto-transfer ipaddr 192.168.200.10 protocol ftp
ftp-dir /backups
```

If you enable automated transfers, your backup files are transferred to the remote server as soon as they are complete, assuming the server is reachable. If the remote server is not reachable, the system waits until the next backup occurs and tries again. After they have been successfully transferred, the backup files are deleted from your Nokia appliance.

Restoring Files from Locally Stored Backup Files

To restore a previously compiled backup, the *set restore* command can be used, provided the backup is located on your Nokia appliance.

```
set restore
manual filename
scheduled filename
```

Before you run the *set restore* command, you must ensure that your backup is located in the /var/backup/ directory. Using the *manual filename* argument allows you to restore a manual backup, whereas the *scheduled filename* argument lets you schedule a restore from a scheduled backup.

For example, suppose you want to restore the *nokia_backup_20080805.tgz* backup we compiled earlier. Because it is still located in the /var/backup/ directory, we can run the following command to restore our configuration:

```
NokiaIP130:32> set restore manual nokia_backup_20080805.tgz
restore successful
```

WARNING

Restoring from a backup file overwrites your existing files. Also, make sure you have enough disk space available on your Nokia platform before restoring files. If you try to restore files and do not have enough disk space, you risk damaging the operating system.

Restoring Files from Backup Files Stored on a Remote Server

You can also restore a previously compiled backup that resides on a remote server using the *set restore remote* command.

```
set restore remote
filename name
ftp-site ip_addr
ftp-dir path_name
ftp-user user_name
ftp-passwd password
```

NOTE

Even though you can transfer your backups to a remote server using the TFTP protocol, you can only retrieve it using the FTP protocol.

Table 11.10 describes the arguments for the *set restore remote* command.

Table 11.10 *set restore remote* Configuration Arguments

Argument	Description
filename name	Specifies to restore your files from the filename stored on the remote server.
ftp-site ip_addr	Specifies the IP address of the remote server on which the backup files are stored.
ftp-dir path_name	Specifies the Unix path to the directory on which the backup files are stored.
ftp-user user_name	Specifies the name of the user account for connecting to the FTP site on which the backup files are stored. If a username is not set, enter anonymous.
ftp-passwd password	Specifies the password to use when connecting to the FTP site.

NOTE

The system must be running the same version of the operating system and the same packages as those of the backup files from which you restore files for both backup restore methods.

Configuring Network Security and Access

This section describes the commands you can use to manage the security and access features of your Nokia appliance. We will also discuss the ability to add and change users and group membership configurations.

Configuring Network Access and Services

As with the Nokia Network Voyager interface, you can use CLISH to configure network access to your Nokia appliance. Using the *set net-access* command, you can configure ftp, tftp, Telnet, and Web access, as well as access through the onboard serial ports. The *set net-access* command has the following arguments, which are detailed in Table 11.11:

```
set net-access
ftp <yes | no>
port <1-65535>
tftp <yes | no>
telnet <yes | no>
```

```
admin-net-login <yes | no>
cli-http <yes | no>
cli-https <yes | no>
com2-login <yes | no>
com3-login <yes | no>
com4-login <yes | no>
```

Table 11.11 *set net-access* Configuration Arguments

<table>
<tr><th>Argument</th><th>Description</th></tr>
<tr><td>ftp <yes | no></td><td>Enables or disables the FTP daemon.
Default: no</td></tr>
<tr><td>port <1-65535></td><td>Specifies the port that the FTP daemon should be listening on for connections.
Default: 21</td></tr>
<tr><td>tftp <yes | no></td><td>Enables or disables the TFTP daemon.
Default: no</td></tr>
<tr><td>telnet <yes | no></td><td>Enables or disables the telnet daemon.</td></tr>
<tr><td>admin-net-login <yes | no></td><td>Specifies "admin" login for Telnet access to the platform. This will not affect admin connections through Voyager or FTP.
Default: yes</td></tr>
<tr><td>com2-login <yes | no></td><td>Enables or disables connectivity to the serial port ttyd1 com2 that may be connected to an external modem.
Default: no</td></tr>
<tr><td>com3-login <yes | no></td><td>Enables or disables connectivity to the serial port ttyd2 com3 that may be connected to an external modem.
Default: no</td></tr>
<tr><td>com4-login <yes | no></td><td>Enables or disables connectivity to the serial port ttyd3 com4 that may be connected to an external modem.
Default: no</td></tr>
</table>

For example, if you wanted to enable the FTP daemon to listen on port 29, you would use the following command:

```
NokiaIP130:47> set net-access ftp yes port 29
```

NOTE

The default port that the FTP daemon listens on is port 21.

Also, if you wanted to disable Telnet access, you would use the following command:

```
NokiaIP130:48> set net-access telnet no
```

You can use the *set services* command to enable or disable some common services such as *echo*, *discard*, *chargen*, *daytime*, and *time*. The *set services* command has the following arguments, which are detailed in Table 11.12:

```
set services
echo <yes | no>
discard <yes | no>
chargen <yes | no>
daytime <yes | no>
time <yes | no>
```

Table 11.12 *set services* Configuration Arguments

Argument	Description
echo <yes | no>	Enables or disables the echo service, which sends back any data received by the platform to the originating source. Default: no
discard <yes | no>	Enables or disables the discard service, which discards any data received by the platform. Default: no
chargen <yes | no>	Enables or disables the chargen service, which sends back any data without regard to input. The data sent is a repeating sequence of printable characters. Default: no
daytime <yes | no>	Enables or disables the daytime service, which sends the current date and time as a character string without regard to the input. Default: no
time <yes | no>	Enables or disables the time service, which sends back the time, in seconds, since midnight January 1, 1900 the originating source. The value is sent as a binary number. Default: no

For example, if you wanted to enable the echo service, you would use the following command:

```
NokiaIP130:52> set services echo on
```

As with other CLISH commands, you can use the *show* command to list the current configuration settings. To verify which services are enabled, you can use the *show services* command, as follows:

```
NokiaIP130:53>      show services
Service                  On-Off
Echo                     on
Discard                  off
Chargen                  off
Daytime                  off
Time                     off
```

NOTE

Typically, you will only enable these services if there is a good reason to. For most Nokia IPSO installations you will not need to tune these settings.

Managing Passwords and Account Management

An important aspect when securing your Nokia network security platform is establishing user passwords and creating an effective password policy. Remember that having users create strong and unique passwords using a variety of character types and creating a password policy requiring users to change their passwords are often key factors to your overall network security.

To change the password and account management configuration, use the following commands:

```
set password-controls
min-password-length <6-128>
complexity <2-4>
palindrome-check <on | off>
history-checking <on | off>
history-length <1-1000>
password-expiration <never | 1-1827>
expiration-warning-days <1-366>
expiration-lockout-days <never | 1-1827>
force-change-when <no | password | first-password>
```

```
deny-on-fail enable <on | off>
deny-on-fail failures-allowed <2-1000>
deny-on-fail allow-after <60-604800>
deny-on-nonuse enable <on | off>
deny-on-nonuse allowed-days <30-1827>
```

Table 11.13 describes the arguments for the *set password-controls* command.

Table 11.13 *set restore remote* Configuration Arguments

Argument	Description
min-password length <*6-128*>	Specifies the minimum number of characters of a password that is to be allowed for users or SNMP users. Does not apply to passwords that have already been set. Default: *6*
complexity <*1-4*>	Specifies how complex users must make their passwords. The following is a description of the values: 1. disables complexity checking. 2. requires that passwords are comprised of a minimum of two character types—for example, abcABC. 3. requires that passwords are comprised of a minimum of three character types—for example, ab1ABC. 4. requires that passwords are comprised of a minimum of four character types—for example, ab1AB#. Default: *3*
palindrome-check <*on* | *off*>	Checks for passwords that are read the same left to right or right to left, such as *racecar* or the phrase "*straw warts*". Default: *on*
history-checking <*on* | *off*>	Enables a check for passwords being reused. Default: *on*
history-length <*1-1000*>	Specifies the number of past passwords that will be kept and checked against for reuse for each user. Default: *10*

Continued

Table 11.13 Continued. *set restore remote* Configuration Arguments

Argument	Description
password-expiration <*never* | *1-1827*>	Specifies the number of days since the last password change before a user is required to set a new password. Default: *never*
expiration-warning-days <*1-366*>	Specifies the number of days before a password expires that a user starts receiving warnings that the password is due to expire. Default: *7*
expiration-lockout-days <*never* | *1-1827*>	Specifies the number of days after password expiration that a user is locked out if the user has not set a new password. Default: *never*
force-change-when <*no* | *password* | *first-password*>	Specifies whether to force users to change their passwords. ■ *no* disables forcing a user to change an assigned password at login. ■ *password* forces a user to change a password after an administrator sets it with the *set user* command or with the Network Voyager User Management page. The forced password change does not apply to passwords set by the user through a self-password change. ■ *first-password* forces a new user to change their password from the initial password assigned by the administrator when the user account was created. Default: *no*
deny-on-fail enable <*on* | *off*>	Locks out a user after a configurable number of failed logins. When you enable this feature, keep in mind that it leaves you open to a Denial-of-Service attack by someone issuing unsuccessful login attempts. Default: *off*
deny-on-fail failuresallowed <*2-1000*>	Sets the number of failed logins a user can have before being locked out. Default: *10*

Continued

Table 11.13 Continued. *set restore remote* Configuration Arguments

Argument	Description
deny-on-fail allow-after *<60-604800>*	Sets the number of seconds a user must wait before being able to log in after being locked out because of failed logins. Default: *1200*
deny-on-nonuse enable *<on | off>*	Enables locking out users who have not logged in during a configurable amount of time. Default: *off*
deny-on-nonuse alloweddays *<30-1827>*	Sets the number of days after a user has last logged in before they are locked out. Default: *365*

NOTE

Password history checking does not apply to SNMP users.

Managing Users

You can use CLISH to add new users and to set and change user passwords, user ID, group ID, home directory, and default shell. Use the *add user* command to add users to the Nokia appliance:

```
add user username
uid <0-65535> homedir unix_path_name
```

Using the *uid* and *homedir* parameters, you must manually define the desired UID number and home directory path, respectively. For example, if you wanted to add a user named *andrew*, with a UID of *103* (the next available), and a home directory of */var/emhome/andrew/*, you could simply type:

```
NokiaIP130:38> add user andrew uid 103 homedir /var/emhome/andrew/
WARNING Must set password for this user before they can login; use 'set user USER passwd'.
```

This will create the user *andrew* and set their home directory to */var/emhome/andrew/*, as verified by the *ls* command:

```
pint[admin]# ls /var/emhome
admin  andrew  klhay monitor rouser  rouser  rwuser  rwuser
```

You can use the *add user* command to add new users, but you must use the *set user* command to set the password and allow the user to log on to the system. You can also use the *set user* command to change other values such as UID, GID, preferred shell, and so on. The available parameters are as follows and are described in Table 11.14.

```
set user username
passwd
newpass passwd
info string
uid <0-65535>
gid <0-65535>
homedir unix_path_name
shell string
force-password-change <on | off>
lock-out off
```

Table 11.14 *set user* Configuration Arguments

Argument	Description
user username	Specifies the new username or an existing username. The valid characters are alphanumeric characters, dash (-), and underscore (_). Range: 1–32 characters
Passwd	Starts a password change dialog. You will be asked to enter a new password for the user and then asked to verify it by reentering it. The password you enter will not be visible on the terminal.
newpass passwd	Specifies a new password for the user.
info string	Specifies a string describing the specified users.
uid <0-65535>	Specifies the particular user's user ID, which is used to identify the user's permissions.
gid <0-65535>	Specifies the ID for the primary group to which a user belongs.
homedir unix_path_name	Specifies the user's home directory, where the user is placed on login.
shell string	Specifies the user's shell, which is invoked when the user logs in. The default shell is /bin/csh.

Continued

Table 11.14 Continued. *set user* Configuration Arguments

Argument	Description
force-passwordchange <on | off>	On forces the user to change the password the next time they log in. Off overrides any condition forcing the user to change the password.
lock-out off	Clears any lockout conditions that are present on the user account and allows the user to log in.

NOTE

The home directory for all users must be in /var/emhome/.

Use the *delete user* command to delete any user you have added to your Nokia platform. Specify the user you wish to delete as follows:

```
NokiaIP130:45> delete user andrew
```

Configuring Routing

Using CLISH to configure routing makes complex routing configurations a relatively easy task. Static route configurations can be performed with a few simple commands, as can dynamic routing protocol configurations. Because there are many dynamic routing protocols to choose from, we will not walk through every protocol's configuration steps. Instead, we will show you how to create static routes and configure OSPF, one of the most widely implemented dynamic routing protocols available.

Configuring Static Routes

Configuring a static route with CLISH is probably one of the most common tasks you will perform at the command line of a Nokia appliance. To create a static route, the *set static-route* command is used.

```
set static-route ip_prefix
nexthop gateway address gateway_address priority <1-8> on
nexthop gateway logical gateway_address priority <1-8> on
nexthop gateway address gateway_address off
nexthop gateway logical gateway_address off
nexthop reject
```

```
nexthop blackhole
off
rank default
rank <0-255>
```

Table 11.15 describes the arguments for the *set static-route* command.

Table 11.15 *set static-route* Configuration Arguments

Argument	Description
nexthop gateway address gateway_address priority <1-8> on	Specifies the static route and the gateway address. The priority value determines the order in which the next hops are selected, and multiple next hops are defined with different priorities.
nexthop logical if_name priority <1-8> on	Specifies the static route and the logical gateway. For a logical gateway, enter the interface name. For example, if your gateway is an unnumbered interface, use its logical interface as the gateway.
nexthop gateway address gateway_address off	Disables the gateway address only for the IP address configured as the endpoint of the static route from your system. This option does not delete the route itself.
nexthop gateway logical if_name off	Disables the gateway only for the logical interface configured as the endpoint of the static route from your system. This option does not delete the route itself.
nexthop reject	Specifies for packets to be dropped rather than forwarded and for unreachable messages to be sent to the packet originators.
nexthop blackhole	Specifies for packets to be dropped rather than forwarded. Unlike the reject option, however, the blackhole option does not result in unreachable messages being sent to the packet originators.
Off	Deletes the specified static route and deletes any next hops associated with the route.
rank default	Specifies the rank for the specified static route that the routing system uses to determine which route to use when there are routes from different protocols to the same destination.
rank <0-255>	Specifies the rank for the specified static route that the routing system uses to determine which route to use when there are routes from different protocols to the same destination.

Configuring OSPF

You can use the following group of commands to set and view parameters for OSPF.

To properly configure your Nokia appliance, you will have to define your OSPF areas and then configure your OSPF interfaces.

NOTE

OSPFv2 is used with IPv4, and OSPFv3 is used with IPv6. The commands for OSPFv3 are similar to those for OSPFv2, except that in place of *ospf* you enter *ipv6 ospf3*.

Defining OSPF Areas

To configure your OSPF areas, including backbone and stub areas, use the following commands:

```
set ospf area
backbone <on | off>

set ospf area ospf_area
<on| off>
stub <on | off>
stub default-cost <1-677215>
stub summary <on | off>
nssa <on | off>
nssa default-cost <1-677215>
nssa default-metric-type <1-2>
nssa import-summary-routes <on | off>
nssa translator-role <always | candidate>
nssa translator-stability-interval <1-65535>
nssa redistribution <on |off>
nssa range ip_addr [restrict] <on | off>
```

Table 11.16 describes the arguments for the *set ospf area* commands.

Table 11.16 *set ospf area* Configuration Arguments

Argument	Description
backbone <on | off>	Specifies whether to enable or disable the backbone area. By default, the backbone area is enabled.
<on | off>	Specifies the area ID for a new OSPF area. Nokia recommends that you enter the area ID as a dotted quad, but you can use any integer as the area ID. The area ID 0.0.0.0 is reserved for the backbone.
stub <on | off>	Specifies the area ID for a stub area. Stub areas are areas that do not have AS external routes.
stub default-cost <1-677215>	Specifies a default route into the stub area with the specified cost.
stub summary <on | off>	Specifies the OSPF area as totally stubby, meaning it does not have any AS external routes and its area border routers do not advertise summary routes.
nssa <on | off>	Specifies the area ID for an NSSA.
nssa default-cost <1-677215>	Specifies the cost associated with the default route to the NSSA.
nssa default-metrictype <1-2>	Specifies the type of metric. The default, type 1, is equivalent to the Default ASE Route Type on the OSPF Voyager page. A type 1 route is internal and its metric can be used directly by OSPF for comparison. A type 2 route is external and its metric cannot be used for comparison directly.
nssa import-summaryroutes <on | off>	Specifies if summary routes (summary link advertisements) are imported into the NSSA.
nssa translator-role <always | candidate>	Specifies whether this NSSA border router will unconditionally translate Type-7 LSAs into Type-5 LSAs.
nssa translatorstability-interval <1-65535>	Specifies how long in seconds this elected Type-7 translator will continue to perform its translator duties once it has determined that its translator status has been assumed by another NSSA border router. Default: 40 seconds
nssa redistribution <on | off>	Specifies if both Type-5 and Type-7 LSAs or only Type-7 LSAs will be originated by this NSSA border router.
nssa range ip_addr [restrict] <on | off>	Specify the range of addresses to reduce the number of Type-5 LSAs for the NSSA border router. To prevent a specific prefix from being advertised, use the *restrict* argument.

NOTE

The backbone area cannot be a stub or NSSA area.

Configuring OSPF Interfaces

The following commands can be used to configure a backbone and other areas, such as stub areas, for specified interfaces.

```
set ospf
area <backbone | ospf_area> range ip_prefix <on | off>
area <backbone | ospf_area> range ip_prefix restrict <on | off>
stub-network ip_prefix <on | off>
stub-network ip_prefix stub-network-cost <1-677722>
interface if_name area <backbone | ospf_area> <on | off>
interface if_name hello-interval <1-65535>
interface if_name hello-interval default
interface if_name dead-interval <1-65535>
interface if_name dead-interval default
interface if_name retransmit-interval <1-65535>
interface if_name retransmit-interval default
interface if_name cost <1-65535>
interface if_name priority <0-255>
interface if_name passive <on | off>
interface if_name virtual-address <on | off>
interface if_name authtype none
interface if_name simple password
interface if_name md5 key authorization key id secret md5 secret
interface if_name md5 key authorization key id
```

Table 11.17 describes the arguments for configuring the OSPF interfaces.

Table 11.17 OSPF Interface Configuration Arguments

Argument	Description
area <backbone | ospf_area> range ip_prefix <on | off>	Specifies the OSPF area to which the specified interface range belongs. Select an area from the areas already configured.
area <backbone | ospf_area> range ip_prefix restrict <on | off>	Any area can be configured with any number of address ranges. These ranges are used to reduce the number of routing entries that a given area transmits to other areas. If a given prefix aggregates a number of more specific prefixes within an area, you can configure an address range that becomes the only prefix advertised to other areas.
stub-network ip_prefix <on | off>	Specifies a stub network to which the specified interface range belongs.
stub-network ip_prefix stub-network-cost <1-677722>	Configure a stub network to advertise reachability to prefixes that are not running OSPF. The advertised prefix appears as an OSPF internal route and is filtered at area borders with the OSPF area ranges.
interface if_name area <backbone | ospf area> <on | off>	Specifies the OSPF area to which the specified interface belongs.
interface if_name hello-interval <1-65535>	Specifies the interval, in seconds, between hello packets that the router sends on the specified interface.
interface if_name hello-interval default	Specifies the default value for the hello interval, which is ten seconds.
interface if_name dead-interval <1-65535>	Specifies the number of seconds after which a router stops receiving hello packets that it declares the peer down.
interface if_name dead-interval default	Specifies the default value for the dead interval, which is 40 seconds.
interface if_name retransmit-interval <1-65535>	Specifies the number of seconds between link state advertisement transmissions for adjacencies belonging to the specified interface.
interface if_name retransmit-interval default	Specifies the default default for the retransmit interval, which is five seconds.

Continued

Table 11.17 Continued. OSPF Interface Configuration Arguments

Argument	Description
interface if_name cost <1-65535>	Specifies the weight of the given path in a route. The higher the cost, the less preferred the link.
interface if_name priority <0-255>	Specifies the priority for becoming the designated router (DR) on the specified link.
interface if_name passive <on | off>	Enabling this option puts the specified interface into passive mode—that is, hello packets are not sent from the interface. Putting an interface into passive mode means no adjacencies are formed on the link. Default: off
interface if_name virtual-address <on | off>	Enables OSPF on the virtual IP address associated with this interface. This option functions only if this router is a VRRP master. You must also configure VRRP to accept connections to VRRP IPs. Default: off
interface if_name authtype none	Specifies not to use an authentication scheme for the specified interface.
interface if_name authtype simple password	Specifies to use simple authentication for the specified interface. Enter an ASCII string that is eight characters long.
interface if_name authtype md5 key authorization key id secret md5 secret	Specifies to use MD5 authorization. Enter at least one key ID and its corresponding MD5 secret. If you configure multiple key IDs, the largest key ID is used for authenticating outgoing packets.

Changing Global OSPF Settings

Use the following commands to configure settings that apply to all configured OSPF areas, including the backbone and stub areas.

```
set ospf
rfc1583-compatibility <on | off>
spf-delay <1-60>
spf-delay default
spf-holdtime <1-60>
```

```
spf-holdtime default
default-ase-cost <1-677215>
default-ase-type <1 | 2>
```

Table 11.18 describes the arguments for changing global OSPF settings.

Table 11.18 Changing OSPF Global Settings

Argument	Description
rfc1583-compatibility <on | off>	The Nokia implementation of OSPF is based on RFC 2178, which fixed some looping problems in an earlier specification of OSPF. If your implementation runs in an environment with OSPF implementations based on RFC 1583 or earlier, enable this option, which is on by default. Setting compatibility with RFC 1583 ensures backward compatibility. Default: on
spf-delay <1-60>	Specifies the time, in seconds, to wait before recalculating the OSPF routing table after a change in the topology.
spf-delay default	Specifies an spf-delay time of two seconds.
spf-holdtime <1-60>	Specifies the minimum time, in seconds, between recalculations of the OSPF routing table.
spf-holdtime default	Specifies an spf-holdtime of five seconds.
Default-ase-cost <1-6777215>	Specifies the cost assigned to routes from other protocols that are redistributed into OSPF as autonomous systems external. If the route has a cost already specified, that cost takes precedent. Default: 1
Default-ase-type <1 | 2>	Specifies the type assigned to routes from other protocols that are redistributed into OSPF as autonomous systems external. If the route has a type already specified, that type takes precedent. Default: 1

Using Route Summary Commands

The route summary commands show information about active, inactive, or both active/inactive routes on your system for the various routing protocols.

You can use the *show route* command to show information for BGP, IGRP, and RIP protocols using the following arguments:

```
show route
igrp
rip
bgp <aspath | communities | detailed | metrics | suppressed>
inactive <bgp | igrp | rip>
all <bgp | igrp | rip>
```

You can also use the *show route* command to show information about the OSPF routes on your system as well by using the following arguments:

```
show route
ospf
inactive ospf
all ospf
```

Finally, you can use the *show route* command to show aggregate route information using the following arguments:

```
show route
aggregate
inactive aggregate
all aggregate
```

Tools & Traps...

Show Routing Daemon (IPSRD) Commands

In addition to using the route summary commands, you can also poll the Ipsilon Routing Daemon (IPSRD) for information that could be used to troubleshoot routing issues.

Use the following commands to view general information recorded by the IPSRD:

```
show ipsrd
   memory
```

Continued

```
    resources
    krt
version
```

The *memory* argument displays the memory usage of the routing daemon. It shows information for each routing protocol running on the system, such as total memory usage, MFC- memory, core memory usage, and per-protocol memory usage breakdown.

The *resources* argument displays system information such as total uptime, total user time, total system time, page faults, page reclaims, file system writes, file system reads, message writes, message reads, signals received, total swaps, voluntary context switches, and involuntary context switches.

The *krt* argument displays statistical information about the messages sent and received on the raw sockets between the kernel and IPSRD.

The *version* argument displays the IPSRD version, system start time, current time, and system uptime. The *show ipsrd version* command, and sample output, is as follows:

```
NokiaIP130    :3> show ipsrd version
Ipsrd version : ipsrd-IPSO-4.2-BUILD081a03-04.14.2008-14:11:02
Started at    : Sat Jul 26 21:46:15 GMT 2008
Current time  : Mon Aug 04 19:47:55 GMT 2008
Up time       : 8 days 22hrs 1min 40secs
```

Summary

This chapter covered some of the more common CLISH configuration commands you might find yourself using on a day-to-day basis. We did not cover every command since a full walkthrough of every command can be found in the *CLI Reference Guide for Nokia IPSO 4.2*, which is available for download from the Nokia support site.

When configuring interfaces, you must know the IP address and netmask of each interface you plan on using. Physical interfaces exist for each physical port on a NIC installed on the appliance. Before you assign IP address and subnet information to an interface, you must configure the physical interface. This is done using the *set interface phys_if_name* command. When a physical interface is installed, the system automatically creates a corresponding logical interface. The *add/set interface* command, and its arguments, can be used to create and configure the logical interfaces on your Nokia appliance.

Advanced tuning options are available from the CLISH interface, which lets you adjust the way your Nokia appliance handles sequence validation, MSS for TCP, and the stripping of the router alert IP option before passing packets to the firewall.

Using the *show summary* command will provide a detailed list of the current system configuration options on your Nokia appliance. The configuration summary provides details for IP interfaces, ARP, Traffic Management, Router Services, System, Security and Access, IPSec, SNMP, Monitoring, and Licenses. Before configuring your DHCP server information, you must enable the DHCP server service. You must then set DHCP-related information, such as lease time, DNS information, and so on, that your Nokia appliance will use in its leased DHCP IP addresses. With the DHCP server settings configured, the final step is to configure the DHCP IP address scope. Set the time on your Nokia appliance manually by connecting to a NTP server for a one-time synchronization, or by constantly synchronizing to a NTP server. You can back up your Nokia appliance manually or by configuring a scheduled backup. By default, the backup file contains all the configuration (/config), cron (/var/cron), etc (/var/etc), and IPSec files (/var/etc/ipsec).

CLISH allows you to configure ftp, tftp, Telnet, and Web access, as well as access through the onboard serial ports. You can also use the *set services* command to enable or disable common services such as echo, discard, chargen, daytime, and time. User and group management can also be performed using CLISH. Having users create strong and unique passwords using a variety of character types and creating a password policy requiring users to change their passwords are often key factors in your overall network security.

Using CLISH to configure routing makes complex routing configurations a relatively easy task. Static route configurations can be performed with a few simple commands, as can dynamic routing protocol configurations. Configuring a static route with CLISH is probably one of the most common tasks you will perform at the command line of a Nokia appliance.

Solutions Fast Track

Configuring Interfaces

☑ When a physical interface is installed, the system automatically creates a corresponding logical interface.

☑ Use the *show interfaces* command to list information about all interfaces on the platform.

☑ Delete a logical interface from your IPSO configuration by using the *delete interface* command.

Applying Security Tuning

☑ To change the maximum segment size (MSS) for TCP, use the *set advanced-tuning tcp-ip tcp-mss <512-1500>* command.

☑ To optimize the forwarding of unidirectional UDP traffic on IP1260 platforms, use *set advanced-tuning ethernet-options on.*

☑ Do not enable the *ethernet-options* option if more than two Gigabit Ethernet interfaces are installed in the system. Doing so can impair system performance.

Configuring System Options

☑ Using the *show summary* command will provide a detailed list of the current system configuration options on your Nokia appliance.

☑ Set the time on your Nokia appliance manually, by connecting to a NTP server for a one-time-synchronization, or by constantly synchronizing to a NTP server.

☑ By default, the backup file contains all the configuration (/config), cron (/var/cron), etc (/var/etc), and IPSec files (/var/etc/ipsec).

Configuring Network Security and Access

☑ Using the *set net-access* command, you can configure ftp, tftp, Telnet, and Web access, as well as access via the onboard serial ports.

☑ Use the *set services* command to enable or disable some common services such as echo, discard, chargen, daytime, and time.

☑ Use CLISH to add new users and to set and change user passwords, user IDs, group IDs, home directories, and default shells.

Configuring Routing

- ☑ Configuring a static route with CLISH, using the *set static-route* command, is probably one of the most common tasks you will perform at the command line of a Nokia appliance.
- ☑ OSPFv2 is used with IPv4, while OSPFv3 is used with IPv6. The commands for OSPFv3 are similar to those for OSPFv2, except that in place of *ospf* you enter *ipv6 ospf3*.
- ☑ Use the *show route* command to show information for BGP, IGRP, and RIP protocols.

Frequently Asked Questions

Q: Where can I get more information about CLISH commands?

A: The *CLI Reference Guide for Nokia IPSO 4.2*, which is available for download from the Nokia support site, provides a thorough walkthrough of every possible CLISH command available.

Q: What is a jumbo frame?

A: An Ethernet frame larger than 1,518 bytes is commonly known as a "jumbo frame." This is because Ethernet was originally designed to handle frames of 1,518 bytes or less.

Q: When I create another logical interface, why does it ask me to specify a VLAN ID?

A: This is because you already have at least one IP address assigned to this interface. If you need one interface to handle multiple IP addresses, you must assign a VLAN ID so the upstream switch knows to which logical interface to route the Ethernet frames.

Q: How can I increase the TCP MSS on my Nokia appliance?

A: Using the *set advanced-tuning tcp-ip tcp-mss* command lets you tune the MSS for your appliance.

Q: What is the default MSS value?

A: The default MSS value for TCP on your Nokia appliance is 1024.

Q: Do I need to tune settings such as MSS and sequence validation?

A: You generally will not need to modify these settings unless there is a requirement for an application installed on your Nokia appliance or an upstream device requires the change.

Q: Should I use the Nokia appliance as a DHCP server?

A: This is entirely up to you. Keep in mind that the more services you enable on your Nokia appliance, the fewer system resources will be available for other critical system functions. If you plan on using this appliance as a core firewall at the edge of your network, you may want it to only worry about passing, and protecting, network traffic.

Q: Which date and time synchronization method should I use?

A: It is recommended that you ensure that your Nokia appliance is continuously synchronizing with an internal NTP server. This ensures that your system logs are timestamped correctly in the event of an incident.

Q: Should I keep my Nokia backups on the Nokia appliance?

A: No, you should not. Should the Nokia suffer a catastrophic hardware failure, you will find it extremely difficult, if not impossible, to retrieve the backup from the appliance. You should always create an extensive backup and restore policy that includes your Nokia appliances.

Q: Can I enable and disable network access via CLISH?

A: Using the *set net-access* command, you can configure ftp, tftp, Telnet, and Web access, as well as access through the onboard serial ports.

Q: I have changed the FTP daemon port using CLISH but now I cannot access the Nokia appliance using FTP.

A: Remember, if you are using firewall software on your Nokia appliance and have defined an explicit FTP rule, you must ensure it is allowing your newly configured FTP daemon port. The default port for FTP is port 21 and your firewall may be blocking FTP access on other ports.

Q: What settings can I specify when I add a user using CLISH?

A: You can use CLISH to add new users and to set and change user passwords, user IDs, group IDs, home directories, and default shells.

Q: What dynamic routing protocol should I use on my network?

A: Unfortunately, this is not a straightforward question to answer. The decision can only be made after reviewing the business requirements and the capabilities of your current hardware.

Q: How can I create a static route using CLISH?

A: You can create a static route using the *set static-route* command.

Q: What are the differences between OSPFv2 and OSPFV3 commands?

A: The commands for OSPFv3 are similar to those for OSPFv2, except that in place of *ospf* you enter *ipv6 ospf3*.

Appendix A

UNIX Basics

Solutions in this chapter:

- Understanding Files and Directories
- Understanding Users and Groups
- Using the Shell and Basic Shell Utilities
- Using *vi*

Introduction

For readers who have little or no experience with UNIX, this appendix explains the basic concepts and commands to quickly get you up to speed with Nokia's (or any UNIX, for that matter) command-line interface. This foundation will also help you when you read some of the chapters in this book.

Here you will learn the basic form of the UNIX file system, including how files and directories are a part of that system. We make our examples Nokia-specific where appropriate. You will also learn about the UNIX user and group permission concept and the commands that manipulate file ownership and access permissions. We round out this appendix with some sections on shell usage and basic shell utility commands, and a section on *vi* editor basics.

Understanding Files and Directories

When working with UNIX-based systems, you must understand the concept of files and directories. This is no easy task, especially if you do not have a background or substantial training in UNIX or Linux. In this section, we look at the fundamentals you need to know to operate within the UNIX environment and demonstrate how to navigate through the file and directory structure. Let's begin with the basic concepts of the file and directory system.

The UNIX Directory Hierarchy

With UNIX, the main concept of understanding files and directories is learning the hierarchical structure, which is based on a tree. Trees have roots on the bottom that go into the ground, and their branches stretch out at the top. The UNIX file system hierarchy concept flips a tree upside down. Now the roots, which for UNIX are really one root, are on top and the branches reach down.

Figure A.1 shows a simple diagram of the root with its branches flipped upside down.

Figure A.1 UNIX Hierarchical Structure

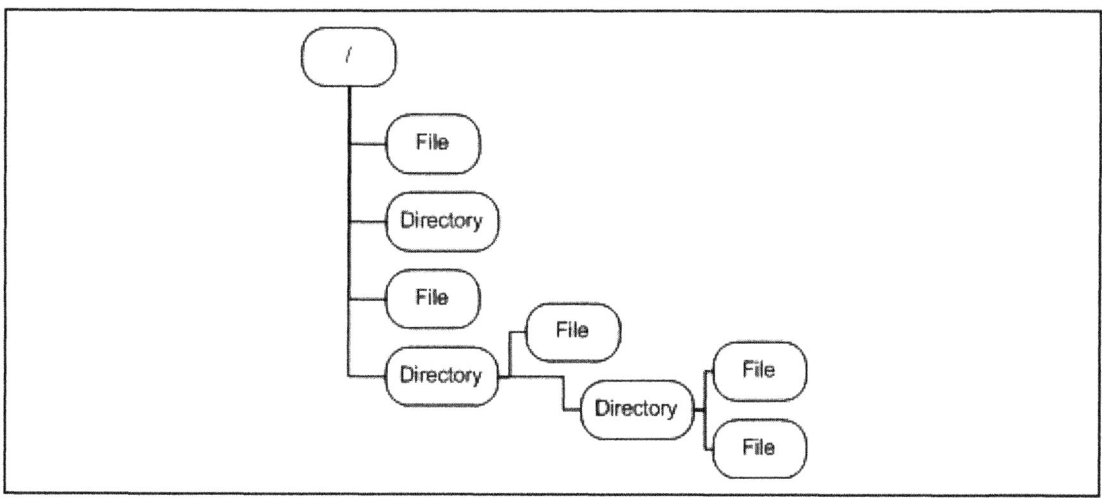

With Figure A.1 in mind, consider this concept from a more technical perspective. If you understand this concept, all you have to do is start naming your branches. The first thing we have to name is the root itself. In Figure A.1, it is simply named root and is represented by a slash (/) when we use it in a command or pathname.

NOTE

It is very important that you know the UNIX-based operating system is case-sensitive and anything you type must be in the proper case. If you make a case-based mistake, your commands will not work. For example, the command *ls* gives you a directory listing when typed in lowercase, but when typed LS, a syntax error is returned.

With UNIX, data, disk, and program information are stored as files organized within the tree. You cannot get far without knowing the location of what you need and how to find it. Let's now look at where everything is in the system and start giving the tree branches some logical names.

In Figure A.2, you are shown the actual layout of the UNIX hierarchy, with the root at the top and the tree expanding down. For now, do not be concerned with what each branch represents; we will explain that in a moment. Familiarize yourself with the idea of how the hierarchy is laid out. You must remember this layout because when you log in to a UNIX-based system using the command line, you must know this information to quickly find your way around.

Figure A.2 Viewing the UNIX-Based Hierarchy

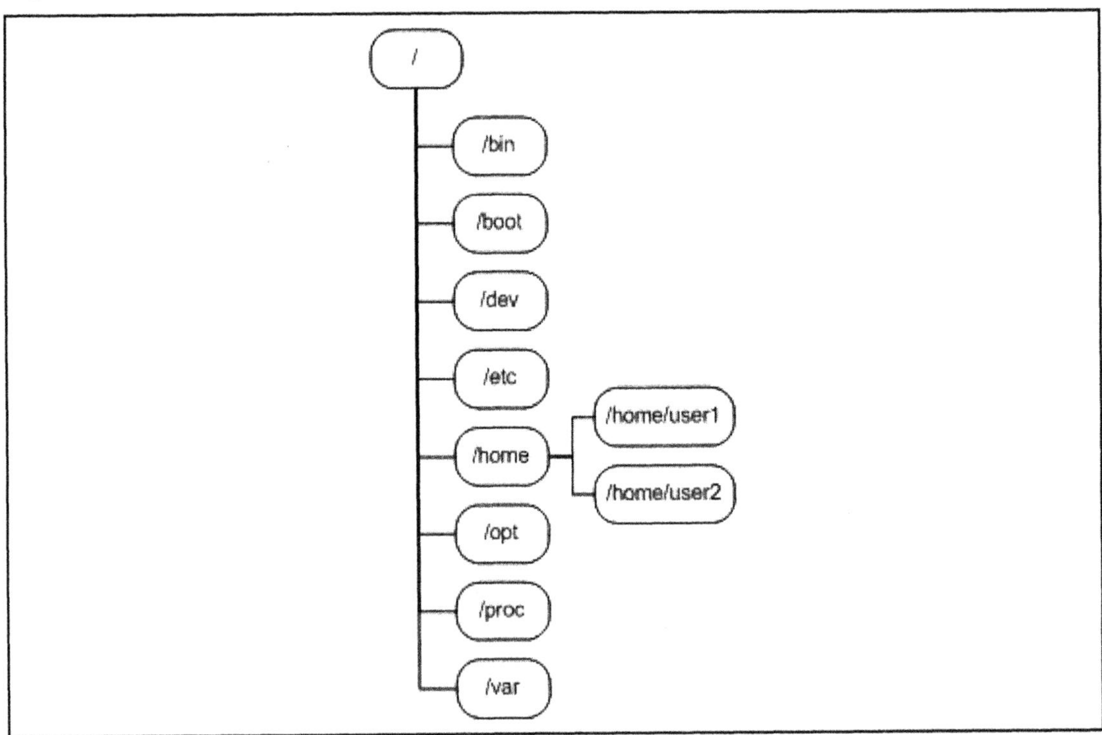

NOTE

This is not a complete listing of the directories available on a UNIX operating system. Instead, this is an example displaying some of the possible directories.

A *directory* is a special type of file that contains information about other files. You can also make directories within other directories, as long as you have the proper permissions to do so. This means that the layout you see in Figure A.2 can actually change and become very deep. For instance, in the home directory, User1 and User2 have their own home directories on the system. What if you had more than just root, User1, and User2? What if you have 20 users? The point here is that you need to master the layout quickly or you could become lost or confused as the system grows.

NOTE

There is no theoretical limit to the number of levels you have within your hierarchy. Therefore, if your directory is heavily populated, you will want to know the location of the root of the hierarchy and how to navigate from it as your starting point. The system can become very populated and quickly get very deep.

To add to the confusion, you must understand that when working with UNIX-based operating systems, *everything appears as a file*. A good example of this concept is when you want to look at running processes and system memory. This information is accessible through various files in the file system.

NOTE

Depending on your terminal type, it might be possible to *colorize* your directory listing output. For example, you can color-code directory names to display in a different color than regular filenames. When you use your Nokia system, however, connecting from a console will not normally display colorized directory outputs. A good tip is to use *ls –F*, which makes directories stand out on any terminal by appending the directory name with a forward slash.

You might think that this information would be difficult to remember, but it really is not once you know what each directory contains. Table A.1 explains what each directory does and their most important features.

Table A.1 The UNIX Hierarchy in Detail

Directory Name	Function
/	This is the system root directory.
tmp	This directory is used for creating system temporary files. Many systems delete the contents of this directory during the boot process.
etc	This directory contains global system configuration files.
usr	This directory contains a majority of your system files and typically is broken down into the lib and bin directories. Program libraries and executable binaries are stored here.
var	This directory is responsible for holding most of the volatile system information such as logs and print spooling that are constantly in a state of change.
boot	This directory holds system startup files and the kernel image. On some other systems, you might also see these files in /.
home	This is the main directory that holds the user's home directories. On Nokia systems, /var serves this purpose.
sbin	This directory is responsible for holding system files and programs such as mount and fdisk.
dev	This directory contains many special files that allow access to physical devices such as your hard disk or diskette drive.
opt	This is the optional software directory.

Depending on which flavor of UNIX you are working with, you might find other directories visible, but Table A.1 shows the most common directory layout you will encounter. Other directories you could see include /proc, which contain specialized runtime kernel information. The directory structure truly does depend on the flavor of UNIX/Linux/BSD you are using.

Basic Directory Commands

Before working with a UNIX system, you must know some basic commands. Again, remember that everything is case-sensitive when working with UNIX. This is the biggest problem people face in learning UNIX basics. You have to be very conscious of the fact that a capital *S* is not the same as a lowercase *s*, for example. The case of a letter you use as a command-line argument could mean very different things, depending on whether it is upper- or lowercase.

UNIX commands will be easy to master if you have a command-line background (DOS, Cisco IOS, and so on), because it is only a matter of memorizing new commands and relating them to what you already know. Let's take a look at some of the most common UNIX commands used to navigate the file and directory system.

Command: *cd*

The *cd* command is used to change directories. If you are familiar with the old DOS command, this command is easy to remember. Let's look at the actual command syntax to change to the directory one level up. In this example, we look at the mild differences between working with UNIX and DOS.

Open a UNIX session and log in. After logging in, try changing to the /home directory (which should be one level up) using the *cd* command. The syntax for this command is *cd* with a space and two dots following it. It looks like this:

```
cd ..
```

Remember that there is a space between the *cd* and the two dots. If you do not include the space, you will not execute the command, generating instead a syntax error.

Here, you can see that when you try to use the *cd* command with the two dots directly adjacent to it, it results in an error and a suggestion. You can use the suggestion from the system to use the *cd* command with two dots placed correctly:

```
rshimonski@BEAST:~> cd..
Error: Try: cd ..
rshimonski@BEAST:~> cd ..
rshimonski@BEAST:/home>
```

Command: *pwd*

The *pwd* command is used to print the working or current directory. The *pwd* command is often mistakenly referred to as the *primary working directory*, but it really stands for *print working directory*. Use whatever mnemonic device helps you to remember the command.

The commands are used as follows: Open a UNIX session and log in. After logging in and moving up one level with *cd ..*, enter **pwd** at the prompt:

```
rshimonski@BEAST:/home> pwd
/home
rshimonski@BEAST:/home>
```

By using the *pwd* command, you have printed to the console the directory you are currently working within. This directory was included with the prompt, but if you were unsure, you would use the *pwd* command to determine the directory. Not all UNIX prompts show you which directory you are currently in.

Let's get a little more creative and use the *cd* command with the *pwd* command. Change directories from /home to your current user (in our case, rshimonski) directory. Here is the syntax you would use:

```
rshimonski@BEAST:/home> cd ~
rshimonski@BEAST:~> pwd
/home/rshimonski
rshimonski@BEAST:~>
```

The most important thing to remember here is that you are learning how to navigate through the hierarchy and to see where your place is within it.

Command: *ls*

The *ls* command is also heavily used within the UNIX system. This command will probably become one of your most used commands when you work within the directory structure. The *ls* command lists filenames, sizes, modification and access times, and file types for you. There are also many options you can use with it. When you use *ls*, the default sort order of the directory listing will be alphabetical by name. You can, however, use options like *-t* to change the sort order to list files by time instead of by name. Table A.2 shows some of the more common options you will most likely use with the *ls* command:

Table A.2 *ls* Command Options

Option	Description
–l	This option provides for a longer listing or a full listing.
-a	This option shows all files, even hidden ones.
-t	This option sorts the output by time instead of by name.
-d	This option lists only directories.

Note that you can use options together for more flexibility. In other words, you can use the *–l* and *–d* options together, as shown in the following commands:

```
rshimonski@BEAST:~> ls -d
.
rshimonski@BEAST:~> ls -ld
```

```
drwxr-xr-x  12 rshimons users    1208 Sep  2 13:37  .
rshimonski@BEAST:~>
```

Working with and navigating around the directory structure and UNIX-based system hierarchy is not really that difficult. It just takes a little knowledge and patience.

Now let's look at the file structure.

UNIX File Basics

In this section, we look at the basics of UNIX-based files and how to work with them. There are a few important things you should remember about working with the file system. First, you should know that an *inode* is a data structure used by the file system to uniquely represent a file and its associated attributes. An inode contains the file type (for example, plain file, directory, symbolic link, or device file); its owner, group, and public access permissions; the owner and group ID numbers; its size in bytes; the number of links (directory references) to the file; and the last access and last modification file times. In addition, there is a list of data blocks claimed by the file. It is critical that you understand the basics of an inode when learning the UNIX system. Other items to note are:

- UNIX file systems will support long filenames (more than eight characters and typically much longer), and the filenames are case-sensitive.
- Only one file system is allowed per disk partition, although one physical disk can have many different partitions and therefore many different file systems on it.
- Each file system has its own inode table.
- The file system uses inodes to uniquely identify files with the system.
- Files are referenced internally by inode number, not names (although you see names in an *ls* output).

That's it! This is the most important information you need to know about UNIX files and how they are managed in your UNIX system.

Symbolic and Hard Links

Before we work directly with the file structure and look at what you can do with it, let's examine links. *Links* are references to a file or a directory and can be very useful. There are two link types: *symbolic* (sometimes called *soft*) and *hard*. You can use links for filename aliasing purposes because sometimes filenames can be hard to remember. The *ln* command creates hard or symbolic links. The following is the syntax of the *ln* command (your command-line options might be slightly different, depending on which flavor of UNIX you use):

```
rshimonski@BEAST:~> ln --help
Usage: ln [OPTION]... TARGET [LINK_NAME]
```

```
or: ln [OPTION]... TARGET... DIRECTORY
or: ln [OPTION]... --target-directory=DIRECTORY TARGET...
```

You can also remove a link or a file with the *rm* command, as shown in this syntax:

```
rshimonski@BEAST:~> rm --help
Usage: rm [OPTION]... FILE...
Remove (unlink) the FILE(s).
```

Hard Links

Hard links are used only on files, not on directories, and are created using *ln <target file> <link>*. When you create a hard link, both the source and target of the link must be provided and must be within the same file system. A hard link always refers to the same inode number, so you can have many hard links to a file, but each link really points to the same underlying inode. Use *ls –i* to see inode numbers.

Symbolic Links

Symbolic links are created with the *ln -s* command. When you create a symbolic link, you create a link to the path of a source file. In this case, the link has its own inode, so you can delete the link without deleting the file it points to, much like a Windows shortcut.

Understanding Users and Groups

After you now know how to connect to a UNIX system, you need to know how to log in, who to log in as, and what control over the system you have. Most of this information is not very difficult to understand, but it can be a little complicated due to the highly flexible use of the UNIX command line. Let's take a look at all the basics you should know to work with users and groups on a UNIX-based system.

Users and Groups

To log in to the system, you need a user account, which has its own password. The UNIX system employs user accounts to keep the system secure from unauthorized access. The user is authenticated to the system through a certain process:

1. You must first be at the console of the system or use a remote access protocol such as SSH or Telnet.
2. After you connect to the system, you will be prompted with a banner:

   ```
   Red Hat Linux release 6.2
   Kernel 2.4.12 on an i686
   login:
   ```

3. When prompted, you can enter the user account you have configured on the system. For example: **rshimonski**.
4. After you enter an account name, the system prompts for the password with the password banner.
5. If you enter the proper credentials, you are authenticated and gain access to the system. If you do not enter the proper credentials, you are prompted to reenter your username. After you are authenticated, you will see the prompt where you can begin working:

```
Red Hat Linux release 6.2
Kernel 2.4.12 on an i686
login: rshimonski
Password:
bash$
```

That's it! So what else is there to know? Now that you know how to log in to a system, you should be aware of the various levels of systems permissions you have, based on who you are logged in as. Now let's look at the two basic types of users.

User Types

When working with UNIX, remember that you can use different kinds of user accounts: privileged and unprivileged. There is the *superuser* account, also known as the *root user* (or the *admin user*, specific to the Nokia platform), which is a privileged user. There are also *normal users*, which you create. Each user has their own varying levels of permissions and rights, often called *unprivileged users*. Frequently, administrators log on to the system with the superuser account. This habit is problematic in a security sense for several reasons:

- Administrators get so used to using the root account that they make the password easy to log in with. The administrator usually picks a password that is quick to type and remember. This usually means it is also easy to crack with most automated password-cracking tools.
- Administrators often use the root account over Telnet to connect to the server they want to administer, which makes the password susceptible to capture with any standard packet-capture device.
- Because it is constantly used, the root password is not changed often enough, which opens up the possibility that the password can be gained through some form of social engineering (*shoulder surfing*, for example).

The list goes on, but you must remember that the root account is really a superuser account. It has more rights and permissions to the system than any normal account and it is for this reason that you should not take its security lightly. Remember, a superuser has full access to the system and can damage it very easily. The recommended way to administer a system is to log in as an unprivileged user and use the *su* command to become root as necessary.

As a Nokia administrator, you should also consider the following information. Nokia has parted from the long-standing security mantra not to log in directly as the root user. Nokia takes the view that you should have only one user on a system, and that user is admin with root privileges. Not having other users on a system prevents other users from logging in and gaining some privilege that they do not have. Both views have some merit, but we still recommend the *su* method, especially because Nokia has taken strong measures to prevent the types of local root exploits that would give unprivileged users root access.

UIDs and GIDs

UID is the abbreviation for *user identification* or *user ID*. *GID* stands for *group ID*. When you log on, your account is given a numerical ID number that is known as the UID. The rule of thumb is, the lower the number, the more privileged the account. The superuser (root) has a UID of 0, where ordinary users typically have a UID higher than 100.

More detailed information about UIDs and GIDs can be helpful in your overall understanding of the UNIX system. UIDs are uniquely indicated within the */etc/passwd* file. You can view this password file by navigating to the /etc directory and using the *vi* editor on the file.

NOTE

In your Nokia box, you can view usernames and UIDs in the /etc/master.passwd file.

You will learn how to use the *vi* editor at the end of the appendix. To view the file, issue the following commands:

```
rshimonski@BEAST:/etc> vi passwd
root:x:0:0:root:/root:/bin/bash
bin:x:1:1:bin:/bin:/bin/bash
daemon:x:2:2:Daemon:/sbin:/bin/bash
lp:x:4:7:Printing daemon:/var/spool/lpd:/bin/bash
```

The third field in the previous file view is the UID. So the bin user has UID 1. Also specified in the system password file are the user's home directory and login shell—in this case, /bin and /bin/bash. The GID is also indicated, but it is located within the file /etc/group. The following is the view of a standard group file:

```
rshimonski@BEAST:/etc> vi group
root:x:0:root
bin:x:1:root,bin,daemon
daemon:x:2:
sys:x:3:
tty:x:5:
disk:x:6:
lp:x:7:
wwwadmin:x:8:
kmem:x:9:
wheel:x:10:
mail:x:12:cyrus
```

The GID is the third field in the previous file view. Adding a user to a group is just a matter of appending the username to the appropriate line in /etc/group. In the preceding example, you can see that the users root, bin, and daemon are all members of the bin group, which has GID 1.

Wheel Group

The *wheel group* is a group that exists for added security. Only users in the wheel group can execute commands such as *su*, or *superuser*, which we look at in the next section. Most standard UNIX systems already have this group added by default, so you only need to edit the group file to add your username to the wheel group. Nokia systems do have the wheel group already created for you.

To add a user to the wheel group, edit the /etc/group file and add the username to the line that begins *wheel:*. This is not overly difficult, but remember that commas delimit the list of login names:

1. Open the /etc/group file again with the *vi* command. (If you are having problems using *vi*, skip to the last section of the appendix to read up on how to use it.) You can now add the users to the wheel group as follows:

   ```
   rshimonski@BEAST:/etc> vi group
   root:x:0:root
   bin:x:1:root,bin,daemon
   daemon:x:2:
   sys:x:3:
   tty:x:5:
   wheel:x:10:root,rshimonski
   ```

2. Now you can *su* to root using the user you just added to the wheel group in /etc/group:

```
rshimonski@BEAST:/etc> su
Password:
BEAST:/etc #
```

File Access Permissions

When you look at the output of the *ls –l* command, you will see a group of letters or characters along the left side of your screen. The characters specify the type of file and how it can be accessed:

```
drwxr-xr-x   2   root   root   2168   Aug 31   15:40   bin
```

The first letter, *d*, indicates that this file is really a directory. The next nine characters specify the file access rights. These rights are divided into three groups: owner, group, and world, for the owner of the file, the primary group of the file, and everyone else, in that order. Each group has three *access specifiers*, which can be present or not. These are read, write, and execute—the *rwx* you see in the example line. Any specifier that is not present is represented by a dash, which means that group of users does not have that access right. So the permissions string *rwxr-xr-x* means that the owner of the file has read, write, and execute permissions, the members of its primary group have read and execute permissions, and everyone else has read and execute permissions (the last group of three, *r-x*). Some terminology you often see used is that each access specifier is a *bit*, so you can say "That file has its execute bit set."

Table A.3 explains the various permissions when referred to regular files or directories.

Table A.3 Permissions and Meanings

Permission	Regular File	Directory
Read	Read permission	Directory list permission
Write	Modify, rename, or delete permission	Create, rename, or delete permission
Execute	Execute permission	Permission to *cd* into directory

The file owner and group are also in the *ls –l* output. In this case, we see that the bin directory is owned by the root user and groups, so only the root user has permission to list the contents of the bin directory, *cd* into it, or delete it. All other users can *cd* into the bin directory and list its contents, but they cannot modify it in any way.

File access specifiers are modified using the *chmod* and *chgrp* commands. There is much more to learn regarding permissions, so refer to the man pages of your system for details.

setuid and setgid Binaries

Executable files in a UNIX system can sometimes assume the identity of their owner or primary group when they are executed. This is different from the way UNIX processes normally decide which access rights they have. Typically, a file assumes the permissions of the user who executed it.

Files that take on the permissions of their owner or group are termed *set UID* or *set GID* files, respectively. You will often see them named simply *setuid* or *setgid* files. An example will probably make this clearer. On my Linux workstation, the *su* binary looks like this when I enter **ls –l /bin/su**:

```
-rwsr-xr-x   1 root   root 23176  Apr  7 11:59 su
```

Notice the *s* in the string *-rwsr-xr-x*. This letter means that this executable file is setuid. When I run it as an unprivileged user, it would normally (if it were not setuid) take on the permissions and access rights of whomever I was logged in as. It instead assumes the permissions of the root user, because it is owned by root. Because *su* is designed to give unprivileged users root access (after entering the root password), this works nicely. There is a potential security problem here, though. A malicious user can sometimes take advantage of poor programming practices in setuid or setgid files to obtain privileges that they would not normally have. This is what security professionals call an example of a *local root exploit.* For this reason, more modern or security-conscious Unices attempt to reduce the dependence on setuid or setgid files, or at least audit the source code of binary files, that must have these special permissions.

Using the Shell and Basic Shell Utilities

This section looks at the fundamentals of a shell and how to use it. It also takes a look at some of the more common commands. The term *shell* is a UNIX term that stands for the user interface you use to interact with the system. The shell is also called the *command interpreter.* It is the layer of programming and the code with which you interact and is highly modifiable in a UNIX-based system. The shell can be considered the skin that surrounds the core of your operating system and interacts with it. There are many types of shells, but for now we take a look at one in particular: *csh* or *C-shell*, which is the default shell used by Nokia.

C-Shell

The C-shell (csh) is a command interpreter with syntax similar to the C programming language. Because most UNIX gurus are (or were) C programmers, they feel right at home with the advanced features of this shell. The C-Shell was created by Bill Joy at the University of California at Berkeley as an alternative to the original UNIX shell, the Bourne shell.

Command: *mv*

The *mv* command is used to rename a file or move it from one directory to another directory. You can do this by entering the following at the console prompt:

```
mv file.txt directory/
```

This command moves the file *file.txt* to the directory named *directory*.

Command: *cp*

The *cp* command is simply used to copy files:

```
cp file.txt dir/
```

This command copies the file *file.txt* to the *dir* directory.

Command: *cat*

Using the *cat* command lets you look at, modify, or combine one or more files in your UNIX system:

```
cat fileA.txt fileB.txt > fileC.txt
```

This command reads fileA.txt and fileB.txt and combines (concatenates) the files to make fileC.txt.

Command: *grep*

The *grep* command is used to find text within a file. In other words, if you *grep* for a term, UNIX searches for that term. For instance, if you are interested in finding every occurrence of *index.html* in a large number of files in your current directory, you could *grep* for it:

```
grep * 'index.html'
```

This command searches all the files in the current directory for any reference of *index.html* and prints results to the console.

Command: *more*

The *more* command displays blocks of text one screen at a time. The following command would begin displaying the file file.txt at line 4:

```
more +4 file.txt
```

Press **Spacebar** to page through the file on screen, and type **q** to quit.

Command: *tail*

The *tail* command displays the last few lines of the file given to it as an argument. Performing this command lists the last lines of the file file.txt:

```
tail file.txt
```

The default number of lines to display is ten, but you can specify more lines using the *-l* switch.

Command: *head*

The *head* command displays the first ten lines in a file given to it by default. The *head –n* command displays the first *n* lines in a file to the screen. The following example specifies that we want to see the first 12 lines of the file file.txt:

```
head -12 file.txt
```

Command: *tar*

The *tar* program provides the ability to create tar archives and various other kinds of manipulation. For example, you can use *tar* on previously created archives to extract files, to store additional files, or to update or list files that were already stored. Using *tar* to extract files is quite a common occurrence:

```
tar zxvf archive.tgz
```

Using *vi*

vi is a very flexible and powerful editor, but it can also be very confusing. The *vi* editor is invoked on the UNIX system console with the following command:

```
rshimonski@BEAST:/etc> vi
```

vi is a *modal* editor, which means that it uses one mode for entering editor commands and another for actually editing text. You can always go back to command mode by pressing the **Esc** key. The *vi* editor lets you edit files by using simple mnemonic keystroke combinations while in command mode.

To get around in *vi*, you need to know a few basic commands. Here are some of the easiest to remember to get you started navigating and using the *vi* editor:

- **Arrow keys** Moves the cursor. You can also use the **h**, **k**, **j**, and **l** keys if you are at a terminal that does not recognize arrow keys.
- ***x*** Deletes a character.
- ***dw*** Deletes a word.

- ***dd*** Deletes a line.
- ***u*** Undoes previous change.
- ***yy*** and ***pp*** Useful to cut and paste lines.
- **Ctrl-u** (page up) **Ctrl-d** (page down) Useful for screen movement.
- ***H*** Moves to the top line of the screen.
- ***L*** Moves to the last line on screen.
- ***M*** Moves to the middle line on screen.
- ***U*** Undo; used to restore the current line.

That's it! With a little work and patience, you will be a UNIX pro in no time. The following are a few other commands you can use to exit your *vi* session:

- ***ZZ*** Used to quit, after saving the current file.
- ***:wq*** Used to quit, after saving the current file.
- ***:q!*** Used to quit while making no changes.

NOTE

For more information on UNIX commands, please see the *Sysadmin's Unixersal Translator (ROSETTA STONE)* document at:
http://bhami.com/rosetta.html
You can also view the *Manual page (UNIX)* Wikipedia entry at:
http://en.wikipedia.org/wiki/Manual_page_(UNIX)

We fully acknowledge use of Appendix A, "UNIX Basics," from Nokia Network Security Solutions Handbook, 978-1-931836-70-8

Appendix B

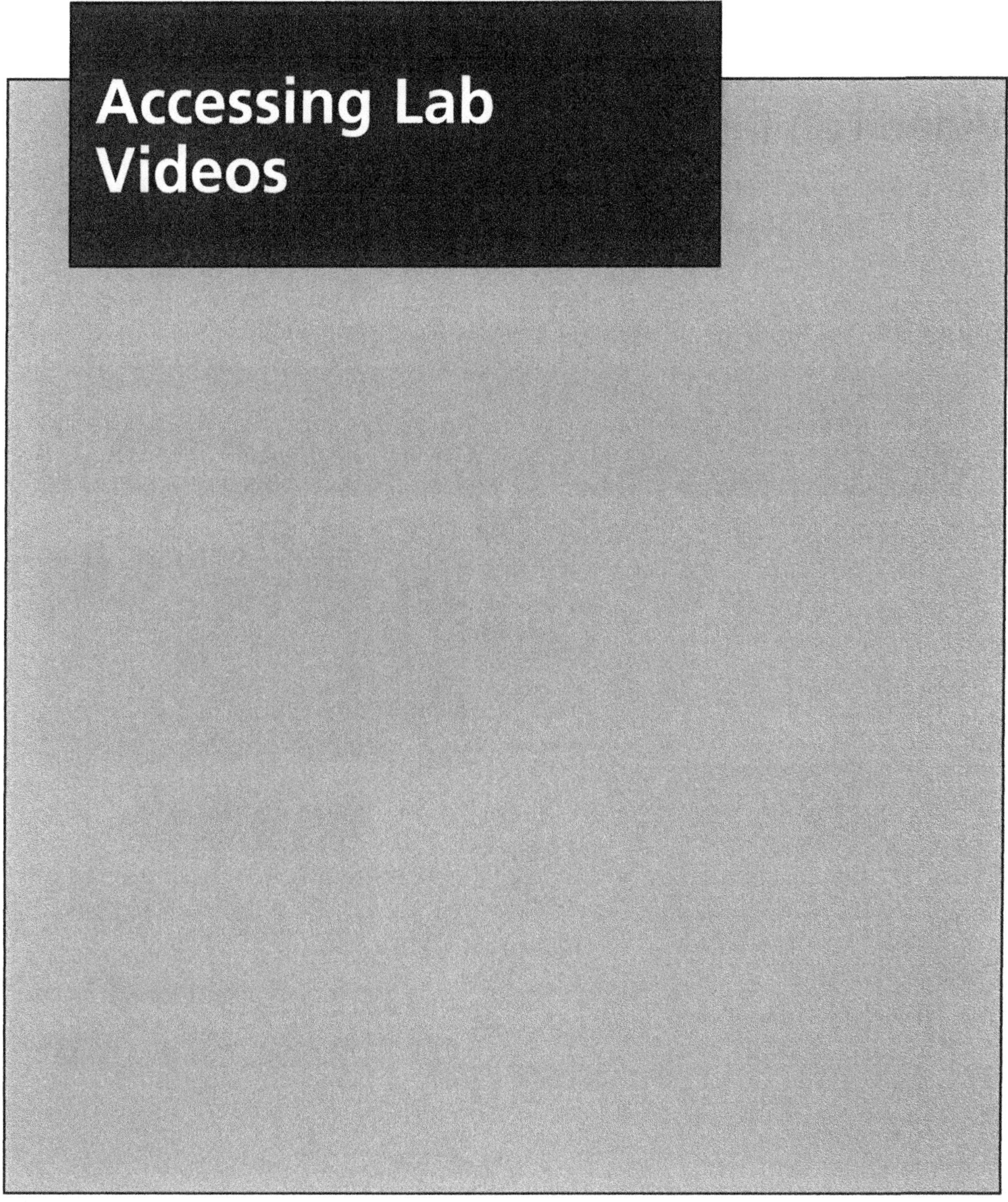

Accessing Lab Videos

Introduction and System Requirements

Many of the configuration steps described throughout this book are available as instructional videos from The Academy Web site located at www.theacademy.ca. To view the video content you must be using a compatible Web browser and have the Adobe Flash Player plug-in installed. Compatible Web browsers include Internet Explorer, Firefox, and Safari.

Video Lab Instruction

The first step is to navigate to www.theacademy.ca and create an account. Registration is free but required to view the video content. The Academy home page is shown in Figure B.1.

Figure B.1 The Academy Home Page at www.theacademy.ca

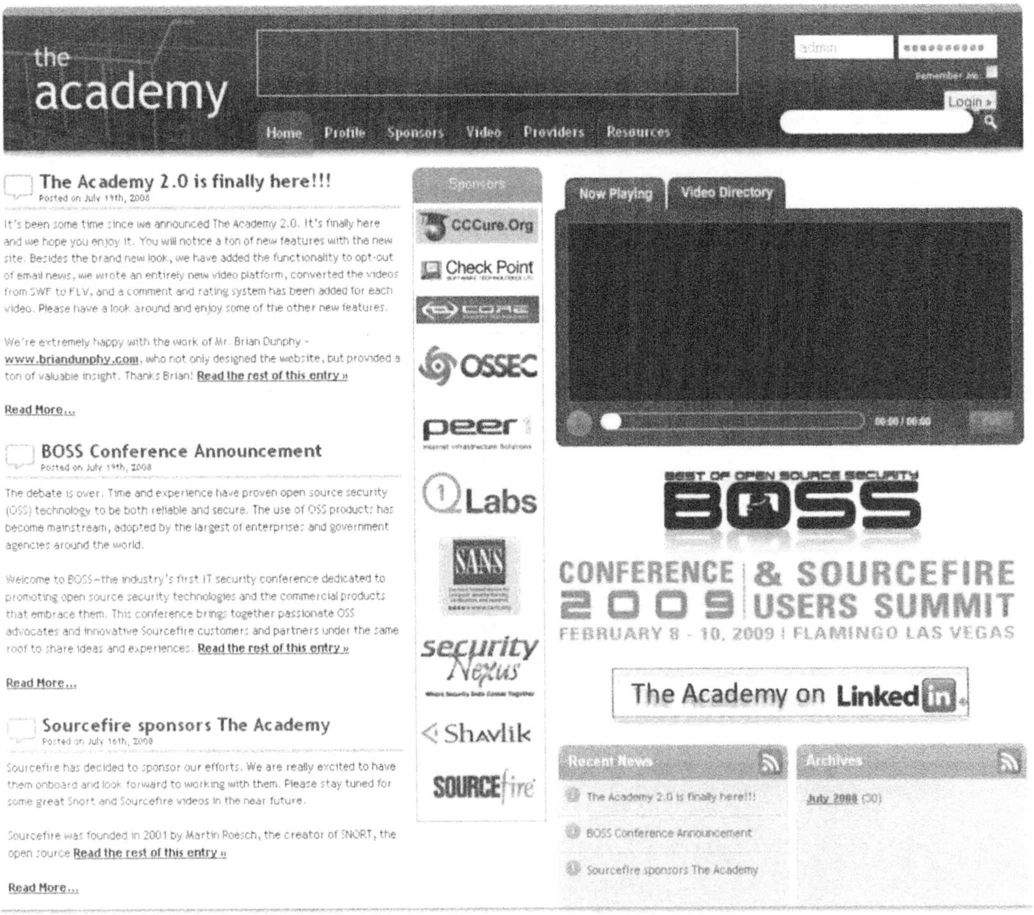

To create an account, click the **Video** tab (see Figure B.2).

Figure B.2 The Academy Registration Page

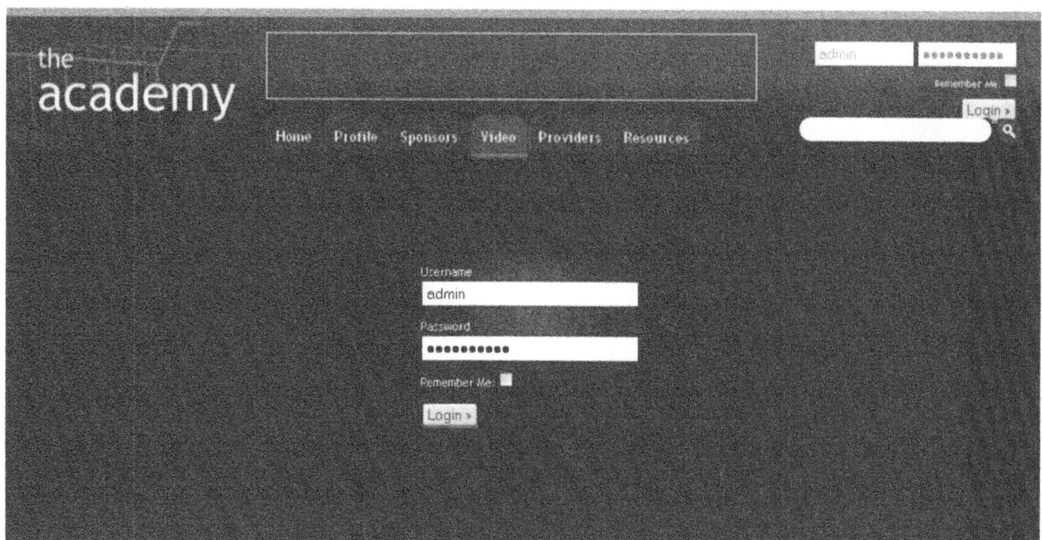

After receiving your password, you can log in to the Video page and select the videos you would like to view. To view Nokia-specific videos, select the **Video Directory** tab, **Firewalls**, and then **Nokia**. You can now navigate through every Nokia video on the site (see Figure B.3).

Figure B.3 The Academy Video Directory

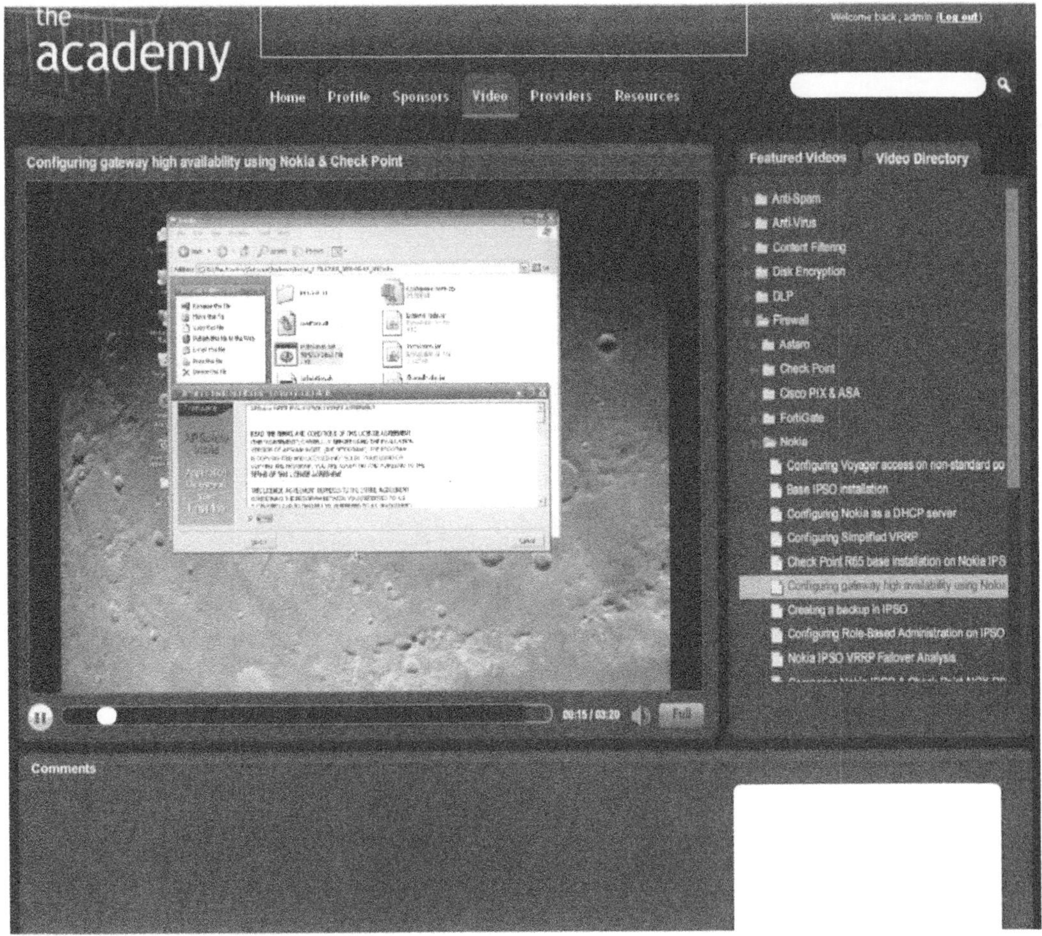

If you have any questions or concerns, or require further information about The Academy, e-mail Peter Giannoulis at peter@theacademy.ca.

Index

H

I

O

W

Printed and bound by CPI Group (UK) Ltd, Croydon, CR0 4YY
03/10/2024
01040343-0013